THE I TATTI
RENAISSANCE LIBRARY

James Hankins, General Editor

SALUTATI

ON THE WORLD AND
RELIGIOUS LIFE

ITRL 62

COLUCCIO SALUTATI
✦ ✦ ✦
ON THE WORLD AND
RELIGIOUS LIFE

TRANSLATED BY

TINA MARSHALL

INTRODUCTION BY

RONALD G. WITT

THE I TATTI RENAISSANCE LIBRARY
HARVARD UNIVERSITY PRESS
CAMBRIDGE, MASSACHUSETTS
LONDON, ENGLAND
2014

Series design by Dean Bornstein

Library of Congress Cataloging-in-Publication Data

Salutati, Coluccio, 1331–1406.
[De seculo et religione. English]
On the world and religious life / Coluccio Salutati ; translated by
Tina Marshall ; introduction by Ronald G. Witt.
pages   cm — (The I Tatti Renaissance Library ; ITRL 62)
English translation with Latin text on verso.
Includes bibliographical references and index.
ISBN 978-0-674-05514-8 (alk. paper)
1. Monastic and religious life — Early works to 1800.   2. Humanism.
I. Salutati, Coluccio, 1331–1406. De seculo et religione.   II. Title.
BX2436.S2513 2014
248.8′94 — dc23   2013032966

Contents

ༀৡৡৡ

Introduction

ॐऽ२ॐ

On the World and Religious Life (*De seculo et religione*) is the first sur-viving treatise of Coluccio Salutati (1332–1406), chancellor of the Florentine Republic (1375–1406) and the leader of the humanist movement in Italy in the generation after Petrarch and Boccaccio. The work was dedicated to Niccolò Lapi of Uzzano in the Valdi-nievole, a former canon lawyer and canon of Santa Maria del Fiore in Florence, who on February 25, 1379, joined the Camaldolese monastery of Santa Maria degli Angeli, located in the heart of the city.[1] Salutati, whose birthplace, Stignano, was located less than a mile from Uzzano, apparently knew Niccolò and his family, and shortly after Niccolò entered the monastery, he visited him. In the course of the visit, Niccolò, who had taken the religious name of Jerome, prevailed on Salutati to write a treatise encouraging him to persevere in the course he had chosen.

Perhaps Jerome's request was at least partly motivated by events outside the monastery as well as by the unsettling atmosphere within Santa Maria degli Angeli itself. Not only was the urban monastery surrounded by political and social unrest following the revolt of the Ciompi, a popular uprising in Florence in 1378, but also the order itself was rent with internal discord. In 1380, in fact, a dissident group of monks appealed to the pope against the head of the order, and Florence's chief governing body, the Signoria, was forced to write to the pope defending the general who had gov-erned the Camaldulensians for almost thirty years.[2] Salutati was well aware of these disturbing elements as he wrote to Jerome.[3]

The treatise can be dated only approximately. In the prologue Salutati excuses his tardiness in keeping his promise. Among other things the pressure of his duties has caused him to put off complying for a long time. Scholars have generally dated the work

to 1381, because, in a letter written after 1390 to Antonio degli Alberti, Salutati referred to his having composed the work shortly after Jerome entered the monastery.[4] It is also unlikely that the work was written before early 1381, because Salutati quotes Propertius (1.5.2), an ancient author whose poetry probably arrived in Florence from Padua only late in 1380.[5]

The *De seculo et religione* forms a part of the venerable medieval tradition of ascetic literature which endeavored to condemn the sensual life of man in the world. Like previous treatments of this subject, the *De seculo* focuses on man's misuse of God's creation, which was in itself good. The error of men is that they confine their goals to achievement in the worldly sphere. While intrinsically good, the world is still of much less value than the spiritual realm, and by concentrating on the world, men are consistently opting for an inferior rather than a superior good.

As with some of his more extreme predecessors, Salutati does not always keep his distinctions clearly in the foreground.[6] Like them, he appears at points to introduce Manichaean tendencies into his work. When this occurs, the justification for flight from the world appears to stem not only from man's failure to orient his life according to a proper hierarchy of values but also from the fact that the world has no value at all; indeed, that it is an evil place, intolerable to anyone truly seeking God. "What is more unwholesome than this world, what is more foul, what more obscene?" Salutati asks. "Let us pass over the great vileness of the bodies in the midst of which we breathe and live. One of these (the one in particular in which it befalls us to linger), is sediment, by its own nature the heaviest of all corporal things" (1.6.2).

In the proemium of the work Salutati explains the diffidence he feels writing on such a theme. Not only does he know that far greater men have written on the subject in the past but he also realizes the inappropriateness of a layman, immersed in worldly

affairs, offering arguments in support of the monastic life. "For what is more repugnant than to live shamefully and yet to offer oneself to others as an instructor of upright behavior? . . . For what is more laughable than for a blind man to guide the steps of one who can see and for someone to offer counsel in matters of which he is known to be ignorant?" (1.proem.5–6). Besides this, as a layman who has devoted his life to secular studies, how can he hope to treat the theme with the proper degree of religious eloquence?

Nonetheless, as a Christian he must do what he can to help his fellow man, and he has made a specific promise. Perhaps in writing, the author himself might be led to improve his own life, or at least he might be like one who, falling into a pit from whence he is unable or unwilling to escape, calls out to others so that they avoid the same danger by taking a better path (1.proem.9). In any case, relying on God's grace and Jerome's prayers, he now intends to keep his promise.

The plan of the treatise is to describe in the first book the world from which Jerome has fled and then, in the second, to praise the way he now follows and to inspire him to pursue it with enthusiasm and alacrity. In the first thirty-two chapters of Book 1, he describes the world as the devil's playing field: it is a palestra of temptations; a workshop of evils; a factory of vices; a ship's hold, full of the bilge of turpitude; a treacherous birdlime snare; a baleful happiness, false joy, and empty exultation; a threshing-floor of tribulation; a pit of miseries; a shipwreck of virtues; kindling for evils; an incitement to crime; a blind and blinding journey. The list of accusations continues in this vein.

By contrast, the four final chapters (1.33–36), before the short summary at the end, are designed to insure "that, in my zeal for accusing the world, God's creation, I don't leave it entirely without praise, but spare it, and deal with it more mildly" (1.1.6). The

chapter titles suggest this approach: "The world is a highway for mortals"; "The world is the inn of our pilgrimage"; "The world is a provider of necessities"; "The world is the most abundant supplier of pleasures." These chapters place the blame for evil squarely on the shoulders of man. Nature itself is a guide when it comes to deciding which of the things of this world we should accept. Nature requires the allaying of hunger, the quenching of thirst, covering against the rain and cold, protection from the violence of winds and heat. That these few things are sufficient is shown by the simplicity of life in early times, and by that of primitive people and of sailors in the modern age. By foregoing all but necessities, by subjugating our bodies, we hasten our journey to the eternal home (1.35.1–23).

Hardened sinners who ask why God put pleasures into the world to ensnare our souls can easily be answered (1.36.5). God gives us intelligence; he showed himself to our first parents and to the sacred fathers; he instructed us through the prophets and revealed himself to us in the person of his own son. Thus, we must all believe in him and cannot sin without secret condemnation from our conscience. We ourselves therefore admit that love of the world for pleasure's sake causes us to offend our Creator and to draw away from him. God gave us the power of desiring to abandon the world, conquer the flesh, and overcome the devil. If we feel this desire, he helps us. The more obstacles there are in our path, the more glory we attain by surmounting them. Besides, the manifold things of the world should help us to realize and admire the power of him who created them.

Salutati's characterization of the human predicament in the first book is a traditional Christian one. As might be expected in a work dealing with the merits of monastic retreat, the predominant emphasis is on man's ability to cooperate with divine grace and merit salvation. Whereas our first parents were created by God so

that they were able not to sin, we have been born in a state where we cannot not sin. But so gracious is God that he

> rouses sleeping reason and, once reason has been roused, subjects the good will to it and, when the will is obeying reason, he causes us, children of wrath, to make better choices and he frees us from slavery to sin. . . . if only we wish it, if only through love we shrink from the ugliness of sin and are moved to desire the beauty of divine justice! (1.10.7–8)

Once in possession of God's grace we cannot lose it unless we want to, i.e., "when with evil intention we deviate from the Prince of all things" (1.36.10).

The mind, that part of the soul capable of contemplation and, through contemplation, of drawing near to our Creator, is corrupted by knowledge of the world. If we abandon the world, we leave the devil no weapon with which to strike at us. We are able to do so if we will, and we can will:

> We have control of our wishes: we direct them where we want and draw them back again from where we directed them. God so moves our wishes that he does not impede our freedom of judgment; not only doesn't he impede it, but he increases the goods that we properly wish for. . . . For indeed God's grace anticipates those who are going to want good things; it helps those who want them, and works with them; and it makes our earth bring forth its fruit. (1.28.6–8)

These fruits are considered merits in God's eyes, and so advantageous is monastic withdrawal to a rich harvest, that, as Salutati states in the proemium of the second book, while the fruits of the average Christian are multiplied thirtyfold and those of the cleric sixty, those of the monk increase a hundredfold.[7]

The second book analyzes the nature of monastic vows and the merits gained from them, and it considers central aspects of the monk's life. Jerome has bound himself to God by a threefold oath of poverty, chastity, and obedience. Indeed, the meaning of religion itself is probably derived from *religatio*, a binding of oneself to God. Through fulfillment of these vows, lust, avarice, and pride are overcome and religious perfection attained.

The one who does good works because of his vows merits more than one who does them unbound.

> For who merits more grace: the one who gives only the fruits of the tree to his superior in such a way that he is not obliged to offer those except insofar as he pleases; or the one who gives both the tree and its fruits on the condition that he cannot revoke them after the giving? No one doubts that the one who gives more merits more; and the one who offers the fruits and the tree gives more than the one who only offers the fruits. The one who gives in perpetuity what he is not able to retract gives more by far than the one who offers in such way that he can with impunity offer nothing further, if he does not wish it. (2.6.11–12)

To do a good work of one's own free will without a vow is meritorious, but he who vows and then does the good work does a good work twice.

Apparently Salutati is aware of critics of monasticism — he calls them "raving," "brawlers," and "prattlers" — who hold that a man gains greater merit when he performs a good deed without a vow than when bound by one.[8] These critics argue that we are more obligated to one who does us good freely than to one who does so because acting under an oath. Against them, Salutati maintains that the analogy will not work. First of all, we can never force God to be obligated, since we owe him everything. Moreover, just as it

is more sinful to leave unexecuted a vow we have made to God than to neglect the same act without a vow, so more merit accrues to the man performing an act under a vow than to someone who does the same thing free of a vow (2.6.16–21).

Salutati then cautions Jerome not to let the devil tempt him by specious reasoning into regretting the step he has taken. After a detailed treatment of the significance of the vows of chastity, poverty, and obedience (2.8–10), he urges Jerome to fortify himself with prayer. In a long chapter (2.11)—about one-eighth of the whole work—Salutati instructs his friend on the nature and purpose of prayer. A listing of some of the beneficent results of prayer follows in three chapters concerning devotion, adoration, and humility in our attitude toward God (2.12–14). The treatise ends with a final exhortation to religion and a contrasting of monasticism and its vows with the evils of this world (2.15).

Salutati's concluding remarks develop the idea of the relative degree of merit attached to the lives of the layman, the cleric, and the monk. Here, as elsewhere in the treatise, he uses etymology extensively in an effort to explicate and justify the argument. In this case, Joseph is associated with the thirtyfold merit of the Christian lay life, Isaac with the sixtyfold merit of the cleric, and Christ with the monk's hundredfold harvest. While conceding that laymen need not despair of salvation, Salutati argues that they must pray and struggle to preserve the merits assigned to their lot. Likewise, clerics must be ever watchful to conserve the sixty allotted to them. In contrast, Jerome and other monks have only to persevere to the end in the path they have chosen to merit eternal peace and glory.

A secondary theme of the treatise is the contrast between pagan and Christian cultures. Although occasionally using examples of ancient virtue to shame modern Christians, Salutati at the same time makes it clear that he regards even the most virtuous of the

pagans as doomed men. Would that the noble, poverty-loving Cincinnatus had known Christ (2.9.27)! But outside the Church there can be no salvation:

> I don't know whether I speak a truth, yet I would most devoutly dare to assert that all who do some virtuous act short of obedience to the divine majesty not only do not earn merit, but even act wrongly; and that all who, for example, accomplish frequent acts of fortitude or temperance only in order to be strong or temperate (and not even just to seem so) are not only thinking carnally, but are not even different from the pagan philosophers. (2.10.18)

Directly inspired by Augustine's judgment on the pagans in the *De civitate Dei* 5.20, Salutati's unambiguous opposition of pagan to Christian morality differs radically from the rather vague relationship between the two found in his other writings during this period.

There is little originality in the treatise. Perhaps the most novel element in the work is found in Salutati's description of Florence as a mirror of the world's vanities (1.27.6–12). Offering a kind of visual perspective foreign to the art of his own generation but common to the next, Salutati urges his readers to imagine Florence seen from the hill of San Miniato on the left bank of the Arno, or from the twin summits of Fiesole's mountain, or from one of the other promontories high enough to behold the panorama. Assuming such a vantage point, he describes the city generally spread out below and particularly the Palazzo della Signoria and the cathedral, while he reflects on their glorious construction and their impermanence. The Palazzo is already settling on its foundations, and gaping cracks are visible in its walls. The viewer's eye then falls on the private houses, many of which were destroyed in the Ciompi Revolt. The whole scene reflects progressive decay.

Whether by coincidence or by design, Leonardo Bruni, Salutati's closest disciple, more than twenty years later offers a similar view from the heights in his *Laudatio urbis Florentine*, but the younger man gives a much more positive assessment of the sight.[9]

Speaking generally, Salutati's main contribution to the literature in the *de contemptu mundi* tradition lay in his organization of the material into a relentless diatribe against life in the world and in favor of monastic retreat. Filippo Villani aptly characterized the work as having so many arguments "that no one could say anything more on the subject than he did."[10] For Villani the *De seculo et religione* compared with Plato's treatment of the immortality of the soul, which had such persuasive force that many killed themselves after reading it. In the case of the former, "I do not doubt that anyone who listens to or reads the book . . . will retire to the solitary and monastic life leaving the vanities of the world behind and, burning with desire for it, be totally immersed in that form of existence."[11]

Quite understandably, such a treatise, composed by the chancellor of the Florentine Republic, a layman, a husband, and the father of a large family, raises puzzling questions about motivation. The work pronounces easily—too easily—on issues that concerned Salutati deeply in later life: the relationship between the active and contemplative life and the value of ancient literature for the Christian. The treatise both minimizes the merits of the ancients and denigrates life in the world. How could Salutati reconcile these conclusions with his career and his passionate love of ancient letters?

Was the *De seculo et religione* only a kind of elaborate *declamatio?* Salutati wrote a number of works in this genre in the form of separate speeches speaking for and against a certain proposition. But these *declamationes* were undisguised rhetorical exercises, whereas in the *De seculo et religione*, Salutati clearly intended the reader to

interpret the work as if the author believed in the arguments presented. Of course, this could be viewed as part of the rhetorical dressing. Yet in a matter of such religious significance, this approach would have been inexcusable. Salutati was a born debater and loved to win arguments. But there was more involved in his motivation for writing the work.

While Salutati at the outset of the *De seculo et religione* might honestly have been expressing his motives for writing at that time, the period of its composition (1381–82) suggests that he was also impelled by immediate personal concerns. The political instability that followed the Ciompi Revolt came to a climax in Florence in 1381, and Salutati was well aware of the threat posed to his safety by the growing dangers of mob violence. Were the present regime to collapse, how would the victors treat a collaborator with the old government? His ascendency to the chancellorship in 1375 had been a personal triumph; he had surrendered to an infatuation with glory, and he feared a reckoning was at hand. His diatribes against the world in the *De seculo* were partly motivated by the bitterness and self-recrimination he felt at abandoning himself to fortune.

But how could the humanist not see that by extolling a life of withdrawal and by censuring ancient culture so severely, he was contradicting his own scholarly enterprise? As has been suggested, however, while sincerely and deeply felt, his religious conceptions were quite unoriginal. In defending monasticism he proceeded with the confidence of one who tapped into a well-established stream of ideas, and the intensity of his own anxieties coupled with his rhetorician's desire to make a strong case pushed him toward the more extreme representatives of the tradition. In letters prior to and contemporary with the treatise, moreover, the assumptions behind his praise of the study of ancient letters had not yet been submitted to careful scrutiny. The two tendencies in his thought remained unreconciled for the time being.

Salutati's increasing involvement in Christian literature after 1368–69, however, had been instrumental in frustrating his efforts to finish the treatise entitled *De vita associabili et operativa*, apparently a defense of the active life. Begun in 1370–71, the writing was interrupted by the death of his first wife, Caterina, in 1372.[12] But even if he had interrupted writing owing to a depression following her death, he did not return to the manuscript in 1373 or 1374, when his fortunes drastically changed for the better. It would seem that he found himself in these years unable, as a Christian, to make a robust defense of the active life. Probably Ciceronian in inspiration, the original draft would have been quite compatible with his earlier attitudes, but in the Christian tradition, as he came to understand it, there were no strong arguments against the view that monasticism was the highest kind of life. In short, whereas earlier the problem of lifestyle had been primarily a moral one, given his increasing absorption in Christian thought, he could no longer treat this issue without paying heed to its theological implications. The humanist defense of the active life would have to await a later time and a later generation less concerned with theology.

R. G. W.

Durham, North Carolina

This translation could not have come to be without the kind and long-enduring support of James Hankins, who, drawing on his storehouse of treasures old and new (cf. Matthew 13:52), provided guidance and encouragement at every stage, along with rich supplementation of the notes to the translation. I owe a great debt to Ronald G. Witt for agreeing to write the Introduction. Finally, I am grateful to Andrew R. Dyck for his close reading of the first draft and his many improvements to the translation, as well as for his notes to the translation and emendations to the Latin text. It has been an honor to be part of such a collaborative effort. I dedi-

cate the volume to the memory of Virginia Brown. *Fulgebunt et tamquam scintillae in harundineto discurrent* (Wisdom 3:7).

T. M.

Guelph, Ontario, Canada

NOTES

1. *Annales camaldulenses*, ed. G. B. Mittarelli and A. Costadoni, 9 vols. (Venice: G. B. Pasquali, 1755–73), 6:134–35. See *Epistolario di Coluccio Salutati*, ed. Francesco Novati, 4 vols.; Fonti per la storia d'Italia, vols. 15–18 (Rome: Istituto storico italiano per il Medio Evo, 1891–1911), 3:10 n. 4.

2. Florence, Archivio di Stato, Archivio della Repubblica, Signori, I Cancelleria, Missive 19, fol. 83ʳ–83ᵛ.

3. For Salutati's relationship with Niccolò Lapi and Santa Maria degli Angeli, see the recent articles of Cécile Caby cited in the Bibliography, and her *voce* on the *De seculo et religione* in the catalog of the 2008 Laurenziana exhibition (also cited in the Bibliography), pp. 137–39.

4. *Epistolario*, 2:10–11; for Novati's dating, see Ullman, *The Humanism of Coluccio Salutati*, 26. In *Epistolario* 2:335 (1392?), Salutati explains that he wrote it for Jerome "soon after" (*nuper*) the latter had joined the order.

5. Ullman, *Studies in the Renaissance*, 178.

6. This tendency of medieval treatises is emphasized by Robert Bultot, *Christianism et valeurs humaines. A. La doctrine du mépris du monde en Occident, de S. Ambroise à Innocent III*, vol. 4.1–2: *Le xiᵉ siècle* (Louvain: Éditions Nauwelaets, 1963–64). Such an attitude seems much less prevalent in the work of nonmonastic writers like Innocent III.

7. This statement, first introduced at 2.proem.18, is explicated in detail in 2.15.

8. The approach of these unidentified fourteenth-century critics of monasticism is in general like that of Valla in the *De professione religiosorum*: Trinkaus, *In Our Image and Likeness*, 2:670–71.

9. Hans Baron, *The Crisis of the Early Italian Renaissance*, revised edition (Princeton: Princeton University Press, 1966), 200, sees the *Laudatio* as

"the first attempt . . . to discover the secret laws of optics and perspective that make the Florentine landscape appear as one great scenic structure."

10. *Epistolario*, 4:492.

11. Ibid., 4:493.

12. Witt, *Hercules at the Crossroads*, 100.

DE SECULO ET RELIGIONE

ON THE WORLD AND
RELIGIOUS LIFE

LIBER PRIMUS

*Incipit feliciter liber primus de seculo et religione
editus a Colucio Pyeri de Stignano cancellario Florentino
ad fratrem Ieronimum de Uzano ordinis Camaldulensi
s in monasterio Sancte Marie de Angelis de Florentia.*

Et primo prohemium.

1 Memor semper fui, venerabilis et karissime frater, postquam te
mundo subtractum in sanctissimo cenobio tuo letus et avidus visi-
tavi, rerum omnium principi per religionis vinculum adherentem,
quod tue caritati promiseram aliquid ad te scribere quo alacrius
prosequereris incepta, quodque te in huius seculi fuga ferventer
accensum ad illius summi et inenarrabilis boni dilectionem, quod
toto corde, tota mente, tota anima, totisque viribus diligere iubemur, pararet ardentius, imo iam paratum solidius confirmaret.
2 Debemus quidem proximo tam naturali ratione, qua simul omne
genus hominum alligamur, quam Christiane religionis glutino, qua
sumus omnes fratres in Christo, ut correctione subveniamus er-
ranti, lapsum erigamus, moneamus ignarum, et viam salutis per
3 dei gratiam eligentem nostris exhortationibus adiuvemus. In qua
re fateor me, quamvis in multis occuper, pro ingenii parvitate (que
utinam minima non foret!) potuisse tamen promissa persolvere
illiusque naturalis obligationis precepta per exhortationis officium
adimplere.

BOOK ONE

Here begins the first book On the World and Religious Life
*composed by Coluccio di Piero of Stignano, Chancellor of Florence,
for Brother Girolamo of Uzzano of the Camaldolese Order,
of the Monastery of Santa Maria degli Angeli, Florence.*

First, the proem.

I have always been mindful, venerable and cherished brother— 1
ever since I happily and eagerly visited you in your holy community after you had withdrawn from the world and were adhering to
the Prince of all by the bonds of the religious life—that I had
promised your dear self to write something for you so that you
might pursue more keenly the life you had begun, something that
would prepare you, fervently inflamed in the flight from this secular world, more ardently (or rather, that would ground you, already prepared, more solidly) for the love of that highest and ineffable good, which we are commanded to love with all our heart, all
our mind, all our soul, and all our strength.[1] Indeed, we owe it to 2
our neighbor both by natural reason (by which we of all the human race are bound together) and by the bond of the Christian
religion (by which we are all brothers in Christ) that we come to
the aid of the errant with correction, lift up the fallen, advise the
ignorant, and assist with our exhortations the one choosing, by
God's grace, the way of salvation. In this matter I confess that I, 3
although occupied with many things, have been able nevertheless
to discharge my promise according to the smallness of my talent (I
pray that it not be the smallest!) and fulfill the precepts of that
natural obligation by the service of exhortation.

4   Plura tamen me diutius tenuerunt. Cogitans enim multos sanctorum patrum et precipue Ieronimum tuum, Augustinum, et Ambrosium huiusmodi materiam felici stilo altissimisque sententiis tum libris, tum epistolis attigisse, temerarius michimet esse videbar rem tantis viris pertractatam et tritam reptanti calamo scribere, quam non possem observatis etiam ipsorum vestigiis expli-
5   care. Quid enim dicere vel cogitare possim quod illi spiritu sancto afflati reliquerint intentatum? Affundebatur insuper michi rubor quod, cum mundo implicitus, tremulis honorum illectus splendoribus, deo longinquus (et utinam non adversus!), in harum caducarum atque corruptibilium rerum salo ad naufragium usque submergar et iacter, michi te quod deum sequaris et mundum fugias hortaturo, mea vita, imo vite mee turpitudo possit opponi et memet teste valeam in cunctis que sequor quibusve damnabiliter implicor condemnari. Quid enim fedius quam turpiter vivere seque
6   preceptorem honestatis aliis exhibere? Accedebat etiam quod tibi et reliquis ista legentibus futurum me videbam esse ludibrio, utpote qui cecus et errans illuminato et viam rectam sapientissime prosequenti conarer iter salutis, quod neglexero quodve prorsus nescivero, demonstrare. Quid enim ridiculosius quam exoculatum videntis vestigia regere et aliquem ea que nescire cognoscitur admonere? Addebatur preterea quod, licet secularibus imbutus lit-
7   teris inani quodam strepitu scribendi inter privata tractantes et notantes publica videar ob cancellariatus officium numerari, attamen hec, que sine divinarum scripturarum noticia explicari non

But a number of considerations held me back for quite some 4
time. For, reflecting that many of the holy Fathers (especially Augustine, Ambrose, and your own Jerome) treated material of this
kind in fine style and with most penetrating thought both in
books and in letters, I seemed even to myself to be rash to write
with creeping pen on a subject dealt with so thoroughly and worn
out by such great men — a subject that I could not expound even
though I were to follow closely in the footsteps of those very
men! What could I say or think that those men, inspired by the 5
Holy Spirit, have left untouched? In addition, this embarrassment
poured over me: since I — entangled in the world, seduced by the
tremulous splendors of public offices, far from God (though not, I
trust, against him) — am tossed and submerged to the point of
shipwreck on the sea of these transient and corruptible things,
my life — more precisely, the turpitude of my life — could be held
against me in my intention to urge you to follow God and flee the
world, and, with myself as witness, I could be condemned in all
that I pursue and in which I am damnably implicated. For what is
more repugnant than to live shamefully and yet to offer oneself to
others as an instructor of upright behavior? Furthermore, I saw 6
that I would be ridiculous to you and to the rest of my readers,
inasmuch as I, blind and lost, was trying to point out the way of
salvation, which I have neglected, or been altogether ignorant of,
to one who is enlightened and pursuing most wisely the correct
path. For what is more laughable than for a blind man to guide the
steps of one who can see and for someone to offer counsel in matters of which he is known to be ignorant? Moreover, while it is 7
true that I am steeped in secular literature and am regarded, on
account of my office of chancellor, as one of those who treat private matters and record public affairs with an empty din of writing, up until now I have never tackled material like this, which
cannot be expounded without knowledge of the sacred scriptures;

possunt, nunquam hactenus attigi, propter quod sperare non poteram ea per me posse debita cum ornatus dignitate tractari.

8 Sed nimie sunt amoris vires! Id enim scribere compulit inconsulte caritas quod melior ratio sapientius dissuadebat. Nam quamvis honestius et tutius foret tacere quam scribere, iussit tamen potens amor temere promissa servare. Licet igitur periculosius sit,

9 scribam tamen, et eo maxime, quia laudans quam elegisti vitam et eam quam fugis quaque detineor horrendam periculis et plenam temptationibus disputando per dei gratiam, cuius quidem factura sum, ad meliora forte componar, vel saltem, sicuti qui ruendo ceciderim in baratrum unde non possim aut nolim exire, clamando te et reliquos viam meliorem admoneam doceamque malum et

10 pericula fugere que demens ipse nesciverim evitare. Nec ambitionis, ut arbitror, aut presumptionis crimine condemnabor qui post sanctissimos illos viros, quibus nec preferri desidero nec equari posse confido, quorum tamen aliquamdiu studiis delectatus vestigia non sequor sed veneror et adoro, sim eandem viam inculto stilo quam illi magna cum venustate hominum admiratione et divina cum laude cucurrerint, ingressurus. Erit enim decori et illis et aliis

11 qui per me dicenda tractarunt ruditas mea. Erit et forte nimis de se confidentibus in exemplum, ut qui mea legerint maiores illos michi preferant nec, quamvis me facile superent, se pares illis futu-

12 ros esse presumant. Denique, licet facultas non suppetat, adiuvabit

therefore, I could not hope to handle the subject with the dignity of embellishment it deserves.

Yet the strength of love is exceedingly great! Love compelled me 8 to write, ill-advisedly, what better policy wisely counseled against. For although it had been more respectable and safer to remain silent than to write, powerful love nonetheless ordered me to keep the promise rashly made. Therefore, even though it is perilous, I 9 shall write nonetheless, and especially for this reason: in praising the life you have chosen and arguing against the life you are fleeing (and in which I am stuck, a life bristling with perils and full of temptations) I may, perhaps, be fashioned for better things by the grace of God, whose creature I am; or at least, just as one who has tumbled and fallen into a pit from which I am unable or unwilling to escape, by crying out I may advise you and others to follow a better path and teach you to flee the evil and perils that I myself, in my madness, did not know how to avoid. And I shall not be 10 condemned for the crime of ambition, I think, or of presumption, since, after those most holy men, to whom I neither desire to be preferred nor trust to be able to equal — yet having delighted in studying them for some time I do not follow their footsteps but rather venerate and adore them — I am about to enter the same path, with an unpolished style, that they have run with great elegance to the admiration of men and with divine praise. My roughness will be an honor both to them and to others who have treated my subject. Perhaps the fact that those who have read my work 11 prefer the great men of the past to me will also serve as an example to those who trust in themselves to an excessive degree not to presume, however easily they surpass me, that they themselves are equal to those men. Finally, although ability may be in short 12

tamen pure caritatis affectus, auxiliabitur fides, opitulabitur ipsa divina gratia in qua michi spes est quamque tu michi tuis devotis orationibus impetrabis, quod ut sedulo coneris et facias te deprecor et exoro.

Explicit prohemium.

: I :

*Incipit tractatus in quo premisso ordine
dicendorum quid sit mundus multis
diffinitionibus explicatur.*

1 Hec igitur tantisper exordiendo prefatus, vir merito venerande, redeam ad promissa et, ut clarius pateat dispositio dicendorum, ostendam primo quid fugeris; explicabo postmodum quid sequaris; deinde, qua potero brevitate, conficiam ut ad id te impellam et 2 horter quod laudabiliter incepisti. Ad religionis igitur amenissimum portum de turbulento presentis seculi baratro et ad exitium usque circumsilientibus fluctibus, tue vite multis hactenus iactate procellis naviculam impegisti. Felix hac tue vite commutatione, Ieronime, felix terque quaterque felix qui potuisti mundi blandientis illecebras superare! Quid enim est mundus iste quo tantopere delectamur nisi campus diaboli, temptationum palestra, officina 3 malorum, et fabrica vitiorum? Quo magis admiror quosdam carnales, ut ita loquar, philosophos secularibus inflatos litteris, in

supply, nevertheless the emotion of pure love will come to my assistance, faith will come to my aid, and that very divine grace wherein lies my hope, and that you will obtain for me by your devout prayers, will help me; I pray and beseech you to earnestly try and do this.

Here ends the proem.

: I :

The treatise begins, in which the nature of the world
is explained in many definitions, once the
order of topics has been set out.

So, then, having said these things for the time being by way of introduction, my deservedly venerable man, let me return to my promise and, so that the order of topics may be more clearly revealed, I shall show first what you have fled; afterward I shall explain what you are pursuing; next, with as much brevity as I can muster, I shall conclude by urging and exhorting you to pursue what you have laudably begun. From the turbulent depths of the present age and its waves thrashing round about to the point of destruction, you have landed the skiff of your hitherto storm-tossed life at the most pleasant haven of religious life. Blessed in this transformation of your life, Girolamo, blessed thrice and four times, blessed you who were able to conquer the enticements of the smoothly coaxing world! For what is that world in which we so greatly delight but the devil's playing field, the palestra of temptations, the workshop of evils, and the factory of vices? So much the more do I wonder that certain carnal (if I may express it thus) philosophers, puffed up with secular literature, yet in

1

2

3

multis tamen vero proximos et acutos, mundum hunc rationale et
eternum animal astruxisse, quosdamque adeo admiratione eius
deceptos et captos quod nedum animal nedumque rationis particeps et perpetuum voluerunt sed ipsum deum esse dicentes ausi
sunt illum, cum impurissimus sit, ad tam purissime rei maiestatem
4 et altitudinem sublimare. Qui profecto michi visi sunt non disputare sed desipere, delirare, insanire, et nedum ineffabilem illam dei
essentiam non novisse sed etiam hunc ipsum sensibilem mundum,
qui manibus tangitur et videtur oculis, ignorasse. Sed illorum vanitatem et ineptias dimittamus.

5 Est igitur mundus immundissima sentina turpitudinum, fallax
viscum, tristis leticia, falsum gaudium, exultatio inanis, area tribulationum, lacus miseriarum, naufragium virtutum, malorum fomes, incentivum scelerum, iter cecum, trames salebrosus, saltus
insidiarum, carcer horridus, scena iniquitatum, arena laborum,
theatrum inhonestatum, spectaculum delictorum, horribile precipitium, domus anxietatum, mare turbidum, vallis calamitatum,
erumnarum domicilium, speculum vanitatis, corruptio mentium,
laqueus animarum, parens mortis, infernus viventium, et aggrega-
6 tio caducorum. Et, ne accusandi studio mundum, dei creaturam,
dimittam penitus illaudatum sed parcendo sibi mitius secum
agam, mundus est via mortalium, peregrinationis nostre diversorium, ministrator necessariorum, et suppeditator etiam abundantissimus voluptatum.

many matters acute and near to the truth, conceived of this world as a rational and eternal living being; and I am amazed that some of them were captivated and deceived to such an extent by their admiration for it, that they maintained that the world was more than a living being and more than a sharer of reason and a perpetual thing. Claiming that it is God himself, they dared to raise it up to the majesty and heights of the purest thing, although it is utterly impure. These men really seemed to me not to dispute but to be foolish, delirious, raving mad, and not only to be ignorant of that ineffable essence of God, but even of this very perceptible world that is touched by hands and seen by eyes. But let us dismiss the vanities and nonsense of those men. 4

The world, then, is the most unwholesome hold of turpitude, deceptive birdlime, baleful happiness, false joy, empty exultation, a threshing floor of tribulations, a pit of miseries, shipwreck of virtues, kindling for evils, incitement to crime, a blind journey, a rugged path, a ravine of plots, a horrible prison, a stage of iniquities, an arena of labors, a theater of disgraces, a spectacle of wrongs, a horrible precipice, a house of anxieties, a turbid sea, a vale of calamities, the home of hardships, the mirror of vanities, the corruption of minds, the snare of souls, the parent of death, the inferno of the living, and a pile of transient things. And (so that, in my zeal for accusing the world, God's creation, I don't leave it entirely without praise, but spare it, and deal with it more mildly) the world is a highway for mortals, the inn of our pilgrimage, a provider of necessities, and even the very abundant supplier of pleasures. 5 6

: II :

Quod mundus est campus diaboli.

1　Audisti brevissimis diffinitionibus et quasi quibusdam punctulis, frater karissime, quid sit mundus. Nec sit quod de his que strictim attigi forte quid dubites. Verissima quidem sunt planeque etiam sine rationum adminiculo non neganda. Campus enim diaboli mundus est, in quo cum mortalibus pugnam conserit et quasi leo rugiens circuit terram et perambulat eam querens quem devoret et 2　extinguat. Cuius insidias qui formidare noluerit quique congressum eius concupiverit non timere, se mundo subtrahat, se mundo occidat, blanditiis suis non credat; non sit in hoc mundo corruptibili tanquam civis sed tanquam peregrinus et advena; non dormiat cum debeat vigilare, et, cum eundum sit, necubi pedem figat, caveat circumspiciatque ne antiquus hostis et continuus insidiator alicunde latenter et improvisus exiliat, ubique cogitet eum adesse; et quicquid invenerit oculis gratum, auribus mellifluum, suave olfactui, gustu dulce, aut delectabile tactu, vel in quo mens capiatur, detineatur animus, aut excitetur appetitus, quicquid, inquam, tale invenerit escam infixam hamis putet et ibidem latere noverit inimicum. Quicquid enim in hoc campo est diaboli telum est.

3　Quis igitur sane mentis mundum, in quo oporteat diabolo congredi, non exhorreat et condicionem tam dure pugne, cuius eventum periculosum et ancipitem videat, non pavescat? In campum istum natura parens, imo ipsius nature autor, deus, nostra corpora seminavit, quibus spirituales infudit animas que cum illo

: II :

The world is the devil's playing field.

You have heard in very brief definitions and in a sort of point 1
form, dearest brother, what the world is. And you should have no
doubt about what I have dealt with cursorily. Indeed these matters
are very true and, even without the support of arguments, clearly
not to be denied. For the world is the devil's playing field: there he
joins battle with mortals and like a roaring lion circles the earth
and ranges over it, seeking whom he may devour and annihilate.[2]
Whoever has no desire to tremble at his snares and longs not to 2
fear an encounter with him should withdraw from the world, kill
himself to the world, not trust in its blandishments. Let him be in
this corruptible world not as a citizen, but as a pilgrim and
stranger; let him not sleep when he ought to keep watch, and,
when it is time to depart, let him fix his foot nowhere; let him be
wary and circumspect lest the ancient Enemy and perpetual plot-
ter stealthily and unexpectedly leap out from some quarter; let
him consider that the devil is everywhere present. Whatever this
person finds pleasing to the eyes, soothing to the ears, fragrant to
smell, sweet to the taste, or enjoyable to the touch, or whatever
captivates the mind, detains the soul, or stimulates the appetite—
whatever of this kind he finds, I say, let him regard as bait fastened
to the hook and know that in that very place lurks the Enemy. For
whatever is in this field is the devil's weapon.

Who, then, in his right mind would not shudder at the world, 3
in which one must meet the devil? And who would not quail at
the terms of a battle so hard, whose outcome he sees to be perilous and dubious? Into that field Mother Nature—or rather, the
Author of nature herself, God—planted our bodies, and into
these he poured spiritual souls to do battle with that spiritual

spirituali hoste pugnarent, si in mundum non descenderint per affectum sique sibi non cesserint per consensum, gloriosam repor-
4 tature victoriam. Si vero in hunc campum carnalia concupiscendo declinent, hosti potentissimo de quadam altitudine terribiliter imminenti et occasionem pugne et spem victorie prebiture, tunc ille ferox et audax quasi in iniquo deprensos loco irruit, fulminat, furit, et improvisos, incautos, et nil tale verentes et, quod periculo-
5 sius est, suis exultantes malis opprimit et devincit. Elevemus igitur mente nos et hunc campum tendentes in celestia fugiamus, memores mundum istum utpote temptationum palestram nunquam nos tranquillos et sine sollicitudine, si in hoc campo mente versati fuerimus, dimissurum.

: III :

Quod mundus sit temptationum palestra.

1 Palestra quidem temptationum est mundus iste quem fugis. Palestra namque, sicut placet vocabulorum tractatoribus, locus luctationis est. Lucta vero certamen erat quo duo brachiis per mutua se stringentes alterutrum sternere conabantur. Qui ne capi atque teneri possent, nudabantur et nudi pingui perfundebantur oleo. Arene autem aut pulveris iactu, ne constricti laberentur e manibus,
2 faciebant. Sicut igitur nudi in palestra concurrunt, sic in hoc mundo diabolus cum homine luctando congreditur. Qui si passionum et desideriorum vestibus nudus sit, facile complexus illos

Enemy, souls destined to bring back glorious victory if they do not descend into the world through the emotions and if they do not yield to it willingly. But if they descend into this field by desiring carnal things, they are destined to offer the most potent Enemy, who looms terribly overhead, both the chance of a fight and the hope of victory; then he, fierce and audacious, rushes down upon them, caught, as it were, on unfavorable ground. He thunders, rages, and finally crushes and utterly defeats the unwitting and incautious people who fear no such thing, and—what is more dangerous—who exult in their own evils. Therefore let us raise ourselves up with our mind and, aiming for the heavens, let us flee this playing field, mindful that this world, inasmuch as it is a palestra of temptations, will never leave us at peace and without worry, once we have wandered on this field with our mind.

4

5

: III :

The world is a palestra of temptations.

This world you are fleeing is indeed a palestra of temptations. For a palestra, as the lexicographers have it, is a place for wrestling.[3] Now wrestling was a competition in which two men, holding each other fast with their arms, tried to throw each other down. And in order to avoid being caught and held, they stripped, and, once naked, they smeared themselves with rich oil. Yet by scattering sand or dust, they made it so that their opponents, when caught, could not slip from their hands. Therefore, just as naked men compete in the palestra, so in this world the devil joins with man in wrestling. If man is stripped of the garments of passions and

1

2

spirituales evadit, et precipue si oleo, hoc est pinguedine bonorum
3   operum, perfundatur. Hoc quidem est oleum illud quod quinque
virgines sapientes in expectatione sponsi suis in vasis et lampadibus detulerunt.

Quid sunt enim quinque virgines nisi quinque nostre vite mortalis etates, quibus possumus animi nostri iam perfecto iudicio
⟨spretis⟩ per libere voluntatis arbitrium malis operibus demereri?
4   Distinxerunt siquidem antiquorum nonnulli creature rationalis et
moriture durationem in sex etates. Quarum prima infantia est,
cui, cum non insit animi iudicium secundum communis nature
cursum, non est meritum vel demeritum ascribendum. Quinque
igitur sequentes etates, hoc est puericia, que et doli capacitas dicitur, adolescentia, iuventus seu virilitas, gravitas, et senectus, bonis
malisve operibus possunt lucrari premia et hominem suppliciis
5   obligare. Si quis enim virtuosis operibus has quinque etates imma-
culatas vitiorum contagiis ac velut virgines sine peccatorum labe
transegerit, securus expectabit sponsum, et oleum, hoc est, sicut
dixi, pinguedinem bonorum operum, secum in vasis et lampadibus
deportabit.

6   Quid autem est oleum in lampadibus et vasis habere nisi taliter
bona facere quod luceant opera nostra sicut lumen super cande-
labro, non ad popularis aure captationem sed ut laudetur pater
noster qui in celis est, et quod ita nos ipsos extimemus quod, cum
nichil simus, non seducamus nos arbitrantes quod aliquid simus?
7   Nam si voluerimus oleum in vasis habere, 'probemus,' ut monet
apostolus, 'unus quisque opus suum, et sic tantum in nobismet
ipsis gloriam habebimus et non in altero,' gloriam quidem non
inanem sed solidam, sed sobriam, non tumidam, non inflatam,

desires, he will easily escape those strangleholds of the spirit, and especially if he has anointed himself with oil, that is, with the grease of good works. This indeed is that oil which the five wise 3 virgins carried in their vessels and lamps in expectation of the bridegroom.

What are the five virgins but the five ages of our mortal life, in which we can earn merit, when the judgment of our mind is already perfect, having spurned wicked deeds by the exercise of free will? Some of the ancients divided the span of the rational, mor- 4 tal creature into six ages.[4] The first of these is infancy, to which neither merit nor demerit should be ascribed, since in accordance with the common course of nature, the mind's judgment is not present. The five subsequent ages, then—that is, childhood (which is also said to be capable of committing crime),[5] adolescence, youth or young manhood, the age of authority, and old age—can win rewards or subject a man to punishment as a result of good or evil deeds. For if anyone has passed through these five 5 ages with good works and so is untainted by the contamination of vices, and like the virgins, is without the stain of sins, this person will await the bridegroom with peace of mind and will carry oil (which is, as I said, the grease of good works) with him in vessels and lamps.

Yet what is it to have oil in lamps and vessels but to do good 6 deeds in such a way that our works shine forth like a light upon a lamp stand, not for the capturing of the popular breeze but so that our Father who is in heaven may be praised and that we reckon ourselves in such a way that we do not deceive ourselves by thinking that we are something, when we are nothing?[6] For if we want 7 to have oil in our vessels, "let each one of us give proof," as the apostle warns, "of his own work, and in this way we shall have glory only in ourselves and not in another,"[7] indeed glory not vain, but solid, sober, not swelling with pride, not puffed up, doing all

omnia deo et non hominibus facientes, ut si pauperi panem frangamus, deo frangamus et ceteras operas misericordie deo, licet erga proximos, faciamus, ut sic habeamus oleum in vasis, hoc est in

8   testimonio conscientie nostre, que quidem est gloria nostra. Etenim qui bona faciunt ut commendationes hominum mereantur, sicut ypocrite tristes qui exterminant ora sua ut appareant hominibus ieiunantes, quique elemosinam facturi canunt ante se tuba ut a multis sciatur ipsos pauperibus subvenire, sicut testatur veritas, 'Receperunt mercedem suam,' et quinque virgines in fatuas convertentes humano contente preconio solum in lampadibus oleum habent, hoc est in propatulo et in hominum conspectu, nichil in vasis

9   suis pinguedinis reservantes. Unde a quinque sapientibus audire merentur, 'Ite potius ad vendentes et emite vobis.' Que dum vadunt humanarum commendationum requirendo suffragia, venit sponsus et cum sapientibus intrans stultas excludit pulsantibusque respondet, 'Amen dico vobis. Nescio vos.'

10   Ungamus igitur nos, sicut sepius dixi, oleo bonorum operum reminiscamurque nos esse in mundo, temptationum palestra, ubi oporteat cum diabolo de salute luctari et luctando aut cum amissione glorie non sine anime morte succumbere aut usque ad ex-

11   itum cum spe corone et successu victorie decertare. Non derelinquat pugnam qui pervenire voluerit ad gloriam. Si enim hosti cesserit, capietur, non hac captivitate terrena qua iure belli victos in servitutem ad nostra servitia reservamus, a qua possint tum manumissione, tum testamento, tum lege, tum postliminio liberari, sed captivitate prorsus eterna in qua non domino serviant sed penis immortalibus affligantur, non iam servati sed mortui.

12   Nec speranda talis domini manumissio; avarissimus quidem est.

things for God and not for men, so that if we break bread for the poor man, we break it for God; and let us do other works of mercy for God (although we do them for our neighbors), so that thus we may have oil in vessels, that is, in the testimony of our conscience, which indeed is our glory. Those who do good deeds 8 in order to earn the approval of men — like the wretched hypocrites who cast down their faces in order to appear to men to be fasting, and who, when they are about to give alms, sound a trumpet before themselves so that it may be known to many that they are coming to the aid of the poor — as the Truth attests, "They have received their reward."[8] And the five virgins turning into foolish ones content with human commendation have oil only in their lamps, that is, out in the open and in the sight of people, preserving none of the grease in their vessels. For this reason they deserve 9 to hear from the five wise ones: "Go, rather, to the vendors and buy some for yourselves."[9] And while they go seeking human approval, the bridegroom comes, and entering with the wise virgins he shuts out the foolish ones and replies to them when they knock, "Truly I tell you, I do not know you."[10]

Let us anoint ourselves, therefore, as I have often said, with the 10 oil of good works, and let us remember that we are in the world, the palestra of temptations, where we must wrestle with the devil for our salvation and in wrestling either succumb with loss of glory (and not without death of the soul), or compete to the death in hope of a garland and with victorious result. Let whosoever 11 wishes to attain glory not give up the fight. For if he yields to the Enemy, he will be captured, not in this earthly captivity whereby through the law of war we relegate the vanquished for our own service to slavery, from which they can then be freed by manumission, by testament, by law, or by right of recovery, but in that eternal captivity in which they do not serve a master but are afflicted by never-dying punishments, no longer saved, but dead. Neither can manumission be hoped for from such a master (he is 12

Nec expectandum testamenti beneficium quod iuxta leges vires ex morte capit; immortalis enim est. Nec lege que irrevocabiliter condemnavit speranda libertas est; nam cum lapidea sit, in ea stilo
13 ferreo perditorum est impressa damnatio. Cumque nullus limes positus sit ultra quem fugiens, postquam hinc excesserit, se in libertatem valeat vendicare, nulla quidem in postliminio spes habenda; semel enim post carnis depositionem adamantinas illas tue damnationis cathenas accipiens, quocunque te verteris, te sequentur.
14 tur. Unicum est, dum in hac peregrinatione degimus, presens et salubre remedium quod ad petram illam que Christus est (qui, mediator dei et hominum, ut vinctos solveret et captos liberaret, mortale coniunxit eterno, viam ostendit, et de sue bonitatis immensitate se ipsum resilientibus miseris peccatoribus viam fecit) per penitentiam fugientes exuamus nos carnis affectus nosque oleo bonorum operum perfundamus caveamusque ne hostis noster pul-
15 verem sive arenam nobis affundat. Quid est iste pulvis, quid est hec arena nisi vane glorie falsissimus splendor, que in hoc cursu mortalium quasi pulvis inter pedes currentium elevatur? Dum enim bonum aliquid operamur superbie tenebras noster hostis affundit et super nos proicit quasi pulverem inanis glorie vanitatem, qua pinguedo bonorum operum exiccatur.
16 Non tamen desperanda venia est ob magnitudinem peccatorum. Christus enim, ad quem fugiendum dixi, benignus et omnipotens est et cui nec hostis et victor noster nec infernus resistere possunt, tanteque benignitatis et gratie quod lapsos erigit et nullis precedentibus meritis devios reducit in viam, dummodo dimittamus gratie sue locum nec obstinatione peccandi nos indignos
17 gratia faciamus. Quod autem sit signum, quis limes ultra quem

extremely avaricious); nor can benefit be expected from a will, which, according to the laws, comes into effect after the master's death (the Master is immortal); nor can freedom be hoped for by a law that has condemned irrevocably; for since it is a law written in stone, damnation of lost souls is engraved on it with an iron stylus. And since no boundary has been set by passing beyond which a fugitive can claim his freedom, no right of recovery can be hoped for; for once you lay the flesh aside and receive those adamantine chains of your own damnation, they follow you wherever you turn. There is only one present and wholesome remedy, while we spend our time in this pilgrimage: that we flee in repentance to the rock that is Christ (who, the mediator between God and men, joined mortal and eternal in order to release the bound and liberate the captives, who showed the way, and out of the immensity of his goodness made his very self the way for wretched, recalcitrant sinners) and divest ourselves of carnal passions, anoint ourselves with the oil of good works, and be on guard lest our Enemy sprinkle us with dust or sand. What is that dust, what is this sand but vainglory's falsest splendor, that vainglory which in this race among mortals is raised like dust from the runners' feet? For while we are doing some good deed our Enemy pours on the shadows of pride and casts over us like dust the vanity of hollow glory, whereby the grease of good works is dried up. 13 14 15

However, we need not despair of forgiveness on account of the magnitude of our sins. Christ, to whom I said we must flee, is kindly and all-powerful and someone against whom neither our Enemy and conqueror nor hell can stand; his kindness and grace are so great that he raises up the fallen and leads back the lost to the right path although no merits of their own precede them, if only we leave room for his grace and do not make ourselves unworthy of it by our persistence in sinning. Yet we do not know 16 17

transeuntes sic dei gratiam amittamus quod non recuperetur ulterius, ignotum est, et ob id cavendum diligentissime ne peccemus; et, si aliquando vel fragilitate carnis vel hostis astutia vel mundi, de quo nunc disputatio est, blanditiis in crimina delabamur, penitentie nos remedio, dum adhuc aliquis divine gratie radius in tenebris nostris effulserit, revocemus; semperque timendum ne misericordie sue gratiam subtrahat, ita tamen quod non desperemus quin inenarrabili sua misericordia nostris erroribus saltem cum debite purgationis pena veniam, si penitentes voluerimus, non concedat, dummodo de hac officina malorum nos ad illud summum bonum totius mentis affectibus erigamus.

: IV :

Quod mundus sit officina malorum.

1 Dixi mundum esse officinam malorum. Quis hoc ignorat? Quis hoc non fateatur? Quota mundi particula Christum colit! Ceteri quidem abominabili et horrenda vanitate decepti non Deo, cuius nomen Christum negando blasfemant, serviunt sed diabolo famulantur. Bonos itaque extra ecclesie nostre corpus, cuius caput
2 Christus est, frustra quesiveris. At inter Christicolas, me miserum, quot videmus bella fervere, quot convenire malarum gentium officinas, quot perditorum hominum manus, qui ius ponentes in armis proximos spoliant, incendiis delectantur et cedibus! Inter quos

what is the sign, what is the boundary by the crossing of which we so completely lose God's grace that it cannot be recovered; consequently, we should be especially careful that we do not sin. And, if now and then because of the weakness of the flesh, or because of the cleverness of the Enemy or the blandishments of the world that is our present theme, we slip into sins, let us restore ourselves by the remedy of penitence, as long as some ray of divine grace still shines in our shadows. And we must always fear lest God withdraw the grace of his mercy, in such a way, however, that we do not despair that he will, by his ineffable mercy, grant forgiveness to our errors (at least, after the punishment of purgation that we owe), if we repent and desire his forgiveness — provided that with the striving of our whole mind we lift ourselves up to that highest good out of this workshop of evils.

∶ IV ∶

The world is a workshop of evils.

I have said that the world is a workshop of evils. Who is unaware   1
of this fact? Who wouldn't concede this? What a minute particle
of the world worships Christ! Indeed, the rest, deceived by abominable and horrendous vanity, do not serve God — whose name
they blaspheme by denying Christ — but wait upon the devil. And
so you will seek in vain good people outside the body of our
church, of which Christ is the head. Yet among Christians —   2
alas! — how many wars we see aboil, how many workshops of
evil peoples congregating, how many bands of desperadoes, who,
placing what is right in weapons, despoil their neighbors, delight
in conflagrations and slaughter! Among them, those who prowl

qui crassantur ardentius, crudelius seviunt, opulentiusque rapiunt,

3 clariores habentur, publice latrociniis implicantur. Aspice reges, considera principes, examina res publicas: quos invenies subditorum utilitati consulere? Quos dabis qui sub iusti presidatus vocabulo tirannidem non exerceant, qui non sanciant id fore iustissimum quod sibi putaverint esse lucrosum, quos iura que tulerint transgredi pudeat quique cum divis illis principibus, Severo et Antonino, dicere velint et possint, 'Licet legibus soluti simus, legibus tamen vivimus'?

4 Sed cur hec temporalia conqueror? Aspiciamus statum nostre spiritualis ecclesie. Nonne omnes unum ludum ludunt? Nonne verissimum esse videmus quod apud prophetam legimus, 'A minore quippe usque ad maiorem omnes avaricie student; a propheta usque ad sacerdotem cuncti faciunt dolum'? Quid ambitionem, quid luxurie complectar illecebras? Nonne videmus eos quos animarum custodes habemus cunctis fetide carnis flagiciis inquinari, ut dignitates quas concupiscunt obtineant, nichil turpe nichilque

5 detestabile devitare? Denique, licet deum videantur labiis honorare, si quis operas ipsorum aspiciat, nonne putet quod illi aut deum esse non credant aut, si deum negare non audeant, ipsum dormientem, cecum, vel humana contemnentem penitus arbitrentur? Nec sufficit peccare privatim et se solum, paucos, vel domum propriam suarum impuritatum testem habere nisi monstruosi, deformes, horrendi cogitationibus, voluntatibus, et operibus in om-

6 nium oculis ostendantur. Ecce quales se toti mundo prebent qui se fore mundi cardines gloriantur! Post exhibitum quidem fidelibus unum Christi vicarium, sive, ut plures arbitrantur, solenniter

around more keenly, rage more cruelly, and plunder more extrava-
gantly are held to be more famous, being involved in acts of brig-
andage in a public way. Look at kings, consider princes, examine   3
states: whom will you find taking thought for their subjects' inter-
ests? Whom will you cite who, under the title of just governance,
do not practice tyranny, who do not ordain as most just what they
think most profitable to themselves, who are ashamed to transgress the laws that they have passed, and who are willing and able
to say with those august princes, Severus and Antoninus, "Although we have been released from the laws, we nevertheless live
by the laws"?[11]

But why am I complaining about these temporal affairs? Let us   4
look at the state of our spiritual church. Are not all playing the
same game? Do we not see that what we read in the prophet is
quite true, "From the least right up to the greatest all compete in
avarice; from the prophet right up to the priest everyone practices
deceit"?[12] Why should I mention ambition, why the lure of luxury? Don't we see those whom we have as guardians of souls
stained by all the offenses of the fetid flesh, shunning nothing base
and nothing detestable in order to obtain the offices they desire?
Finally, although they appear to honor God with their lips, if any-   5
one were to look at their works, wouldn't he think that either they
do not believe in God, or, if they do not dare to deny God's existence, that they consider him to be asleep, blind, or utterly con-
temptuous of human affairs? It does not suffice for them to sin in
private and to have only themselves, a few others, or their own
household as a witness to their impurities, if they—monstrous in
their thoughts, deformed in their impulses, and horrible in their
works—are not displayed before the eyes of all. See what kinds   6
of people present themselves to the whole world, glorying that
they are the world's axes! After one vicar of Christ has been presented to the faithful (whether, as the majority think, solemnly

ordinatum sive, ut ipsi credi volunt, per impressionem metus assumptum, inaudito atque pessimo exemplo venenum abominandi scismatis effundentes, alterum elegerunt, et Christi sponsam aut hinc aut inde producentes adulterum post fedam prostitutionem fecerunt esse bicipitem. Ab istis igitur ad quem terrarum angulum, ad quam ignotam insulam, ad quam inhospitam heremum, non
7 est, si quis sue saluti consulat, fugiendum? Felix itaque, mi Ieronime, qui seculum relinquens et mundi pompas, quarum studium te poterat huiusmodi feditate scismatis maculare, ex malorum oculis te in congregationem honestam et sanctissimam coniecisti. Simul enim malorum hominum furores et hanc calentem vitiorum fabricam evitasti.

: V :

Quod mundus sit fabrica vitiorum.

1 Fabrica quidem vitiorum est mundus. Nam quicquid mali committitur intra mundi presentis ambitum perpetratur. Hic quidem fornicationes voluptuose, deflorantia stupra, violenti raptus, reverentie sanguinis corruptores incestus, insidiantia nuptialibus thoris adulteria, in deo dicatas sacrilege pollutiones, nefandique affectata sterilitate concubitus et quicquid monstruosum venenum in nos
2 veneris excitat committuntur. Quibus miseri mortales implititi, dum specie qua pereunt decipiuntur, subvertente concupiscentia

ordained, or, as they themselves wish to be believed, accepted under duress), pouring forth the venom of abominable schism in an
unheard-of, wicked example, they elected another, and, produc-
ing an adulterer on either side, after foul prostitution, made the
bride of Christ two-headed.[13] If anyone takes thought for his
own salvation, therefore, to what corner of the world, to what
unknown island, to what inhospitable desert should he not flee
from this corruption? And so, blessed are you, dear Girolamo, you   7
who, abandoning this age and the world's ostentation (eagerness
for which could have tainted you with the filth of this kind of
schism), have taken yourself out of the sight of evils into an honorable and most holy community. For at the same time you have
avoided the raving madness of wicked men and this factory seething with vices.

: V :

The world is a factory of vices.

The world is indeed a factory of vices. For all evil that is commit-   1
ted is perpetrated within the ambit of the present world. Here are
committed acts of pleasurable fornication, deflowering debauchery,
violent rapes, acts of incest corrupting reverence for blood ties,
adulteries that plot against the nuptial bed, sacrilegious pollution
of women dedicated to God, wicked sexual intercourse with con-
trived sterility, and whatever the monstrous poison of sex excites
in us. Wretched mortals are entangled in these acts, deceived by   2
the outward appearance that kills them. With desire subverting

cor rectum cecitate mentis obtenebrantur, dumque amorem, qui, ut Propertius inquit,

> docet castas odisse puellas
> improbus et nullo vivere consilio,

sequuntur, precipitatione quadam consilio subtrahuntur inconsiderationeque sensus suos avertentes recta iudicia non recordantur.

3 Et ipso concupiscentie impetu, licet bona videant, mala sequuntur, ut apud Ovidium impatiens conqueritur amans,

> video meliora proboque,
> deteriora sequor.

Et denique suarum voluptatum studio presens affectant seculum, desperant futurum, et deum odio habentes, cuius maiestate atque metu a suis libidinibus deterrentur, ut diutius venereis perfruantur

4 illecebris, se ipsos plus quam oporteat amant. Hic nos excandescentie fellei motus invadunt; hic amaros atque diuturnos manie pertinacis estus, hic observantes ultionis tempus furoris impetus experimur, ex quibus, cum nos indignos reputamus iniuria, indignatione commovemur. Dum ardore quodam vindictam querimus, mentis tumore concutimur et in clamosa iurgia, contumelias iniuriosas, blasfemiasque abominabiles excitamur. Nec solo maliloquio contenti iracundia provocati inimicicias concipimus sed et bella mortifera preliamur.

5 In hac vitiorum fabrica ut ad inflatam mentis superbiam, que princeps est omnium peccatorum, veniamus, adeo insolenter efferimur quod a nobis habere quod deus ipse tribuit arbitramur, aut si id ab eo recepisse nos dicimus, nostris provenisse meritis cogitamus, aut quod nobis abesse cognoscimus, nos habere mendaciose iactamus, et denique si quid habere nos cernimus, ceteris

the upright heart, they are overshadowed by their mental blindness, and as they pursue love—which, as Propertius says,

> teaches to despise the chaste girls,
> the rascal, and to live recklessly[14]

—in a kind of haste they are drawn away from reason; turning
their senses thoughtlessly away, they are forgetful of right judgment. Upon the very attack of desire, although they see good   3
things, they follow bad, as the impatient lover in Ovid complains:

> I see and approve of the better,
> I follow the worse.[15]

Finally, in their eagerness for their own pleasures they focus on the
present age, abandon hope for the future; hating God (by awe for
whose majesty they are deterred from their lusts), they love themselves more than they should, so that they may the longer enjoy
the allurements of sex. Here the poisonous movements of growing   4
anger attack us; here we experience the bitter daily seething of
stubborn madness, here are fury's impulses watching for the time
of revenge, moving us with indignation when we believe that we
have been undeserving of harm. While we seek revenge with ardor, we are shaken by a swelling of mind and provoked into shouting matches, wounding insults, and abominable blasphemies. Not
content with vilification alone, provoked by wrath, we conceive
vendettas and even wage deadly wars.

In this factory of vices, to come to inflated mental pride, which   5
is the chief of all sins: we are so carried away in our insolence that
we regard what God himself has bestowed upon us as originating with ourselves; or if we admit that we have received it from
him, we consider that it has come to us because of our merits, or
we mendaciously boast that we have what we know we lack. And

6 despectis, videri volumus id singulariter obtinere. Hic curiositate quadam motis obtutibus inordinata circumspectione vagamur. Hic levitate mentis clamosa loquacitate perstrepimus. Hic inepta leticia in risus petulantiam sine moderatione resolvimur. Hic debite
7 taciturnitatis observatione soluta in iactationem efferimur. Hic elati conamur sanctitatem nobis singulariter arrogare. Hic viribus maiora presumimus. Hic per arrogantiam nos anteferimus preponendis. Hic peccata superbe defendimus aut simulate per insolentiam confitemur. Hic contra eos quibus parendum est elatis mentibus rebellamus. Hic dum facere que volumus delectamur, pudentissima libertate peccamus. Et denique cum deum timere debeamus, ipsum habendo contemptui a peccandi consuetudine recedere non curamus.

8 Et ut omnia breviloquio comprehendam, hic hereses, infidelitas, apostasis, blasfemia, hebetudo sensus, et cecitas intellectus; hic aggravans illa tristicia que deprimit mentes humanas ut bonum nichil facere placeat; hic malicia, rancor, pusillanimitas, torpor, vagatio mentis, desperatio, invidia, odium, susurratio, detractio, exultatio in adversis proximi et afflictio in prosperis; hic pacis, quam cuncta quidem appetunt, inimica contentio, discordie, scismata, bella, rixe, seditiones, scandala, imprudentia, precipitatio, temeritas, inconsideratio, inconstantia, dolus, prudentia carnis, as-
9 tutia, fraus, sollicitudo temporalium rerum atque futurorum; hic iniusticia, personarum acceptio, homicidia, cedes, iniurie, sacrilegia, furta, rapine, iniqua iudicia, calumnie, tergiversationes, falsa testimonia, maledicta, derisiones, deceptiones, illicita lucra, usura, simonia, execrationes, maleficia, fascinationes, sortilegia, divinationes, superstitiones, ydolatria, auguria, avaricia, proditio, falsitates, mendacia, periuria, violentie, fallacie, fraudes, simulatio,

finally, if we see that we have something, we despise others and want to be seen as the only one to possess that thing. Here we 6 wander with inordinate circumspection, our gaze excited by inquisitiveness. Here we thoughtlessly raise a din with unremitting shouts. Here with inordinately high spirits we dissolve in laughter's impudence. Here, failing to observe due silence, we are carried away into boasting. Here, elated, we try to arrogate holiness to 7 ourselves alone. Here we undertake things that are greater than our strength. Here in our arrogance we place ourselves before people who ought to be put first. Here we haughtily defend our sins or in our insolence feign confession of them. Here with minds carried away we rebel against those we ought to obey. Here, as we delight in doing as we please, we sin with the most shameful freedom. And finally, although we ought to fear God, we hold him in contempt and do not care to withdraw from the habit of sin.

And to put it in a nutshell: here are heresies, infidelity, apostasy, 8 blasphemy, dullness of sense, and blindness of intellect; here that depression that weighs on human minds so that they don't want to do anything good; here malice, rancor, small-mindedness, lethargy, a straying mind, despair, envy, hatred, whispering, carping criticism, exultation in the misfortunes of a neighbor and affliction in his prosperity; here is contentiousness, the enemy of the peace that all things long for, discords, schisms, wars, quarrels, seditions, scandals, imprudence, haste, rashness, thoughtlessness, inconstancy, guile, carnal wisdom, trickery, fraud, concern for temporal and future affairs; here injustice, regarding of persons, homi- 9 cides, slaughter, injuries, acts of sacrilege, thefts, acts of pillaging, unfair judgments, calumnies, betrayals, false testimonies, slanders, derision, deceptions, illicit gains, usury, simony, curses, misdeeds, spells, casting of lots, divination, superstition, idolatry, augury, avarice, betrayal, falsehoods, lies, perjury, acts of violence, deceit,

10   ypocrisis, iactantia, ironia, adulatio, atque litigia. Sed quid ego ad
     impossibile conor? Nam, ut poeta inquit,

> Non michi si lingue centum sint oraque centum
> Ferrea vox omnes scelerum comprendere formas,
> Omnia penarum percurrere nomina possim.

11   Nam quicquid ab divine legis tramite devians vel hostis insidiis vel
     fragilitate carnis vel deceptione mundi in mortalium mentibus ex-
     citatur aut corrupto lumine rationis in divine maiestatis offensam
     eligitur aut electum opere consumatur, totum in hac mundi coha-
     bitatione delinquimus, tantaque cecitas mentes invadit quod nos-
     tris his malis corrupto iudicio non solum indulgemus sed delec-
     tamur nec nos esse in immundissima sentina turpitudinum
     cogitamus.

: VI :

Quod mundus sit immundissima sentina turpitudinum.

1   Sentina quidem infima pars navis est, ad quam aqua fetens et
    putrida et omnes ipsius navis sordicies congregantur, locus quidem
    tanta obscuritate horrendus tantaque immundicia plenus quod,
    nisi sepius emundetur, totam navim coinquinet et corrumpat,
    et quidquid in ipsum decidat, si animans sit, diu non possit in
    illo fetido fimo vivere; si vero inanimatum, aut omnino in sordis
    illius augmentum se transferat aut limositate fetida ad horrorem
2   usque, si aliquamdiu ibi permanserit, contabescat. Quid autem
    hoc mundo immundius, quid fedius, quid obscenius? Omittamus

cheating, pretense, hypocrisy, boastfulness, irony, adulation, and lawsuits. But why do I attempt the impossible? For, as the poet 10 says,

> Not if I had a hundred tongues and a hundred mouths
> and a voice of iron could I include all the forms of crime,
> run through all the names of punishments.[16]

For whatever deviation from the path of divine law is excited in 11 the minds of mortals by the scheming of the Enemy or the fragility of the flesh or the deception of the world, either is chosen to offend the divine majesty when the light of reason has been corrupted, or, having been chosen, is consummated in the deed. In all of it we offend by this cohabitation with the world, and such great blindness invades our minds that not only do we, in our corrupt judgment, indulge these evils of ours, but we delight in them and fail to consider that we are in the unwholesome hold of turpitude.

: VI :

The world is the unwholesome hold of turpitude.

The hold is the lowest part of the ship. Fetid and putrid water and 1 all the dirt of the ship itself collects in it, a horrendous place filled with such great darkness and unwholesomeness that, unless it is cleaned often, it contaminates and corrupts the entire ship. If what falls into the hold is alive, it cannot survive for long in that fetid filth; but if it is inanimate, either it changes into an accretion to that dirt, or, if it remains there for some time, it decays to a horrific condition with the fetid sliminess. What is more unwhole- 2 some than this world, what is more foul, what more obscene? Let

quanta sit vilitas corporum in quorum regionibus spiramus et vivimus, quorum unum, in quo precipue contigit nos morari, suapte natura gravissimum omnium corporalium fex est, alterum paulo purius multum limositate quam trahit et ipsam terram colluvione sua quasi corruptione quadam videmus inficere, tertium vero nescio qua natura in secundi curva superficie sedem habens, cum tamen exilire videatur, sua gravitate descendit et infectione subita mortalibus grave, pestifero afflatu finitima coinquinat elementa.

3 Ultimum autem illud ceteris tum nobilius, tum purius, quamvis evolare credatur, ab impuriorum tamen confinio non discedit et plerumque sui veneni tabe creditur desevire. Omittamus hec, inquam, et ad id quod intendimus veniamus.

4 Quid enim inquinatius mundo, quid limosius, quid denique turpius? In hoc enim spacio intra quod mortales versamur anima nostra, que ab illo rerum omnium opifice infunditur et creatur, imo de nichilo dum creatur infunditur, pura, simplex, recta, innocens, et eterna conversatione mundi quasi in fetidam sentinam delapsa fit immunda, maliciosa, perversa, culpabilis, et, quantum ad incorruptibilem pertinet gloriam, mortua penitus et extincta, ut iam bonum esset homini illi si natus non fuisset. Hic enim quicquid inficit, maculat, et corrumpit ⟨quaecumque⟩ cogitamus, perficimus, operamur. Et cum, sicut proxime dictum est, sit hic mundus cunctorum fabrica vitiorum, que quidem feditate sua ab eterne legis pulcritudine discedentia, imo penitus adversantia, turpissimos nos efficiunt et immundos, merito dicimus mundum istum olentem, fetidam, et immundissimam sentinam turpitudinum,

us pass over the great vileness of the bodies in the midst of which we breathe and live.[17] One of these (the one in particular in which it befalls us to linger) is sediment, by its own nature the heaviest of all corporal things. We observe that the second, a little purer, infects much with the sliminess that it carries, and the earth itself with its swill, as if it were a kind of corruption. A third body has its seat on the curved surface of the second by some law of nature; although it is seen to rise up, it sinks by its own weight, and with sudden infection dangerous to mortals, contaminates the neighboring elements with its disease-bearing breath. Although the last body, both nobler and purer than the others, is believed to ascend, it does not depart from the boundary of the impure bodies and is believed generally to seethe with the decaying of its poison. Let us pass over these things, I say, and come to our goal. 3

What is more defiling than the world, what is slimier, what, finally, is more base? For in this space within which we mortals dwell, our soul, which is poured into us and created by that Craftsman of all things (more precisely, it is poured into us when it is created out of nothing), is pure, simple, upright, innocent; yet in its constant interaction with the world, as if it has sunk down into a fetid hold, it becomes unclean, wicked, perverse, guilty, and, as far as incorruptible glory is concerned, wholly dead and extinct, so that by now it were good for that man never to have been born.[18] For here is whatever infects, sullies, and corrupts whatever we think about, perform, and accomplish. Since, as was said in the preceding chapter, this world is the factory of all vices — vices that depart by their disgusting nature from beauty's eternal law, or indeed are thoroughly opposed to it — these vices render us extremely base and unclean; with good reason we call this stinking, fetid, and very dirty world the hold of turpitude. To flee from it is 4 5

quam fugere mundicia mentis est, purificatio cordis, intellectus il-
luminatio, et ad huius aggravantis corporis futuram glorificatio-
nem, quam speramus et credimus post adventum domini, sola via,
ut iam, postquam hinc emerserimus, nunquam sit decepta mente
ad huius fallentis visci glutinum, si recte vivere voluerimus, redeundum.

: VII :

Quod mundus est fallax viscum.

1 Si quanto amore cupiant miseri mortales in hoc mundo sui exilii
immemores permanere, si quantum nos decipiat contemplemur,
nemini iam vertetur in dubium quod mundus iste sit fallacissi-
mum viscum. Quid enim fallacius, quid viscosius mundo? Blanditur enim, allicit, mulcet, delectat, et, quod horum consequens est,
suis illecebris nos inviscat; tantaque ipsius deceptio est ut, quamvis
post gustum dulcedinis amarissima venena permisceat et id ipsum
cui fomenta ministrare videtur corpus humanum inficiat et corrumpat, ad se tamen nos falsa illa et fallaci mulcedine sua rapiat et
2 convertat. Quo cautius meditandum et obnixius agendum est ut
ab illo semel decepti (semper enim decipit) factique cautiores ulterius non fallamur. Habet inertissimum animal et inter bruta bru-
tissimum illud rudibile insitam naturaliter mirabilem cautionem.
Ubicunque quidem semel ceciderit, longiusculum capit horrorem
et, si post multos etiam annos ad eundem locum redierit, retro
vertitur, transire formidat, et, nisi cogatur verberibus, locum illum

cleanliness of mind, purification of heart, illumination of intellect, and the only way to the future glorification of this body (which we hope and believe will happen after the Lord's coming) that now drags us down. Consequently, now, after we have extricated ourselves from this world, we must never, with mind deceived, return to the glue of this deceptive birdlime, if we want to live correctly.

: VII :

The world is deceptive birdlime.

If we contemplate with what great love wretched mortals, forgetful 1
of their exile, desire to remain in this world, if we contemplate
how much it deceives us, nobody will doubt that this world is the
most deceptive of birdlime. For what is more deceptive, what
stickier than the world? It blandishes, allures, sweet-talks, delights, and, as a consequence, ensnares us with its enticements. Its
deception is so great that it snatches and turns us to itself with its
false and tricky soothing, even though, after the taste of sweetness,
it mixes in the bitterest poisons, infecting and corrupting that
same human body to which it appears to supply lenitives. We 2
must reflect all the more carefully and act all the more vigorously
in order that, once we have been deceived by the world (for it always deceives) and thus put on guard, we are not tricked any
more. The most indolent animal and the most brutish among
brutes possesses a marvelous caution implanted by nature. Wherever he has fallen once, even at a great distance, terror grips him,
and, if he returns to that same place even after many years, he
turns back; he is afraid to cross it, and, remembering his earlier

3 memor prioris casus adire renuit et evitat. Aviculas etiam tradunt, postquam alis semel viscatis effugerint, locum eundem et apparatum similem abhorrere. Quibus irrationalibus rationales admonemur non minus evitandam a nobis fore nostrarum animarum iacturam quam fugiant illa corpoream.

4 Tu autem, mi Ieronime, ut ad te redeam, dirupisti vincula, contrivisti laqueum, et liberatus mundi viscum taliter posuisti quod hinc elevatis alis ad religionis altitudinem evolasti, ut maxima tibi sit indicta perseverandi necessitas cavendique ne per precipitia rediens et ruinam ad mundum, ubi, cum tristari debeas, leteris, imo ad mundi labes et quas fugisti miserias revertaris.

: VIII :

Quod mundus est tristis leticia, falsum gaudium,
et exultatio inanis.

1 Et, ut inceptum redeamus ad ordinem, cum dixerim mundum fore tristem leticiam, falsum gaudium, et exultationem inanem, hec tria simul, licet proprietate vocabulorum differant, explicemus. Circa idem enim versantur obiectum. Nam, ut secularium quidam ait, 'Cum animus movetur placide atque constanter, tum illud gaudium dicitur. Cum autem inaniter et effuse animus exultat, tum illa leticia gestiens et nimia dici potest.' Hec ille. Exultatio autem
2 coniunctus mentis et corporis motus est. Et quia hec tria scimus

fall, he avoids that place, refusing to approach unless compelled by blows. They even relate that little birds, when they have once escaped with sticky wings, keep clear of the same place and a similar device. We rational beings are admonished by these irrational creatures to shun the loss of our soul no less than they flee that of their bodies.   3

But, dear Girolamo (to return to you), you have broken your chains, crushed the trap, been liberated, and have laid aside the world's birdlime to such an extent that you have flown forth from here on wings soaring to the heights of religious life. Therefore the utmost need is imposed upon you to persevere and be on guard lest, crashing down headlong in ruin, you return to the world in order to enjoy merriment when you ought to be sad, or rather to the world's disgraces and miseries, which you have fled.   4

: VIII :

The world is baleful happiness, false joy,
and empty exultation.

To return to the order we began: when I said that the world is a baleful happiness, false joy, and empty exultation, let me explain these three things together, although the meaning of the words differs. All three have to do with the same object. For, as a certain secular author says, "When the soul is moved peacefully and constantly, then that is called joy. But when the soul exults in an empty and extravagant way, then that happiness can be said to be excited and excessive."[19] Exultation is the conjoined movement of the mind and the body. And since we know that these three things   1

2

animis humanis contingere ex recordatione presentiaque bonorum, ideo ea simul, ut diximus, pertractemus. Letamur igitur, gaudemus, et exultamus nostrarum cupiditatum facti compotes cum voluptatibus nostris perfruimur — imo, ut verius loquar, non fruimur, non utimur, non potimur, sed corrumpimur, inficimur, effe-

3 minamur, occidimur. Tristis quidem est leticia que, cum ad rationem venerimus cumque absconditam acutiori nobiscum examine claram excusserimus veritatem, non solum est nobis allatura tristiciam sed super his in quibus letati fuerimus lugendum fuisse, do-

4 lendum, et lacrimandum ratione validissima cognoscemus. Falsum est proculdubio mundi presentis gaudium quia cum, prout fuit superius diffinitum, motus animi constans et placidus gaudium esse dicatur, inter hec corruptibilia nos ipsi mortales non possumus constanter, ut patet intuentibus, iocundari. Inanis est etiam exultatio inter ista mundana adeo gaudio resolvi quod animi vanitatem, imo irrationabilitatem, ut videmus in brutis animalibus, ostendamus.

5 Videamus, si placet, quoniam plus est omnia quidem dicere quam totum aliquid explicare, quid in mundo nos relaxet in gaudium, leticiam moveat, et ad exultationem impellat. Hoc superius in expletionem cupiditatum et voluptatum confluentiam compre-

6 hendi. Quid autem in hoc mundo concupiscimus aut quidnam desiderare solemus? Perscrutemur maris tractus planaque et montuosa terrarum. Certe aut his omnibus dominari cupimus aut que in eis sunt ad superfluitatem nobis et voluptatem gliscimus obve-

7 nire. Optavit quondam Alexander magnus, Macedonum rex, totum orbem sue subdere monarchie. Qui tamen cum Persarum superasset imbelliam et Indos prospero fortune flatu bellis felicibus

happen to human souls as a result of the memory and presence of good things, I will deal with them at the same time, as I said. We are happy, then, we rejoice, and we exult when we have come into the possession of the objects of our desires and are enjoying our pleasures — rather, to speak more truly, we do not enjoy, use, have possession of, but we are corrupted, infected, emasculated, slain by them. When we have arrived at reason and investigated the 3 hidden truth, clear upon subtler examination, not only is happiness that is destined to bring sadness to us baleful indeed, but we will acknowledge with sound reason that we should have lamented, mourned, and wept about these things over which we rejoiced. The joy of the present world is undoubtedly false: accord- 4 ing to the above definition, constant and peaceful motion of soul is called joy; yet amid these corruptible things we, ourselves mortal, cannot rejoice constantly, as is clear to the observer. Exultation amid those worldly affairs is empty — to dissolve in joy to such an extent that we show the vanity, or rather irrationality, of our soul, as we observe in brute beasts.

Let us see, if you please (since it is more valuable to survey ev- 5 erything than to explain one thing in its entirety), what in the world releases us into joy, stirs happiness, and drives us to exultation. I included this topic above when I spoke about the satisfaction of desires and the flowing together of pleasures. What do we 6 long for in this world, or what do we habitually desire? Let us examine the tracts of the sea, the plains and mountains of the earth. Certainly, we either desire to dominate all of them, or we yearn to come into possession of their contents for our superabundance of pleasure. Alexander the Great, the king of the Macedonians, once 7 wished to subject the whole world to his monarchy. When he had conquered the unwarlike Persians and subjugated the Indians in successful wars with an auspicious blast of fortune, and had added

subiugasset et pene cunctas Asie et orientis oras dicioni Macedonum addidisset, quasi toto orbe quesito et huius unius mundi sa-
8 tietate correptus cogitabat ad anthipodas penetrare. Cum tamen
apud nos adhuc vincendus restaret occeanus, ubi non cum fugaci-
bus Parthis, divitibus Persis, effeminatis Assiriis, non cum relictu-
ris urbes et ad petras male etiam defendendas pre formidine fugi-
turis, non cum his qui solo Alexandri nomine et fama, que ingens
et gloriosa per totum orbis ambitum ferebatur, intra propugnacula
murorum attoniti victis iam animis se dedebant pugnandum erat,
sed contra Romanos, durum bello genus hominum, ferro non
fama, consilio non fortuna, sobrietate non vino (cuius ille appeten-
tissimus fuisse traditur) erat eventu dubio dimicandum, cum Romanis, inquam, quorum auspiciis, ut gentili utar vocabulo, domi-
natus orbis dispositione celestis numinis debebatur, quive per id
tempus non tam aurum habere volebant quam aurum habentibus
imperare noverantque non solum uti victoriis sed adversis bello-
9 rum casibus non prosterni. Quid autem ille tot bellis, tot laboribus, tanta superbia, tanto fastu, non deus, cuius sibi decerni postulabat honores, sed mortalis exhausit? Certe apud suos venenum
mortiferum, apud externos contemptum, suis quoque temporibus
nedum victarum gentium sed etiam suorum militum odium, apud
posteros vero inter optimi ducis famam avaricie, crudelitatis, et
ebrietatis infamiam, extimationem ancipitem, et rumorem ambi-
10 guum dereliquit. Cum igitur ille victoriis exultaret, letaretur prosperis, et gauderet ac potiretur optatis, satis nobis exemplo sit tris-
tissime letatum, gavisum false, et inaniter exultasse qui in vita

almost all the regions of Asia and the Orient to the dominion of
the Macedonians, as if he had gained the whole globe and was
seized by surfeit of this one world, he was planning to penetrate
the antipodes. But the ocean near us[20] remained to be conquered,   8
where he did not have to fight with flighty Parthians, wealthy Persians, effeminate Assyrians; not with peoples prone to abandon
their cities and flee in fear to rocks difficult to defend; not with
peoples who, thunderstruck by Alexander's name and fame alone,
which was borne huge and glorious through all the globe's ambit,
surrendered with spirits already conquered within the bulwark of
their walls. No, at that time he would have had to fight a war of
uncertain outcome against the Romans, a race of men hardened by
war; he would have had to fight by steel not fame, by counsel not
fortune, by sobriety not wine (to which Alexander is reported to
have been addicted) — with the Romans, I say, to whose auspices
(to use a pagan word) world domination was due by the disposition of the celestial Deity, and who throughout that time wanted
not so much to have gold as to rule those who had it,[21] and knew
not only how to use victories but also how not to be laid low by
mischances of war. Yet what did Alexander — not a god, whose   9
honors he demanded be decreed to him, but a mortal — drink up
with so many wars, so many labors, such great haughtiness, such
great arrogance? Truly, death-dealing poison among his own people, contempt among foreigners, and even in his own times the
hatred not only of vanquished races but also of his own sol-
diers; and to posterity he left behind, along with the fame of being
the most excellent general, the infamy of avarice, cruelty, and
drunkenness, an ambivalent reputation, and ambiguous rumor.
Since, then, he exulted in victories, rejoiced in prosperity, and was   10
happy in and in possession of what he wished for, let this be a sufficient example for us that he was very sadly happy, that he rejoiced falsely, and that he exulted vainly — he who accumulated

odium, ad mortem venenum, et post fata tantam infamiam congregavit.

11   Que autem in mundo sunt, quando ille superbia spiritus est, ut paulo ante diffinitum fuit, quid aliud dici possunt quam concupiscentia carnis et oculorum? Ve igitur miseris mortalibus qui mundum sequentes seque convertentes in beluas carni serviunt, carni student, et, ut expleant gulam, aerem, terram, et maria, quibus delicatos venentur cibos, diligenti faciunt indagine perscrutari. Ve cunctis respicientibus filias hominum ad libidinem et divitias ad avariciam, quique splendores ceteros istos fugaces et falsos ad am-
12   bitionem respiciunt vel livorem. Quid enim aliud istis eventurum esse credi debet quam quod audiant verbum illud terribile contra ipsorum quemlibet proferendum, 'Ligatis pedibus suis et manibus mittite eum in tenebras exteriores'? Cum enim terrena ex toto corde, tota anima, et tota mente dilexerint turpes et infecti vitiis, non splendidi luce bonorum operum, sicut iusti qui fulgebunt velut scintille ignis in arundineto, licet cogantur, ut evangelii parabola monet, non intrabunt ad regii filii nuptias vestes nuptiales
13   induti. Unde dicetur eis in die illa districti iudicii cum separabuntur a damnatis electi, 'Amici, quomodo huc intrastis non habentes vestes nuptiales?' et demum ligatis manibus atque pedibus proicientur in tenebras exteriores ubi erit fletus et stridor dentium. Hoc est, miseri mortales, superbie, cupiditatum, libidinum, et voluptatum nostrarum lucrum; hic est huius corruptibilis et corrumpentis
14   mundi fructus. Hunc igitur, non quod ante oculos nobis in hac carnis fragilitate positum est sed ventura pensantes, ac velut beluam crudelissimam evitemus iustamque in hac area tribulationum formidinem capientes ad mundum reverti, quicunque vel elevatione mentis vel dei benignitate et gratia filii dei per lavacrum

hatred in life, poison for his death, and such great infamy after his demise.

What else can worldly things be called than concupiscence of the flesh and eyes, when that world is arrogance of the soul, as it was defined above? Woe, then, to wretched mortals, who, pursuing the world and transforming themselves into beasts, serve the flesh, are zealous for the flesh, and cause air, earth, and seas to be searched with utmost care, for places in which to hunt delicacies to fill up their gullets. Woe to all who ogle people's daughters to fulfill lust and eye wealth to satisfy avarice, and all who look at the rest of those evanescent and false splendors with ambition or envy. What else should one suppose will happen to those people than that they will hear those terrible words proclaimed against any one of them: "Bind his feet and his hands and send him into the outer darkness"?[22] For since those base and vice-infected men love earthly things with their whole heart, their whole soul, and their whole mind, and do not shine with the light of good works as do the just who will glow like sparks of fire in a bed of reeds,[23] they will not enter the prince's wedding feast wearing wedding clothes, although they are required to do so. Therefore, this will be said to them on that day of severe judgment when the elect will be separated from the damned: "Friends, how did you enter here without wedding clothes?"[24] Finally, they will be thrown with hands and feet bound into the outer darkness, where there will be weeping and gnashing of teeth. This, wretched mortals, is the reward of our pride, desires, lusts, and pleasures; this is the fruit of this corruptible and corrupting world. Let all of us, then, who, made children of God through the bath of rebirth, have escaped by the elevation of our mind or by the beneficence and the grace of God, recoil with all the senses of our mind and body at this world, considering not what has been placed before our eyes in this fragility of the flesh, but the things to come. Let us avoid this world as we

11

12

13

14

regenerationis effecti forsan effugimus, totis anime corporisque
sensibus horreamus.

: IX :

Quod mundus sit area tribulationum.

1 In mundo quidem, sicut in area frumentum multis verberibus tri-
turatur ut hinc grana statuantur, hinc palee, sic nos multis anxietatibus, angustiis, tribulationibus, et erumnis vexamur, premimur,
2 affligimur, et torquemur. Principio quidem respice condicionem
nostre carnis, examina corporis fragilitatem, et considera quot cir-
cum morbis, dum in mundo sumus, quotve calamitatibus agite-
mur. Discurre per urbes, circumeas oppida, perambula vicos: quot
invenies captos oculis, abscisos naribus, evulsos dentibus, lingua
3 cesos vel impeditos, et denique privatos auditu? Hic estuat febribus, ille podagris, deliciarum ultricibus, cruciatur; hic morbo dis-
torquetur iliaco, ille dolore capitis infestatus giros, vertigines, et
caliginosa volumina patitur ac viscido sanguine de fellis nigredine
vitiato cerebrum conturbante cervicem tremit et contractione manuum atque pedum amissis sensibus sternitur aut ore spumante
4 cum pectoris sonitu supinatur. Alii dum urgentur febribus alienata
mente decidunt in furorem, aut febribus non correpti timentes,
iracundi vel hilares insaniunt, seviunt, vultuque mestissimo tris-
tantur, fletu irrationabili deliquescunt, et plerumque mori cupiunt
5 vel asciscunt. Sed quid ego enumerare connitor multimodas

would the cruelest beast, taking hold of a righteous fear of returning to it on this threshing floor of tribulations.

: IX :

The world is a threshing floor of tribulations.

In the world, just as on a threshing floor, threshing is done with 1 much beating so that the grain falls to one side and chaff to the other; so we are vexed with many anxieties, stressed by many trials, afflicted with many tribulations, and tortured with many sorrows. First, look at the condition of our flesh, examine the fragility 2 of the body, and consider how many diseases and disasters harry us while we are in the world. Canvass the cities, go around the towns, wander through the neighborhoods: how often will you discover people with eye injuries, noses cut off, teeth pulled out, tongues cut or maimed, and, finally, deaf? This person boils with 3 fever, that one is tormented by gout, the avengers of luxuries. This one is racked with bowel disease. That one, attacked by pain in the head, suffers from dizzy spells, vertigo, and blackouts; viscous blood tainted by black bile throws this one's brain into confusion; that one has tremors in the neck; with convulsions of hands and feet, this one falls down senseless, or lies prostrate with wheezing, foaming at the mouth. Others, goaded by fever and out 4 of their minds, fall into frenzy. Or, though unaffected by fever, they rave and rage, fearful, wrathful, or manically high-spirited; and with terribly sad countenance they are depressed, they melt with irrational weeping, generally desiring to die or bring death upon themselves. But why do I strive to enumerate the manifold 5

diversitates morborum, quas vix potuerunt pater optimus et infal-
libilis Hypocras, venerabilis Galienus, Avicenna mirabilis, et autores infiniti post illos plus quam mille voluminibus explicare?
Sufficiat igitur dicere infinitis morborum qualitatibus corpus nostrum nunc ad internicionem, nunc ad languorem et egritudinem
alterari.

6   Sed dicet quispiam, 'Cur non ita laudas mundum propter sanos
qui corporibus integri sunt, stomaco valent, et cunctorum membrorum sospitate fruuntur, quorum ingentior est multitudo, sicut
eum propter infirmos vituperas et condemnas?' Facerem id plane si

7   possem et si ratio ipsa permitteret. Sed illi ipsi quos sanos vides,
aut iam multa perpessi sunt aut iam multa passuri, et, si nobis
constare voluerimus, ista nostrorum corporum sanitas infirmitas
est, infirmitas quidem tanto maior quanto suavior tantoque peri-

8   culosior quanto latentior. Dicere non possum quantis sit ista,
quam incolumitatem dicimus, si eam conservare voluerimus, admi-
niculis fulcienda. Cibo famem, potu sitim, veste frigus, umbris et
flabellis estum, sopore vigilias, excubatione somnum, lassitudinem
ocio, torporem opere, saturitatem inedia, cibationeque ieiunium

9   restauramus. In quorum vicissitudine illud dignum admiratione
contingit, quod, si aliqui predictarum necessitatum quas retuli
supplemento diutius insistamus, quod fuit ante remedium mox
convertitur in venenum indeque datur morbos incipere unde prius

10   instanti morbo cogitavimus obviare. Denique hec ipsa sanitas et
salubritas corporis quotidie quasi quadam diluvione descrescit et
in se ipsa corrumpitur. Que si, ut putamus, sanitas esset, quanto
foret diuturnior, tanto fieret dierum accessione robustior et ad in-
corruptibilitatis statum, si foret possibile, deveniret.

diversity of diseases, which the excellent father, infallible Hippocrates, the venerable Galen, the wonderful Avicenna, and an infinite number of authors after them could scarcely explain in more than a thousand volumes? Let it suffice, therefore, to say that our bodies are altered by infinite kinds of diseases, sometimes leading to annihilation, at other times to lethargy and illness.

But someone will say, "Why don't you praise the world on account of the healthy people who are whole in their bodies, strong in stomach, and enjoy the well-being of all their limbs, who form the majority, in the same way that you blame and condemn the world on account of the infirm?" I would, of course, do that if I could and if reason itself allowed it. But those very people whom you see healthy either have already endured, or presently will endure, many sufferings. And (if we want to be consistent) the health of our bodies is in fact infirmity, indeed an infirmity that is all the greater the sweeter it is, and all the more dangerous the more it is hidden. I cannot say on what great supports that thing that we call well-being depends if we wish to preserve it. We treat hunger with food, thirst with drink, cold with clothing, heat with shade and fans, late nights with sleep, sleepiness with staying awake, fatigue with rest, listlessness with work, overeating with fasting, and fasting with eating. In the alternation of these states, it is a wonder that if we somehow rely upon the supplement to the aforementioned necessities for too long, what was previously a remedy is soon converted into a poison, and diseases begin from the same source whence we earlier thought to avoid disease when it threatened. Finally, this very health and well-being of body diminishes daily as if by a kind of deluge and is corrupted in itself. And if this were health, as we suppose, then the longer lasting it was, the more robust it would become with each passing day, and if it were possible, it would attain a state of incorruptibility.

6

7

8

9

10

11   Est itaque infirma nostra sanitas, imo, ut verius loquar, non infirma sed infirmitas, a nostris tamen remota sensibus et absconsa,
nec aliter sanum possumus quempiam affirmare quam si, cum
tertianam, quartanam, vel quintanam febrem aliquis patiatur, eum
12   diebus remissionis incolumem asseramus. Quid enim refert cessare
una die, duobus vel tribus aut pluribus an mensibus aliquot, sicut
de Anthipatre poeta legitur, qui quotannis die sui natalis febribus
vexabatur, postquam mox est ad morbum sensibilem redeundum
et illud medium respirationis tempus transitus est in morbum?
13   Certe quantum ad sanitatem attinet, nichil refert. Adde quod, licet
innumerabilia sint que corporibus nostris contingunt ex ipsius
fragilitate nature, multa tamen exstrinsecus imprimuntur. Et ut de
feris bestiis, venenosis reptilibus, aquarum inundationibus, terrarum hyatibus, incendiis, concussionibus, et ruinis, que non solum
unum hominem oppresserunt sed urbes maximas atque regiones
totas, plerumque leguntur ad vastitatem aut solitudinem de-
duxisse, hei michi, quanta, qualis, et quam perniciosa pestis est
homo homini! Heu quam lacrimosum et flebile spectaculum est
videre quot artibus, quot ingeniis, quot machinationibus rupta
14   naturali societate mortalium nobis invicem noceamus! Et cum
homo ad hominis auxilium sit propagatus quia non est inventum
adiutorium simile sibi, cumque tum natura, tum lege proximum
sicut nos ipsos diligere iubeamur, in parvo iracundie nostre fervore
ut iniurias (et utinam veras; tolerabilior enim error esset!), imo ut
que ad iniuriam ducimus ulciscamur, vel solo nocendi studio
proximum ledimus, diffamamus, decipimus, spoliamus, odio habemus, et contra omnem humanitatem occidimus, nec perpendimus

And so our health is infirm, or rather, to be more accurate, it is 11
not infirm but infirmity itself, yet one that is removed from our
senses and concealed. We are no more able to declare that anyone
is healthy than we can assert that someone who is suffering from
three-day, four-day, or five-day fever is fine during his days of remission. For what does it matter that the fever ceases for one day, 12
for two, three, or more days, or even for some months (as we read
concerning the poet Antipater, who was vexed with fevers every
year on his birthday),[25] when soon we must return to feel the disease, and that the intermediate time of remission is but a transi-
tion into disease? Truly, in relation to health, it doesn't matter. In 13
addition, although innumerable things affect our bodies as a result
of the fragility of their very nature, many external things impinge
upon them. To say nothing of wild beasts, venomous reptiles,
floods, chasms opening in the earth, conflagrations, earthquakes,
and devastation, evils that have oppressed not only a single man
but great cities and entire regions as well, and are generally reported to have reduced them to wastelands and deserts — woe is
me! how great and how pernicious a plague man is to man![26] Alas,
how pitiful and lamentable a spectacle it is to see with how many
tricks, how many schemes, how many machinations we hurt each
other, breaking the natural social bond among human beings!
Man is born to help his fellow man (since no other help is found 14
that matches him), and both by nature and by law we are commanded to love our neighbor as ourselves. Yet in a brief flare-up of
our wrath, to avenge ourselves for an injury (and would that it
were a true injury; for then the error would be more tolerable!) —
rather, to avenge ourselves for the things that we deem as injury —
or simply out of zeal for doing harm, we hurt, vilify, deceive, despoil, hate our neighbor; against all humanity we kill him, and,

miseri quod deus nos a deliciarum paradiso in mundum quasi in lacum miseriarum transgressione primi parentis damnabiliter relegavit. Et tanta tamen est mentium nostrarum deliratio quod in hoc miseriarum miserrimo lacu intumescimus et proximis insultamus.

: X :

Quod mundus sit lacus miseriarum.

1 Recordare, o miser homo, quod, sicut innocens Daniel invidorum factione eo quod fuerit in colendo deum transgressor regie iussionis positus fuit in lacum leonum, ita et tu transgressione primi parentis in hunc mundum, omnium miseriarum lacum, iustissima et divina fuisti sententia deportatus, ubi, nisi mittat deus angelum suum et concludat ora leonum, antequam pavimentum attigeris, 2 devoreris. Vade igitur, o miser, letare in miseria, gloriare in fedo isto loco supplicii et dei tui ac humane fragilitatis immemor adhereat anima tua pavimento, hoc est terrenis illecebris, et istis rebus fugacissimis immoretur. Recordare, miser, qualis fuerit ante ruptam mandati divini legem status condicioque mortalium, qualis sit ad presens, qualisque post mortem hinc exeuntibus reservetur. 3 Poterant quidem ante inobedientiam parentes nostri, in quibus corrupta et damnata fuit hominum futura propago, si paruissent divinis iussionibus, non peccare; nunc autem, quod cum lacrimis referendum est, tantam ex illa infectione labem nascendo

wretches that we are, we do not consider that God sent us from the paradise of delights into the world as if into a pit of miseries as punishment for the transgression of our first parent. And so great is the delirium of our minds that we swell up in this wretched pit of miseries and trample our neighbor.

: X :

The world is a pit of miseries.

Recall, O miserable human, that just as Daniel, although inno- 1 cent, was put into the lions' den by a faction of envious persons because in his worship of God he was a transgressor of the king's command, so you too, as a result of the transgression of your first parent, have been banished to this world, the pit of all miseries, by the most just divine sentence. Here, unless God sends his angel and closes the jaws of the lions, you may be devoured before you have reached the bottom of the pit. Go, then, miserable man, re- 2 joice in misery, glory in this foul place of punishment and, forgetful of your God and of your human frailty, let your soul adhere to the bottom of the pit — that is, to earthly enticements — and let it linger among those fleeting pleasures. Recall, miserable man, what the state and condition of mortals was like before the law of the divine command was broken, what it is at present, and what sort of state and condition is reserved for us after death when we depart from here. Before their disobedience, our parents, in whom 3 the future progeny of the human race was corrupted and damned, would have been unable to sin, if they had obeyed the divine commands; now, however (something I must weep to report), by being born we contract such a great stain from that infection that we

4 contrahimus quod non possumus non peccare. Nam si dixerimus
quia peccatum non habemus, seducimus nos ipsos et veritas non
est in nobis. Scriptum est enim, 'Septies in dies cadit iustus,' 'et
nunquam in eodem statu permanet.' Testante quidem propheta,
'Non est qui faciat bonum, domine, non est qui faciat usque ad
5 unum.' Quid autem miserius, quid infelicius, quidve flebilius hac
impossibilitate non peccandi? Gloriatur genus mortalium quod liberum habeat sue voluntatis arbitrium, quo voluntate sua peccare
possint, declinare autem a malo et facere bonitatem sua fragilitate
et prime transgressionis nostre pena non possint, nisi emittat deus
lucem suam nos sanantem ad hoc, ut a peccatis tum abstinendo,
tum recedendo inter antiqui hostis insultus, carnis nostre stimu-
lum, et mundi blanditias liberemur.

6 Nec sit tamen quod de huiusmodi condicione pene impoten-
tiaque non peccandi mortalium inobedientia conqueratur. Iustissimum quidem fuit quod qui, cum posset non peccare, sua sponte
peccavit, innata teneretur cupiditate peccandi, ut et ille rerum parens cuius infinita est bonitas et immensa misericordia hoc nobiscum ageret gratiosius quo benignius gratiam suam exhiberet offen-
7 sus. Ipse enim nos, ire filios, dum, ut lapsi resurgamus, sopitam
excitat rationem, excitate rationi bonam subicit voluntatem, et voluntate rationi obtemperante facit ut melius eligamus et a peccati
8 liberat servitute. O mira, o ineffabilis dei misericordia, que cunctos
humane condicionis defectus supplens, dummodo velimus, dummodo per caritatem peccati deformitatem abhorrentes ad con-
cupiscientiam pulcritudinis divine iusticie moveamur, in fidei lu-
9 mine nos sua gratia preveniendo iustificat et exaltat! Sed huius

cannot fail to sin. For if we say that we do not have sin, we deceive 4
ourselves and the truth is not in us. For it is written "Seven times
a day the just man falls,"[27] "and never remains in the same state."[28]
The prophet attests, "There is no one who does good, Lord, there
is not even one."[29] What is more miserable, what is more unhappy, 5
or what more lamentable than this impossibility of not sinning?
The human race glories that it has free power over its own will,
whereby people can sin willingly; yet as a result of our own frailty
and the punishment of our first transgression, they are unable to
turn away from evil and do good unless God sends his light that
heals us, so that by abstaining from sin and withdrawing from the
attacks of the ancient Enemy, we are freed from the goad of our
flesh and the world's blandishments.

However, let us not complain about the terms of such a pun- 6
ishment and the powerlessness of mortals to refrain from sin as a
result of disobedience. Indeed it was most just that he who sinned
of his own accord when he had the power not to sin, was gripped
by an innate desire to sin, so that the Parent of the world, whose
goodness is infinite and whose mercy is immeasurable, might deal
with us more graciously, and, although offended, might reveal his
grace all the more generously. For he himself, in order that, though 7
fallen, we may rise again, rouses sleeping reason and, once reason
has been roused, subjects the good will to it and, when the will is
obeying reason, he causes us, children of wrath, to make better
choices and he frees us from slavery to sin. O wonderful, O inef- 8
fable mercy of God, which makes good all the defects of the human condition, if only we wish it, if only through love we shrink
from the ugliness of sin and are moved to desire the beauty of divine justice! O mercy that justifies and exalts us, in the light of
faith, that comes to us in advance by God's grace! But as we try to 9

mundi, quo utendum est ad necessitatem, illecebris dum ad voluptatem in eo ponendo nobis finem ultimum frui conamur, detes-
tande cecitatis tenebris adeo cecutiendo decipimur quod dei et
nostri veri finis obliti ab ipso, quamvis summe bono, excitari, di-
rigi, et roborari, dum mundum sequimur, demeremur. Nec cogitamus quod post sarcinam nostre mortalitatis depositam, si nunc
mundum dimiserimus et, quod in fidei nostre salutifero sacramento promittimus, non verbo sed opere abrenuntiaverimus Sa-
thane et omnibus pompis eius, que solum inter mundanos istos
deceptiosos futilesque splendores in oculis nostris versantur, sic
per dei gratiam confirmabimur in futuro taliterque divine iusticie
per dilectionis habitum coniungemur quod nedum mala non poterimus facere vel etiam velle sed, quod verissimum et excellentissi-
mum libertatis arbitrium est, nefas habebimus cogitare. Mundum
autem istum, verum omnium virtutum naufragium, dum sequimur, dum amamus, ea necessitate damnabimur ut bonum nec velle
nec operari, postquam hinc exiverimus, valeamus. Cogitemus itaque quam certum sit omnium virtutum, secundum quas vivere nos
oportet si eternam illam incorruptibilem gloriam volumus, inevita-
bile publicumque naufragium mundus iste et, cum cognoverimus
nos simul mundum et virtutes amare non posse vel sequi, fugiamus hunc terribilem scopulum et, ut veram illam beatitudinem
mereamur, hoc relicto virtutibus nos tradamus.

enjoy the enticements of this world (which we should use only as far as is necessary) for the sake of pleasure, placing in it our final goal, we are so deceived in our fumbling around in the shadows of detestable blindness that, forgetful of God and our true goal, as we pursue the world, we deserve to be roused, directed, and invigorated by him, supremely good as he is. We do not consider that 10 once we have laid aside the burden of our mortality and have dismissed the world, and (as we promise in the salvation-bringing sacrament of our faith)[30] we have renounced, not in word but in deed, Satan and all his works, which parade before our eyes among those deceptive and futile worldly splendors, we will be so strengthened in the future through God's grace, and we will be so joined through the habit of love of divine justice that not only will we be unable to do or even wish to do evil, but we will hold it to be wrong even to think about it—which is the truest and most excellent exercise of liberty's discretion. Yet as long as we pursue that world, the true shipwreck of all virtues, as long as we love it, we will be condemned by the necessity that we can neither wish to do nor do good after we have departed from here. And so let us 11 consider how certain, inevitable, and public a shipwreck of all virtues (in accordance with which we ought to live if we want that eternal, incorruptible glory) this world is. Once we have recognized that we cannot love or pursue the world and virtues at the same time, let us flee this terrible reef, and, once we have left it behind, let us devote ourselves to virtues in order to merit that true blessedness.

: XI :

Quod mundus sit naufragium virtutum.

1   Naufragantur enim in hoc mundo cuncte sine differentie preroga-
tiva virtutes. Volumus et hoc, licet planum sit, clarius exequi. Incipiamus a rerum consideratrice, prudentia, que in omnium visibilium et invisibilium cognitione versatur. Videamus an apud
amatores mundi hec divinarum humanarumque rerum possit esse
2   prudentia. Quomodo autem potest ad res intelligendas acies intellectus illorum emergere qui irresolubili mentium nubilo in tanta
caligine et cecitate versantur quod rem vanam atque caducam
queve nos decipiat, nos seducat, summe diligere damnabiliter in
animum induxerunt? Excutiat hanc dilectionis nubem qui mundum voluerit plene cognoscere quive illud prudentie lumen concu-
3   piverit obtinere. Male quidem de rebus temporalibus, cum illas
diligis, iudicatur. Cognoscende prius sunt et, quantum ratio patitur postquam cognoveris, diligende. Preposterum enim est hec
4   mundana prius diligere quam cognoscas. Quod si in hac societate
mortalium bene et utiliter preceptum est plures salis modios cum
homine comedendos priusquam in amiciciam asciscatur, quidnam
in amando mundum debemus facere? Omnes certe vescendo ex-
hauriende salinarum apothece sunt antequam mundum diligere
5   statuamus. Cum igitur diligendo mundum ipsum cognoscere non
possimus, eclipsatur proculdubio in eius amore illud prudentie lumen quo, duce ratione, cuncta discernimus, aut ipsum cognos-
6   centes, si rationi consenserimus, non amamus. Hec est enim eternorum et temporalium precipua et magna diversitas, quod hec,

: XI :

The world is a shipwreck of virtues.

All virtues without exception are shipwrecked in this world. I wish   1
to expound this subject more clearly, even though it is obvious. Let
us begin from the power of considering things, discretion, which
consists in the understanding of all things visible and invisible. Let
us see whether this discretion in matters divine and human can
exist among world lovers. How can the sharpness of intellect   2
needed for understanding things emerge in those people who wander in a thick mental cloud, in such great darkness and blindness
that they have convinced themselves, to their own damnation, that
they utterly love hollow and evanescent matter that deceives and
seduces us? Whoever wants to know the world fully or whoever
desires to obtain that light of discretion must shake off this cloud
of love. In truth, you make bad judgments about temporal affairs   3
when you love them. First you must understand them and then, as
much as reason allows after you have understood them, you may
love them. It is backward to love these worldly things before you
understand them. But if in this community of mortals a good and   4
useful precept is that we must eat several measures of salt with a
man before he is admitted into our friendship, what then ought
we to do in loving the world? Indeed, we must devour and exhaust
all salt reserves before we decide to love the world. Since, there-   5
fore, we cannot understand the world by loving it, there is no
doubt that by the love of the world that light of discretion is
eclipsed, by which, with reason as our guide, we discern all things,
or by which, understanding the world, we do not love it, if we are
in accord with reason. For this is the particular and great differ-   6
ence between eternal and temporal things: the more we understand

quanto magis cognoscimus, minus sine dubitatione diligimus, illa vero, quanto pleniori luce percipimus, tanto tenacioribus amoris

7 nexibus adamamus. Iam enim quis in hac concupiscentis carnis sarcina et inter huius mundi blandientis illecebras illius moderatricis passionum, temperantie scilicet, rationem novit aut potest, si se

8 mundo dederit, observare? Quid iusticiam memorem? Cuius cum principale sit et unicum institutum reddere que dei sunt deo, nos ipsos a deo creatos, dum mundum sequimur, autori nostro subtrahimus, dumque mundum diligimus, proximum non amamus.

9 Quis autem fortitudinis nervus esse potest in horum corruptibilium et fluxorum societate? Caro quidem nostra fragilis et infirma vigori fortitudinis obstat et in magnarum rerum aggressibus obtremit et formidat, et mundus ipse, dum ad terrena nos trahit, mollit, effeminat, et enervat.

10 Fides vero, que in rerum non apparentum affirmatione versatur, a mundi quidem amatoribus non habetur. Hec enim nos erigit ad eterna; ille vero nos retrahit ad terrena. Hec nos facit sine titubantia invisibilia credere; illo autem duce non possumus etiam in his visibilibus non errare, quoque certius nos in his sensibilibus errasse percipimus, tanto dubitabilius de his que nunquam vidimus

11 cogitamus. Quid autem caritati, qua deum diligere iubemur et proximum, adversantius mundo? Qui enim mundum diligit deum odit. Audi veritatem: 'Qui mecum non est contra me est.' Non est cum deo qui mundum amat, quoniam qui diligit mundum non est caritas patris in eo. Per solam enim dilectionem cum deo sumus; nam increata illa caritas solum create caritatis merito possidetur.

12 Nec cogitemus posse deum simul cum mundo diligere nisi propter

the latter, the less we love them unreservedly; the more we perceive the former in a fuller light, the stronger become the bonds of love with which we love them. Now, who in this bundle of desiring 7 flesh and among the enticements of this sweet-talking world knows how or is able to keep the rational order of that moderator of passions, namely self-control, if he has surrendered to the world? Why should I mention justice? The first and only stipula- 8 tion of justice is to render to God the things that are of God.[31] Therefore, we withdraw ourselves, God's very creatures, from our Creator when we pursue the world; and when we love the world, we do not love our neighbor. Who can be a sinew of fortitude in 9 partnership with these corruptible and changeable things? Indeed, our fragile and weak flesh stands in the way of fortitude's vigor, and trembles at and fears the approach of great events; and the world itself, as it drags us down to earthly affairs, softens us, emas- culates us, enervates us.

But faith, which consists in the affirmation of things unseen, 10 the world lovers do not have. For faith raises us to eternal things; but the world draws us back to the earthly. Faith makes us believe in invisible things without wavering; but with the world as our guide, we cannot fail to err even in these visible things. The more surely we perceive that we have erred in these tangible things, the more skeptically do we ponder those things that we never see. What is more opposed to charity, according to which we are com- 11 manded to love God and neighbor, than the world? For whoever loves the world hates God. Listen to the Truth: "He who is not with me is against me."[32] A person who loves the world is not with God, since the love of the Father is not in the person who loves the world. For we are with God through love alone; that uncreated charity is only possessed by means of the merit of created charity. And let us not think it possible to love God together with the 12 world unless we are determined to love the world on account of

deum mundum decreverimus nos amare. Actionum enim nostrarum unus et ultimus finis statuendus est, ad quem quicquid agi-
13 mus quicquidve cogitaverimus dirigatur. Cum autem ex dilectione
spes perfecta, que tamen incipiens amorem generat, oriatur, mundum diligendo quid sperabimus? Certe mundo perfrui, abundare
divitiis, explere voluptates, et aliis presidere, que quidem via sunt
14 ad Tartarum, non in celum, ad diabolum, non ad deum. Fugiamus
igitur istud horrendum naufragium in quo virtutes non iactantur
sed pereunt, non vexantur solummodo sed opprimuntur invales-
centibus in hoc mundo vitiis, que quidem in ipso modis omnibus
confoventur.

: XII :

Quod mundus sit malorum fomes.

1 Omnium equidem vitiorum, que sola mala sunt et ad quorum
deformitatem infinita et omnifica dei bonitas, licet cooperetur, ipsis actibus non concurrit, mundus iste proculdubio fomes est.
Tolle namque divitias mundi ut omnino de mortalium oculis aufe-
rantur: radicem malorum omnium, avariciam, et omnium peccato-
2 rum reginam, superbiam, extirpabis. Redeat genus humanum
unde plurimi discessisse crediderunt, ad glandes et flumina, ut ille
cibum, hec pocula subministrent, ut non explicet tellus fructus
pulcros visu et ad vescendum suaves, nec mortale genus instet bestiis terre, volucribus celi, et piscibus maris ad viscera replenda sua:

God. For we must have a single and final goal of our actions, according to which whatever we do or have planned is directed.[33] Since perfect hope, which in its beginnings generates love, arises 13 out of love, what will we hope for in loving the world? No doubt to enjoy the world to the full, to abound in riches, to indulge in pleasures, and to be in charge of others—things that are the way to hell, not to heaven; to the devil, not to God. Let us flee, there- 14 fore, that frightful shipwreck in which virtues are not tossed but perish, are not only troubled but oppressed by vices that are increasing in strength in this world—indeed, whose flames are being fanned in the world in all ways imaginable.

: XII :

The world is kindling for evils.

This world is without a doubt the kindling of all vices, which are 1 the sole evils. Although the infinite and all-creative goodness of God cooperates toward their deformity, it does not agree with the evil acts themselves. Take away the world's riches so that they are removed from mortal eyes altogether: you will extirpate avarice, the root of all evils, and pride, the queen of all sins. Let the hu- 2 man race return to the condition whence many believe it departed, to acorns and rivers, so that the one may provide food, the other drink; so that the earth may not unfold fruits beautiful to see and sweet to eat, and the race of mortals may not threaten the beasts of the earth, the birds of the sky, and the fish of the sea for the

penitus evanescet illa gustus delectandi cupiditas et nullum eius in
3 nobis vestigium remanebit. Ut etiam si intemperatus ille Philose-
nus Erixius forte rediret, qui teste Aristotile legitur in votorum
suorum desiderio deum orasse collum sibi collo gruis longius ob-
venire quo diutius posset saporibus delectari, collibrevium rana-
rum guttur aut si quod reperitur brevius exoptaret. Sicut autem
sublatis divitiis avaricie sitis et tumor superbie comprimuntur, sic
4 repressa ventris ingluvie flama libidinis extinguetur. Eoque modo
ad tantam sanctitatem redigeretur mortalium genus ad tantamque
concordiam quod iracundie locus non esset utpote quam nulle
prorsus iniurie commoverent, quod alique lites aut invidie livor,
qui de proximorum opulentia, quam prosperitatem credimus,
instillatur, inter pauperes, sobrios, et pudicos locum nullatenus
inveniret, sed mentibus liberis nec ad hec transitoria, dum indulgemus passionibus, occupatis nulla tepesceremus tristicia ab arduo-
que virtutum tramite nulla pusillanimitas nullaque diffidentia re-
5 vocaret. Heu heu, munde corruptibilis, munde corrupte, munde
corrumpens, quis te cognoscet, quis te spernet, quis te fugiet? Non
amator tui, quem exoculas et excecas; non admirator tuus, cui te
dulci blanditiarum lenocinio carum facis; non cultor et fruitor,
quem illecebris variis illaqueas atque capis. Utinam nudetur in
oculis hominum turpitudo tua, ut te, incentivum scelerum, meliori
consilio fugiant et evitent!

sake of filling their own guts. That desire for delighting the taste
buds will disappear and no vestige of it will remain in us. Conse- 3
quently, even if that intemperate Philoxenus, son of Eryxis, were
by chance to return—who, as we read in Aristotle, in the desire of
his prayers prayed to god that he might be granted a neck longer
than a crane's in order to savor flavors for a longer time—he
would long for the gullet of a short-necked frog or whatever neck
is found shorter than that.[34] Just as the thirst of avarice and the
swelling of pride are held in check when riches are eliminated, so
the flame of desire will be extinguished when the stomach's gluttony is suppressed. In this way the human race would be led back 4
to such great holiness and such great concord that there would be
no place for irascibility, inasmuch as no injuries would incite it
anymore, because quarrels or envy's malice—which seeps into us
from our neighbor's opulence, which we believe to be prosperity—
would find no place at all among poor, sober, and chaste people.
Instead, with minds free and not occupied with these transitory
things (as they are so long as we indulge our passions), we would
not become tepid with depression, and no pusillanimity or diffidence would call us away from the steep path of the virtues. Woe, 5
woe, corruptible world, corrupt world, corrupting world, who will
see you for what you are, who will spurn you, who will flee you?
Not your lover, whose eyes you knock out and whom you make
utterly blind; not your admirer, to whom you endear yourself by
the sweet pandering of your charms; not your cultivator and con-
sumer, whom you trap and capture with various enticements.
Would that your turpitude be laid bare before the eyes of men,
that they may take better counsel and flee and shun you, you incitement to crime!

: XIII :

Quod mundus sit incentivum scelerum.

1 Incitat enim mundus ad scelera quos facit sue false pulcritudinis spectatores. Bona sunt, fateor, que in mundo cernimus si nos ad ipsorum originem referamus; creature quidem dei sunt. Post omnium namque creationem et productionem scriptum est, 'Et vidit

2 deus cuncta que fecerat valde bona.' Verumtamen spiritus promptus est, caro autem infirma, que, cum de terra sit, terrena desiderat et terrenis in sua natura corruptibili delectatur. Et ideo, dum cupiditatibus habenas relinquimus, de re bona malum nostris erroribus

3 perpetramus. Non putemus antiquum hostem usum fuisse mundi bonis solum in superatione primi parentis; quotidie quidem hec arma contra nos movet, hoc telum in nos vibrat, hoc nos gladio ferit, quique tunc nos vicit in esu nunc etiam auditu capit, visu detinet, olfactu trahit, tactu permulcet. In quibus omnibus hec

4 mundana velut escam deceptionis ubi laqueos ponat ostendit. Non expedit explicare quid nos ad scelera, dum mundum amamus, alliciat. Clare cunctis, si ad mentem redierint, clariusque tibi et reliquis qui a mundi blanditiis consultissime profugistis, clarius, inquam, patet. Qui si vere de mundo corrumpente ad vivificantem Christum per dei gratiam confugistis, ac velut in portum recepti post imminens in hac mundi tempestate naufragium, ad estuantis maris fluctus adhuc pectore trepidante conversi, videbitis mundum

: XIII :

The world is incitement to crime.

The world incites to crime those whom it makes spectators of its 1
false beauty. I acknowledge that the things we observe in the world
are good if we refer them to their origin; indeed, they are God's
creatures. For it is written that after the creation and production
of all, "And God saw everything that he had made, and it was very
good."[35] Nevertheless, the spirit is willing, but the flesh is weak;[36] 2
since the flesh is from the earth, it desires earthly things and takes
pleasure from them in its own corruptible nature. For this reason,
when we give free rein to our desires, by our errors we turn a good
thing into a bad. Let us not think that the ancient Enemy used the 3
world's good things only to overpower our first parent; daily he
brandishes these weapons against us, wields this missile against us,
strikes us with this sword, and he who once conquered us with
food now also seizes us with sounds, detains us with sights, draws
us with smell, soothes us with touch. In all of these ways he displays these things of the world like deceptive bait in order to set
his snares there. It is not useful to elaborate on what entices us to 4
crimes as long as we love the world: that is patently obvious to everyone once they have returned to their senses, and even more
obvious to you and to others who have wisely taken refuge from
the world's allurements; it is, I repeat, more patently obvious. If
you have truly fled by the grace of God from the corrupting world
to life-giving Christ and, as if received into the harbor after imminent shipwreck in this storm of the world, you have turned
with still trembling breast to the waves of the seething sea, you

istum quem reliquistis quasi vitiorum materiem periculosissimos
5 mentibus excitare tumultus. Dulcibus enim cibis insatiandam
ingluviem, rerum opulentie cupiditatem, mulierum ficta specie et
caduca formositate libidinem, tremulorum honorum splendore
falso superbiam, tetrum proximorum de felicitate livorem, deliciarum affluentia luxuriam facile cognoscetis, cum illum dilexistis
dumque sequebamini, vestris mentibus incussisse, et cum in illo
creaturam amantes vos creatorem offendisse videritis, gaudebitis
profecto vos, quantum in hoc itinere ceco licuerit, ab eius insidio-
sis commotionibus liberatos.

: XIV :

Quod mundus sit iter cecum.

1 Iter cecum et, quod periculosius est, cecum faciens mundus est.
Quid enim obscurius, quid tetrius, quam per hec mundana pergere, putantes immarcescibilem illam gloriam, dum in his animum
ponimus, obtinere? Tanta tamen diligentes mundum caligine cecitatis offundimur quod, cum hic assequi non posse veram illam
beatitudinem cognoscamus, nitamur tamen in mundo, stulti atque
dementes, esse beati et, quod inanius est, inter hec mundana, falsa,
2 atque caduca nos beatos ac felices et credimus et iactamus. Non
licet in hoc sanctorum exempla proponere, quorum diversum fuit
a mundo propositum, dividuum iter et mentis conversatio sepa-
rata. Principio quidem, o miser homo qui mundo deditus deum

will see that the world you left — the raw material, as it were, of vices — excites extremely perilous upheavals in the mind. You will easily recognize that, when you loved and followed the ways of the world, insatiable gluttony for sweet foods, desire for material wealth, lust for dolled-up women with their evanescent beauty, pride in the false splendor of fragile honors, loathsome envy of a neighbor's good fortune, and luxury in an abundance of delights used to beat against your minds. When you see that you offended your Creator by loving his creature in the world, you will really rejoice that you have been freed from its insidious commotion — as far as one may be, on this blind journey.

: XIV :

The world is a blind journey.

The world is blind journey and, what is more dangerous, a blinding journey. For what is darker, what more loathsome, than to make one's way through these earthly things with mind fixated on them, all the while thinking that we possess unfading glory? Loving the world, we are enveloped in such a great fog of blindness that, although recognizing that here it is impossible to attain true happiness, we nevertheless strive, stupid and senseless, to be happy in the world, and, what is even more inane, we believe and boast that among these worldly, false, and unstable things we are happy and blessed. Here is not the place to hold up the examples of the saints, whose way of life was different from the world, whose journey was distinct and whose habit of mind was separate from it. In the first place, O wretched man, who in your devotion to the

reliquis, putasne te celum fugaces possidendo divitias obtinere? Audi veritatem: 'Difficilius est divitem intrare in regnum celorum quam camelum per foramen acus.' Ardua quidem et arcta via est 3 que nos celo genitos ducit in patriam. Quis autem adeo demens est quod iter arduum intraturus impedimenta et onera non deponat? Si divitie nobis aperirent celi ianuam et inter beatos, ut nobis hic persuadere videmur, hec rerum opulentia collocaret, quot reges, quot principes, quot privati, quos ad fastidium usque videmus opibus abundare, ad celestem illam patriam devenirent! Sed dives evangelicus in inferno positus quondam mendicantem Lazarum vidit in sinu Abrahe et refocillari beneficio olim neglecti et spreti 4 pauperis exorabat. Unicus est divitiarum, si obvenerint nobis, gloriosus et certissimus fructus, ut nostris opibus proximorum indigentiis succurramus. Requiret enim deus a nobis in die iudicii divitiarum quas concesserit usum, et qui mendicanti pauperi, qui siquidem personam Christi, postquam sedit in gloria, representat, in hoc mundo neglexerit subvenire, mittetur in ignem eternum. Qui vero fuerit elemosinarum occultus et largifluus dispensator 5 recipietur in gloriam sempiternam. O infinita dei bonitas, quis te satis poterit admirari? Concedit nobis deus divitias finitas, corruptibiles, et fugaces. Quarum si nos non dominos sed dispensatores esse cognoverimus et eas refundendo pauperibus, veris exactoribus Iesu Christi, benigne reddiderimus creditori, infinitam, incorruptibilem, et permanentem eternaliter remunerando gloriam elargitur. 6 Hec est vera divitiarum felicitas, eas non multiplicare in terris sed thesaurizare nobis in celis. Iam enim honores, dignitates, potentias, gloriam, voluptates, et si quid aliud, dum ad mundanam hanc beatitudinem suspiramus, appetimus, quoniam illa inflant,

world leave God behind, do you think that you have a hold on heaven by possessing fleeting riches? Listen to the Truth: "It is more difficult for a rich man to enter the kingdom of heaven than for a camel to go through the eye of a needle."[37] Steep indeed and narrow is the way that leads us, born for heaven, into our homeland. Who is so crazy that he would not lay down his baggage and 3 burdens when he was about to embark on a difficult journey? If riches opened heaven's gates for us and if this material opulence placed us among the blessed (as we seem to persuade ourselves here), how many kings, how many princes, how many private citizens, whom we see at the pinnacle of abundant wealth, would reach that celestial homeland! But the rich man of the Gospels, sitting in hell, saw Lazarus, once a beggar, in the bosom of Abraham, and was praying to be revived by the favor of the once spurned and neglected pauper. The only glorious and dependable 4 fruit of riches, if they have come to us, is that with our resources we come to the help of our neighbors in need. On the Day of Judgment God will ask after our use of the riches he granted to us, and he who in this world failed to come to the aid of the poor beggar (since indeed he represents the Person of Christ after Christ has taken his seat in glory) will be sent to the eternal fire. But he who has been a hidden and generous dispenser of alms will be received into eternal glory. O infinite goodness of God, who could 5 marvel at you enough? God bestows upon us finite, corruptible, and fleeting riches. If we realize that we are not their owners but their stewards, and if by showering them in turn upon the poor — who are the true collectors for Jesus Christ — we generously pay back our Creditor, he grants us infinite, incorruptible, and enduring glory, remunerating us eternally. This is true blessedness in 6 riches, not to multiply them on earth but to store up for ourselves treasure in heaven. Now let us forsake honors, distinctions, powers, glory, pleasures, and anything else we seek as we sigh for this earthly happiness, since some of these puff us up, while others

7 hec inquinant, dimittamus. Satis enim omnibus persuasum est, et etiam illis ipsis qui rebus huiusmodi delectantur et affluunt, ea non esse viam in celum sed in infernum, et tamen tanta mentium nostrarum cecitas est quod illa querimus et ad ea quasi beatifica totius mentis nixibus anhelamus. Excutiamus igitur has tenebras et mundum relinquentes nos ad illud lumen inextinguibile convertamus, et, dum hoc itinere ceco pergimus, huius intercisi tramitis salebras caveamus.

: XV :

Quod mundus sit trames salebrosus.

1 Salebrosus equidem trames mundus est, in quo, si recti voluerimus pergere, multa nos oporteat nostris occurrentia gressibus evitare. Considera tecum quot vitiorum capita sunt, quot ramuli, quot cespites, quot radices, et totidem scito scrobibus atque fossis pre-
2 sentis mundi tramitem intercidi. Hinc enim cupiditatis insatiabile baratrum, dum pecuniam plus equo congerimus, nobis obstat, et cum transeundum sit, nos detinet ac retardat, quantoque plus senescimus, tanto magis hoc monstrum oculis nostre mentis opposi-
3 tum iuvenescit. Hinc se nobis implicitis obicit, ne emergamus, inflata superbia, que iuxta desipientis vulgi iudicium pulcerrimum esse persuadens minores opprimere, maiores horrere, nec parem alterius potentiam tolerare, mundanorum splendorum, quibus etiam lumina bene compositarum mentium offuscantur, fulgoribus

taint us. All agree — even those who delight and abound in things   7
of this kind — that these are not the way to heaven but to hell;
however, such is the blindness of our minds that we seek those
things and pant for them with the efforts of our whole mind as if
they led to our happiness. Let us, then, shake off these shadows
and, abandoning the world, let us turn to that inextinguishable
light. While we make our way on this blind journey, let us watch
out for the ruts in this rugged path.

: XV :

The world is a rugged path.

The world is indeed a rugged path, on which, if we want to pro-   1
ceed on a straight course, we must avoid the many obstacles lying
in our way. Consider how many sources of vice there are, how
many branches, clumps of earth, and roots, and know that the
path of the present world is sliced by just as many ditches and
holes. On one side, the insatiable pit of desire stands in our way,   2
as we pile up more money than is right; when we must cross it, it
detains and delays us, and the older we get, the younger this monster becomes, an obstacle before our mind's eye. On the other side,   3
inflated pride stands in our way, and we become so entangled in it
that we cannot escape — pride that, according to the opinion of the
ignorant mob, convinces us that it is the finest thing to oppress
those below us, to tremble before those above us, and not to tolerate another person's having power equal to ours. Pride eats away at
us with its brilliant beams of earthly splendors, by which even the
lights of well-ordered minds are darkened, and does not allow us

nos inescat, nec sinit effici sicut parvulos quo ad celestis regni glo-
4 riam ascendamus. In quo tantus error mentibus nostris obrepit
quod, cum decepti scandere nos putemus, in obscure profunditatis
caliginem demergamur. Hinc dum temporalia nimis appetimus et
ea proximis evenire dolemus, tristi defossione tramitem mundi
presentis intersecat cecutiens invidie tabes et iussam caritatem,
qua proximos debemus diligere propter deum, veneno sue impieta-
tis inficiens, dum liventi oculo iugiter terrena respicimus, iter nos-
5 trum exasperat et ad superna dirigere gressus vetat. Hinc autem
quis nescit ad omnem levem iniuriam excandescentibus animis
iram cum vindicte cupidine derivari? Que cum infelicem invaserit
animam, ne discernere verum possit impediens et ipsa non parve
profunditatis abruptum opponens, viam qua debemus pergere de-
6 molitur. Quid edacitatem atque libidinem memorem, quarum una
vas luteum sine fundo, sicut de Belidibus in fabulis legitur, replere
sollicita omnium que recondit reddit calculum in secessu, altera
gignendi vim atque potentiam ad conservationem humani generis,
quod in mortali individuo non durabat, nobis consilio divini numinis attributam voluptate depravat? Que quidem ingenti fossarum
amplitudine nos in terrenorum quasi quandam insulam relegantes
7 desiderium inhibent eternorum. Vade nunc, o miser homo, et spe-
rans tuam innocentiam conservare elige mundi viam in qua tot
impeditus obstaculis totque salebris circumventus, quamvis coneris exilire, non possis, nec nisi omnipotentis dei manu translatus
8 valeas ad destinatum terminum pervenire. Ergo meliori consilio, ex
quo per tot difficilia transitum nos oportet habere, et instet nobis

to become as children so that we may ascend to the glory of the celestial kingdom. In this matter, such great error creeps over our minds that although, in our deception, we believe that we are climbing, we are sinking into the darkness of an obscure depth. On the one side, as long as we seek temporal things to excess and are upset when they accrue to our neighbors, envy's blinding infection, with its baleful digging, cuts through the path of the present world. With the poison of its own impiety it infects the charity that has been enjoined upon us (by which we ought, for the sake of God, to love our neighbors). This disease makes our journey rough and prevents us from directing our steps toward heaven, as we are constantly looking back to earthly things with envious eye. But on the other side, who is unaware that anger combined with a desire for revenge comes from spirits set ablaze by every slight injury? When anger has invaded the unhappy soul and prevented it from being able to discern the truth and interposes a precipice of considerable depth, it demolishes the way by which we ought to proceed. Why should I mention gluttony and lust? The first is a bottomless clay vessel, as is recounted in the tale about the descendants of Belus: when bidden to fill up, of all the things that it had stored, it rendered up a stone in a privy. The second perverts by means of pleasure the strength and power of procreation — a power granted to us, according to the Deity's plan, for the preservation of the human race, which could not endure in the individual mortal. Both of these inhibit our desire for the eternal, relegating us to a kind of island of earthly things, surrounded by enormous gaping ditches. Go now, O wretched man, and, hoping to preserve your innocence, choose the way of the world! On this path, impeded by so many obstacles and surrounded by so many ruts, you cannot extract yourself, try as you will; unless you are carried across by the hand of all-powerful God, you cannot reach your destination. Therefore, with better judgment (which should give us safe passage through so many difficulties, even if the

inseparabile carnis onus, hoc salebrosum iter et locum insidiosum totis nixibus evitemus.

∶ XVI ∶

Quod mundus sit saltus insidiarum.

1 Mundus enim magna cum fragilitatis humane sarcina transeundus insidiarum importunissimus saltus est; insidiarum quidem quas non solum homo homini carnaliter instruat sed antiquus hostis spiritualiter moliatur. Heu miseri, quid in mundo tot periculis

2 pleno tam avide commoramur, imo commorimur? Habemus hostem invisibilem, non solum actuum sed cogitationum nostrarum, quantum percipere potest ex exterioribus signis, accuratissimum observatorem, ut capiat et occidat. Qui si nos viderit mirabundos rei cuipiam immorari, impellit, instigat, cogit, inescat, et nos ab illo summo bono rerum omnium tam opifice quam rectore in

3 admiratione creature detinens distrahit et elongat. Elongat enim; nam cum illam superiorem mentis vim qua eterna et, quantum in hoc mortali carcere possumus, divine statum essentie contemplamur ad sensuales illecebras inclinamus, sic ab illo rerum omnium principe, deo, recedimus quod ad bestialis condicionis vilitatem nos miserabiliter deducamus in humani corporis nostri simulacro, quantum ad mentem intus attinet, in bestias transfor-

4 mati. Adest et maxima pestis homo homini, quorum infinitus numerus tum seductiosis hortatibus, tum illecebrose vite spectaculo

5 ad inhonesta et turpia tum sermonibus, tum exemplis inflectit. Et ne parum insidiarum sit in hoste gemino, et ipse mundus suis

inseparable burden of the flesh weighs us down), let us avoid with all our might this rough journey and place of plots.

: XVI :

The world is a ravine of plots.

The world, which we must pass through with a great burden of human fragility, is a troublesome ravine of plots — not only plots that man contrives against man carnally, but plots that the ancient Enemy devises spiritually. Woe to us wretches, why do we tarry — rather, why do we so eagerly perish — together so eagerly in a world full of so many dangers? We have an invisible Enemy, a most accurate observer not only of our actions but of our thoughts (as far as these can be perceived from exterior signs), intent on capturing and killing us. If he sees us, bedazzled, fixated on something, he drives us on, goads us, forces us, entices us, and, detaining us in our admiration of the creature, he separates and draws us far away from the supreme good, the Creator and Ruler of all things. He draws us far away: for when we turn our superior strength of mind (with which we contemplate eternal things and, as much as is possible in this mortal prison, the state of the divine essence) to sensual allurements, we so withdraw from the head of all things, God, that we miserably reduce ourselves in the likeness of our human body to the baseness of bestiality, transformed, as to the inner workings of the mind, into beasts. The greatest plague to man is also present — man.[38] Countless people turn us to dishonorable and shameful deeds both by word (their seductive urgings) and example (the spectacle of their enticing life). And lest there be too few snares in the double foe, the world itself also

copiis et deliciis insidiatur. Obambulant enim ante oculos nostros pulcerrime rerum facies, que nos decipiunt et fragilem illam anime nostre potentiam, que per sensus corporeos explicatur, adeo movent et oblectant quod plerumque nedum inferiorem rationis vim, qua hec terrena disponimus et curamus, sed etiam illum defecatum peneque angelicum et celestem mentis vigorem quo petimus et contemplamur eterna, ad obedientiam trahat et ordine perverso
6 dominetur et presit appetitus inordinatio rationi. Nec secum aliquis glorietur hanc adversantem spiritui membrorum legem (ad quod non attigit apostolus) domuisse. Quod si se fecisse forsitan arbitretur, tunc se maxime victum et prostratum sciat. Et tanto gravius quanto periculosius morbo quem non sentimus aut non
7 cognoscimus egrotamus. Iuxta dominicum itaque consilium vigilemus et oremus ut non intremus in temptationem; spiritus quidem promptus, caro vero infirma. Et non solum sciamus nos esse circumventos insidiis sed in hoc mundo ac velut in horrido carcere fore clausos.

: XVII :

Quod mundus sit carcer horridus.

1 Nec sit quod, quamvis latissime videatur tellus extendi et maris tractus per amplissimorum litorum curvamina sinuari, que duo, illam scilicet nostris pedibus, hoc vero classium vehiculo pera-
2 gramus, nos inclusos carcere non credamus. Omittamus enim illam philosophorum et mathematicorum disputationem qua tenaciter

waits in ambush with its resources and delights. For exceedingly
beautiful appearances parade before our eyes. These deceive us,
and so move and delight that fragile power of our soul (which is
unfolded through our bodily senses) that most of the time an inordinate appetite drags into obedience not only the inferior power
of reason (by which we arrange and manage these earthly affairs),
but also the pure, almost angelic and celestial vigor of the mind
(by which we seek and contemplate eternal matters).[39] And, by an
inversion of the proper order, the appetite dominates and has
charge of reason. No one should boast that he has tamed this law   6
of the members in opposition to the spirit — this the apostle did
not achieve.[40] But if by chance someone thinks that he has done
so, then he should know that he has been utterly conquered and
laid low: we are more seriously and dangerously ill with the disease that we don't feel or recognize. And so, following the Lord's   7
counsel, let us keep watch and pray that we don't enter into temptation; for the spirit is willing, but the flesh is weak.[41] Let us know
not only that we are surrounded by plots, but also that we have
been shut up in this world as if in a horrible prison.

: XVII :

The world is a horrible prison.

Although the earth is seen to extend far and wide and the tracts of   1
the sea to bend round the curves of great shores — which two bodies we traverse, the one with our feet, the other by the conveyance
of ships — there is no reason to disbelieve that we have been shut
up in a prison. Let me set aside the well-known thesis of philoso-   2
phers and mathematicians, by which they adamantly assert that

astruunt terram omnem ad ambitum celestis voluminis puncti quodam modo indivisibilis speciem obtinere. Omittamus, inquam, hec, ne contra sensibilem telluris magnitudinem spinosiore ratio-
3 nis argumento nitamur. Nam quamvis sit illa parvitas respectiva, patet nichilominus omnis terre periferia non ad palmorum, cubito-rum, vel pedum sed ad miliarium maximam quantitatem, utpote que relata ad ambitum firmamenti trecentos sexaginta zodiaci gra-dus, quorum quilibet super terram perpendiculariter se extendit, ut voluerunt optimi geometrarum Alphagranus atque Campanus, ad quinquaginta sex miliaria et parum plus in sua superficie com-plectatur atque distinguat, ut, quamvis inter mediam terre zonam, continui caloris violentia vastam, et extremam aquilonarem, assi-duo frigoris rigore torpentem, unica zona restet que mortalium quos scire possumus et quorum habuimus hucusque commertium incolatum acceperit, et hec ipsa occeani circumfluentis alluvione, inundatione marium, lacuum, et stagnorum tractibus, vastitate Sirtium, multitudine perniciosa serpentum, et ipsorum montium et silvarum asperitate magna ex parte cohabitationem hominum non admittat, ipsam tamen ad carceris angustias redigi perridicu-lum videatur.
4   Sed per quantacunque terrarum spacia protendatur terrarum orbis et quantacunque latitudine pateat, carcer proculdubio anima-rum est. Quarum cum sit ad suum creatorem per operum merita, gratia tamen dei adiuvante, reverti, in hoc mundo posite quasi carcere diro concluse ad illum pergere prohibentur, ut per quod-cunque virtutis iter conentur exire, terribiles vitiorum facies se

the entire earth has the appearance of a somehow indivisible point at the circumference of the rolling movement of the heavens. Let me, I repeat, set these things aside, so as not to struggle against the earth's perceptible magnitude with a rather thorny rational argument. For whatever its relative smallness, it is nevertheless clear 3 that the periphery of the entire earth is not a matter of palms, cubits, or feet, but of a very great number of miles, since in relation to the circumference of the firmament, 360 degrees of the zodiac, each one of which extends perpendicularly over the earth, as the best geometers, Alphagranus and Campanus have claimed,[42] the earth encompasses and marks out a little more than fifty-six thousand miles on its surface. Hence, although between the middle zone of the earth (a wasteland because of the violence of continuous heat) and the most northern one (rigid because of frost's perpetual stiffness), a single zone remains that is habitable by mortals we are familiar with and with whom we have had dealings up to the present day, this zone too is for the most part not amenable to human communities on account of the flooding of encircling Ocean, the inundation of the seas and lakes, the swaths of swamps, the immensity of sandbanks, the pernicious multitude of serpents, and the great harshness of the mountains and forests. Nevertheless, it seems utterly ridiculous that the earth should be reduced to the confines of a prison.

But however great the tracts of land through which the globe 4 extends and with however great a breadth it lies open, it is beyond a doubt a prison of souls. It is the nature of the soul to turn back to her Creator by the merits of her works (albeit with the help of God's grace). Yet souls are placed in this world as if shut in a dreadful prison and are prevented from proceeding to him, so that on whatever journey of virtue they try to embark, terrible forms

5 opponant. Non oportet explicare quomodo prudentie ignorantia et cecitas intellectus, frugalitati temperantieque voluptas et gula, castitati libido, sobrietati ebrietas, fortitudini tum gestiens leticia in prosperis, tum consternatio et anxietas in adversis, iusticie iniquitas, fidei repugnans infidelitas, corrumpens heresis et retrocedens apostasis, desperatio spei, caritati tum invidie livor, tum iracundie fervor, magnanimitati pusillanimitas, clementie crudelitas, humilitati superbia, et singula vitia singulis virtutibus opponantur.

6 Notissima quidem sunt hec et hoc properanti stilo minime complectenda. Satis enim constat etiam ingenii parvi viris perdita profanaque vitia cum sacratissimis virtutibus obluctari.

Periculosum quidem hoc certamen quod cum manifestis vitiis decertamus, periculosius tamen quod inferunt vitia sub facie mentita virtutum. Pugnat enim cum fide, latenti mucrone sub habitu

7 sanctitatis, heretica pravitas, cum spe inordinata presumptio de divino favore, cum caritate cogitans de bono proprio carnalis et

8 mundana dilectio. Prudentiam vero conantur extinguere sollicitudo temporalium, fraus, dolus, astutia. Contra iusticiam autem decertat inexorabilis et austera severitas. Fortitudini congreditur comes temeritatis, audacia. Magnanimitatem demolitur ambitio eamque et presumptionis virus et inanis glorie venenum inficit et

9 occidit. Constantie pertinacia repugnat et, quod summa cum diligentia cavendum est, subit recte factorum conscientiam inanis glorie tumor et, dum in memoria virtuose gestorum miser homo gloriabundus exultat, premium perdit meritaque virtutum, ut non incongrue dici possit nos in hoc mundi carcere vitiorum muris propugnaculisque conclusos et hanc vitiorum congestam nobis hinc inde maceriam gladium esse versatilem et rumpheam flamam nobis oppositam in introitu paradisi, quam non liceat homini

of vice oppose them. It is not necessary to elaborate upon how   5
individual vices are pitted against individual virtues:[43] ignorance
and blindness of understanding against discretion; pleasure seeking and gluttony against frugality and self-control; lust against
chastity; drunkenness sobriety; how now excessive happiness in
prosperity, now consternation and anxiety in adversity, are pitted
against fortitude; iniquity against justice; recalcitrant infidelity,
corrupting heresy, and backsliding apostasy against faith; despera-
tion against hope; how now envy's spite, now wrath's fervor is
pitted against charity; pusillanimity against magnanimity; cruelty
clemency; pride humility. All this is very well known, and need   6
not be included by my hastening pen. For it is generally agreed
even among men of small intellect that depraved and profane vices
struggle with the holiest virtues.

This struggle we engage in with manifest vices is indeed dangerous, yet more dangerous is that which the vices wage under the
false appearance of virtues. For heretical error, its blade hidden in   7
the clothes of holiness, fights against faith; inordinate presumption of divine favor fights with hope; carnal and earthly love that
thinks only of its own good fights with charity. Deception, guile,   8
cunning, and concern for temporal matters try to extinguish discretion. Inexorable and austere severity battles against justice. Au-
dacity, comrade of temerity, attacks fortitude. Ambition topples
magnanimity, and the venom of presumption and the poison of
vainglory infect and kill it. Stubbornness resists constancy, and—   9
something to avoid with utmost diligence—the swelling of vainglory follows closely upon the heels of consciousness of righteous
deeds. As wretched man exults, glorying in the memory of actions
done with virtue, he loses the reward and merits of virtues. Thus
it could aptly be said that we have been enclosed in this prison of
a world by the walls and bulwarks of vices, and that this wall of
vices piled up on either side of us is the revolving sword and fiery
javelin set before us at the entrance of paradise, which man may

pertransire nisi cum omni comitatu virtutum et perfecte caritatis ignitus incendio divina manu per oppositas vitiorum flamas inco-
10 lumis transmittatur. Quo fugiendum est ad virtutum libertatem et ad Christi crucifixi iugum tam leve quam suave, ut ruptis carceris horrendi vinculis ex hac iniquitatum scena quanto mundiores possumus educamur.

: XVIII :

Quod mundus sit scena iniquitatum.

1 Scena locus erat in theatro coopertus et tectus ex quo recitabantur lascivie comice et scelera tragedorum, et non solum cantibus instrumentisque musicis edebantur sed ea etiam histriones et mimi larvatorum hominum gesticulationibus ad delectationem populi figurabant, ubi fraudes, stupra, adulteria, homicidia, et pudenda flagitia tum verbo, tum gestu ad horrorem forte sapientum sed delectationem lascivorum et corruptionem plebecule canebantur.
2 Quis autem adeo demens et sui oblitus qui talem esse mundum ratione certa non noscat? Exeas quicunque mundo implicitus hec nostra qualiacunque percurres; exeas domum, precor, et medium procedas in vulgus. Aut tu idem, mi Ieronime, vel a cellule tue quiete vel a confratrum tuorum sacro collegio per recordationem
3 ad mundi colloquia revertaris. Qui solent mundanorum istorum hominum esse sermones? Certe ubicunque te volveris, ubicunque duos vel plures aut memineris aut inveneris colloquentes, hi de

not cross unless, with an entire entourage of virtues and fired with the blaze of perfect charity, he is conveyed unharmed through the opposing flames of vices by the divine hand. Therefore, we must 10 flee to the liberty of the virtues and to the yoke of Christ crucified that is both sweet and light, so that, once the chains of this horrible prison have been broken, we may be as pure as possible when led off from this stage of iniquities.

: XVIII :

The world is a stage of iniquities.

The stage was a place in the theater, covered and roofed, from 1 which comic lewdness and the crimes depicted by tragic poets were recited. These were produced not only with songs and musical instruments, but actors and mimes portrayed them with gestures of masked men for the people's delight. Here acts of deceit, debauchery, adultery, homicide, and shameful crimes were sung both in word and in gesture—most likely to the horror of the wise, but to the delight of the lascivious and to the corruption of the common people. Who is so crazy and forgetful of himself that 2 he does not know with certainty that the world is like this? Go out, whoever you are, entangled in this world, and run through these assorted activities of ours. Leave your house, please, and proceed into the midst of the common crowd. Or you yourself, dear Girolamo, return in memory from the quiet of your little cell or from the holy college of your brothers to the world's conversation. What are, in general, the topics of conversation of those 3 men of the world? Wherever you turn, wherever you remember or discover two or more people speaking together, they will be

proximorum fraudibus, impuritatibus, et flagitiis predicabunt. Et
utinam, ut peccata corrigerent, utinam, ut auditores a vitiis deter-
4 rerent, de talibus loquerentur! Sed omnes huiusmodi fabulantur
ut proximo detrahant, infamiam conflent, et nomen eius, si forte
clarum extiterit, maculent et confundant. Sunt etiam plerumque
nonnulli qui vitia illa commendant et detestanda facinora per astu-
tie aut mundane prudentie admirationem illustrent laudibus et
improbos auditores ad similia perpetranda moveant et hortentur.
5 Nec satis est vitia aliena aut laudando aut detrahendo referre,
sed tanta morum impudentia est quod plurimos audies de suis
sordibus et flagitiis contionari. Narrat vulgo quilibet splendidas
dapes et exquisita convivia quantaque qualique parasside cenet,
quibus se vinis ingurgitet, que iantacula summo mane, que demum exactis cenarum solennibus mensis absumat accubiturus ob-
sonia, tantaque depravatis moribus in his gloria ducitur quod qui
faciunt referunt, nec sola relatione contenti quasi virtuosissimum
6 aliquid conantur augere. Qui vero aut rei familiaris inopia ne-
queunt vel per avariciam nolunt, ne viles reputentur et sordidi, hec
eadem simulant et confingunt. O tempora! O mores! O vanorum
hominum fugienda colloquia! Nunc quasi in preclaro facinore de
mensarum nostrarum nitore et copia cum iactantia gloriamur;
priscis vero temporibus extra domos, ne quid legibus vetitum aut
forte delicatius ederetur, solebant cenare Romani glorieque duce-
7 bant modica cenare palam olus omne patella. Inexpiabile quidem erat moribus illis mulieres vinum bibere virosque aut delicata

proclaiming the deceptions, impurities, and crimes of their neighbors. And would that they were speaking about such things to
correct sins, would that they were doing so to deter their listeners
from vices! But all tell tales of this kind to denigrate their neigh-   4
bor, to stir up infamy, and to stain and confound his name, if it
should happen to be well known. There are also some people who
commend those vices, and through their admiration for cunning
or worldly wisdom praise detestable crimes; they incite and encourage their wicked listeners to perpetrate similar acts.

Nor does it suffice to relate others' vices either in praise or in   5
blame, but so great is the shamelessness of their ways that you will
hear very many people holding forth about their own crimes and
dirty deeds. Whoever you like tells publicly of splendid dinners
and choice parties, and how great are his feasts and on what kind
of plate, what wines he swills, what breakfasts he consumes early
in the morning, what snacks before bed, when at last the regular
courses of the meal have been finished. Our morals being depraved, there is held to be such great glory in these acts that those
who do these things tell about it; and not content with the telling
alone, they try to embellish their story as if it were the most virtuous thing in the world. But those who either are unable, through   6
lack of resources, or unwilling, through avarice, to do such things,
simulate and fabricate them, lest they be regarded as cheap and
shabby. O the times, O the morals![44] O conversation of vain men,
to be shunned! These days, we boastfully glory in the splendor
and abundance of our tables as if it were a brilliant deed. Yet in
ancient days, the Romans used to dine outside their homes, in
order to discourage the eating of any delicacy forbidden by the
laws; and they considered it glorious to eat a vegetarian meal publicly on a modest dish. It was unforgiveable according to the cus-   7
toms of that time for women to drink wine and for men to eat

comedere aut sobrietatem inter convivia non servare. Quid autem hic optem? nisi Oratianum illud,

> Hos utinam inter
> heroas natum tellus me prima tulisset.

Sed frustra hec opto. Aletur enim vitiis suis seculum nostrum.

8   Et utinam, postquam nobiscum correctionem non spero, non faciant saltem deteriora nepotes! Narrabit itaque unus splendidas dapes sed, quod impudentius est, referet alter illicitos concubitos suos et totius rei seriem quasi honestissimam narraturus hysto-
9 riam explicabit. Non tacebit qua petulantia visus quave prima sermonis lascivia suorum furorum spem conceperit, quibus internuntiis usus sit, quo verborum lenocinio labantem impulerit animum, quibus in insidiis steterit, qua fraude maritum puella deceperit in sua turpitudine et dedecore curiosa, qui primi titubantium sermonum congressus, quis oscula primus impresserit, que murmura, que suspiria, qui gemitus intercesserint, quam arctis dulcibusque complexibus mutuo se insana mentium affectione coniunxerint, qui motus, que alternationes, quotiensque reportaverint de certa-
10 tione triumphum. Nec satis est (tantus furor tantaque oblectatio vitiorum mentes excecat) se duos cum internuntiis et infelicem illum maritalem thorum, in quo alterius viri vestigium sit impressum, et denique deum ipsum testem habere flagitii, nisi hoc etiam
11 cum amate mulieris infamia populi totius auribus ingeratur. Nec solum adolescentuli, quorum minor est autoritas, talia predicant sed assunt maiores plaudentes illis mali gaudii recitatione ipsa facti participes, nec suos quamvis senes proferre verecundantur amores.

dainty items or fail to keep sober at parties. But in this context what should I aspire to but Horace's famous wish,

> Would that the first earth
> had borne me among these heroes?[45]

Yet my wish is in vain. For our age will be fed by its vices.

I have no hope for correction among ourselves, but would that 8 at least our descendants do no worse! One man will tell of splendid dinners, but (what is even more shameless) another will talk about his illicit amours and will unfold the details of the entire affair in order, as if he were going to narrate the most edifying history. He will not keep silent about the impudent sights and wan- 9 ton words that caused him to conceive hope for his mad project; what intermediaries he used; with what verbal pandering he incited her flagging spirit; in what ambushes he lay; by what trick the girl deceived her husband in her turpitude and overly-inquisitive disgrace; what was the first exchange of faltering conversation; who gave the first kiss; what murmurs, what sighs, what moans were uttered; how with tight and sweet embraces they were mutually joined in an insane state of mind; what movements there were, what alternations, and how many times they returned triumphant from the battle. It is not enough (such great madness and 10 delight in vices blinds their minds) that they have their two selves as witnesses to their crime along with their intermediaries, the sad marriage bed on which another man's traces have been imprinted, and finally God himself, unless this crime, along with the bad reputation of the beloved woman, is also brought to the ears of the entire populace. It is not only teenagers (who have less authority) 11 who proclaim such things, but older people are present applauding them, made participants in the evil joy by the recitation itself. However old they are, they are not ashamed to offer the crowd an account of their own love affairs.

12   Sed, ut aliquando a voluptatibus discedamus, quas etiam saty-
rice pertractatas (tot blandiuntur illecebris) periculosum est legere
vel audire, hos libidinosos homines relinquamus, quibus si daretur
electio, non sapientiam, non regnum, non divitias Salomonis sed
septingentas illas reginas et trecentas concubinas optarent, ut diebus singulis possent multa variaque tentigine suos concubitus re-
novare, relinquamus, inquam, et ad viros honestioris habitus ve-

13   niamus. Adeamus, si placet, inclite patrie nostre celebre forum
novum et nos mercatorum nostrorum colloquiis inferamus. Quid
apud eos nisi de augendis et conservandis facultatibus audiemus?

14   Narrant enim et iugiter fabulantur quanta sollicitudine, quanta
previdentia, quali astutia, quantisque laboribus suas divitias con-
gregarint, in hoc sicut in ceteris solita mortalium cecitate decepti,
qui se putant suis operis et virtutibus querere quod manifestum

15   est deum clementia sua ingratis hominibus indulgere. Nec contenti
sunt, dum errant, de se solis loqui, sed narrant etiam aliorum
fraudes et aliena mendacia, cum tamen in conscientiarum secreto,
nisi se voluerint decipere, se non sentiant puriores. Et si quem in
fraudem creditorum fallendo fidem viderint aufugisse, mordent,
lacerant, diffamant, et illi pungentius qui mox sunt illos deceptis
creditoribus secuturi.

16   Hec itaque recitantur in huius mundi scena, hec non ab histrio-
nibus, quorum iuxta simiarum morem proprium est quicquid geri
viderint assimilare, sed ab ipsis autoribus in omnium oculis expli-
cantur, ut, quoniam corrumpant mores bonos colloquia prava
et ad impellendum animos nil potentius nichilque efficacius sit
exemplo, remis et velis sit mundane cohabitationis scenicum istud

But to move on, finally, from the subject of pleasures, which are   12
dangerous to read or hear about even if treated satirically (with so
many charms do they flatter us), let us leave these libidinous men:
if a choice were given to them, they would choose not the wisdom,
kingdom, or wealth of Solomon, but those famous seven hundred
queens and three hundred concubines, in order to be able to renew
their sexual exploits each day with many and various kinds of lust.
Let us leave these men, I say, and turn to men of more honorable
way of life. Let us approach, if you will, the bustling new forum of   13
our renowned homeland and betake ourselves to the conversations
of our merchants. What will we hear from them but conversations
about augmenting and preserving resources? They tell and con-   14
stantly recount with what great trouble, foresight, cunning, and
toil they have heaped up their riches. In this, as in other matters,
they are deceived with the usual blindness of mortals, who think
that they are pursuing by means of their own works and virtues
what God in his mercy obviously lavishes upon ungrateful men.
They are not content, in their error, to speak only of themselves,   15
but they also recount the tricks and lies of others, although in the
hidden recesses of their conscience (if they do not wish to deceive
themselves) they recognize that they themselves are no purer. And
if they see that someone has defaulted, deceived his creditors, and
run off, they carp at, excoriate, and vilify him—and those do so
most harshly who are soon to follow in his footsteps by deceiving
their own creditors.

And so these are the things recited on the world's stage. These   16
things are not narrated by actors (whose nature it is to imitate, in
the manner of apes, whatever they see going on), but are unfolded
by the agents themselves for all to see. Evil conversations corrupt
good morals,[46] and nothing is more powerful, nothing more effective in provoking minds to action than example. Consequently, we
must flee as speedily as possible this stage show of living together

spectaculum fugiendum. Quod, ni fallor, libentius faciemus si hunc quo adeo delectamur mundum arenam esse laborum certiori cognoverimus argumento.

: XIX :

Quod mundus sit arena laborum.

1 Quis autem negaverit hunc mundum arenam esse laborum qui divinum illud oraculum legerit cum homini dictum fuisse scribitur, 'In sudore vultus tui vesceris pane tuo donec revertaris in terram de qua sumptus es, quia cinis es et in cinerem reverteris'? 2 Hanc quidem penam inflixit deus homini pro transgressione precepti, ut qui sine labore vescendo fructibus sponte creatis in sue immortalitatis semine se poterat eternaliter conservare, inevitabili necessitate moriendi peccati contagio teneretur et id ipsum quod vite durationisque prestaretur per infinitorum laborum seriem 3 consumaret. Hoc autem facile quidem videbit quicunque multas atque varias nostrarum manuum operas considerabit quive quid ventri quidque lateri debeamus secum voluerit ratione perspicua 4 contemplari. Non referamus quantum in superfluis occupemur, quot castra, quot urbes, quot villas, quot domos, quot turres atque palatia humanum genus mirabiliter excitaverit, quotque, dum voluptatibus indulget, edificiorum ornatus cogitaverit atque perfecerit, quos pontes superiecerit fluviis, que propugnacula menibus

in the world. Unless I am mistaken, we will do this more willingly
if we recognize by stronger evidence that this world, in which we
take such delight, is in fact an arena of labors.

: XIX :

The world is an arena of labors.

Who would deny that this world is an arena of labors? Surely no   1
one who has read that divine pronouncement, when, as it is written, man was told, "In the sweat of your brow you will eat your
bread until you return to the earth from which you were formed,
since you are dust and to dust you will return."[47] This punishment   2
God inflicted upon man for the transgression of his precept; as a
result, he who would have been able to preserve himself eternally
in the seed of his immortality by eating spontaneously created
fruits without labor was held by sin's contagion to the inevitable
necessity of dying, and used up whatever portion and duration of
life he was granted in a series of infinite labors. Anyone will see   3
this easily if he considers the many and various works of our
hands, and is willing to contemplate in the clear light of reason
what we owe to the stomach, and what to the body in general. Let   4
us not recount how much we are occupied in superfluous activities; how many camps, cities, villas, homes, towers, and palaces the
human race has miraculously built; how many embellishments of
buildings it has planned and perfected, indulging in pleasures;
what bridges it has cast over rivers; what bulwarks it has furnished

quasve circumfuderit fossas, et quas cloacas, purgamentorum re-
ceptacula, subterranea fabricatione firmaverit, quos fluminibus al-
veos etiam parva indignatione succensi principes militum labore
deduxerint, que stagna mortalium cura siccaverit, quos lacus colle-
gerit, quos portus classibus accipiendis armaverit, et infinita huiusmodi que ad architecturam spectant; que quidem nedum fecisse
labor fuit sed esset laboriosissimum numerare.

5   Hec, inquam, non referamus sed solum quantum exigit etiam
evangelice vite consilium attingamus. Sine pane quidem et vestibus
(licet aliquos et sine his vixisse legamus) vitam transigere durissi-
mum et inhumanum est, quorum unum agricolationem exigit, al-
6   tere lanificium complectuntur. Quantis autem laboribus queratur
panis qui semel viderit, quotiens sit versandus ager aratro ut bis
frigora sentiat mota tellus, bis etiam estu maximo gleba putris in
pulverem redigatur, quo sudore mox arva receptura semen divi-
dantur in sulcos, qua diligentia credita sulcis semina subtegantur,
quas aves arcere sit opus, qualiter purgentur iam nata frumenta,
qualiter sarculentur, et, ut messionem omittam, cuius labores le-
gendorum fructuum demit alacritas, qui viderit quorum verberum
fulmine triturentur, qualiter invehantur in horrea, quantaque sollicitudine conserventur facile iudicabit.

7   Iudicabit etiam de laboribus mortalium quisquis lanificium
conabitur intueri. Tondentur enim oves et lavatur sucidum vellus,
mundatur, eligitur, extricatur, mollitumque et excultum plurimo
dente, pinguefactum oleo per pensa dividitur aut a nentibus

for walls and what moats it has surrounded them with; what sewers, receptacles for waste, it has strengthened with subterranean structures; what riverbeds military leaders, angered by even a small offense, have diverted with their labor; what swamps the work of mortals has dried up; what lakes it has created; what harbors it has equipped to receive ships; and countless things of this kind that pertain to architecture. Not only was it labor to have built them, but it would also be extremely laborious to enumerate them.

Let us not recount these things, I say, but let us merely touch 5 on how much the plan of the evangelical life demands. It is very hard and most inhuman to go through life without bread and clothing (although we read that some people lived even without these): the former requires agriculture; the latter is the product of spinning. Yet anyone who has once seen it will easily judge with 6 what toil bread is acquired: how many times the field must be plowed in order for the disturbed earth to feel frost twice, and the putrid clod be twice reduced to dust by the extreme heat; with what sweat the lands, when they are ready to receive the seed, are divided into furrows; with what care the seeds are entrusted to the furrows and covered over; what birds must be fended off; how the grain, once it has appeared, is cleaned and hoed. Finally (to leave out the harvesting, the toils of which are reduced by our eagerness for gathering the fruits) whoever has seen with what thunderous beatings the grain is threshed, how it is conveyed to the barns, and with what care it is stored, will easily ascertain the labor involved.

Whoever sets out to observe the process of making wool will 7 also get an idea of the toils of mortals. The sheep are shorn and the fresh fleece is washed, cleansed, plucked, disentangled, and, once it has been softened and worked carefully with much combing, it is treated with oil and divided into units for spinning;

imponenda colis aut in girum currente netorio in subtegminis fra-
8 giliorisque fili longitudinem deducenda. Ordiuntur illo telas, isto
vero contexunt; et iam pannus effectus cadentibus malleis traditur
solidandus. Omitto sciens multa que tum avarorum agricolarum
cura, tum delicatorum hominum luxus, quos mollior et splendi-
9 dior delectat vestis, invenit. Quis autem quot artibus opus sit
quantumque laboris exigatur ut instrumenta parentur rustica aut
mille instrumenta lanificum habeantur poterit recensere? Ut etiam
si nichil aliud quam vestitus procuretur et victus abunde satis,
iuxta nostri creatoris oraculum, in sudore nostri vultus sit quoti-
dianus iste panis quem sepius orando petimus comparandus.

10   Sed misera mortalium concupiscibilitas occupari solum neces-
sariis non contenta, ut fugaces divitias cumulet, voluptates expleat,
fruatur deliciis, et aliquo tempore miserabili non vexetur inopia,
agros parat, urbes cingit, oppida struit, maria sulcat, bella gerit, et,
ut corpori morituro, quod esca vermibus reservatur, bene sit, infinitis laboribus implicatur. Et cum agrum quam optimum atque
frugiferum quilibet conetur habere, cuncti tamen vitam pessimam,
plenam periculis, bonis fructibus sterilem, vitiorumque feracissi-
11 mam eligunt et sequuntur. Cum itaque infinitos, si mundum sequimur et si his que in mundo sunt abundare cupimus, nos oporteat subire labores, fugiamus omnes qui laboramus mundum et ad
deum, qui nos in refectionem evocat, sine more dispendio convertamur. Et cum solummodo Christum sequi sit vivere, illum
imitando vitam nostram, si sumus iuvenes, inchoemus, si senes,

the wool must either be put on spinning distaffs, or it must be drawn down, with a circling movement as the spindle rotates, into a length of fragile weft thread. With the one they establish rows of 8 upright threads, and with the other they weave; the cloth now made is given over to falling mallets to be compacted. I am leaving out on purpose many things that the care of greedy farmers and the luxury of spoiled men, who delight in the softer and more splendid variety of clothing, have discovered. Who could make an 9 inventory of how many techniques are necessary and how much labor is demanded in order to provide farm implements or the thousands of pieces of equipment for spinning? Consequently, even if nothing other than clothing were to be provided and food were abundant enough, according to the word of our Creator, that daily bread that we regularly ask for in prayer would have to be acquired in the sweat of our brow.

But mortals' wretched susceptibility to desire, not content to be 10 concerned only for the essentials — with the result that it heaps up fleeting riches, experiences pleasures, enjoys delights, and for a certain time is not vexed by wretched poverty —, purchases fields, surrounds cities with walls, builds towns, plows the seas, wages wars, and, in order that the body, destined to die, which is ear-marked as food for worms, might be well, entangles itself in infi-nite labors. And however much a person may try to have as excel-lent and fruitful a field as possible, all people choose and pursue the worst life, full of perils, bereft of good fruits, yet most fertile in vices. And so since we must undergo infinite labors if we follow 11 the world and desire to possess an abundance of the things in it, let all of us who labor flee the world and without delay turn to God, who calls us to refreshment. And since the only way to live is to follow Christ, let us, if we are young, begin our life by imitat-ing him; if we are old, let us be ashamed to have put off doing so;

pudeat distulisse et flagitiosum putemus aut aliquando, licet sero, non incipere aut mortem antequam inceperimus obivisse diligenterque respiciamus in hoc inhonestatum theatro nos nichil nisi fugiendum, si recte senserimus, intueri.

: XX :

Quod mundus sit theatrum inhonestatum.

1 Quis autem mundum negaverit esse theatrum in quo cuncta ad plausum circumfuse multitudinis agitantur? Quis eum negaverit fugiendum cum inhonestissimum esse certissima concluseris ratione? Nonne et talem esse mundum scimus et in ipso talia quidem cernimus et audimus? Et ut hoc, licet clarum sit, levi nostra disputatione clarius faciamus, consideremus hominum mores et in unica 2 solum differentia ponderemus. Videmus pene cunctos sua occultare consilia et quecunque gerunt ab oculis hominum removere et ea solum auribus aut oculis aliorum credere, ac velut in theatris fieri consuevit, quibus commendationum preconia vel bone extimationis famam sperant, ut manifeste pateat in hac conversatione mortalium nichil aspici nisi quod propter inhonestatem occulitur aut quod propter inanis glorie fumum, quo nichil est vanius, pro- 3 palatur. Nam habent honesta decorem suum ex quo in lucem prodire nituntur; inhonesta vero turpitudine sua latebras semper querunt. Et si aliquando recte facta volumus apparere, sequitur a tergo glorie vane splendor, et dum hominibus placere gaudemus, a remuneratoris eterni gratia sequestramur. Et hec quidem apud illos qui fronti student et non virtutem sed virtutis simulacrum

let us consider it shameful either not to begin sometime, however late, or to die before we have begun. Let us carefully consider that in this theater of disgraces we behold nothing but what, if we judge correctly, we must flee.

: XX :

The world is a theater of disgraces.

Who would deny that the world is a theater of disgraces in which   1
everything is done for the applause of the surrounding multitude?
Who would deny that we must flee it, when one has concluded on
the surest of evidence that it is utterly disgraceful? Don't we know
that the world is such, and haven't we seen and heard that such
things are in it? To make this clearer with our superficial argument
(although it is already clear), let us consider people's ways and
evaluate them only in a single aspect. We see that almost all people   2
conceal their plans and remove their activity from public view;
they only entrust to the eyes and ears of others — as generally occurs in theaters — what they hope will bring them public praise or
a reputation of high esteem. Consequently, it is abundantly clear
that in human relations, we discern nothing but what is concealed
on account of its shamefulness, or what is broadcast for the sake
of the smoke of vainglory — than which nothing is more vain.
Honorable actions have their own beauty as a result of which they   3
strive to come out into the light; but disgraceful actions, in their
turpitude, always seek hiding places. And if at some point we want
correct actions to be apparent, the splendor of vainglory follows
after: rejoicing that we are pleasing to men, we cut ourselves off
from the grace of our eternal Remunerator. This is clearly the case
with people who strive for a good image, not seeking virtue, but

4 querunt plane vera sunt. Sunt autem corruptis nostris moribus plurimi quos occultandarum, ut supra dixi, turpitudinum cura non tenet, sed adeo peccatis delectantur quod et publice peccent et que celare possunt quadam mentis insania et impurissime loquacitatis impetuoso pruritu gaudeant quasi rem pulcerrimam predicare.

5 Quos autem amatores mundi dabis qui se magis esse bonos eligant quam videri, qui non gaudeant occuluisse flagitia, qui non aure popularis flatibus agitentur? Nec perpendit miserie nostre miserrima cecitas quod, cum boni videri volumus, hoc ipsum quod

6 bene facimus depravamus. Videmus enim homines nostri temporis, quando ieiunant, cum proximis loqui et hora pransionis instante, dum reliqui vocantur ad mensam, aut illos increpare quod non ieiunent aut, si exhortentur ad prandium, se gloriabun-

7 dos quod ieiunium celebrent excusare. Quid autem inter illorum abstinentiam et refectionem istorum intersit ego non video, nisi quod plerumque comestores illi, dum audiunt nominari ieiunium, compunguntur et erubescunt deprehendi preceptorum ecclesie transgressores, isti vero prandia que dimittunt recogitantes in suis

8 ieiuniis affliguntur. Quis vero dispensaturus elemosinam non querit sicut ludius in theatro vulgum testem habere? Nec cogitamus quod de cunctis que ad ostentationem facimus mercedem nostram recepimus cum videmur, et eo ipso quod apud homines gloriam desideramus in bonis, nos eterne damnationi per elationis culpam et inanis glorie maculam obligamus, ut iam sine dubitatione liceat affirmare quod aut turpia auditu percipimus in hoc mundi theatro, qui proculdubio est spectaculum delictorum, aut oculis inhonesta videmus aut bona que fiunt vane glorie contubernio (tanta est hominum fragilitas) inquinantur.

rather a semblance of virtue. Since our morals are corrupt, there   4
are very many people who are not bound by concern for concealing
their shameful acts (as I said above),[48] but so delight in their sins
that they both sin publicly and, with insane and prurient loquac-
ity, enjoy proclaiming things that they could hide, as if these were
extremely attractive business.

What world lovers will you cite who choose rather to be good   5
than to seem good;[49] who do not rejoice to have hidden their
crimes; who are not excited by the gusts of popular breeze? The
miserable blindness of our wretchedness does not consider that
when we want to seem good, we subvert that very thing we have
done well. We see men of our time who, when they fast, converse   6
with their fellows; when mealtime is near and the others are called
to the table, they either chastise them for not fasting, or, if they
themselves are urged to dine, they boastfully make the excuse that
they are keeping the fast. I do not see the difference between the   7
abstinence of those men and the refreshment of the others, except
that generally the eaters, when they hear the word *fast*, feel compunction and are ashamed to be caught as transgressors of the
church's precepts; the others, however, are afflicted in their fasting,
perpetually thinking about the meals they are missing. And who,   8
when about to give alms, does not seek, just like a player in the
theater, to have the crowd as a witness?[50] We do not consider that
we have received our reward for all the things we do for ostentation's sake when we are seen, and by that very thing—that we long
for glory among men for our good deeds—we make ourselves liable to eternal damnation through the fault of elation and the stain
of vainglory. Therefore, we can now unhesitatingly assert that either we perceive things shameful to hear in this theater of the
world—which is indeed a spectacle of wrongs—or we see things
disgraceful to the eyes, or (so great is human fragility) the good
things that are done are tainted by contact with vainglory.

: XXI :

Quod mundus sit spectaculum delictorum.

1 Si enim delictum est dei eterni derelinquere legem et creatori nostro aut committendo vetita aut negligendo precepta damnabiliter adversari, nonne manifestum est mundum istum fore spectaculum

2 delictorum? Quid autem, licet te undique vertas in mundo, tuis poterit ocellis occurrere nisi triplex illa partitio, concupiscentia carnis, concupiscentia oculorum, et superbia vite? Quid videbis

3 nisi delictorum sceleribus cuncta fervere? Adi, si placet, palatia regum, atria pontificum, et curias populorum: quid ibi cernere datur nisi venenate livorem invidie, contentionum incendia, iracundie flamas, superbie tumorem, calumniarum insidias, blanditiarum laqueos, assentationum applausus, et, ut hystorici dictum, imo Catonis sententiam referam, ambitionem omnia virtutis premia pos-

4 sidentem? Pergas ad ecclesias, me miserum, pudet dicere tedetque videre quam pessimo exemplo templum domini, domus orationis, quam olim Christus increpuit factam esse speluncam latronum, conversa sit in diversorium procacionis, vanitatum confabulatorium, et oportunum promptuarium voluptatum.

5   Adest, postquam omiserunt episcopi monere populos aut per suos presbiteros ad virtutis tramitem exhortari, adest, inquam, religiosus quispiam et sublimis in pulpito, post angelicam Marie salutationem iocundo quodam sermocinationis preludio suis moribus introductam, aliquod divinarum scripturarum oraculum reassumens pulcerrimum totum in sua, ne dicam turpia, membra discerpit, et equisillabis canticis puerili labore compositis auriculas

: XXI :

The world is a spectacle of wrongs.

If it is a wrong to abandon the law of eternal God and damnably   1
to oppose our Creator either by committing forbidden acts or by
neglecting his precepts, is it not obvious that the world is a spectacle of wrongs? Turn where you will in the world, what will you   2
see but that triple division, concupiscence of the flesh, concupiscence of the eyes, and arrogance of life?[51] What will you see but
everything seething with the criminal wrongs? Approach, if you   3
please, the palaces of kings, the halls of priests, the senate houses
of peoples: what is presented to the sight there but the venom of
poisonous envy, the conflagrations of strife, flames of wrath, swelling of pride, ambushes of calumny, snares of charms, applause of
flattery, and (to use the historian's dictum, or rather, the saying of
Cato) ambition possessing all the prizes of virtue?[52] Make your   4
way to the churches — alas! — it is shameful to say and depressing
to see how with terrible example the Lord's temple, a house of
prayer, which Christ once rebuked for having become a robbers'
den, has been turned into an inn of insolence, a club of vanities,
and a convenient repository of pleasures.

There is present (when bishops have neglected to admonish the   5
people or to exhort them through their priests to enter on the
path of virtue), there is present, I say, one or another religious
man, high in the pulpit, after the angelic salutation of Mary has
been introduced with a jovial preamble of his sermon in his
own character, who takes up again some passage of the divine
scriptures, rips the very beautiful whole apart into its (not to call
them vile) members, and soothes the ears of the crowd with
simple hymns of equal syllables composed with puerile labor.

vulgi permulcet, et eodem observato concentu membra subdividit, subdivisa distinguit, et rebus inops ac sententiis inanis maxima verborum inculcatione lascivit, nuncque acutissime vocis tonitruo totis viribus laterum excitat audientes, nunc graviter insonando submissiore voce proloquitur, nunc candidissimo deprompto sudario frontem tergit, faciem purgat, oculos fricat, nares emungit, tantamque mundiciam delicatus affectat ut non vir, non religiosus

6 sed potius Ciprica mulier videatur. Manicas deinde reiciens summas oras pulpiti candida manu comprendit, digitos in ordinem ponit, seque muliercularum murmuratione gaudet de formositate laudari sicque predicaturus verbum dei totus in ostentationem effusus aut levitatis aut inanis glorie spectaculum prebet. Intuetur interim ab suo pendentem ore plebeculam et in circumstantium silentio gloriabundus incepta prosequitur.

7 Assunt miris ornate vestibus mulieres pictas acu clamides, illitas fuco genas, populatas pilis frontes, afflatos sulfure crines circumfuse virorum multitudini demonstrantes. Adest corona iuvenum quos urit videndo femina. Hic notat oculis quam diligendam assumat. Hic in suam pressos figit obtutus. Ille gaudet oculis paulisper inflexis in se suam amasiam convertisse. Alter aliis in

8 locis vetita sibi petit in templo colloquia. Alter post illius verbalis confessionis solennitatem et benedictionem in domino manu atque ore cum crucis delatam signaculo surgentibus se permiscet ut latus aut manum possit amice contingere vel ei coniuncto corpore pressius adherere.

Maintaining the same harmony, he subdivides the members and adorns the subdivided parts. Devoid of material and empty of thought he frisks about, cramming in as many words as possible. Now he excites his audience with the thunderclap of a high-pitched voice, using all the strength of his lungs; now he speaks out, deeply resounding in a lowered tone; now he takes out a white handkerchief, wipes his brow, mops his face, rubs his eyes, blows his nose, and affects such great delicacy that he seems to be not a man, not a religious person, but a woman of Cyprus. Then, 6 throwing back his sleeves, he grasps the edges of the pulpit with his white hand, arranges his fingers, and rejoices that he is praised for his good looks by the murmuring of little females; thus, when about to preach the word of God, he pours himself completely into ostentation and offers a spectacle of either triviality or vainglory. Meanwhile, he beholds the riffraff hanging on to his every word. Glorying in the silence of the congregation, he continues the discourse he began.

In attendance there are women adorned with magnificent cloth- 7 ing, displaying to the surrounding multitude of men their embroidered cloaks, cheeks smeared with rouge, brows plucked of hair, and coiffures tinged with sulfur. There is present a gathering of young men who burn at the sight of a woman. This youth marks out with his eyes the one he will take as a lover. That one fixes his gaze on his own girl. This takes pleasure in having turned his beloved's attention to himself by staring at her a little while. Another 8 seeks in church conversations forbidden to him in other places. Yet another, after the solemnity of verbal confession and the blessing in the Lord conferred with the sign of the cross on hand and mouth, mingles in the rising crowd so he may touch the side or hand of his girlfriend or to stick to her more closely with his body pressed to hers.

9   Que cum video, cum mente recogito, miror inter alia mirabilia
dei patientiam nisi quod firmiter teneo ipsum in suo districto iudicio miseris inhonestisque carnalibus debite penam iusticie reser-
10   vare. Postquam igitur in terrestribus ac manu factis nostris istis
templis, que propter dedicationem nos deberent in deum speciali
consideratione dirigere, tot et tanta videmus flagitia perpetrari,
cumque vicos et plateas cernamus obscenitatibus abundare, quid
putare debemus intra septa domorum et in secretis penetralibus
11   agitari? Ut quocunque direxeris oculos aut mentem converteris
nichil occurrere possit nisi turpe, culpandum, reprehensibile, de-
testandum, sicque, cum omnia quecunque videmus in mundo non
ex deo sint sed ex Mamona iniquitatum, mundum fugere sicut
horribile precipitium remis et velis perniciter debeamus.

: XXII :

Quod mundus sit horribile precipitium.

1   Quicunque naturalem humani generis super animalia cetera digni-
tatem, in qua deus sublimis et bonus nos constituit, diligenter
examinat facile perpendet in quod profunditatis chaos huius
2   mundi conversatione labamur. Minuit enim deus nos paulo minus
ab angelis, ut illud non solum de Christo sed etiam de universo
humano genere dictum sit, 'Et constituit super omnia opera manuum suarum; omnia subiecit sub pedibus nostris, oves et boves
universas, insuper et pecora campi,' deditque nobis de creaturis
perditis atque rebellibus potestatem filios suos fieri si crediderimus

When I see these things, when I think them over in my mind, 9
among other wonderful things, I wonder at God's patience — except that I firmly believe that in his strict judgment he is reserving
a punishment of deserved justice for wretched and disgraceful,
carnal people. Therefore, when we see so many and such great of- 10
fenses being perpetrated in these earthly temples of ours made by
hands — temples that we ought to devote to God with special
consideration on account of their dedication — and when we see
villages and town squares abounding in obscenities, what ought we
to think goes on within the confines of homes and in secret inner
chambers? Wherever you direct your eyes or turn your mind, you 11
can encounter nothing but what is base, culpable, reprehensible,
and detestable. So, since all that we see in the world is not from
God but from the mammon of iniquities, we ought to flee the
world energetically and with oars and sails just as we would a horrible precipice.

: XXII :

The world is a horrible precipice.

Whoever carefully considers the natural dignity of the human 1
race, in which a lofty and good God established us above the other
animals, will easily ponder into what a depth of chaos we sink
through dwelling in this world. For God made us a little less than 2
the angels, so that it is said not only of Christ but of the entire
human race that "he set him over all the works of his hands; he
put all things under our feet, all sheep and oxen, and also the animals of the field"[53] and from our condition as lost and rebellious
creatures he gave us the power to become his children if we believe

3 in nomine eius. Nos autem, ne solummodo de primi parentis transgressione queramur, cuius inobedientia merito supplicio totum genus humanum affecit, mundum diligentes in nomine suo non credimus qui dixit, 'Regnum meum non est de hoc mundo.' Non credimus quidem, nam huius blandientis mundi contagione non solum consilia sed precepta quidem dei nostri, creatoris et

4 salvatoris nostri, nullatenus observamus. Positi itaque inter angelos et bestias, si mundum dimiserimus, cogitantes et facientes que ex deo sunt, benignitate plasmatoris nostri per caritatem illi infinito et beatifico bono, ac velut angeli secundum mensuram meritorum elevati, liberalitate et gratia sua coniungimur; carnalia vero et terrena sequentes, quasi ignorantes ad quid geniti fuerimus, in vi-

5 litatem bestiarum per huius mundi precipitium declinamus. Unde de nobis non immerito dictum fuit: 'Homo cum in honore esset non intellexit. Comparatus est iumentis insipientibus et similis

6 factus est illis.' Heu, heu, miser, cur hic maneo? Cur non assumo gladium separationis et relinquens uxorem atque filios hinc elevor, hinc fugio? Cur non surgo, cum fame peream positus in custodiam porcis et cupiam de ipsorum siliquis satiari, et revertor ad

7 patrem meum? Heu miser! Heu miser! Notas fecisti michi, domine, vias vite. Ego autem corruptus sum et factus sum abominabilis in studiis meis. Spero tamen quod aliquando respicies in me et misereberis mei. Iudicium dabis puero tuo et salvum facies filium ancille tue, ut in hoc precipiti positus, imo iam perturbatus in preceps, surgam et sitiam ad te, fontem irriguum pietatis, et hunc mundum, domum anxietatum, ereptus et elevatus tuis manibus derelinquam.

in his name. But we (lest we only complain about the transgres- 3
sion of our first parent, for whose disobedience God inflicted deserved punishment on the entire human race), loving the world,
do not believe in the name of him, who said, "My kingdom is not
of this world."[54] Indeed we do not believe, for because of the contagion of this wheedling world, we in no way keep either the
counsels or the precepts of our God, Creator, and Savior. Placed, 4
then, between angels and beasts, if we cast off the world, thinking
and doing things that are of God, by the kindness of our Creator
we are through love by his liberality and grace united to his infinite and beatific goodness, and raised up like angels according to
the measure of our merits; but if we pursue carnal and earthly
things, as if ignorant of what we were born for, we sink down by
way of the precipice of this world to the vile nature of beasts.
Therefore not without reason has it been said of us, "Although 5
man was in honor, he lacked understanding. He has been likened
to senseless beasts and made similar to them."[55] Woe, woe, wretch, 6
why do I stay here? Why do I not take up the sword of separation,
leave wife and children, be lifted up from here, flee from here?
Why don't I rise and return to my Father, as I am perishing with
hunger — appointed to tend pigs, I long to be filled with their
husks?[56] Woe wretch! Woe wretch! You have made known to me, 7
O Lord, the paths of life.[57] Yet I have been corrupted and have
become an abomination in my pursuits. I hope, however, that you
will at length look on me and have mercy on me. You will give
judgment to your servant and you will save your handmaid's son,
so that perched on this precipice — or rather, already thrown headlong — I may rise and thirst for you, well-watered font of piety.
Taken and lifted up by your hands, may I abandon this world, this
house of anxieties.

: XXIII :

Quod mundus sit domus anxietatum.

1   Si enim anxietas premens est egritudo, quod et ipsum vocamen, ab
'angor' inflexum, dat intelligere, ut egritudinem hic accipiam non
corporis sed animi dolorem ex presentis mali opinione prove-
nientem, sicut multi diffiniunt, quis negabit domum anxietatum
2   prementium mundum esse? Intra in mundum, stude opibus, stude
successioni, stude ambitioni, stude denique voluptatibus: heu quibus mentis anxietatibus opprimeris! Anguntur equidem amatores
3   mundi coniugalibus stimulis, anguntur etiam celibatu. Nam sive
uxor forma niteat sive deformitate sordescat, continuis stimulis
agitantur. Hinc enim subit meror assiduus, inde timor. Et si forte
coniuge careat aut sterilem sit sortitus, fortunarum et laborum
suorum se cariturum dolet herede; si vero proles obtigerit, affliguntur in filiis tum educandis, tum instruendis, et cum ambulent
quandoque cum impiis in viam iniquitatum maximo parentibus
4   sunt dolori. Omittamus languores et mortes, que non solum filios
sed quotidie ceteras necessitudines rapiunt, ut verissimum sit satyricum illud,

> hec data pena diu viventibus ut renovata
> semper clade domus multis in luctibus inque
> perpetuo merore et nigra veste senescant.

Et attingamus, si placet, divitiarum studiosos et ne, inextricabile
5   quidem opus, singula designemus. O per quot anxietates mentis

: XXIII :

The world is a house of anxieties.

Anxiety is an illness that presses us; the word itself, formed from   1
angor ["to be pressed"] gives us to understand this. Here I take the
illness in the way that many define it, as a pain not of the body
but of the mind, originating from an opinion of present evil.[58] If
this is so, then who will deny that the world is a house of pressing
anxieties? Enter into the world, pursue wealth, pursue success,   2
pursue ambition, and finally pursue pleasures: alas, by what mental anxieties you will be oppressed! World lovers are, to be sure,
tormented by conjugal goads, but they are also tormented by celi-
bacy. Whether a wife shines with beauty or is soiled by ugliness,   3
world lovers are driven by continual goads. Constant sorrow arises
from the latter, fear from the former. And if a person does not
have a spouse or has been allotted one who is sterile, he grieves
that he will lack an heir to his fortunes and his labors; but if children fall to their lot, people are troubled in raising and educating
them, and when the children walk someday with the impious
along the path of iniquity, they are a very great pain to their parents. Let us say nothing of illnesses and deaths, which snatch away   4
not only children, but other relatives and friends on a daily basis.
The saying of the satirist is very true:

> These things are given as punishment to those who live a
> long time, so that with domestic disaster ever renewed in
> many lamentations, they grow old in perpetual mourning
> and black clothing.[59]

Let us speak, if you please, of those who are zealous for riches
—yet not by depicting the details one by one, which would be an
endlessly complicated task. O, through how many anxieties of   5

et labores corporis qui cumulare divitias pulcrum putant miserum vite tempus transigunt! Exardescunt enim cupidine congregandi, pallescunt et tremunt sollicita perdendi formidine et amissorum

6 dolore inconsolabiliter cruciantur. Ambitiosi vero, qui dignitatibus, potentie, et (quod summum arbitrantur bonum) dominationibus student, quibus urgentur angoribus, quas non effundunt preces, quibus, dum horum aliquid assequi nituntur, se supplices

7 non submittunt? Est opere precium videre quanta humilitate (si tamen humilitas dici potest quam non honestatis dilectio sed mundi cura extorquet) superbas ambitiosi cervices inclinent, capita nudent, et ante aliorum pedes se prosternant dignitatum expetitores, quanta subiectione, imo servitute, verborum blandiantur, rogent, instent, polliceantur, mox tamen adepto quod querunt in

8 intolerabilem elationis insolentiam evasuri. Quibus autem dominantes premantur angustiis, qui videt illorum ipsorum palatiis armatos stare pro foribus, nullos intus nisi prius an occultum ferrum habeant diligenti discussos indagine recipi, quique videt pregustationes in mensis, armatorum excubationes ad thalamos ingentesque turritarum arcium fabricas, facile iudicabit.

9   Hoc autem admonitus fuit non ignobili documento Siracusanus ille Damocles, qui deceptus in splendore purpure et alio quem circa Dyonisium tirannum apparatu mirabatur non dubitavit pa-

10 tronum suum beatissimum appellare. Quam vocem cum derisisset Dyonisius, et ille perstans in proposito multa sue beatitudinis munera recenseret, 'Faciam,' inquit, 'Damocles, te iam esse beatum.' Moxque iussit ipsum in sede statui sua, purpura et bysso vestitum, parari regifico luxu mensas et omnem servorum familiam sibi tanquam domino ministrare, et denique curiam et omnem

mind and labors of body do those who think it a fine thing to accumulate riches pass their wretched time of life! For they burn with desire for acquiring things; they grow pale and tremble with anxious fear of loss and are inconsolably tortured by pain when they have lost things. Ambitious people, however, are eager for 6 distinctions, power, and domination (which they think the highest good): by what torments are they driven, what prayers don't they pour out, to whom do they not submit themselves as suppliants when they are trying to get something from them? It is useful to 7 see with what great humility (if you can call it humility when not the love of integrity but concern for the world compels it) the ambitious bend their haughty necks, bare their heads, and prostrate themselves before others' feet when they are aiming at political office; with what great verbal subjection (or rather, servility) they flatter, beseech, insist, promise—and yet soon, when they have got what they want, they break forth into intolerable insolence of elation. But anyone will easily judge into what straits rulers are 8 pressed when he sees that armed guards stand before the gates of their palaces, and that nobody is let in unless he is first submitted to a careful search to see whether he is hiding a sword, and when he sees the pretasting of foods at table, the night watch of armed men at the bedroom doors, and the huge works of turreted castles.

Damocles the Syracusan was warned by this famous example— 9 Damocles, who, deceived by the splendor of the purple and in awe of the rest of the ostentation surrounding the tyrant Dionysius, did not hesitate to call his patron the happiest man in the world. Dionysius laughed in derision at this pronouncement, but Damo- 10 cles, persisting in his opinion, enumerated the many gifts of the tyrant's happiness. So Dionysius said, "I will make you happy now, Damocles." Right away he ordered Damocles to be placed on his throne and dressed in purple and fine cotton; the tables to be set in luxury fit for a king, and all the household servants to attend him as if he were their master; and finally, the court and all the

11 civitatem ac velut regi deferre. Cumque Damocles cuncta que domino suo familiaris ille timore plenus et reverentia famulatus pre-
bere solebat sibi conspiceret exhiberi, iamque sibi non Damocles
sed rex et dominus videretur, voluptuose et splendide discumbenti
demissus est ab auratis laquearibus gladius seta, ut dicitur, equina

12 retentus, qui iugulo cepit et cervicibus imminere. Tunc ille morte
propinqua perterritus, utpote que sibi non longe sed ad paucos
digitos adhereret queve non cathenis ferreis sed retinaculo sete
fragilis arceretur, desideratas fastidire dapes et regiam pompam,
quam paulo ante tam cupide mirabatur, mutata sententia cepit

13 horrere, et compulsus stare flens orabat: 'Gloriose Dyonisi, cui
Iuppiter et omnis celitum ordo dedit Siracusis, urbi quidem nobi-
lissime, dominari, per deos omnes, per maximi parentis tui um-
bras, per dexteram tuam, per spem unici filii tui, quem tibi conces-
sere dei futurum glorie successorem tantarumque fortunarum
heredem, parce misero, ignosce desipienti, et me supplicem fortune mee, qualiscunque sit illa, restitue. Liceat tante formidinis
plena palatia securitate mee domuncule commutare. Satis enim
agnosco errorem meum. Nunc video sollicitudinem regum et im-
pendentium periculorum metus, que michi cuspis huius mortiferi

14 gladii representat.' Nec dubitem ipsum impetrata licentia splendores illos regios properantiore gradu fugisse quam expeti soleant,
et post illa cum sue condicionis statu longe melius et equanimius
convenisse.

15   Age vero, deditos voluptatibus quis ignorat per tela, per ignes,
et per immensa transire pericula? Quis nescit hos, quibus urgean-
tur stimulis, quibus vexentur angoribus, ut delectationibus suis

citizenry to obey him as a king. When Damocles saw everything 11
that he — as part of the royal household, and full of the fear and
reverence of servitude — used to give to his master being offered to
him, and he seemed to himself to be no longer Damocles, but king
and lord, just then, as he lay down in voluptuous splendor, a
sword was lowered from the gilded paneled ceiling (suspended, it
is said, by a horse's hair), which began to hang over his throat and
neck. Then Damocles, utterly terrified by the nearness of death 12
(inasmuch as death was not far from him, but standing at a distance of a few inches, and was not being kept at bay by iron chains
but held back by a fragile hair), changed his mind and began to
feel disgust at the once-desired feasts and recoiled at the royal
pomp that he had so avidly marveled at a little earlier. Getting to
his feet, he prayed tearfully, "Glorious Dionysius, to whom Jupiter 13
and all the order of celestial beings gave dominion over Syracuse, a
city most noble — by all the gods, by the shades of your very great
parent, by your right hand, by the hope of your only son, whom
the gods granted to you as successor to your glory and heir of such
great fortunes — spare miserable me, forgive stupid me, and restore
me, a suppliant, to my fortune, such as it is. Allow me to exchange
a palace full of such great fear for the security of my own little house. For I recognize my error well enough. Now I see the
worry of kings and the fear of impending dangers, which the tip of
this death-dealing sword brings home to me." I wouldn't doubt 14
that, after being given leave, he fled those regal splendors with a
quicker step than they are generally sought, and that after that
experience he accepted his status in life far better and with far
more equanimity.[60]

But come, who is unaware that those dedicated to pleasures 15
pass through missiles, through fires, and through immense dangers? Who doesn't know by what goads these people are driven,
by what torments they are vexed in order that they may be able

16 queant iuxta insane mentis cupidinem indulgere? Ite igitur, ite mortales, in exitium vestrum proni, ite et mundum istum diligite, et, ut animam, que ad imaginem creatoris de nichilo facta est, perdatis, anxietatibus, quarum infinita sunt agmina, vos cece mentis erroribus implicate! Cur non melius huius turbidi maris fluctus, quibus hinc inde iactamini, in anime vestre salutem et eternam beatitudinem devitatis?

: XXIV :

Quod mundus sit mare turbidum.

1 Respicite, miseri mortales, quos usque adeo mundus iste delectat, circumque respicite diligenter et scitote vos in huius vite miserande curriculo magnum hoc et spaciosum mare manibus navigare, in quo, sicut psalmista testatur, 'reptilia sunt quorum non est numerus'; nichil enim huic mundo mari turbido convenientius com-

2 paratur. Si enim mare, ut legiferi prophete, imo dei, digito scriptum legitur, congregatio aquarum est, que quidem instabiles sunt, labiles, atque fluxe, nonne mundum istum tremulum, caducum, et

3 effluentem iure maris nomine possumus appellare? Si vero mare, ut plerique volunt, ab 'amaritudine' dictum est, et hoc blandiente mundo nichil amarius, quid potest congruentius in designatione mundi huius quam maris vocabulum adaptari? Hinc Ysaias propheta inquit, 'Ve multitudini populorum multorum ut multitudo maris sonantis,' et alter sed eodem tamen spiritu dixit, 'Cor impii autem quasi mare fervens quod requiescere non potest, et redundatio fluctus eius in conculcationem et lutum.' Nam et nisi congregasset dominus aquas que sub celo sunt in locum unum, et

to indulge in their delights according to the lust of their unsound mind? Go, then, mortals, go on hands and knees to your destruc- 16 tion, go and love this world, and, by the errors of your blind minds, entangle yourselves in anxieties, whose armies are infinite, so that you lose your soul, which was made out of nothing in the image of its Creator! Why not better avoid the waves of this turbid sea, by which we are tossed every which way, for the safety of your soul and eternal blessedness?

: XXIV :

The world is a turbid sea.

Look, wretched mortals, you whom this world delights so much 1 —look around carefully and know that in the course of this miserable life you are navigating this great and spacious sea with your hands, a sea in which, as the psalmist attests, "there are reptiles without number."⁶¹ Nothing is a more fitting object of comparison for this world than a turbid sea. If the sea is the gathering of the 2 waters (as we read in the text written by the finger of the lawgiving prophet, or, to be more precise, by God himself),⁶² and the waters are unstable, slippery, and fluctuating, can we not rightly call this wavering, fleeting, and passing world by the name of *sea?* But if *sea* 3 [*mare*], as many have it, is derived from *bitterness* [*amaritudo*],⁶³ and nothing is more bitter than this blandishing world, what is more appropriately used to designate the world than the word *sea?* Hence the prophet Isaiah says, "Woe to the multitude of many peoples like the multitude of the sounding sea";⁶⁴ and another said in the same spirit, "The heart of the impious is like the seething sea that cannot rest, and the overflowing of its waves into mire and mud."⁶⁵ And if the Lord had not gathered up the waters under the

apparuisset arida, quid esset omnis mundi presentis ambitus nisi
4 mare? Quod si non incongruenter de parte maiore precipue vel
nobiliore totum appellamus, cumque maiores et nobiliores aquas
esse videamus, in quarum medio apparuit arida et factum est fir-
mamentum, id est celum, quis neget mundum maris vocabulo de-
5 signari? Sed quid ego quod clarissimum est apud omnes divinarum scripturarum tractatores conor astruere? Hoc igitur pro re
notissima relinquamus. Nam sicut rebus obscuris pauciloquio vi-
tiosum est tenebras densiores affundere, ita res claras sermonis et
verborum multitudine pertractare et vanum et tediosum est.

6 Est itaque mundus mare turbidum, in quo quicunque mortalium extra ecclesie catholice naviculam se direxerit naufragus sub-
mergetur. Nec sit quod in hoc mari sine ecclesie sancte navigio
7 portum speres salutiferum invenire. Olim enim filii Israel, populus
dei, in circumcisionis sacramento mare Rubrum facto tramite in
medio aquarum omnipotentis dei gratia incolumes evaserunt in
repromissionis terram sicut prenuntiatum erat ipsorum patribus
8 perventuri. Egiptii vero illud idem iter ingressi, quia dei fedus et
illum preparantis in remissione peccatorum ad salvationem caratherem non habebant, in eodem mari submersi sunt, ut in illa
figurali hystoria Veteris Testamenti satis apte possit intelligi sine
dei sacramento, quod ille qui circumcisionem instituit nova faciens
omnia, cumulatiore tamen gratia in baptismi lavacrum commutavit, in hoc mari neminem posse salvari.

9 Sed ne, postquam ortus nobis fuit sol iusticie, putemus et hoc,
sicut fuerunt plurima, renovatum, evangelica figura nos admonet

sky into one place, and dry land had not appeared, what would the area of this entire present world be but sea? If we appropriately 4 take the name of the whole from its greater or nobler part, and since we observe that there are greater and nobler waters, in the middle of which dry land appeared and the firmament (that is, the sky) was made, who would deny the world the designation of *sea*? But why do I try to add to what is utterly clear in all commenta- 5 tors on divine scripture?[66] Let us abandon this topic, then, as something very well known. For just as it is bad to spread even denser shadows over obscure matters by saying too little, so it is both useless and tedious to treat clear matters with a plethora of talk and words.

And so the world is a turbid sea, in which any mortal who has 6 steered himself outside of the ship of the Catholic Church is wrecked and drowned. And there is no reason to hope to find a safe harbor on this sea without the vessel of the holy church. For 7 once the children of Israel, the people of God in the sacrament of circumcision, escaped the Red Sea unharmed after a path had been made in the middle of the waters by the grace of all-powerful God, they were destined to arrive in the Promised Land, as it had been foretold to their fathers. But the Egyptians who entered 8 upon that same route, since they did not have a covenant with God and the mark of one preparing for salvation in the remission of sins, were drowned in that same sea. So in the figurative story of the Old Testament we can understand quite well that without the sacrament of God—who, making all things new, instituted circumcision, yet with grace compounded exchanged it for the bath of baptism—in this sea no one can be saved.

But lest we think that now, when the Sun of Justice has risen 9 for us, this sea, too, has been made new (as were a great many things), the figurative story in the Gospels admonishes us that

navim ad illum portum salutis quem Christum crucifixum intel-
10 ligo donec ad ipsum pervenias appellendam. Legimus quidem
quod Christus orans stetit in monte, et navicula cum discipulis in
medio mari tota nocte fluctibus iactabatur (erat enim eis contrarius ventus), et quod videns eum quarta vigilia Petrus super
mare deambulantem, ceteris autem timentibus quasi fantasma vi-
derent, Christo clamante, 'Habete fiduciam. Ego sum. Nolite ti-
11 mere'; dixit ei, 'Iube me, si tu es, venire ad te super aquas.' Quod
cum fecisset et homo purus super mare deambularet, videns ventum validum timuit et cepit mergi, nisi Christus ipsum appre-
hendisset manu, proculdubio periturus; moxque cum ascendisset
naviculam, cessavit ventus et facta tranquillitate adorabant eum
dicentes, 'Vere filius dei es.'

12   Hec verba, licet sicut cetera divine scripture plenissima sint
misteriis, quantum ad presentem tamen tractatum pertinet, statum militantis et triumphantis ecclesie satis aperte demonstrant.
Iam enim ab omnibus usurpatum est ut communi locutione cor-
13 pus ecclesie appellatione navicule figuretur. Ecclesia vero militante
Christus orat et manet in monte, hoc est in divine celsitudinis
maiestate, orans, sicut et ipse testatus est, pro petra illa ecclesie
14 principe ut non deficiat fides sua. Quid enim? Indigebatne Christus, verus deus et verus homo, et ita verus homo quod, cum venis-
set princeps mundi huius, in eo non invenerit quicquam, indige-
15 batne pro sua salute orationum suffragiis? Non profecto. Orabat
igitur et orat pro ecclesia sua, pro sponsa sua, pro dilecta sua,
quam tam ardenter amavit quod, ut institueret ipsam et in ea genus mortale salvaret primi parentis transgressione damnatum, humanitatem assumpsit, nec dedignatus est de eterno et creatore
16 temporalis effici creatura. Orat enim pro salute ecclesie, que quidem tota nocte fluctibus iactabatur, id est in hoc mundo, qui vere

we must drive our ship on toward that port of salvation (by which I understand Christ crucified) until we reach it. Indeed, we read 10 that Christ stood praying on the mountain, while a boat carrying the disciples was being tossed by waves all night in the middle of the sea (for the wind was against them). At the fourth watch of the night, Peter saw him walking on the sea; all the rest were afraid, as if they were seeing a ghost. Christ cried out, "Have faith. It is I. Don't be afraid." Peter said to him, "If you are he, command me to come to you over the waters." Jesus did this, and the pure 11 man was walking on the sea, but when he saw the strong wind he was afraid and began to sink; if Christ had not taken hold of his hand, Peter surely would have perished. As soon as Christ had boarded the boat, the wind ceased; when all was calm, the disciples worshipped Christ, saying, "Truly you are the Son of God."[67]

Although the rest of sacred scripture is full of mysteries, yet as 12 far as they pertain to the present subject, these words demonstrate quite clearly the state of the church militant and triumphant. For it is now generally accepted that in common parlance the body of the church is figured as a boat. While the church is doing battle, 13 Christ prays and remains on the mountain—that is, in the majesty of divine elevation, praying, just as he himself attested, for the "rock," the leader of the church, that his faith not fail. Tell me: was 14 Christ in need, Christ, true God and true man—so true a man that, when the prince of this world came, he had no hold on him[68]—was he in need of the support of prayers for his own salvation? Certainly not. Therefore he was praying and prays for his 15 church, for his spouse, for his beloved, whom he loved so passionately that he took on humanity in order to establish her and in her save the mortal race, damned by its first parent's transgression; and he did not disdain to become a temporal creature instead of the eternal Creator. He prays for the safety of the church, which indeed 16 was being tossed by waves all night—that is, in this world,

nox est et densissima obscuritas tenebrarum. Erat enim navicule contrarius ventus, nam in hoc mari multa contra salutem ecclesie quotidie quasi ventus insurgunt, ut hereses, scismata, persecutiones, et alia plura que tedium est referre.

17   Quarta autem vigilia, hoc est extrema nocte, in fine videlicet seculi, videt eum Petrus, caput ecclesie, super aquas ambulantem, et ceteris putantibus se fantasma videre et ipsum dei filium non agnoscentibus, solus Cephas petit ut iubeat quod ad eum super aquas accedat, nec illud verbum, 'si tu es,' dubitantis est sed omnino credentis. Nam si non cognovisset illum Petrus, non petisset

18 imperium ut se inter fluctus proiciens mergeretur. Exivit igitur Petrus, et qui tota nocte salvatus est in navi, relinquens illam et ad Christum properans, validum afflare cernens ventum timuit et mergi cepit, hac hystorie veritate nos admonens extra ecclesie sancte naviculam omnibus pereundum, licet iter ad Christum cre-

19 dulus moliatur. Unde merito sequitur increpatio Christi dicentis, 'Modice fidei, quid dubitasti?' Vere modice fidei qui in navi salutem quodam modo desperabat: 'Cur dubitasti et in navicula nostra perire et in meo conspectu ventum licet validum timuisti?' Pius itaque salvator noster eum manu capiens reduxit in navim, quoniam, ut volunt sanctorum patrum autoritates, in fine temporum

20 omnes reducentur in navim et erit grex unus et pastor unus. Tunc igitur intrat Christus in navim, hoc est sue unitur ecclesie, sicut erit in statu iam exacta militia triumphante, et statim cessabit ventus. Amplius enim non iactabitur fluctibus sicut in hoc mari

which is truly night and a very thick cloud of shadows. The wind was against the boat, for on this sea many things rise up daily like a wind against the church's safety, such as heresies, schisms, persecutions, and many more things which it would be tedious to name.

But at the fourth watch of the night (that is, at the end of night, namely, at the end of the age), Peter, the head of the church, sees him walking over the waters. The others think that they are seeing a ghost and do not recognize the very Son of God: only Cephas asks Jesus to command him to come to him over the waters; and the phrase "if it is you" is not said by one who doubts, but by one who fully believes. For if Peter had not recognized him, he would not have asked for the command to cast himself into the waves and drown. Peter, therefore, went out. The whole night he was safe in the boat, but he left it and hastened to Christ. When he saw that a strong wind was blowing, he was afraid and began to sink. With this true story he warns us that outside of the boat of the holy church, all must perish, although the believer works his way to Christ. For this reason it is fitting that Christ's rebuke follows, when he says: "You of little faith, why did you doubt?" Truly of little faith is the one who somehow despaired of his safety while in the boat: "Why did you doubt and fear that you would perish in our boat and in my sight, even though the wind was strong?" And so our faithful Savior caught him by the hand and led him back into the boat, since (as the authoritative holy fathers believe) at the end of time all will be led back into the boat and there will be one flock and one shepherd. Then Christ boards the boat, that is, he is united with his church, just as it will be in the church's triumphant state, after its military service is finished; and at once the wind will cease. It will be tossed no further by the

videmus dum sumus in via, sed tranquillitate facta apertis oculis Christum cognoscentes adorabimus, quod erit in patria.

21 Cum igitur videamus Petrum extra naviculam pene submersum, non sit quod temere confidamus extra corpus ecclesie, que navicula quidem est, debere salvari. Latent enim in hoc mari magno, quod manibus, hoc est nostris operibus, navigamus, innumerosa reptilia, hostis videlicet diabolus, inimica caro, et carnis plene illecebris voluptates, quibus inspiratur ventus ille submergens, et damur reptilibus ipsis in predam, que nos extra navim capiunt, que tamen, dum sumus in illa, dimisso reticulo capiuntur,

22 non ut noceant sed ut cibent. Illorum enim insidiis et temptationibus, si in vias ambulaverimus domini, sic exercemur quod dei benignitate et gratia cumulatius mereamur. Mare igitur hoc relinquentes ascendamus naviculam que nos ad portum deducat

23 incolumes. Huius autem navis compago est sola caritas qua proximis coniungimur, deo unimur. Vitam enim eternam possidebimus deum et proximum diligendo. Mundum autem diligentes quomodo deum amare possumus, qui dixit, 'Ego non sum de hoc mundo'; cum scriptum sit, 'Qui diligit mundum non est caritas

24 patris in eo'? Blandiuntur ergo sibi et se blandiendo decipiunt quicunque se et deo servire et mundum diligere posse confidunt. Quo fugiendum est mare turbidum istud et per ecclesie dei naviculam transmittendum, ne in hac calamitatum valle torpentes et devii, privati gloria in eternam miseriam demergamur.

waves that we experience as long as we are traveling on this sea, but all will be made calm: our eyes will be opened, and, recognizing Christ, we will worship him since he will be in our homeland.

Therefore, when we see Peter almost drowning outside the 21 boat, we shouldn't rashly trust that we ought to be saved outside the body of the church (which is the boat). For concealed in this great sea that we navigate with our hands (that is, by our works), are countless reptiles. These are our Enemy the devil, the inimical flesh, and pleasures of the flesh full of enticements over which that drowning wind blows, and we are given to the reptiles themselves as prey. They seize us outside the boat, but as long as we are in it, we cast our nets and catch them so that they do not harm us, but feed us. If we walk in the way of the Lord, we are harassed by 22 their plots and temptations to the extent that we earn all the more merit by the kindness and grace of God. Leaving this sea, then, let us board the boat that will lead us to harbor unharmed. The 23 framework of this boat is charity alone, by which we are joined to our neighbors and united with God. For we will possess eternal life by loving God and neighbor. But if we love the world, how can we love God, who said, "I am not of this world,"[69] and when it is written that "Whoever loves the world, the love of the Father is not in him"?[70] Therefore those who are confident that they can 24 both serve God and love the world flatter themselves, and, by so doing, they deceive themselves. For this reason we must flee this turbid sea and be conveyed by the boat of God's church, lest, languishing and wandering in this vale of calamities and deprived of glory, we sink into eternal misery.

: XXV :

Quod mundus sit vallis calamitatum.

1 Calamitas equidem vel a 'casu calamorum,' hoc est 'frugiferarum palearum,' dicta est, sterilitas scilicet et caritudo frumenti, vel, ut aliqui profitentur, miseria est spe vacua et rebus inanis aut, sicut alicubi iura civilia sumunt, recidivatio est in miseriam servitutis.
2 Ex quo quis negare audeat mundum esse vallem calamitatum? Omnis equidem virtutum seges, ne fructum afferat in tempore suo, taliter in mundo corrumpitur quod in summa sterilitate meri-
3 torum societas mortalium reperitur. Mundo quidem dediti, harum visibilium rerum amore decepti, nichil supra corporeos sensus cogitant et si cogitant non intelligunt, aut si intelligunt non dili-
4 gunt. Quare quid sperare possunt nisi quod, cum visi fuerint in connubiali convivio, non habentes vestem nuptialem ligatis manibus et pedibus proiciantur in tenebras exteriores, ubi sit fletus et stridor dentium, aut exclusi pulsantes ad ianuam audiant vocem
5 illam tremendam, 'Amen dico vobis, nescio vos'? Nesciuntur enim in gloria quos hec terrena delectant, et mundum dum vixerint dilecturi in eternam miseriam presciuntur, ut manifeste pateat mundum esse spe vacuum et certissime rebus inanem, cum que in mundo sint putrescant, dilabantur, et effluant et ea que bona fece-
6 ris, si ad mundum retuleris, mala fiant. Oportet enim cuncta que facimus facere propter deum et ad eius gloriam quicquid agimus

: XXV :

The world is a vale of calamities.

Calamity [*calamitas*] is derived either from the fall of reeds [*casus* 1
calamorum], that is, "the fall of fertile grasses," that is, sterility and
lack of fruit; or, as some people claim, it is misery devoid of hope
and empty of resources,[71] or, as civil law has it somewhere, it is a
relapse into the misery of slavery.[72] And so who would dare to 2
deny that the world is a vale of calamities? Indeed the entire crop
of virtues does not bear fruit in its season, but is so corrupted in
the world that human society is found to suffer from utmost sterility of merits. People who are devoted to the world and deceived by 3
the love of these visible things think about nothing beyond the
bodily senses. If they do think about eternal things, they do not
understand them; if they understand them, they do not love them.
What, then, can these people hope for except that, when they are 4
noticed to be without nuptial attire at the wedding banquet, with
hands and feet bound, they will be cast into the outer darkness
where there will be weeping and gnashing of teeth; or, locked out
and knocking on the door, they will hear the terrible words "Truly
I tell you, I do not know you"?[73] For those whom these earthly 5
things delight are not known in glory, and, destined to love the
world as long as they live, they are marked out beforehand for
eternal misery. Consequently, it is patently clear that the world is
devoid of hope and most certainly empty of resources: since the
things that are in the world decay, decline, and flow away; your
good deeds, if you have oriented them toward the world, become
bad. For all that we do we should do on account of God, and any- 6
thing we engage in or say we should refer to his glory. For it is a

dicimusve referre. Deformitas est enim et ingens ab eterna lege
defectus non de illo summo rerum omnium principe et fine, deo,
cum aliquid mente concipimus aut conceptum in actum deduci-
7   mus, cogitare. Denique, si calamitas est recidivatio in miseriam
servitutis, quid magis mundo congruit quam ut calamitatum vallis
appelletur? Equidem concepti in iniquitatibus peccato obnoxii
nascimur et lavati per dei gratiam et super nivem regeneratione
baptismatis dealbati, dum in hoc mundo ad cupiditates revertimur
et labimur in terrena cecitate deflenda, et truculento carnis nostre
8   tiranno et tremende nos resubicimus servituti. Dimittendus igitur
mundus iste, calamitatum vallis, cui quicquid operamur vanum, a
quo quicquid speramus inane, ad quem quicquid referimus, quan-
tumlibet virtuosum in se ipso, subsidit et labitur, quo quicquid
lavatur inficitur, cuiusque contagio peccato liberi peccatis iterum
subiugamur. Sed ipsum et erumnarum domicilium sicut vallem
calamitatum consultius horreamus.

: XXVI :

Quod mundus sit erumnarum domicilium.

1   Quamvis enim idem videantur calamitas et erumna, proprietate
tamen quadam ab autoribus distinguuntur. Et de calamitate quidem proxime dictum est. Est autem erumna, si licet in Christianis
eloquiis uti diffinitionibus paganorum, ut refert Cicero, 'mentis
2   egritudo laboriosa.' Ut autem vocabulorum tractatores volunt,
cum dicatur erumna quasi 'extra rumen,' id est extra cibum quem
rumine constat assumi, nichil aliud erit erumna quam miseria

deformity and an enormous falling away from eternal law not to think about the ruler and end of all things, God, when we conceive something in the mind or carry out a concept in action. Finally, if calamity is a relapse into the misery of slavery, what is more appropriate for the world than to be called a vale of calamities? We are born conceived in iniquity, bound to sin; we are washed through God's grace and clothed in white whiter than snow by the regeneration of baptism. As long as we are in this world, we return to our desires and slide back into earthly things with pitiful blindness; we subject ourselves again to the truculent tyrant of our flesh and to terrible slavery. We must leave this world, a vale of calamities; whatever we do for it is in vain; whatever we hope for from it is empty; whatever we orient toward it — however virtuous this thing may be in itself — sinks and falls; whatever is washed by it is infected; although freed from sin, we are subjugated to sins again by its contagion. Let us more wisely shun this home of hardships as a vale of calamities.

7

8

: XXVI :

The world is the home of hardships.

Although calamity and hardship appear to be the same thing, in strict usage authoritative writers make a distinction between them. I have just spoken about calamity. Hardship, Cicero says (if one may use pagan definitions in Christian discourse), is "toilsome sickness of mind."[74] Yet as the lexicographers have it, *hardship* [*erumna*] is, as it were, "outside the gullet" [*extra rumen*], that is, outside food[75] (which, as is well known, is taken in by the gullet). Hardship is likely to be nothing other than misery in need of

1

2

ciborum indiga, qua nichil apud mortales miserius reputatur. Explicemus igitur hoc ultimum, deinde ad laboriosam egritudinem
3 revertamur. Est homo, ni fallor, unum compositum in quo subicitur corpus, ut materia, substantiali forme, anime videlicet rationali, qua vivimus et ad dei similitudinem facti sumus. Non negaverim autem mundum istum corpori nostro cibum necessarium ministrare, sed cibum qui, quicquid apponit corpori quicquidve restaurat in nobis, impurius creditur, unde morborum infiniti tu-
4 multus, sicut cernimus, excitantur. Sed dilatemus corpus et impinguemus carnem istam fetidam hac in vermes transitura sagina, ut pulcer sit color et vividus, nulle in corpore nostro ruge, et a summo verticis usque ad pedes splendor quidam acceptus intuentium oculis affundatur; superemus etiam, si placet, forma et specie pulcritudinis Absalonem: certe nulla poterit esse corporis nostri tanta nobilitas quin, si intra cutem cogitatione vel oculis penetre-
5 mus, plurima nostris displicitura sensibus offerantur. Minimum est quod turpia separat a formosis, et quod oculos insipientis vulgi detinet et suspendit; plurimum autem est et fluxum quod dum in cibum assumimus ad estuantis libidinis voluptatem, huius mundi labilis et caduci dilectores accendit.

6   Abundet licebit igitur mundus et non solum ad necessitatem sed ad superfluitatem cibos suppeditet corporales, cum intus excitet, et exterius, sicut videmus, alliciat fetide libidinis appetitum, quid hec refectio proderit, imo quid non nocebit, postquam corpore saturato interior homo fame periens non nutritur sed offendi-
7 tur, occiditur, non servatur? Alius est panis verus in via cibans animam ut eam cum obedienti corpore deducat in gloriam. Panis

food, than which nothing among mortals is reckoned to be more miserable. Let us develop this last point and then return to hardship as toilsome sickness. A human being is, I believe, a compound in which the body, being material, is subject to the substantial form, that is, to the rational soul, by which we live and have been made in God's likeness. I won't deny that the world provides our bodies with necessary food, but it is food that—whatever it adds to our bodies and whatever it refreshes in us—is believed to be impure. The infinite disturbances of diseases are, as we see, stirred up from this source. Yet let us expand our bodies and fatten that stinking flesh with this rich food that is destined for the worms, so that our color is good and vivid, there is not a wrinkle on our bodies, and from the crown of the head right down to the feet we acquire a sort of glow that shines forth for all to see. Let us, if you will, surpass even Absalom in beautiful physique—truly our bodies could not possess such great nobility that, if we were to penetrate under the skin with our imagination or with our eyes, a great many things would not present themselves bound to offend our senses. Only the smallest difference separates ugly things from beautiful, and what detains and holds captive the eyes of the senseless mob is small indeed; but very great and inconstant is that which, when we take it as food for the pleasure of our burning desire, inflames the lovers of this unstable and fleeting world.

Granted, then, that the world is abundant and supplies food to the body not for necessity, but also to superfluity. But when it stirs us up internally and also entices our appetite for stinking lust externally, as we see, what good is this refreshment—rather, how will it fail to do harm—since, though the body is saturated, the inner man perishes with hunger; is not nourished but offended; killed, not preserved? The true bread is different, the bread that nourishes the soul on its journey so as to lead her with obedient body into glory. This bread is not born in the world but descends

iste non in mundo nascitur sed de celo descendit, Iesus Christus dominus noster, verum dei verbum caro factum, quo per misterium sacramenti reficimur, quique se per doctrinam quotidie manducandum fidelibus exhibet, quam evangelizando regnum dei no-

8 bis tradidit observandam. O felices, o saturi qui audiunt verbum dei et faciunt illud! Plane tamen illud omnes audientes non facimus sed eius precepta negligimus, cum tamen deum nos diligere labiis ostendamus. Non habet igitur mundus iste cibum quo totus homo cibetur et ob id convenienter erumnarum domicilium appel-

9 latur. Sed si laboriosam egritudinem mentis intelligere velimus erumnam iuxta Ciceronis sententiam, cum mundus iste, sicut dictum est, laboribus plenus sit et mentes, sicut in subsequentibus ostendetur, corrumpat et ledat, quis ipsum domicilium erumnarum non affirmet ratione clarissima nominari? Ut hunc mundum, vere speculum vanitatum, quanto magis cognoverimus, tanto minus diligere debeamus.

: XXVII :

Quod mundus sit speculum vanitatum.

1 Speculum siquidem vitrum est, in sperica rotunditate conflatum, quod, ne raritate sua visu penetretur, intra convexum plumbi superficie circumlinitur, cuius obiectu corpus illud dyaphanum videtur obscurum, et in raritate vitrea oppositarum rerum formas mira specierum multiplicatione recipiens conversam fugacemque obiec-

2 torum reddit imaginem. Mundus igitur iste vitro fragilior et obscurior plumbo non res sed inanes rerum imagines representat et,

from heaven—Jesus Christ our Lord, true Word of God made flesh, by whom we are restored through the mystery of the sacrament. Through his teaching he daily shows himself to the faithful as food which, by proclaiming the kingdom of God, he handed down for us to keep. O blessed, sated people who hear the word of God and do it![76] Clearly, however, all of us who hear it do not do it; we neglect his precepts even though we profess with our lips that we love God. Therefore the world does not have food by which the whole person may be fed, and for this reason it is aptly called the home of hardships. But let us try to understand hardship according to Cicero's definition as a toilsome sickness of mind. Since this world of ours (as was said) is full of toils, and (as will be shown below) it corrupts and hurts minds, who will not assert that it is on self-evident grounds that the world is called the home of hardships? So we ought to love this world, truly a mirror of vanities, all the less, the more we come to know it.

: XXVII :

The world is a mirror of vanities.

A mirror is glass melted into a spherical shape. In order that it may not be penetrated by the vision on account of its thinness, the glass is smeared all over with a layer of lead within the rounded hollow. By this obstruction that transparent body appears dark; with its glassy thinness it receives the figures of the things in front of it with a wonderful multiplication of forms and gives back an inverted and insubstantial image of the objects. The world, more fragile than glass and darker than lead, does not present real

quod prestrigiosius est, sinistra in dexterum et in sinistrum dextra commutat. Hec quidem omnia elementa que stare videntur, celum et terra, fluxu tacito dilabuntur aut, si subsistendi forsan influentia subtrahatur, ad nichilum penitus redigentur. Solus enim deus vere

3 est; cetera participatione quadam esse dicuntur. Unde non incongruenter sed verissime sicut cetera propheta dixit, 'Initio tu, domine, terram fundasti, et opera manuum tuarum sunt celi. Ipsi peribunt, tu autem permanes.' Et subdit, 'Tu autem idem ipse es, et anni tui non deficient.' Semper enim deus est idem, reliqua vero non. Differunt enim etiam a se ipsis et, si non aliter, loco, tempore, habitu, et aliis circumstantiis sine quibus esse non possunt. Unde

4 iubebat dominus prophetis, 'Vade et dicas, "Qui est mittit me."' Si igitur, quocunque sensu dictum sit, celum et terra sicut vestimentum veterascent et sicut opertorium mutabit ea dominus et mutabuntur, planum est hec omnia que vitriplumbeus iste mundus ostendit non vere sed imperfecte esse nosque velut in speculo et enigmate non entia sed entium imagines intueri.

5 Et, ne longius queramus exempla, ponamus nobis ante oculos hanc regiam urbem, gloriosam patriam tuam atque meam, que, ni fallor, 'Tantum inter alias caput extulit urbes Quantum lenta

6 solent inter viburna cupressi,' ut ille ait. Ascendamus consecratum pio cruore beati Miniatis ab Arni sinistra ripa colliculum aut antiquarum Fesularum bicipitem montem vel aliquod ex circumstantibus promuntoriis unde per sinus omnes completius videri possit

7 nostra Florentia. Ascendamus, precor, et intueamur minantia menia celo, sidereas turres, immania templa, et immensa palatia, que non, ut sunt, privatorum opibus structa, sed impensa publica vix est credibile potuisse compleri, et demum vel mente vel oculis ad

things, but their empty images. What is even more cunningly deceptive, it changes left to right and right to left. Indeed, all these elements that appear to persist—earth and sky—are in fact sinking away in quiet flux, or, if the stream of their subsistence were to be removed, they would be completely reduced to nothing. For God alone truly exists; other things are said to exist by a certain participation. So not inappropriately but very truly, as elsewhere, 3 the prophet said, "In the beginning you, Lord, established the earth, and the heavens are the work of your hands. They shall perish, but you remain." And he adds, "You are the same, and your years will not run out."[77] For God is always the same, but all else is not. Things differ from each other—if not in other respects, in place, time, condition, and other circumstances without which they cannot exist. Thus the Lord commanded the prophets, "Go and say, 'He who is sends me.'"[78] If, then, in whatever sense it was 4 said, earth and sky grow old like clothes, and the Lord will change them like a garment, and they will be changed,[79] it is clear that everything that this world of glass and lead displays exists not truly but imperfectly, and that we, as if through a glass darkly,[80] behold not beings, but their images.

And (so as not to search for examples far and wide) let us place 5 before our eyes this royal city, the glorious fatherland of both of us, which (if I am not mistaken) "Raises its lofty head above other cities like the cypresses amid the pliant wayfaring trees," as the great man says.[81] Let us ascend the hill on the Arno's left bank 6 consecrated by the pious blood of San Miniato or the twin-peaked mountain of ancient Faesulae, or one of the surrounding ridges whence our Florence may be seen in its entirety, in all its winding curves. Let us ascend, I pray, and let us observe the walls threaten- 7 ing the sky, the turrets in the stars, the enormous temples, and the immense palaces (it is scarcely credible that these could have been completed at public expense, much less built, as they were, by the wealth of private citizens). Finally, returning with either mind or

singula redeuntes consideremus quanta in se detrimenta suscepe-
8 rint. Palatium quidem populi admirabile cunctis et, quod fateri
oportet, superbissimum opus, iam mole sua in se ipso resedit et
tam intus quam extra rimarum fatiscens hyatibus lentam, licet se-
9 ram, tamen iam videtur nuntiare ruinam. Basilica vero nostra,
stupendum opus, cui, si unquam ad exitum venerit, nullum credatur inter mortales edificium posse conferri, tanto sumptu tantaque
diligentia inceptum et usque ad quartum iam fornicem consuma-
tum, qua speciosissimo campanili coniungitur, quo quidem nedum
pulcrius ornari marmoribus sed nec pingi aut cogitari formosius
queat, rimam egit, que videatur in deformitatem ruine finaliter
evasura, ut post modicum temporis resarciendi non minus futura
10 sit indiga quam complendi. Quot autem et qualia civium habita-
cula quotque palatia intestini dissidii civica pestis absumpsit! Quot
tum studiosa, tum fortuita consumpserunt incendia! Quot vetus-
tate in se ipsa (tanta est violentia temporis) corruerunt! Quot mox
sunt, si paulum expectaveris (paululum enim est quicquid tempore
mensuratur si ad eternitatis immensitatem retuleris), peritura!

11 Ex quo, postquam in rebus quas inter mortalia aut perpetuas
aut diutinas reputamus in nostris oculis tot future resolutionis
cernimus detrimenta, quid est de ceteris omnium consensu fragi-
12 lioribus iudicandum? Non oportet maximarum consanguinitatum
que a nostris oculis evanuerunt occasus describere, nam, seu vetera
percurramus sive in nostra tempora venientes moderna narremus
sive urbis nostre revolvamus annales, facilius erit singulorum
viventium capita numerando concipere quam extinctas clarissimo-
13 rum hominum prosapias recensere. Absumpta est Priameia proge-
nies et Eneadum gloriosissimum nomen in ultimo scribitur finiisse

eyes to individual details, let us consider what great harm they have suffered. The Palace of the People earns the admiration of all, and one must confess that it is a most superb work. Yet now it is sinking by its own weight; splitting with gaping cracks both inside and out, it seems already to be announcing slow ruin, however late. Our basilica is a stupendous work: if ever it came to destruction, one would think it impossible that a comparable building existed among mortals. It was begun with such great assiduity and at such great expense, and has been finished up to the fourth bay, where it is adjoined to the most attractive campanile. Nothing could be more beautifully adorned with marble than this campanile; nothing more stunning could be painted or even conceived of. Yet our basilica has shown a crack that appears destined to result in ruin's deformity, so that soon the structure will be no less in need of repair than of completion. How many and what kinds of dwellings of citizens, how many palaces, has the civic plague of internecine strife consumed! How many have fires, both deliberately set and accidental ones, destroyed! How many — so severe is the violence of time — have collapsed as a result of age! How many are soon destined to perish, if you wait a little while (for anything measured by time is very little if you compare it to the immensity of eternity)!

Consequently, when we see before our eyes so many losses of coming disintegration in things that we hold to be perpetual or long lasting in the world of mortals, what should we think about other things that are by common agreement more fragile? We need not describe the fall of the great number of families that have vanished from our sight. Whether we survey ancient events or, coming to our own times, narrate modern ones, or if we read over the annals of our city, it will be easier to record the number of living individuals by counting them than to enumerate the extinct lineages of the most famous men. Priam's progeny is spent, and the most glorious name of Aeneas' descendants is reported to have

Nerone. Incredibilis etiam Arthaxerxis proles, qui centum quinde-
cim filios habuisse dicitur, et incredibilior Erothimi, regis Arabum,
atque miranda propago, quem septingentis superbum filiis legimus
14 Egiptiis bellum intulisse, deperiit. Extincti sunt una die et uno
congressu trecentum et sex Fabii. Una nox quadraginta et novem
fratres coniugum scelere et soceri machinatione delevit. Nox etiam
una totius insule Lenni mares unico solum Thoante per Ysiphilem
conservato feminea cede confecit.

15   Et nedum familie sed urbes et nationes ad internicionem usque
sublate sunt. Gens quidem Numantina contra Africe victorem,
populum Romanum, audax bellum inferre totque duces potens
multarumque legionum exercitus tum vincere, tum fugare, demum
virtute Scipionis Africani, cuius auspiciis et ducatu iam ceciderat
bellicosa Carthago, aliquando compressa et in ultimis clausa adeo
pertinaciter libertatem optavit quod ipsam morte querens, quam
bello tueri non poterat, se et sua tum ferro, tum igne consumpsit,
ut de tot milibus armatorum et tante gentis utriusque sexus po-
16 pulo nec predam victoribus relinquerent nec captivos. Quid memorem, ut sacre testantur hystorie, Pharaonis exercitum in maris
Rubri fundo demersum, et totam unam tribum relictis pene
quingentis viris a ceteris Israel tribubus esse deletam, aut infinitas
urbes in quibus iussu dei non est relictus mingens ad parietem?
17 Quid dicam disiectas et compressas Romanis viribus civitates
Vehios, Fregellas, Samnium, et, ut Italiam dimittam, Corinthum,
Ierusalem, Carthaginem, et alias multas quas ostentatius esset
quam difficile numerare? Infinita sunt hec que docent omnia

ended with Nero as the last. Even the incredible offspring of Artaxerxes (who is said to have had 115 sons)[82] and the more incredible and astonishing posterity of Erotimus, king of the Arabs (who, we read, waged a haughty war against Egypt with his 700 sons) died out.[83] The 306 Fabii were extinguished in one day 14 and in a single engagement.[84] One night destroyed 409 brothers through the crime of their wives and the scheming of their father-in-law.[85] One night also finished off the males of the entire island of Lemnos, slaughtered by their womenfolk, with Thoas alone saved, by Hypsipyle.[86]

And not only families, but cities and nations have been exter- 15 minated. The Numantine race audaciously waged war against the Roman people, conquerors of Africa, and powerfully defeated or put to flight a great many generals and armies of many legions but finally were pressed together and trapped in the worst conditions by the courage of Scipio Africanus, under whose auspices and leadership bellicose Carthage had already fallen. The Numantines so stubbornly desired liberty that, seeking by their death what they could not guard by war, they destroyed themselves and their possessions by fire and sword, with the result that out of so many thousands of armed men and a people of so great a race, men and women both, they left the victors neither booty nor captives.[87] Why should I mention the army of Pharaoh sunk to the bottom 16 of the Red Sea, as the sacred histories attest;[88] and that one whole tribe was wiped out by the other tribes of Israel, with scarcely 500 men left;[89] or the countless cities in which by God's command there was not left one pissing at the wall?[90] Why should I 17 speak of the cities scattered and crushed by Roman strength: Veii, Fregellae, Samnium; and (to leave Italy aside) Corinth, Jerusalem, Carthage, and many others that it would be more ostentatious than difficult to list? Countless examples teach that all things of

mundi huius sic in oculis nostris stare quod aliquando sint aut occasu subito aut defectione latenti ad suum interitum perventura.

18   Nec putemus principatuum et regnorum duratiorem esse gloriam: nichil enim vanius splendore potentum. Vere quidem est

19 vanitas vanitatum fulgor dominantium. Ubi nunc Assiriorum ambitiosum in regno ampliando propositum, qui duce Nino, Beli filio, humani generis federa violantes primum arma contra finitimos extulerunt? Ubi in eodem regno longissima subsequentium series regum qui Babilonicam monarchiam usque ad confectum deliciis et effeminatum voluptatibus Sardanapalum magna cum gloria te-

20 nuerunt? Ubi regni Medorum sublimitas quod in se ab Assiriis cede Sardanapalica transtulerunt? Ubi Persarum illa potentia que oppresso Astiage, Medorum rege, et totius orientis imperio ad Cyrum, Persidis regem, deducto post aliquod tempus etiam tenta-

21 vit Europam? Ubi Xerxis ille stupendus exercitus cui non sufficiebant maria classibus, flumina potui, quique incisis montibus navibus in Greciam penetravit? Ubi illa magni Alexandri, Macedonum ducis, usque in exitum continuata felicitas qua post Persas totum

22 domuit orientem? Et, ut dimittam Iudeos, Arabas, Egiptios, Tyrios, et bellacem illam Carthaginem, ubi ferocitas Romanorum et illa clarissimorum armorum gloria qua totum orbem peragrando triumphis victores gentium et rerum domini etiam hostium confessione meruerunt, sicut a nobilibus confirmatur hystoricis, appellari?

23   Non igitur revocetur in dubium quod mundus iste non sit vere speculum vanitatum, in quo quicquid est, imo, ut verius loquar, esse videtur, in intuentium oculis evanescit. Vere igitur mundus

this world stand before our eyes in such a way that they will reach their destruction at some point, either through a sudden fall or hidden decay.

But let us not suppose that the glory of principalities and king- 18 ships is any longer lasting: for nothing is emptier than the splendor of the powerful. The glitter of rulers is truly the vanity of vanities. Where now is the ambitious plan of the Assyrians for 19 expanding their empire, who, when Ninus, son of Belus, ruled, violated the agreements that bind the human race and first took up arms against their neighbors? Where in that same kingdom is the very long series of successors who with great glory held the Babylonian monarchy down to Sardanapalus, who was worn out with delights and emasculated by pleasures? Where is the 20 lofty kingdom of the Medes, transferred to them from the Assyrians after the slaughter of Sardanapalus? Where is that power of the Persians, which, when Astyages the Median king had been crushed and the rule of the whole East had been given to Cyrus of Persia, after some time even attacked Europe?[91] Where is that 21 awesome army of Xerxes for whose fleets the seas were not big enough and rivers were not enough for drinking, and who penetrated Greece with his ships by cutting through mountains? Where is that good fortune of Alexander the Great, leader of the Macedonians, uninterrupted until his death and by which he tamed the whole East after the Persians? And (not to mention the 22 Jews, Arabs, Egyptians, Tyrians, and that warlike Carthage) where is the ferocity of the Romans and that glory of illustrious arms whereby, going triumphantly through the whole world, they deserved to be called conquerors of peoples and masters of the world even by the lips of their enemies, as noble historians assert?

Let it not be called into doubt, then, that this world is truly a 23 mirror of vanities, in which whatever exists—rather, more accurately, whatever seems to exist—disappears before the eyes of the

fragile vitrum et obscurum plumbum est, in quod si quis mentis obtutum direxerit, que sinistra sunt dextra, que vero dextima sunt

24 sinistra, sicut speculum representat. Secundum enim et paganorum et Christianorum traditiones dextera via ducit in celum, sinistra vero precipitat in infernum. Unde in die iudicii legitur electos a Christi dextera colligendos cum damnandi debeant a sinistro latere

25 convenire. Quod et Maronem nostrum non latuit. Inquit enim divini prorsus ingenii vates: 'Hic locus est partes ubi se via findit in ambas: Dextera que Ditis magni sub menia tendit, Hac iter Elisium nobis; at leva malorum Exercet penas et ad impia Tartara mittit.' Cum igitur poeta incomparabilis per campos Elisios, quos alibi leta arva vocavit, locum intellexerit beatorum, dextra ad illos

26 pergi, sinistra vero in impia mitti Tartara diffinivit. Mundus igitur, vere speculum vanitatum, sinistram viam ostendit delectationum, voluptatum, avaricie, cupiditatum, et reliquorum flagitiorum quibus mundo dediti deum offendunt; que quidem, ut ille ait, 'ad impia Tartara mittit.' Fugiamus igitur mundum, vanitatum speculum et corruptionem mentium humanarum, in quo nichil nisi vana et ad interitum ducentia possumus intueri.

: XXVIII :

Quod mundus sit corruptio mentium.

1 Mens quidem nostra, hoc est eminens et prestantior anime nostre pars, cum anima dum scit mens dicatur, sicut tabula rasa in qua nichil scriptum est imprimendarum litterarum formas est apta

beholder. The world, therefore, is truly fragile glass and dark lead: if anyone looks into it with the eyes of the mind, left is right and right is left, just as a mirror represents things. According to both 24 pagan and Christian traditions, the right path leads to heaven, but the left casts down to hell. For this reason we read that on Judgment Day the elect must gather at the right hand of Christ whereas the damned must assemble on the left. This was not un- 25 known even to our Maro. For the poet of divine talent says, "This is the place where the way splits into two parts: the right, which leads under the walls of great Dis, and our journey to Elysium takes us this way; but the left works the punishments of the wicked and sends them to impious Tartarus."[92] Although, therefore, the incomparable poet understood the place of the blessed to be throughout the Elysian Fields (which he elsewhere called "the happy lands"),[93] he specified that on the right one made one's way to them, but on the left one was sent to impious Tartarus. The 26 world, then, truly a mirror of vanities, exhibits the left way of delights, pleasures, avarice, desires, and the rest of the sins by which people devoted to the world offend God; indeed this way, as the great man says, "sends them to impious Tartarus." Let us therefore flee the world, mirror of vanities and corruption of human minds, in which we can behold nothing but things that are vain and conducive to destruction.

: XXVIII :

The world is the corruption of minds.

Our mind is the conspicuous and outstanding part of our soul 1 (since when the soul is engaged in knowing, it is called *mind*). As a blank slate, on which nothing has been written, is suited to

recipere, sic sensibilium rerum imaginibus et intelligibilium similitudinibus habet potentiam informari ut per creaturarum noticiam

2 in suum autorem tanquam in finem ultimum dirigatur. Ad illum autem etiam in hac corporis mole per contemplationem ascendens anima tam diu bonitatis gradibus emergendo perficitur quod ambulans in lumine vultus dei in nomine suo exultabit tota die et in iusticia eius exaltabitur, quoniam gloria virtutis beatorum deus est et in beneplacito suo exaltabitur cornu eorum.

3 Ergo anima ad illum finem beatificum ordinata, si mundum cognoscat corruptorem suum, si cognoscendo exhorreat, si exhorrendo relinquat, nichil habet quo possit efficaciter impediri quin dei assistente gratia certo tramite ad creatorem suum eterna in eo

4 fruitura gloria revertatur. Exinanivit enim illecebras carnis qui mundum perfecte deseruit, exarmavit hostem ne possit secum aperte congrediendo pugnare, purgavit latebras et nemorosi mundi densitates illas in quibus se occultans diabolus molitur insidias, adeo mundum deserendo subvertit quod non habeat ille telum quo feriat nec ex improviso possit impetum facere aut tendens arcum non videri seu funem extendere in laqueum vel iuxta iter scanda

5 lum ponere transeunti. O felix anima, que mundum deserere potuit!

Potuit autem omnis homo qui voluit. Non blandiamur nobis ipsis nec nos non posse mundum relinquere cavillemur. Possumus

6 plane si volumus. Voluntatum quidem nostrarum moderamen habemus ut illas quo voluerimus deflectamus et unde flexerimus retrahamus. Sic enim movet voluntates nostras deus quod non impediat arbitrii libertatem, et non solum non impedit sed dat bonis que bene volumus incrementa. Infinita est magnitudo bonitatis

receive the forms of the letters that are to be inscribed, so our mind has the power to be formed by images of sensible things and likenesses of intelligible things. Thus, through its acquaintance with the creatures, the mind is directed to their Author as its final goal. Even while in this corporal mass, the soul ascending to him 2 through contemplation by climbing the steps of goodness for so long a time, emerges and is perfected, so that, walking in the light of God's face it will exult in his name the whole day and will be exalted in his justice, since God is the glory of the strength of the blessed and by his good pleasure their horn will be exalted.[94]

The soul, then, is ordered to that beatific end. If it recognizes 3 the world as its corruptor; if in recognizing, it recoils; if in recoiling, it abandons it, there is nothing that can effectively stop it, with the help of God's grace, from returning by a sure path to its Creator, destined to enjoy in him eternal glory. For the person 4 who has perfectly deserted the world has made fleshly enticements empty; disarmed the Enemy so that he cannot engage with him in open conflict; cleansed the lairs and thickets of the well-wooded world in which the devil hides while devising his ambushes; and subverted the world to such an extent by abandoning it that the devil has no weapon with which to strike and cannot make an unexpected attack, cannot be seen drawing his bow or stretching out a rope as a snare or setting a stumbling block in the way of the passerby.[95] O happy soul that has been able to leave the world 5 behind!

Yet everyone who has wanted to has been able to. Let us not flatter ourselves or make the excuse that we cannot relinquish the world. Clearly, if we want to, we can. We have control of our 6 wishes: we direct them where we want and draw them back again from where we directed them. God so moves our wishes that he does not impede our freedom of judgment; not only doesn't he impede it, but he increases the goods that we properly wish for.

7 divine. Longissime patet dei gratia, qua possumus filii dei fieri si
crediderimus in nomine eius, crediderimus quidem fide viva, non
8 mortua, et nedum viva sed fecunda sanctis operibus. Nec dif-
fidamus aut torpeamus ignavi. Gratia namque dei volituros bona
prevenit, volentes adiuvat, cum volentibus operatur, et terram nos-
9 tram facit reddere fructum suum. Tali igitur et tanto freti subsidio,
quo non caremus nisi cum volumus, nisi cum derelinquimus recti-
tudinem voluntatis, quomodo possumus nos, si mundum non relinquimus, excusare?

10 Sed cum superna dimittimus et in hec terrena non cogitando
solum sed diligendo mente demergimur, excitantur vires carnis,
insultant sensus, instat diabolus et per hec mundana rationem,
que in superioribus contemplandis et colendis intendit queve inferiora disponit, trahunt, inescant, impellunt, et demum ut consen-
tiat operantur, sicque corrupta mentis integritate anima, que creata
fuerat ad celum, ducitur ad infernum. Unde quia emergere labo-
riosum est et ultra quam dici valeat operosum, merito corruptor
mentium mundus dici potest laqueus animarum.

: XXIX :

Quod mundus sit laqueus animarum.

1 Illaqueamur siquidem mundo ne in celum possimus ascendere et
ad illum principem beatificum properare. Hinc rerum temporalium nulla copia satianda cupiditas, hinc voluptatum illecebre, hinc

The scope of divine goodness is infinite. Far and wide God's grace 7
lies open, by which we are able to become sons of God if we believe in his name—believe with a living faith, not a dead one, and
not only living but fruitful in holy works. And we shouldn't lack 8
confidence or be idle cowards. For indeed God's grace anticipates
those who are going to want good things; it helps those who want
them, and works with them; and it makes our earth bring forth its
fruit. Relying on help so great and of such a kind (which we only 9
lack if we do not want it or if we abandon rectitude of will), how
can we excuse ourselves if we do not leave the world?

But when we dismiss supernal things and immerse ourselves 10
mentally in these earthly affairs not only by thinking about them
but also by loving them, the strength of the flesh is stirred up, the
senses leap, and the devil approaches. They drag the reason (which
is focused on contemplating and cultivating higher things and
which organizes the inferior) through these mundane things; they
gnaw at the reason, they push it, and finally they achieve its consent. With integrity of mind corrupted in this way, the soul, which
was created for heaven, is led to hell. Since it is laborious to
emerge from there and toilsome beyond words, the world, corruptor of minds, can with good reason be called the snare of souls.

: XXIX :

The world is the snare of souls.

We are ensnared by the world, so we are unable to ascend to 1
heaven and hasten to the beatific Ruler. Hence our cupidity, able
to be satisfied by no abundance of temporal things; hence the allurements of pleasures; hence the chains of spouses, filial bonds,

cathene coniugum, filiorum nexus, et splendores insidiosissimi dignitatum, hinc et alia infinita quibus mentium nostrarum amentia, dum mundum sequimur, quasi veram felicitatem prestantibus

2 implicatur. 'O quam bonum,' inquit avarus, 'abundare divitiis! O quanta providentia est opes quas acquisiveris conservare! Sed omnia transcendit non solum parcere partis sed quotidie multiplicare quesita et languenti consulere senectuti ne tunc, cum lucrari non poteris, vacuus deprendaris et, cum tibi presidio esse non valebis, ludibrio ceteris habearis.'

3 Sed responde, o miser, quis spopondit eas tecum nedum in senium sed usque in crastinum perventuras? An non ignoras sic divitias deum hominibus indulgere quod recipientem, dum acquiruntur, admoneant non minus eas accipientibus posse quam illis a quibus ea receperint deperire? An putas vanum fuisse commen-

4 tum illud rotam volventis sine intermissione fortune? Sed pone divitias, quod rarissimum tamen est, te fideliter usque in interitum sociare: an invenies senex et moriens te ex illarum copia ultra necessitates corporis accepisse? Imo forte (tanta est avaricie potentia)

5 tibi multa subtraxeris que humane vite condicio requirebat. Quid igitur prodest multis abundare pecuniis et continuatis agris, montes cum vallibus occupare, si non potes exinde tibi percipere ultra quam unus venter capiat aut unum corpus pro sue fragilitatis

6 necessitate aut etiam corrupte carnis voluptate requirat? 'Sed,' inquiunt, 'divitias istas superstiti relinquam heredi.' Si filius erit, fateor iocundum esse de futura post mortem filiorum opulentia cogitare. Cave tamen ne, dum pro filio tuo divitias paras, mundum sequeris, et terrena dispensas, ipse tibi celestia perdas neve illum filium tuum cui tanta cum anxietate consulis sis tuarum rerum

and the most insidious splendors of political offices; hence also an infinite number of other things in which we are mindlessly entangled, as long as we follow the world, as if these were offering true happiness. "O how good it is," says the miser, "to abound in riches! 2 O what great foresight it shows to preserve the resources you have acquired! But best of all is not only to be sparing with what you have obtained, but to multiply your gains daily and take thought for languishing old age, so that then, when you are unable to earn, you are not caught empty-handed and, when you are unable to support yourself, others do not make sport of you."

Answer me, O wretch: who has guaranteed that your wealth 3 will go with you into old age, or even until tomorrow? Are you unaware that God grants riches to people such that when they acquire wealth, they are warned that it is just as possible for the recipients of wealth to perish as it is for those from whom they have received it? Do you think the wheel of perpetually revolving fortune an empty fiction? Although it is extremely rare, suppose 4 that riches will faithfully accompany you unto death: as an old and dying man, will you find that you have received from that abundance anything beyond the physical necessities? Or perhaps (so great is the power of avarice) you will have gone without many things that the condition of human life required. What good is it, 5 then, to abound in vast wealth and a string of farms, to occupy the mountains along with the valleys, if you cannot take for yourself any more than one stomach can hold or one body requires for the needs of its fragility — or even for the pleasure of its corrupt flesh? "But," they say, "I will leave those riches to my surviving heir." If 6 the heir is a son, I admit that it is pleasant to think about the future wealth of one's sons after one's death. Nevertheless, while you are assembling riches for your son, pursuing the world, and dispensing earthly goods, take care that you yourself do not lose heavenly goods, and that you are not about to corrupt that son of yours, for whom you are taking thought with such great anxiety,

copia corrupturus. Extraneo vero laborare etiam amatorum mundi
7 sententia miserrimum est. Esto igitur pauper spiritu, ut tua sint
regna celorum. Si contingunt tibi divitie, illis animum non appo-
nas. Fatigant etenim, non quietant, possessoremque efficiunt timi-
8 dum, quem pauperem vidimus esse securum. Nec in eis te putes
esse felicem, que propter te create sunt queve nullo modo sunt vi-
gentis intellectus obiectum, secundum quem oportet beatos perfici
et in statum rei nullius indigum collocari.

9   'Sed o quam dulce.' dicit alter, 'uxoris contubernium.' Quid autem huic respondeam? nisi satyricum illud,

> semper habet lites alternaque prelia lectus
> in quo nupta iacet.

10 Lege sanctum Iob, cui periit substantia omnis, perierunt et filii,
cuique ulcere pessimo tactum corpus ut, si fortunam in eo se-
vientem contempleris, nemo miserior, si letam, nemo felicior. An
habuit dulcem uxoris societatem? An sibi forte defuit temptatio
11 coniugalis? Non certe. Cum enim permittente domino percussis-
set eum Sathan ulcere pessimo a planta eius usque ad verticem,
tunc, cum maxime consolationis indigebat, obiurgans uxor dixit,
'Adhuc tu permanes in simplicitate tua. Benedic deo et morere.'
Maledicat tibi deus, pessima feminarum, que viro sancto te tam
12 molestam et intolerabilem prebuisti! An et Tobiam cecum et pauperem uxor non temptavit? Temptavit enim et dixit, 'Manifeste
vana facta est spes tua et elemosine tue perierunt.' Maledicat et
tibi creator tuus cui, dum vis esse viro tuo infesta, non mediocriter
13 maledixisti. Nec putes hec tantum de duabus scripta fore; prope-
modum omnes tales sunt, omnes unum ludum ludunt. Nichil

with your abundant wealth. Even in the opinion of world lovers, it is a most miserable thing to work for another. So be poor in spirit, 7 so that the kingdom of heaven may be yours.[96] If wealth happens to accrue to you, don't attach your soul to it. The fact is that wealth is tiring, not relaxing; it makes its possessor timid, while we observe that the poor man is carefree. And don't think that in 8 your riches, you are blessed. They were created for your sake and are in no way the object of a vigorous intellect. For the blessed ought to be perfected in understanding and placed in the position of needing no material goods.

"But O how sweet," says another, "is a wife's companionship!" 9 How should I respond to him except with that satirical remark:

the bed on which the wife lies always has disputes and
battles back and forth?[97]

Read holy Job, who lost all his wealth, whose children perished, 10 and whose body was afflicted with severe sores: if you reflect on fortune's raging against him, no one is more wretched; if on his good fortune, no one is happier. Surely he didn't enjoy a sweet companionship with his wife? Surely he didn't lack conjugal trials? Certainly not. When God had allowed Satan to strike him with 11 severe sores from head to toe, then, when he was especially in need of consolation, his nagging wife said, "You have endured till now in your simplicity. Bless God and die."[98] God curse you, most terrible of women, who behaved so annoyingly and intolerably toward your saintly husband! Wasn't Tobit, blind and poor, also 12 tried by his wife? She tested him, saying, "Clearly your hope has proved vain and your own alms have disappeared."[99] May your Creator curse you also, as you immoderately cursed him when you chose to be hostile to your husband. Don't think that such things 13 have been written about two women only: almost all women are such; all play the same game. Nothing is more noxious to men

uxore viris infestius, nichil molestius. Quarum fastidia, si referre
curem, vix multiplicata volumina satis erunt.

14   Sed quis filios non desideret propagare? Restat enim in filiis
memoria parentum et post funera natorum beneficio celebramur.
His quid respondeam? nisi Persianum illud:

O curas hominum, quantum est in rebus inane!

15 Quot dabis qui sciant tritavum nominare aut, si forsitan nomen
eius acceperint, quicquam norint de suarum virtutum meritis fa-
bulari? Ut, quamvis de transferenda memoria cogites, non facile
possis in quarte generationis noticiam filiorum merito pertransire.

16 Nec mirum; obscuratur enim fama viventium, ut non solum ignoti
vitam transigant sed progenitoribus suis tenebras ignorantie cali-

17 gantis affundant. Adde quod filiorum demerita sepe reddunt maiorum nomina non solum non celebria sed cum infamie maculis
odiosa, ut rarissimum esse fateri oporteat maiorum famam in pos-

18 teris renovari. Verumtamen, si rationi decreverimus consentire,
non est querendum occasurum nomen in terris sed perpetuo man-
surum in celis, ut in libro vite stilo ferreo indelebiliter ascribamur,
ad quod possumus non per filiorum multiplicationem sed adiu-

19 vante dei gratia in perseverantia bonorum operum pervenire. Sed
subdet alter, 'Fragiles sumus, subiecti morbis et demum obnoxii
senectuti. Cur ergo non queramus filios nobis astituros futurosque
languentis baculum senectutis?' Maledictus homo qui confidit in
homine. Quis novit an sint tibi priusquam decesseris perituri? An

than a wife, nothing more irritating. Multiple volumes would scarcely be enough to contain their disgusting characteristics, if I chose to relate them.

But who does not desire to have children? For the memory of 14 their parents remains with children, and after death we are celebrated by the favor bestowed by our progeny. What reply should I give to these arguments? — apart from the verse of Persius,

O cares of men, how great is the void in human affairs![100]

How many people can you cite who are able to name their great- 15 great-great-grandfather, or, if by chance his name has come down to them, to recite anything about his merits and virtues? So, although you are concerned about handing down your memory, it would be difficult for you to come to the notice of the fourth generation by the merit of your children. And no wonder: the 16 fame of the living is darkened, so that not only do they pass through life unknown, but they cast the shadows of their shrouding ignorance upon their progenitors. Moreover, the faults of the 17 children often render the name of their ancestors not only not famous, but odious with stains of infamy, so that we must admit that it is extremely rare for the fame of the ancestors to be renewed in their descendants. Nevertheless, if we decide to yield to 18 reason, there is no need to lament that our name is destined to pass away on earth yet perpetually remain in heaven. In the book of life our names are inscribed indelibly with an iron stylus; this we can attain not through multiplication of children, but, with the help of God's grace, by persevering in good works. But someone 19 else will add, "We are fragile, subject to illnesses and finally at the mercy of old age. Why, then, should we not ask for children who will stand by us and be the staff of languishing old age?" Accursed is the man who trusts in man. Who knows whether you will lose them before you have passed away? Surely you are not unaware

ignoras ipsos esse mortales? An novum est et non quotidianum nativitatis ordinem a morte, que omni etati communis est, ut plurimum non servari?

20   Sed quid hec disputatione prosequar longiori? Planum enim est quod mundo dediti his et ambitione et aliis que decepti miramur et admirantes diligimus implicamur, nescientesque relinquere divitias, dimittere coniuges, deserere filios, abominari voluptates, vanum splendorem dignitatum spernere nec lubricam potentiarum altitudinem exhorrere, illaqueati mundo, quem parentem mortis diximus, his terrenis ad animarum perniciem inheremus.

: XXX :

Quod mundus sit parens mortis.

1   Si enim princeps huius mundi primos parentes per Eve seductionem in esu pomi vetiti divini precepti fecit suis suasionibus transgressores, ex quo iuxta iam latam ab illo sententiam mors intravit in mundum, quis negare potest mundum istum fore certissimum

2   mortis autorem? Scriptum est enim, mortem deus non fecit sed precepti divini prima transgressio, cuius equidem causa fuit omne quod in mundo est, concupiscentia videlicet carnis, concupiscentia oculorum, et superbia vite.

3   Audi prophetam, imo ipsum spiritum sanctum, primorum peccatum hominum describentem: 'Sed et serpens,' inquit, 'erat callidior cunctis animantibus terre que fecerat dominus. Qui dixit ad mulierem: "Cur precepit vobis deus ut non comederetis ex omni ligno paradisi?" Cui respondit mulier: "De fructu lignorum que sunt in paradiso vescimur. De fructu vero ligni quod est in medio

that they, too, are mortal? Or is it strange and out of the ordinary that generally speaking, the order of birth is not adhered to by death, which is common to every age?

But why should I pursue this topic any further? It is clear that   20
we, devoted to the world, are entangled in these affairs both by ambition and by other things that we, being deceived, admire, and, in admiring, love. We do not know how to abandon riches, to dismiss wives, to leave children, to detest pleasures, to spurn the empty splendor of distinctions and recoil at the slippery heights of powers. Ensnared by the world — which we have called the parent of death — we fix on these earthly things to the ruin of our soul.

: XXX :

The world is the parent of death.

By seducing Eve with his powers of persuasion, the prince of this   1
world made our first parents transgressors of the divine precept by their eating of the forbidden fruit. As a result, according to a sentence already passed by him, death entered the world. This being the case, who can deny that this world is the most certain author of death? For it is written that God did not make death, but the   2
transgression of the divine precept did. To be sure, the cause of this transgression was all that is in the world: concupiscence of the flesh, concupiscence of the eyes, and arrogance of life.[101]

Listen to the prophet, or rather the Holy Spirit itself, describ-   3
ing the sin of the first human beings: "But the serpent was," it says, "cleverer than all the animals of the earth which the Lord had created. The serpent said to the woman, 'Why did God instruct you not to eat from every tree in paradise?' The woman replied, 'We eat the fruit of the trees in paradise. But the fruit of the tree

paradisi precepit nobis deus ne comederemus et ne tangeremus il-
4 lud ne forte moriamur.'" Hic est primus mulieris lapsus: titubare
quidem temptatori congrediens cepit an divine maiestatis oraculum verum esset. Cum enim dixisset deus, 'In quacunque die
comederis ex eo, morte morieris,' quod tamen Ade dictum et ipsa
didicerat, sub 'forte' posuit quod erat sine dubitatione futurum.
5 Sed ad inceptum redeamus: 'Dixit autem serpens ad mulierem:
"Nequaquam morte moriemini. Scit enim deus quod in quocunque die comederitis ex eo aperientur oculi vestri et eritis sicut
6 dii, scientes bonum et malum."' Hoc audito in superbiam spiritus
elata, 'vidit mulier quod bonum esset lignum ad vescendum,' ecce
concupiscentia carnis, 'et pulcrum oculis aspectuque delectabile,'
ecce concupiscentiam oculorum, 'et tulit de fructu illius et comedit
deditque viro suo qui comedit.' Ecce consumationem peccati in
7 transgressione precepti. Nec putet aliquis Adam non cogitasse de
statu divinitatis per diabolum Eve promisso, licet, ut inquit apostolus, seductus non fuerit et licet elevatione mentis agnoverit non
posse creaturam in divine perfectionis statum ascendere, et quam-
8 vis illud dictum fuerit solummodo mulieri. Nam licet eius principale propositum fuerit non contristare uxorem, quam forte dolore
credebat contabescere si sibi non consensisset, et licet nondum
expertus divine iusticie severitatem veniale forte putaverit quod
erat omnino mortale, prohibitionis tamen preceptum transgressus
est ac muliebris ambitionis se fecit socium, cui prebuit in vetita
9 manducatione consensum. Unde mox eum irridens deus inquit,
'Ecce Adam factus est quasi unus ex nobis, sciens bonum et malum,' licet illa scientia non simplicis noticie sed penalis experientie
fuerit.
10 Nec forte credas, karissime mi Ieronime, tunc solum homines
de ligno vetito comedisse: quotidie quidem mortale genus prohibita

in the middle of paradise God instructed us not to eat or touch lest perhaps we die.'"[102] This is the woman's first mistake: in meeting with her tempter, she began to be in doubt whether the divine majesty's utterance was true. For although God had said, "On the day you eat from it, you will die"[103] (this had been said to Adam, and she had been told about it), she added "perhaps" to what was to happen without a doubt. But let us return to our story. "The serpent said to the woman, 'You will by no means die. For God knows that on the day you eat from it, from then on your eyes will be opened and you will be as gods, knowing good and evil.'"Upon hearing this, raised to a prideful spirit, "the woman saw that the tree was good for eating" (there you see concupiscence of the flesh) and "beautiful to the eyes and an attractive sight" (there you see concupiscence of the eyes); "and took from its fruit, ate, and gave it to her husband, who ate."[104] There you see the consummation of sin in the transgression of the precept. Let no one suppose that Adam had failed to consider the state of divinity promised to Eve by the devil, even though, as the apostle says, Adam was not seduced,[105] and in the elevation of his mind he recognized that a creature cannot rise to a state of divine perfection, and although that was said to the woman alone. Adam's chief intention was not to sadden his wife; perhaps he believed that she would waste away in distress if he did not acquiesce. And since he had not yet experienced the severity of divine justice, perhaps he thought that his sin was venial when it was altogether mortal. Adam transgressed the prohibition, made himself an ally of his wife's ambition, and gave her his consent to the eating of the forbidden food. Hence shortly thereafter, God mocked him, saying, "See, Adam has become like one of us, knowing good and evil"[106] — though that knowledge was not of a simple concept, but of an experience of punishment.

But, dearest Girolamo, do not think that it was only then that people ate from the forbidden tree: daily we of the mortal race eat

manducamus. Habemus legem quam in cordibus nostris ipsa natura prescripsit quamque deus ipse suis oraculis declaravit. Iubemur etenim ut quod nobis nolumus alteri nullatenus inferamus. Quere inter amatores mundi qui hanc pie quidem abstinentie legem servet, qui eadem mensura metiatur aliis qua sibi metiri velit, qui minimas etiam utilitates suas per maxima alterius incommoda non procuret et, quod evangelicum imperavit oraculum, qui diligat proximum ut se ipsum. Non conqueramur igitur de una transgressione parentum, qui pene cunctis horis preceptorum dei sumus manifestissimi transgressores. Et cuius precepti? Certe talis quod, si amatores mundi non negligerent illud, tam suavis foret mortalium status quod hic magnam portionem beatitudinis haberemus. Quod videntes mundani latores legum suis hoc maxime sanctionibus sunt conati, quod quis honeste vivat, alterum non ledat, suumque ius omnibus tribuatur. Quo magis admiror, quoniam, ut satyricus ait,

> exemplo quodcunque malo committitur ipsi
> displicet autori,

quomodo possint miseri peccatores, quos mens sibi conscia facti, sive divina sive humana considerent, noctesque diesque debeat stimulare, cum alacritate comedere panem et bibere vinum quod cum alterius dispendio quesiverunt, quomodo possint domum in leticia possidere alieno damno vel iniuria comparatam, quomodo possint iocundi vestem induere pro quibus habendis recolant se deum et proximum offendisse, quomodo quietos possint capere somnos in lectulo rapinis et flagitiis acquisito. Sed hanc momentaneam alacritatem, inanem leticiam, iocunditatem falsam, et

prohibited things. We have a law that nature itself has written on our hearts and God himself has declared by his holy pronouncements. We are commanded not to do to another what we would   11 not wish done to us. Search among the world lovers for one who piously keeps this law of abstinence; who measures to others by the same measure with which he wishes to be measured;[107] who does not procure even the smallest advantages for himself at the expense of the greatest disadvantages to another; and — as the gospel has commanded — who loves his neighbor as himself.[108] Let   12 us not complain, therefore, about a single transgression of our parents, since we are most obviously transgressors of God's precepts at almost every hour of the day. Whose precept are we talking about? Indeed, a precept of such a Person that, if the world lovers were not neglecting it, the state of mortals would be so pleasant that we would enjoy a good portion of beatitude right here. Seeing this, the legislators of the world tried very hard to   13 achieve by their sanctions that each person lives honorably and does not hurt another, and that all are given their rights. Since, as   14 the satirist says,

> whatever is committed in the way of a bad example
> is displeasing to its very author,[109]

I am all the more amazed that wretched sinners — whose minds, whether they are considering divine or human affairs, conscious of their deeds, ought to goad them day and night — can with enthusiasm eat bread and drink wine that they sought at another's expense; that they can possess a home in happiness when they have acquired it as a result of another's loss or harm; that they can flippantly put on clothing that they recall they offended God and their neighbor to obtain; that they can sleep peacefully on a couch they got by robbery and wrongdoing. Yet God's justice repays   15 wretched sinners for this momentary enthusiasm, empty happiness, false jocundity, and deceptive quiet with eternal sorrow,

quietem deceptiosam dei iusticia merore eterno, tristicia solida, afflictione vera, et molestia punitiva, nisi forsan aliter ad deum re-
16 deant, miseris peccatoribus recompensat. Recompensat quidem non in rigore iusticie sed in benignitate misericordie infinite, non pro magnitudine commissorum sed citra gravitatem et multitudi- nem iniquitatum, quarum turba perterritus propheta dixit, 'Si ini-
17 quitates observaveris, domine, domine, quis sustinebit?' Ex quo sequitur ut reprehensibiliores condemnemur iustiusque plectamur, qui dominum tante benignitatis offendimus quod etiam non sine misericordia condemnati gloriam suam nostris iniquitatibus amit- tamus. Quod tanto magis pudendum est quanto certius mundum, per quem a deo recedimus, oportet nos, nisi penitus desipiamus, nedum fore parentem mortis sed etiam infernum esse viventium confiteri.

: XXXI :

Quod mundus sit infernus viventium.

1 Nam infernum, sive a situ loci considerare velimus, cum mundus iste quem colimus in infimo elemento consistat, sive a cruciatibus quos anime sensibiliter patiuntur tam unite corporibus quam car- nis sarcina liberate infernum ipsum diffiniamus, quis negaverit
2 mundum istum vere ac rationabiliter esse infernum? Inferio- rem enim terram esse ceteris elementis, quam, nisi quatenus dei bonitas iussit in medio aquarum pro habitatione mortalium apparere, mari maximo quod occeanum et Athlanticum dicitur credimus circummergi, quis negaverit? Nam omittamus geome- trarum demonstrationes et rationes philosophorum, quibus solet

unmitigated sadness, true affliction, and punishing annoyance—
unless they return to God. Indeed, he repays us not in the rigor of   16
justice but in the generosity of infinite mercy; not in proportion to
the magnitude of what we have done, but short of the seriousness
and multitude of our iniquities. Terrified by the accumulation of
these, the prophet said, "If you observe our iniquities, Lord, Lord,
who will endure it?"[110] From this it follows that we, being repre-   17
hensible, will be condemned and justly punished. We offend the
Lord of such great generosity, with the result that condemned
(albeit not without mercy), we lose his glory because of our iniquities. This is all the more shameful, the more certain it is that, unless we are utterly stupid, we ought to confess that the world,
through which we withdraw from God, is not only the parent of
death but also the inferno of the living.

: XXXI :

The world is the inferno of the living.

Who would deny that this world, truly and reasonably speaking, is   1
an inferno, whether we want to regard an inferno from the point
of view of its location (since the world that we inhabit consists of
the lowest element); or if we define an inferno on the basis of the
tortures that souls palpably suffer, both united to bodies and freed
from the burden of the flesh? Who would deny that the earth is   2
lower than the other elements? If God's goodness had not ordered
the earth to appear in the middle of the waters as the dwelling
place for mortals, we believe that it would have remained submerged all round by the great sea called the Atlantic Ocean. Let us
leave aside the demonstrations of the geometers and the arguments of the philosophers, which traditionally prove the earth's

3   inferioritas terre probari. Scimus enim et sensui patet terram gravitate sua sedem infimam petiisse et undique circa centrum et gravitatis et molis miris hinc inde librationibus consedisse huicque aquam, undis autem aerem, ignem illum vero qui celo simillimus elementa cuncta complectitur aeri proximo credimus imminere, ut saltem ab illo beatitudinis loco in quo electorum animas fide novimus in eternam gloriam collocari mundus iste quem colimus distantia maxima dividatur, ut quasi ex opposito illic beati deo fruan-

4   tur, hic vero reprobi cum diabolo crucientur. Ex quo nonnulli gentilium putaverunt infernum esse corpora nostra et in his animas pati quicquid de damnatorum suppliciis apud inferos con-

5   fingebant. Nos autem, sicut sancti patres, illuminatores fidei et doctores veritatis, tradiderunt, firmiter teneamus infernum esse aerem istum caliginosum et quicquid in ipso per omnem eius cir-

6   cumferentiam continetur. Nam et infernum fore in concavitatibus terre satis sacre littere manifestant ubi de pena Core, Dathan, et Abiron in libro Numeri tractaverunt. Scribitur enim: 'Disrupta est terra sub pedibus eorum, et aperiens os suum devoravit eos cum tabernaculis suis et universa substantia eorum, descenderuntque in inferno operti humo.'

7   Terra igitur ista et mundus in quo sumus et quem tantopere diligimus infernus est, in quo et vivi iam incipientes damnationis sue penas multis tribulationibus cruciantur. Nullus enim est tam explorate felicitatis qui, dum vivit, aut conscientie morsus aut pe-

8   nas corporeas non patiatur. Unde verissimum est poeticum illud, 'Quisque suos patimur manes.' Ita tamen, dum in mundo sumus, ascribimur in inferno quod, si mundum mente relinquamus et nos in deum per virtutum opera dirigamus, hinc mente, dum in carne vivimus, elevamur omni demum vitiorum fece purgata ad illam

inferior position. For we know, and it is open to observation, that 3
on account of its heaviness earth sought the lowest place and set-
tled everywhere around the center by means of marvelous leveling
of its heavy mass on either side. We believe that water lies over
earth, the lower air over the waves, and that fire which, being most
similar to the heavens, embraces all elements, lies over the lower
air. Consequently, this world we inhabit is divided by the greatest
distance from that place of beatitude, where we know in faith that
the souls of the elect have been assembled for eternal glory. As if
in opposition, then, the blessed enjoy God there, while here the
reprobates are tortured with the devil. For this reason, some of the 4
pagans thought that the inferno was our bodies, and in these the
souls suffer whatever they invented concerning the punishments of
the damned in the underworld. But let us firmly hold, as the holy 5
fathers — illuminators of faith and teachers of truth — have handed
down, that the inferno is that murky air and whatever is contained
within it throughout its entire circumference. Sacred scripture 6
makes it clear that the inferno is in the cavities of the earth when
in the book of Numbers it deals with the punishment of Korah,
Dathan, and Abiram. For it is written: "The earth split under
their feet, and opening its mouth, it devoured them with their
tents and all of their possessions, and, covered over by earth, they
descended to the pit."[111]

This earth, and the world we are in and love so much, is an 7
inferno where even the living already begin the punishments of
their damnation and are tortured with many tribulations. For no
one is of such guaranteed felicity that, while he is alive, he does
not suffer either stings of conscience or corporal punishments.
Hence the poet's famous pronouncement is quite true: "Each of us 8
suffers our own ghost."[112] As long as we are in the world, we are
thus enrolled in the inferno, so that if we mentally leave the world
behind and direct ourselves to God through virtuous works, we
will be lifted from here mentally while we are still alive in the flesh.

9 arcem beatitudinis, postquam mortem obiverimus, volaturi. Sin autem dimiserimus vias domini et mundum decepti secuti fuerimus, iam a deo peccatorum turpitudine recedentes incipimus quasi in inferni carcerem deportari et, si non aliter, conscientie saltem

10 stimulis cruciari. Ex quo de mundi amatoribus dictum est, 'Sinite mortuos sepelire mortuos suos.' Mortui quidem sunt qui mundum diligentes summum illud bonum deserunt ac sepulti etiam donec

11 secundum carnem vivunt hic temporaliter in inferno. Quod si creature rationalis est, quam etiam deus sursum erectam fecit, celum petere, cur mundum, qui infernus est, diligimus? Cur hinc, postquam corpore nexi sumus, mente saltem non conamur emergere? Sed blandienti carni obtemperantes solum carnalia cogitamus et facimus et mundum, qui caducorum aggregatio est, quasi rem mansuram sequimur et amamus.

: XXXII :

Quod mundus sit aggregatio caducorum.

1 Non oportet multis ostendere caduca fore quecunque in mundo cernuntur. Quis enim ignorat quod cuncta sint transitoria que vi-

2 demus? Appareant enim, licet omnia inferiora secundum materiam, quamvis forma corrumpatur, continue permansura, cum tamen nichil esse dicatur nisi per formam ac omnia quecunque cernimus ex materia et forma composita videamus, materia quidem vel ad unam solum disposita formam, ut in corporibus celestibus, licet in potentia sint ad infinitas loci differentias, verisimiliter

With all the dregs of vices purged, we will at last be ready to fly to
the summit of beatitude after we have met our death. But if we   9
leave the Lord's ways, are deceived, and follow the world, already
withdrawing from God by the turpitude of our sins, we begin to
be deported to the infernal prison, as it were, and to be tortured,
if not otherwise, at the very least by pangs of conscience. This is   10
why it was said concerning the world lovers, "Let the dead bury
their dead."[113] Dead indeed are those who in their love of the
world abandon that highest good; they are buried even while they
live according to the flesh here, temporally, in the inferno. But if it   11
is the nature of a rational creature, which God too made to stand
upright, to seek heaven, why do we love the world, which is an
inferno? Although we have been tied here in body, why don't we at
least try to emerge from here in mind? But complying with our
blandishing flesh we think of and do only carnal things. We follow
and love the world—a pile of transient things—as if it were something that is bound to endure.

: XXXII :

The world is a pile of transient things.

There is no need to show with many arguments that whatever is   1
seen in the world is transient. Who doesn't know that all we see is
transitory? Things that are lower according to matter appear des-   2
tined to remain perpetually, however much their form is corrupted. However, nothing is said to exist except through form;
and we see that every discernible thing is composed of matter
and form. It is thought with good reason that matter is disposed
to one form only (as in celestial bodies) although it is poten-
tially subject to infinite local differences. Alternatively, matter is

creditur, vel ad multitudinem formarum, sicut inferiora ista fate-
mur, omnia tamen hec visibilia proculdubio naturaliter resolvi
3 possunt. Hinc videmus rerum inferiorum continuos et mirabiles
4 fluxus et ea omnia nostris in oculis permutari. Omittamus hominum et animantium reliquorum multiformes interitus, siccitates
fluminum, inundationes aquarum, terrarum hyatus, et, sicut testatur Aristotiles in Methauris, montes ubi planum esse consueverit
5 excitatos. Omittamus, inquam, vicissitudines temporum, motuum
varietates, et inter generationem et corruptionem compositarum
rerum illam instantaneam coniuncturam et quicquid in his que
permixtione corporum simplicium componuntur aut separationis
aut interitus possumus cogitare. Nonne iuxta sanctorum patrum
oracula et elementis et celo futurum illud universale incendium
credimus imminere, ut, quamvis aliqua multis seculis stare videamus, ad suum tamen sint exitum perventura?

6   Et quoniam creditur celos corrumpi non posse vel dei voluntate,
sicut Plato testatur, vel sua natura propter unipotentiam materie,
sicut vult Aristotiles, nonne etiam, cum omnia a deo ex nichilo
creata sint sola dei voluntate et bonitate, participando cum ipsis
esse dum illa crearet et continuando dum permanent, potest idem
creator etiam sine sue bonitatis iniuria ipsius essendi influentiam
7 subtrahendo in nichilum cuncta reducere? Sint enim licet pure
forme, sint ex materia que solum uni forme conveniat, si creator et
idem conservator deus continuum esse non influat, annichilata
prorsus esse desisterent, ut, licet verbo corruptionis (que quidem
est incipere fore quod non erat et desinere iam esse quod erat) illorum taliter se habentium proprie fluxibilitas explicari non possit,

disposed to a multitude of forms, as we admit these lower things to be, although all these visible things can undoubtedly be dissolved by nature. Hence we see the continuous and amazing fluc- 3 tuations of lower things, and all of them being transformed before our eyes. Let us leave aside the multiform deaths of humans and 4 the other animate beings, the drying up of rivers, the inundation of the waters, earthquakes, and (as Aristotle attests in his *Meteorology*)[114] mountains raised up where it once was flat. Let us leave 5 aside, I say, the vicissitudes of time, the varieties of movements, and that instantaneous conjunction between the generation and corruption of compounds and whatever separation or destruction we can imagine in the things that are compounded of a mixture of simple bodies. Don't we believe (following the sayings of the holy fathers) that that future universal conflagration is threatening the elements and the sky?[115] Hence though we see some things remain for many centuries, they are destined for destruction.

There is a belief that the heavens cannot be corrupted either by 6 the will of God (as Plato attests)[116] or by their own nature, on account of the single power of matter (as Aristotle argues).[117] Since all things were created by God from nothing, by means of his will and his goodness alone, through his participating with them while he was creating them and continuing with them as long as they remained, cannot the same Creator also, with no harm done to his goodness, reduce everything to nothing by removing the influence of his very being? For although there are pure forms and ones 7 made of matter that is fitted only to a single form, if God, Creator and Preserver, does not stream continuous being into them, they are annihilated and absolutely cease to exist. Consequently, although the state of flux in things that act in this way is not properly explained by the word *corruption* (which means that something that did not exist comes into being, and something that did exist now ceases to be), we nevertheless think that they can be so designated on account of their subjection to time, place, and finally that

sentiamus tamen loco, tempore, et ipsa demum annichilatione posse, cui sua natura resistere nequeant, designari.

8   Timeo tamen, cum similia similibus delectentur, quod homines fragiles et caduci sue eternitatis immemores mundi huius, quem aggregationem noscimus caducorum, fiant ex hac fragilitatis com-
9   munione propensius amatores. Non decipiamur ergo mundi blandientis ad tempus in eternam amaritudinem evasura dulcedine. Corruptibiles sumus. Aliquid incorruptibile cui sustentaturo possimus incumbere deligamus. Tale autem, si invisibilia querimus,
10   deus est; si visibilia magis volumus, Christus est. Igitur ad inhibendam fragilitatis nostre ruinam deo, qui vere solus est immutabilis et eternus, non mundo, quem transire cernimus, innitamur. Maiores hoc mundo corruptibili sumus, quem constat tum ad ne-
11   cessitatem, tum ad utilitatem hominum procreatum. Fortiora vero debent esse sustentacula sustentatis. Ulmis etenim vites adiungimus, ligustra proximis fruticibus implicantur, et edere muris aut arboribus consuuntur. Moneat nos ars, doceat ipsa natura, ut fragiles non transitoria sed perpetua in eternitatem evasuri secundum animam amplectamur. An turrem ruituram, ut maneat, harundine
12   fulciemus? Hereamus igitur deo et Christo, domino nostro, qui vere petra est, et mundum istum transitorium dimittentes, quo fragili fragiles sustentari non possumus, non patriam sed viam fore mortalium cogitemus.

very annihilation which created things, by their own nature, are unable to resist.

I fear, however, since like delights in like, that fragile, decadent 8
people, forgetting their own eternity, have a tendency to become lovers of this world (which we know to be a pile of transient things) as a result of this shared fragility. Therefore, let us not be 9
deceived by the blandishing world's momentary sweetness: it is destined to lead to eternal bitterness. We are corruptible. Let us choose something incorruptible on which we can rely to sustain us. And such, if we seek the invisible, is God; if we prefer the visible, it is Christ. To prevent the ruin consequent upon our 10
fragility, let us depend on God—who alone is truly immutable and eternal—not the world, which we see passing away. We are greater than this corruptible world, which, it is agreed, was created to provide what is necessary and useful to human beings. Props 11
ought to be stronger than what they prop up: we join vines to elms; privets are woven into nearby bushes; and ivy is attached to walls and trees. Let art advise us, let nature itself teach us, that, being fragile, we should embrace not transitory, but perpetual things, if our soul is to reach eternity. Should we shore up a falling tower with sand to ensure that it remains? Let us, then, adhere to 12
God and Christ, our Lord, who truly is the rock. Abandoning this transitory world—which in its fragility cannot support us fragile beings—let us not view it as our homeland, but as a highway for mortals.

: XXXIII :

Quod mundus sit via mortalium.

1 Via, sicut vult M. Varro libro de agricultura, quasi 'vea' dicta est a vehendo, quia per illam curribus res vehantur. Hunc Varronem, licet deum non agnoverit, iuvat inter sermones catholicos admiscere. Quo teste sepius Augustinus et alii doctores ecclesie, sicut
2 legimus, usi sunt. Mundus itaque via est per quam vehimur nostrarum vehiculo voluntatum, quas nos soli possumus ad mala deflectere, divina tamen suffulti gratia valemus etiam ad bona effica-
3 citer applicare. Pone tibi ante oculos, miser homo, statum tue miserabilis voluntatis quam tibi fore liberam gloriaris; vide quid tibi tua voluntate liceat. Quid dixi 'liceat'? Optima quidem sunt que licent. Sed vide quid possis, imo quid non possis. Potes enim,
4 quod summa impotentia est, per te solummodo mala velle. Transgressione quidem primorum parentum hac pena tenetur cuncta posteritas, ut, cum voluntate sua potuerint illi non peccare, nunc non peccare penitus nequeamus, ut fateri oporteat quod quicquid bene volumus, totum movente deo voluntates nostras, si recte sentire voluerimus, exoptemus.

5   Non igitur, cum mundus aut ea que in ipso sunt nostrum excitant appetitum, quamvis facilitate invitent, delectatione alliciant, et fucata quandoque ratione persuadeant, obsequendum est continuo
6 voluntati. Via quidem solius voluntatis rationem deserentis et a dei gratia destitute via mundi est. Mundus autem ad immunda nos trahit, immundas generat voluntates, et lumen obnubilat rationis. Ex quo, cum aliquid volumus, maxima nobis est adhibenda cautela

: XXXIII :

The world is a highway for mortals.

The word *highway* [*via*] (according to M. Varro in his book on ag- 1
riculture)[118] is, as it were, a *vea*, from conveying [*vehere*], since
along it material is conveyed in wagons. We may happily include
this Varro in Catholic literature, even though he did not know
God: Augustine and other doctors of the church (as we read) used
his testimony quite often.[119] And so the world is the highway 2
along which we are conveyed by the vehicle of our wishes. Alone,
we can bend these toward evil; but relying on divine grace, we
can also effectively apply them to good. Place before your eyes, 3
wretched man, the state of your pitiable will that you boast is free;
see what you are permitted by your will. Why did I say "permitted"? The things that are permitted are excellent indeed. But look
at what you can do, or, more precisely, what you cannot do. For
you can, on your own, will only evil: this is the height of powerlessness. All of posterity is liable to this punishment by the trans- 4
gression of our first parents. Though they were able, by their own
will, not to sin, we are now absolutely unable not to sin. We must
confess, if we want to hold the proper view, that whatever good
thing we wish for, we wish for it entirely because God is animating
our wishes.

When the world or its contents excite our appetite, we must 5
not instantly obey the wish, however much they affably invite us,
delectably allure us, and persuade us with counterfeit arguments.
The way of the will on its own, deserting reason and bereft of 6
God's grace, is the way of the world. The world draws us to
unwholesome things, generates unwholesome wishes, and clouds
over the light of reason. Therefore, when we want something,
we must apply the utmost caution and ponder with the greatest

7   maximoque debet examine ponderari. Adest enim nostre voluntatis auspicio insidiator diabolus, deceptor mundus, adulatrix caro.
Incitat diabolus ad divine legis transgressionem, mundus ad sui
dilectionem, blandientis autem carnis fragilitas ad voluptatem. Si
in eo quod vis prevaricaturus es instituta legis eterne, diabolus est;
si ad corruptibilium amorem induceris, mundus est; si ad volup-
8   tates alliceris, caro est. Deus vero, creator noster et redemptor
noster, si bona sunt que volumus, adiuvat ut mereamur; si mala,
dissuadet et admonet ne peccemus. Instigat igitur hostis ut capiat;
delectat mundus ut decipiat; caro blanditur ut inficiat; deus autem
9   nos admonet ut recipiat. Quem ergo sequeris, miser homo, miserabilis homo? An despicies creatorem recipientem et creaturam
imitaberis ad interitum te ducentem? Precedant itaque palpebre
tue gressus tuos. Comprimat ratio voluntatem et, cum ad aliquid
10   illa movetur, consule rationem. Si rectum est, sequere; si vero
iniquum, coneris mala desideria declinare et quotidie tecum repu-
tans mundum esse viam, te vero natum ad patriam, noli abuti via.
Tunc autem via abutimur cum in ea quasi simus in patria delectamur.

11   Heu miseros homines! Solent cives extra hanc patriam terrenam positi semper de reditu cogitare. Abundent enim licet extra
patriam opibus, extollantur honoribus, et quacunque velint splen-
deant dignitate, natalis tamen soli dulcedo mentibus semper inhe-
12   ret vixque sui patitur oblivisci. Tantum mortali patrie mortales
damus; eterne autem et perpetuo mansure pene nichilum exhibemus, imo, quod reprehensibilius est, patriam negligimus et ipsius
vie amenitate decepti venire in patriam non curamus, cumque

discernment. For the wily devil, trickster world, and sycophant 7
flesh are present at the onset our will. The devil incites us to
transgress divine law; the world, to love of itself; the blandishing
flesh's fragility, to seek pleasure. If in what you wish for you are
going to deviate from the provisions of eternal law, that is the
devil; if you are led into love of corruptible things, that is the
world; if you are seduced by pleasures, that is the flesh. But if the 8
things that we want are good, God, our Creator and Redeemer,
helps us, so that we are rewarded; if the things we want are bad,
he dissuades us and admonishes us not to sin. The Enemy, then,
incites us to catch us; the world delights us to deceive us; the flesh
flatters us to infect us; but God admonishes us to receive us.
Whom, then, will you follow, wretched man, pitiable man? Will 9
you despise your Creator, who receives you, and will you mimic
the creature that is leading you to your doom? Let your eyelids,
then, precede your steps.[120] Let reason restrain your will and,
when the latter is moved to anything, consult the former. If it is 10
right, follow it; but if it is unjust, try to reject bad desires. Reflect
daily that the world is the highway, but that you were born for
your homeland: don't misuse the highway. We misuse the highway
when we delight in it as if we were in our homeland.

Alas, wretched human beings! Citizens who find themselves 11
outside their earthly homeland always think about their return.
Even if outside their homeland they have abundant wealth, are
exalted with honors, and shine with all the status they wish for,
nonetheless the sweetness of their native soil always sticks in their
mind and scarcely allows them to forget it. We mortals grant 12
so much to our mortal homeland; yet we present almost nothing to the homeland that is eternal and will perpetually endure.
More accurately — and this is more reprehensible — we neglect our
homeland; deceived by the pleasantness of the highway itself, we
don't care about arriving in our homeland. Although we see that

videamus mundum esse peregrinationis nostre diversorium, ipsum veluti patriam errore maximo colimus et amamus.

⁝ XXXIV ⁝

Quod mundus est peregrinationis nostre diversorium.

1 Si enim, sicut sacra testatur hystoria, dum in hoc mundo manemus peregrini sumus et advene coram domino et nostrum est inquirere patriam, cum simus hospites super terram, in eo divertimus, non manemus, nam dies nostri sicut umbra super terram et 2 nulla est mora. Que cum ita sint, cur non patriam veram inquirimus, cur non ad illam celestem ad quam sumus geniti properamus? Cur in itineris nostri diversorio non solum retardantes viam sed perdentes patriam cupimus permanere et, quoniam diversorium duo nobis significat, aut locum in quo viatores mox recessuri declinant aut locum in via ubi plures semite reperiuntur ita quod per unam euntes ab alia declinamus, quid facimus amatores mundi? Quam stultum est in diversorio spem et mentem apponere 3 unde mox simus etiam si stare voluerimus recessuri! O quanta dementia tenet in hac mundi dilectione mortales! Diligimus exilium, negligimus patriam; mansura spernimus, transitoria vero 4 transeuntes amamus. Non possumus, fateor, corpore mundum istum exire. Hic enim gignimur, hic vivimus, hic nutrimur. Mentem tamen hinc valemus, dummodo voluerimus, elevare. Respiciamus dum in mundo pergimus ante pedes. Mundus iste diversorium est; plures ante oculos vie sunt, via voluptatis, via virtutis, via

the world is the inn of our pilgrimage, by a colossal error, we worship and love it as if it were our homeland.

: XXXIV :

The world is the inn of our pilgrimage.

Sacred history attests that as long as we remain in this world, we 1
are pilgrims and strangers before the Lord, and our task is to seek
our homeland. Since we are guests on earth, we sojourn here; we
do not abide, for our days are like a shadow over the earth and
there is no lingering.[121] Accordingly, why don't we seek our true 2
homeland? Why don't we hasten to the celestial country for which
we were born? Why do we desire to remain at our journey's inn,
where we not only slow our progress, but lose our homeland? *Diversorium* signifies two things for us: it is either an inn where travelers turn aside and whence they soon will depart, or a fork in the
road, so that by going along one path we turn away from the
other.[122] Since this is so, what are we world lovers doing? How 3
stupid it is to put our hope in an inn and attach our mind to a
place we are soon to leave, even if we wanted to stay! What great
madness holds mortals in this love of the world! We love exile and
neglect our homeland; we despise things that will last, but we love
transitory things, since we ourselves are transient. Granted, we are 4
unable to depart this world in body: here we are born; here we
live; here we are nourished. Yet if only we wish it, we can raise our
mind from here. While we are making our way in the world, let us
look in front of our feet. This world is an inn, and several roads
are before our eyes: the road of pleasure, the road of virtue; the
road of transgression, the road of obedience; the road of hell, the

5 transgressionis, via obedientie, via inferi, via celi. Quid facimus, o
mortales? Ad voluptates infirma caro nos trahit, ad transgressionem diabolus, ad inferum mundus; continentia autem in deum
nos dirigit, obedientia ducit, mundique abrenuntiatio deo nos
unit. Non dormiamus in diversorio expectantes donec eiciamur. Si
6 venire in patriam volumus, surgendum est et properandum. Via
enim longa, arcta, ardua, et laboriosa superanda est: longa quidem
amatoribus mundi, qui a deo in viam longissimam abierunt; arcta
divitibus, quos oportet divitiarum dimittere sarcinas si volunt ad
celorum principem pervenire; ardua voluptuosis, quibus opus est
mentem a sensibus revocare et delectationem suam erigere in celis
quam habebant in terris; laboriosa vero negligentibus, qui habeant
7 pugnare cum carne, luctari cum mundo, certare cum diabolo. Surgamus igitur, nam brevem et compendiariam viam nobis efficiet
caritas, amplam paupertas, planam sobrietas, facilem et amenam
quotidiana victoria et, quod victorie premium est, immarcescibilis
glorie spes non vana; sufficiatque nobis de mundo necessaria
sumere et a malo quicquid fuerit amplius reputare.

: XXXV :

Quod mundus sit ministrator necessariorum.

1 Ministrat equidem necessaria nobis mundus, necessaria quippe ad
vitam hanc corruptibilem transigendam. Quid autem oporteat
de his que mundus habet assumere, naturam ipsam, ducem opti-
mam, consulamus: famem enim reprimi, sitim extingui, imbres et
frigora pelli, ventorumque et estuum vim arceri natura desiderat.

road of heaven. What are we doing, mortals? The weak flesh 5
draws us to pleasures; the devil, to transgression; the world, to
hell. But continence directs us to God; obedience leads us to him;
and renunciation of the world unites us with God. Let us not fall
asleep at the inn waiting until we are evicted. If we want to come
into our homeland, we must get up and make haste. A long, nar- 6
row, steep, and toilsome road must be overcome. It is long indeed
for the world lovers; they have departed on the road furthest from
God. For the rich it is narrow; they must lay aside the burden of
their riches if they want to reach the prince of the heavens. It is
steep for the pleasure seekers; they need to call their mind back
from their physical senses and to lift up to heaven the enjoyment
they were taking on earth. For the negligent it is toilsome; they
have to fight with the flesh, wrestle with the world, and contend
with the devil. Let us rise, therefore, since charity will make our 7
way short and abbreviated; poverty will make it broad; sobriety
will make it flat; daily victory and — victory's reward, the sure hope
of imperishable glory — will make it easy and pleasant. Let it suffice for us to take what is necessary from the world and consider
anything more than that an evil.

: XXXV :

The world is a provider of necessities.

The world serves up to us necessary things, things necessary for 1
passing this corruptible life. Let us consult nature itself, the best
guide,[123] about what we ought to take up from the world's contents: nature desires hunger to be checked, thirst to be quenched,
rain and frost to be driven away, and the force of wind and heat to

2 Quicquid ultra est a malo est. Quam facile vero his necessitatibus
satisfiat, docuit etas prima, que famem, ut legitur, glande replevit,
sitim compressit undis, frigora depulit pellibus, imbres, ventos, et
estus antris ac specubus evitavit. Hec est illa innocentissima etas
quam poete multis laudibus extollentes tum auream, tum Satur-
3 niam vocaverunt. O felices glandes! O saluberrima flumina! Non
excitavit tunc estuantium ciborum virus suo calore libidinem; non
tentavit cerebrum insanie simillima marcens ebrietas; non fuit cum
4 proximo de finibus controversia, non de regno. Omnia communia
erant. Thoros herba, domos antra non custodita, non clausa, sed
cunctis patula ministrabant. Sublata tunc erant, imo nondum re-
perta, illa duo litigiosa vocabula que mortalium pacem turbant
queve claudunt hominibus viam in celum, que sunt avaricie fo-
mites et contentionum autores, scilicet 'meum' et 'tuum.' 'O utinam,' ut Severinus ait,

> modo nostra redirent
> in mores tempora priscos!

5 Sed adeo mundo et deliciis dati sumus quod illa nostris moribus, imo non moribus sed abusibus ac flagitiis, comparantes fabu-
losa, non hystorica, reputemus, dicimusque fragiliorem fore temporis nostri etatem ut ad asperitatem illam impossibile sit redire.
Fragilior autem est, fateor, quia vitiosior et, quod vitiorum fomes
6 est, quia delicatior. Impossibilis profecto videtur reditus ad frugalitatem et prisci temporis communionem quia, sicut predictis versi-
culis subditur,

> sevior ignibus Ethne,
> fervens amor ardet habendi.

be kept off. Anything beyond this is bad. The earliest age has 2
taught us just how easily these needs can be satisfied: we read that
people satisfied hunger with acorns, suppressed thirst with water,
drove off chills with pelts, and avoided rainstorms, winds, and
heat by means of caves and hollows. This is that most innocent
age; the poets extolled it with many praises and called it golden or
Saturnian.[124] Blessed acorns! Wholesome rivers! At that time the 3
poison of sizzling food did not excite lust by its warmth; drooping
drunkenness most like insanity did not assault the brain; there was
no dispute with neighbor over boundaries or sovereign rule. All 4
things were held in common. Grass served as beds, and caves —
unguarded, not closed but open to all — as homes. Gone at that
time (more precisely, not yet discovered) were those two conten-
tious words that disturb the peace of humankind and bar people's
way to heaven, words that are the kindling of avarice and the authors of disputes, namely *mine* and *yours.* "Would that our times,"
as Boethius says,

> could just go back
> to ancient ways of life![125]

But we are so given to the world and its delights that when we 5
compare earlier times with our ways (or rather, not our ways but
our abuses and offenses), we take the former era for fairy tales, not
historical facts; we say that our generation is more fragile, so that
it is impossible to return to the former austerity. More fragile it is,
I admit, since it is more wicked and more effeminate — since ef-
feminacy is tinder for vice. A return to frugality and the common 6
holdings of the pristine age certainly seems impossible, as the
aforementioned verses go on:

> more savage than Etna's fires,
> seething greed burns.[126]

7   Tolle cupidinem, miser homo, depone divitias, abrenuntia mundo, duc vitam tuam sub preceptis, coneris adimplere consilia, subde voluntatem tuam voluntati divine, imo non subdas (subdita quidem est) sed subditam teneas; incipe diligere deum, odire mun-

8   dum, amare paupertatem, horrere divitias. Non potes hec relinquere nisi odio habeas; non potes ad illa transire ni diligas. Nec iam etatis nostre fragilitatem accuses. Potens est enim corpus nostrum per omnes incommoditates transire.

9   Non referam tibi Danielem et socios in legumina regie mense delicias commutantes. Non proponam tibi in exemplum maximum illum inter natos mulierum domini precursorem; non anachoritas, de quibus mirabilia legimus in vita patrum; non heremitas etiam nostri temporis; non cenobitas, quorum multos videmus eligere

10   paupertatem, amare ieiunia, et omnem fugere voluptatem. Scio enim quod, cum istos obiecero, respondebit amator mundi illos spiritus sancti gratia suffultos hec facere nunc posse et hactenus potuisse, et spiritum spirare quando, quantum, et ubi vult hocque

11   a nostre voluntatis arbitrio non pendere. Opponam igitur tibi montanos agricolas; opponam tibi totam Carintiam et orbis plurimas nationes; opponam tibi, quod super omnia mirum est, etiam temporis nostri nautas.

12   Cibus est monticolis agrestibus, quos ab urbanis deliciis Alpium separat altitudo, aut panis insuavissimus medice, quam nostri saginam vulgo dicunt per antifrasim, ut arbitror, eo quod homines non saginet; aut milii quidem hyulcus aut ordei siliquosus panis; potus autem aqua pura, lectus vero stramenta durissima.

Get rid of your desire, wretched man, lay down your riches, re- 7
nounce the world, lead your life according to the precepts, try to
fulfill the counsels, subject your will to the divine will—rather,
you are not to subject it (for it is already subject), but to keep it
subject; begin to love God, to hate the world, to love poverty, and
recoil at riches. You cannot relinquish these things unless you con- 8
sider them hateful; you cannot pass over to the old ways unless
you love them. Stop blaming our generation's fragility. For our
body has the power to go through all inconveniences.

I will not cite Daniel and his companions to you, who ex- 9
changed the delicacies of the king's table for legumes.[127] I will not
put before you the example of the greatest among those born of
woman, the Lord's precursor; not the anchorites, about whom we
read miracles in the lives of the fathers; not even the hermits of
our time; not the cenobites, many of whom we see choose poverty,
love fasting, and flee all pleasure. For I know that when I bring 10
these people forward as proof, the world lover will reply that they
have been up until now, and are still, able to accomplish these
things because they rely on the grace of the Holy Spirit; that the
Spirit blows when, how much, and where it wills,[128] and that this
does not depend on the determination of our will. I will set before 11
you as proof the mountain-dwelling farmers; all of Carinthia and
very many nations of the world; and I will set before you, what is
most incredible, even the sailors of our time.

For the rustic mountain dwellers, whom the altitude of the 12
Alps separates from urban delights, food means either the most
unpleasant clover bread we commonly call *fattening* (by antiphra-
sis, I think, because it does not fatten people), cracked millet
bread, or lumpy barley bread; their drink is pure water, and
their bed is a hard straw mat. Their clothing, amid continual

Vestis est inter continuos ventos et perpetuas nives singulis singula

13 asperrimo vellere setosaque lana contexta. In Carintia vero, regione
Germanica, que montibus nostris, quibus furor Theutonicus ab
Italico solo mira nature discretione seiungitur, adiacet, stupenda

14 nostris deliciis paupertas est. Illic sterile vitibus solum, multis ob-
sessum nivibus, ordei et avene potius quam frumenti ferax. Illic,
sine solennitate qua nostri pueri recenter editi calore precario
confoventur, de matris utero nudi communiter exponuntur in pa-
leis et antequam frigora noscant frigoribus assuescunt; tantaque
est vis consuetudinis quod perpetua quodam modo gaudeant nu-
ditate, ventos spernant, delectentur nivibus, et asperitate vite ip-

15 sam quodam modo superent paupertatem. Quid Dalmatas, Illiri-
cos, et Pannonios, quos Hungaros dicimus, quid Sicambros aut
Hunnos referam? Quid Polanos, Saxones, Silandos, et Scithas, et
alias infinitas gentes quorum solennissimus victus aut inops sordi-
cies est aut sordidissima copia?

16 Aspice nautas nostros, qui per remos et transtra dormituri fes-
sos artus exponunt, sub aere puro galbana veste contenti, et considera quot quantosque labores, qualia et quam horrenda pericula
subeunt etiam parvissimi lucri temporalis amore et quanta cum

17 victus asperitate minima stipendia promerentur. Bis decocti panis
alimonia cum modico casei Sardi vel Siculi et leguminum ferculis
prandia celebrant; cenas vero sine parasside pisciculis sale plurimo
conservatis, quos sardellas vocant, aut parcissima dispensatione
casei cum eodem pane vere lapideo transigunt; aqua et aceto non
nuper hausta sed diu ad putrefactionem usque servata aridam sitim aspergunt, solumque bis in Sabbato carne salita decocta cum

18 fabis in prandiis epulantur. Quid potest igitur eis deliciarum sub-
trahi vel laboris augeri? Vinum ignorant, imo, quod durius est,

winds and constant snow, is a single garment woven of rough
fleece and bristly wool. Carinthia is in the German region that lies   13
adjacent to our mountains, which by nature's marvelous discrimi-
nation separate Teutonic frenzy from Italian soil: the poverty there
is stupefying to our own decadence. There, the soil is devoid of
vines, besieged by copious snow, and fertile in barley and oats
more than corn. There — without the ceremony in which our new-   14
borns are, by request, warmed up with heat — infants are commu-
nally exposed, naked, on straw, as soon as they are born; they become accustomed to frost before they know what it is. So great is
the force of custom that they rejoice in a kind of perpetual nudity;
they spurn the winds, delight in snow, and in a way surpass poverty itself in harshness of life. Why should I mention the Dalma-   15
tians, the Illyrians, and the Pannonians (whom we call Hungari-
ans)? Why the Sicambri or the Huns? Why the Stirians, Saxons,
Silandi, Scythians, and countless other peoples whose customary
way of life is either destitute filth or utterly filthy abundance?

Behold our sailors, who, as they go to sleep along the oars and   16
thwarts, expose their tired limbs, content with a yellow garment
under the open sky; consider how many and what great toils, what
kinds of horrible dangers they undergo for the love of even the
smallest temporal reward, and with what great harshness of life
they earn their minimal stipend. The Sardinians and Sicilians eat   17
twice-baked bread and a little cheese along with platters of legumes for lunch. For supper, they have little fish preserved in a lot
of salt (these they call sardines) unaccompanied, or a tiny portion
of cheese with the same truly rock-hard bread. They quench their
dry thirst with water and vinegar, not recently drawn but preserved for a long time to the point of putrefaction. Only twice, on
Saturday, do they feast on salted meat cooked with beans. What,   18
then, can be taken away from them in the way of delights or added
in the way of toils? They are ignorant of wine, or they dismiss

cum agnoscant dimittunt. Nam vinum et omnia gule irritamenta videntes navis prepositos bis in die tum abundanter, tum splendide
19 capere, vinum tamen publica dispensatione non potant. Et tamen, cum inter omnia victus versentur incommoda, remis imminent, sentinam exhauriunt, vela suspendunt, suspensa deponunt, et nunc pede facto per omnes in levam, nunc in dexteram flectunt. Maximi ponderis demittunt anchoras, dimissas colligunt, et imo
20 plerumque fundo defixas se plurimum demergentes evellunt. Sed cur frustra conor cunctos labores naviculariorum expromere? Levius enim esset quot turbato mari naves ipsorum circumquassentur fluctibus explicare.

21   Non igitur blandiamur nobis. Mundum quidem relinquere possumus et deo servientes ad extremam illam necessitatem nature
22 nostra corpora subiugare. Imo pudeat mortale genus, cui benigna dei clementia ratio desuper est infusa, post sensus usque adeo deviare quod cum videamus non unum sed totam unam gentem nativi soli dulcedine captam ut terrenam hanc et corruptibilem patriam non relinquant, aspera cuncta pati per omnia quecunque dici possunt incommoda, ad celestem illam et eternam patriam
23 minime properare. Cumque videamus nautas vilissimi et transitorii lucri questu tot labores tanta cum asperitate subire, pudeat eterne atque beate vite propositis premiis adeo deliciis obtorpere quod mundum relinquere non velimus, maxime cum videamus ipsum non solum ministrare necessaria sed ad voluptates quibus occidimur sua nos etiam abundantia suisque blanditiis invitare.

it even though they are familiar with it (which is harder). For though they see the ship's captains take wine and all other stimuli of the throat twice daily in splendid abundance, nevertheless, by public dispensation, they do not drink wine. Yet however well- 19 versed they are in all of life's inconveniences, they press on with their oars; they drain the bilge water; they hang the sails and take them down again; and, with the sheet set by all, they steer the ship now to starboard, now to port. They lower anchors of great weight and lift them up again — more precisely, they generally dive deeply to pull out anchors fixed on the bottom of the sea. But why 20 am I trying in vain to describe in detail the labors of seamen? It would be easier to elaborate on how many of their ships are tossed around by the waves of the turbulent sea.

Let us therefore not flatter ourselves. We can indeed abandon 21 the world and, serving God, subjugate our bodies to nature to reach that state of extreme need. Rather, the human race should 22 be ashamed, although, by the kindly clemency of God, reason has been poured over us, to wander so far after the senses that we do not in the least hasten to our celestial and eternal homeland, when we see not one person but an entire people so taken by the sweetness of their native soil that they suffered through a gamut of all the hardships that can be named in order not to leave their earthly and corruptible homeland. And when we see sailors submitting 23 themselves to so many toils under such harsh conditions in their quest for vile and ephemeral lucre, we should be ashamed, with the rewards of the eternal and blessed life set before us, to be so numbed by our pleasures that we refuse to leave the world behind — especially since we see that it not only serves up necessities, but also invites us with its abundance and its charms to indulge in the pleasures that kill us.

: XXXVI :

Quod mundus sit suppeditator abundantissimus voluptatum.

1 Suppeditator enim, ut ultimo loco dixi, abundantissimus voluptatum mundus est et, ne per singula discurram, infinita quidem sunt
quibus mundus nos ad voluptates invitat. Creator optimus et deus
noster quam mellifluas voces in parvis etiam aviculis excitavit!
Quantam iocunditatem oculis nostris obiecit dum singula visibilia

2 tum unico, tum vario colore depinxit! Quantam suavitatem statuit
in olfactu, iubens odorabilia diversos naribus accipiendos exhalare
vapores! Quantam dulcedinem attulit gustui, tot educens in fructibus, tum ex plantis, tum ex herbis, tum in aliis concessis ad esum

3 multiplici cum varietate sapores! Quot etiam animalibus non solum ad cibi necessitatem sed etiam ad voluptatem hominum pro-
creatis iussit terram, aquas, et aerem abundare! Quantam autem
delectationem esse decrevit in tactu et in eo precipue quem novi-

4 mus ad gignendam sobolem pertinere! Quocunque te volveris, instat mundus, insidiatur diabolus, blanditur caro, ut creaturas se-
quens obliviscaris cum damnatione perpetua creatoris. Quo fit ut
nichil tutius, nichil securius, nichilque consultius, si properare volueris ad gloriam (omnes autem velle debent), quam mundum relinquere, relinquendo domare carnem, mundoque relicto et carne

5 domita diabolum exarmare. Quid enim antiquo illi hosti reliqueris
quo tibi nocere queat si carne subacta mundum duxeris totius
mentis viribus deserendum?

Sed dicent miseri peccatores qui falsa mundi dulcedine laqueati
in malis propriis delectantur, 'Cur posuit deus bonus, qui cuncta

: XXXVI :

The world is the most abundant supplier of pleasures.

As I have just said, the world is a most abundant supplier of plea- 1
sures, and (not to canvass the particulars) infinite indeed are the
means by which the world invites us to pleasure. How mellifluous
are the songs that our excellent Creator and God stirred in even
the smallest of birds! What great gaiety he put before our eyes
when he painted each visible thing with color both unique and
various! What great pleasantness he planted in our sense of smell 2
when he ordered odorous things to give off various aromas to be
taken in by the nostrils! What great sweetness he brought to the
taste when he brought out so many flavors of manifold variety in
fruits, plants, herbs, and other things granted to us as food! In 3
how many animals did he order the earth, waters, and air to
abound, animals created not only to supply the need for food but
also for the pleasure of humans! How much delight did he decree
to be in the touch, and especially in that which we know pertains
to the begetting of children! Wherever you turn, the world looms, 4
the devil plots, the flesh entices, so that if you follow creatures,
you forget your Creator — to your perpetual damnation. Hence, if
you want to hasten to glory (and everyone should want this),
nothing is safer, nothing more secure, and nothing more prudent
than to tame the flesh by relinquishing the world, and, once the
world has been relinquished and the flesh tamed, to disarm the
devil. What will you leave for that ancient Enemy to be able to 5
harm you with if, having subdued the flesh, you consider the
world as something to be deserted with all of your mind's power?

But wretched sinners — who, ensnared by the world's false
sweetness, take pleasure in their own evils — will say, "Why did the

bona fecit, tot in mundo decipulas ad mortalium animas capien-
6   das?' Quibus facile responderim cum ipsorum aliquo sic inquiens:
deus tibi, qui ad gloriam natus eras, lumen indidit intellectus seque primis parentibus in specie corporali, quam volens sibi forma-
verat, audiendum prebuit et videndum; et postea sanctis patribus
se multis ostendens modis et formis cunctisque per prophetarum
oracula se revelans, demum nobis per suum unigenitum filium, ad
eam parvitatem secundum humanitatem assumptam minoratum
de qua homo superbiens ad divinitatis altitudinem anhelaverat, se
monstravit, omniumque creatorem adeo doctrina ac miraculis fore
se docuit quod, sicut Augustinus vult, nulla tam aspera tamque
inculta barbaries remaneret que deum, rerum cunctarum opificem,
7   non firme crederet et teneret. Ut, cum eius beneficio fore quicquid
sumus sine dubitatione firmiter sentiamus nichilque carius sit
nobis hac essentia qua constamus et vivimus, non possumus delectatione vel admiratione creature ab essentie nostre principe tam
leviter mente discedere quin nos ipsos in secreto conscientie con-
demnemus.
8   Vides ergo etiam te iudice, cum mundum diligis ad delectationem vel propter aliud quam propter deum, te principium omnium
offendere, cumque sic creaturam sequeris, te a tui creatoris reve-
9   rentia deviare. Et cum tamen ita sit, fecit nos deus potentes velle
mundum relinquere, carnem vincere, et diabolum superare dummodo velimus. Continue gratia sua nos prevenit et preventos
comitatur et adiuvat ut tanto gloriosius triumphemus tantoque
iuxta beneplaciti sui legem meritabilius operemur quanto maiorem
10   difficultatem in certamine collocavit. Illam autem gratiam non nisi
volentes amittimus quando voluntate mala ab illo rerum omnium

good God, who made all things good, put so many tricks in the
world to capture the souls of mortals?" I could easily reply to them   6
by speaking to one of their number in this way: God endowed
you, who were born for glory, with the light of understanding. He
showed himself to our first parents, in a corporeal shape he had
willingly fashioned for himself, as someone to be heard and seen.
Afterward, he showed himself to the holy fathers in many ways
and forms and revealed himself through the sacred pronouncements of the prophets. Finally, he showed himself to us through
his only-begotten Son, diminished to that smallness in accordance
with the humanity he assumed — the humanity out of which ar-
rogant man had avidly sought the heights of divinity. He taught by
his precepts and miracles that he was the Creator of all, and consequently, as Augustine has it, there remained no barbarous people
so rough and crude that they did not firmly believe and hold that
God was the Maker of all things.[129] Without hesitation we firmly   7
believe that we are whatever we are by his favor, and nothing is
dearer to us than this essence by which we exist and live. Therefore, we cannot so lightly depart in mind from the Prince of our
essence by loving or admiring his creature without condemning
ourselves in our innermost conscience.

You see, then, with even yourself as judge, that when you love   8
the world for your own pleasure or on account of something other
than God, you are offending the Origin of all things; and when
you follow a creature in this way, you are turning yourself away
from reverence for your own Creator. And although this is the   9
case, God made us capable of wanting to relinquish the world,
conquer the flesh, and defeat the devil, if only we want to. He
continuously anticipates us with his grace, and then accompanies
us and helps us, so that we triumph all the more gloriously and
work according to the law of his good pleasure all the more meritoriously, the greater the difficulty he has put in the struggle. We   10
do not lose that grace unless we want to lose it, when with evil

principe, in quem quicquid cogitamus aut facimus tanquam in fi-
11 nem optimum debemus dirigere, deviamus. Non igitur frustra
preposuit hec nobis creator noster, que si fugimus aut bene, non
inconvenienter, illis utamur, ad glorie future cumulum prosunt,
quarumque admiratione perterriti debemus autorem super omnia,
si recte vivimus, admirari, qui novit corpulenta tanta colorum varietate depingere, esculenta potuit tanta saporum varietate condire,
olfactibilia voluit tam diversorum odorum redimire fragrantia, so-
nora curavit tanta discrepantium vocum componere melodia, que
vero subiecit tactui tot delectationum illecebris sociavit, et, cum
tam vehementer trahentia cunctis obiecerit sensibus, relinquenti-
bus ipsa et eosdem superantibus sensus, qui non gladiis, non ner-
vorum viribus sed adiuvante dei gratia solius libere voluntatis
nostre robore subiugantur, eterne vite premia, que nec extimare
nec cogitare possumus, preparavit.

: XXXVII :

Epilogus libri primi.

1 Vides, ni fallor, mi Ieronime, quid sit mundus iste quem fugis
quove nos sensibus dediti tam perdite delectamur ut iam videre
videar te sicut naufragum quem mare fluctisonum deiecit in portum fessum, attonitum, et paventem, adeo mundi presentis insidias exhorrere quod iam ille religionis tue status, obedientie iugum, paupertatis votum, et ipsa victus asperitas tibi tum iocunda,
2 tum dulcissima videantur. Et quoniam de mundo satis disputatum

intention we deviate from the Prince of all things, to whom we ought to direct whatever we think or do as to the best end. Our 11 Creator, then, did not put these things before us to no purpose. If we flee them, or use them not inappropriately but well, they are of benefit for the accumulation of future glory. Trembling with admiration for them, we ought, if we live correctly, to admire their Author above all things: for he knew how to paint physical things with such a great variety of colors; he was able to season food with such a great variety of flavors; he wanted to crown aromatic things with the fragrance of such diverse odors; he took pains to compose sonorous things with such a great melody of distinct voices; he bound up palpable things with so many delectable allurements; and, although he put before all our senses things so powerfully attractive, he prepared for those who relinquish them and overcome those same senses — which are defeated not by swords, not by muscular strength, but, with the support of God's grace, by the strength of our free will alone — the rewards of eternal life, which we can neither estimate nor imagine.

꞉ XXXVII ꞉

Epilogue to Book One.

You see, I believe, dear Girolamo, what the world you are fleeing 1 is. We who are devoted to it with our senses delight in it so recklessly that now I seem to see you as a shipwrecked person whom the wave-resounding sea has cast into harbor: exhausted, dazed, and fearful, you are so horrified by the snares of the present world that now the state of your religious life, the yoke of obedience, the vow of poverty, and the very harshness of your way of life seem to you both pleasant and very sweet. The world has been sufficiently 2

est, cuius fallacias utilissimum arbitror denudasse, ut, sicut tibi proposui, licet non plene (opus enim esset maiore quam michi concedatur ocio et volumine longiore et, quod omnino michi non est, copiosa scientia et ingenio perspicaci), saltem aliqualiter videas quod fugisti, et ut ego et reliqui sectatores mundi, quid amemus quove tam miserabiliter implicemur, discussis nebulis agnoscamus, dicendum restat amodo quid sequaris, sed, quoniam hec disputatio me longius quam arbitrarer traxit, dicenda in sequentem libellum prosequar, quantum dederit omnipotens deus, cui honor et gloria in secula seculorum. Amen.

Explicit liber primus feliciter. Incipit secundus.

discussed. I think it has been very useful to expose its tricks, so that, as I proposed to you, you may see, albeit not completely — that would take leisure greater than is granted to me, a bigger volume, and copious knowledge along with perspicacious genius, which I altogether lack — at least to some degree, what you have fled. Now it remains to speak about what you are pursuing, in order that, the clouds parted, I and the other adherents of the world may recognize what we love and in what we are so pitifully entangled. However, since this disputation drew me further than I intended, I will continue the discussion into the following book, as far as all-powerful God grants it. To him be honor and glory, world without end. Amen.

Here ends the first book. The second begins.

LIBER SECUNDUS

Incipit liber secundus De seculo et religione
ad fratrem Ieronimum ordinis Camaldulensis
in monasterio Sancte Marie de Angelis de Florentia,
editus per Colucium Pyeri de Stignano, cancellarium Florentinum.

Et primo prohemium.

1 Non sine divini numinis dispositione factum puto quod, cum quicquid in maiore quam premisimus opusculi nostri parte tractavimus consulte reliqueris, id totum ad dimissi tui primi nominis proprietatem significationemque vocabuli pertineret. Quod qui-

2 dem eo michi mirabilius fuit quod illud nomen quod in baptismate recepisti non a parentibus vel illius sacramenti testibus ad aliquod futurum misterium impositum fuit, sed quia sic illis placuit te vocari.

3 Nicholus etenim, quod tibi primum nomen imposuere parentes, licet formam habeat diminutam, nichil aliud est quam Nicholaus. Quid autem huius nominis interpretatio sonet, palam est. Nicholaus enim 'stultum populum,' ut vult Papias, vel, ut ponit nominum Biblie quisquis ille fuerit non contemnendus interpres, 'stultum ecclesie' vel 'ecclesiam languentem' vel 'stulticiam ec-

4 clesie languentis' importat. Quod autem tibi quondam in seculo et in rebus mundi non occupato sed perdito nomen convenientius donari potuit quam ut stulti vocabulo notareris? Stultus eras, mi Ieronime, qui pro transitoriis dimittebas eterna, pro occidentibus vivificantia; et denique creatorem pro creatura deserens, a celesti patre, suscepta portione substantie que te contingebat, profectus eras in regionem longinquam ubi denique cupivisses fame facta de

BOOK TWO

Here begins the second book On the World and Religious Life,
composed by Coluccio di Piero of Stignano, chancellor of Florence,
*for Brother Girolamo of the Camaldolese Order,
of the Monastery of Santa Maria degli Angeli, Florence.*

First, the proem.

Now that you have wisely left behind what I have discussed in the 1
preceding part of my little work,[1] I reckon that all that pertains to
the proper significance of your first name, which you have shed,
has been done by divine arrangement. This was all the more amaz- 2
ing to me because the name you received in baptism was not given
to you by your parents or godparents for the sake of a future secret
significance, but simply because it pleased them so to call you.

Niccolò, the first name your parents gave you, is nothing other 3
than a shortened form of *Nicholaus*. The meaning of this name is
clear. *Nicholaus* means "the stupid populace," according to Papias;[2]
or it has the sense of "stupid man of the church," "languishing
church," or "stupidity of the languishing church" (according to the
interpreter of biblical names, not to be despised, whoever he was).
What name could more fittingly have been granted to you — who 4
were once not so much occupied in the secular world and its ap-
purtenances, but lost in them — than that you be designated by
the word *stupid?* You were stupid, dear Girolamo, since you cast
aside the eternal for the transient, the life-giving for the deadly.
Finally, deserting the Creator for the creature, taking your allotted
portion of wealth, you had set out from your heavenly Father into
a far-off land, where in the end, famished, you longed to be filled

5 porcorum siliquis saturari. Ad te itaque reversus divine tibi gratie
   lumine in tenebris effulgente, sine qua nedum bona facere non
   possumus sed etiam velle presertim efficaciter non valemus, et
   stulticiam et nomen stulticie dimisisti et, sicut vite statum, ita
   etiam tui nominis vocabulum immutasti proque secularibus occu-
   pationibus tranquillitatem religionis, pro mundi deliciis asperitatem ordinis, pro transacte vite superbia, in qua superiores gradus
   elatis affectibus cupiebas, obedientie iugum non verbo solum sed
   per effectum operis elegisti, gloriosissimum nomen assumens ut
   deinceps pro Nicholo Ieronimus vocareris.

6   Nec iam stultum te non fuisse contendas qui solum carnalia
   sapiens temporalia cogitabas. Quid enim faciebas in seculo nisi
   congregare divitias, insanire gloria, frui deliciis, ambire honores, et
7 appetere dignitates? Quod si sapientes sapientia mundi huius,
   quam deus, ut testatur apostolus, stultam fecit, hec quibus occupa-
   tus eras stulticiam iudicant, quid hec relata ad veram et ineffabilem
   dei sapientiam dicenda sunt nisi stulticia stulticie, sicut tu de Ni-
8 cholao Nicholus dicebaris? Quod si forte magis Grecorum appel-
   lationibus delectaris, cum Nicholaus a 'nichos,' quod est 'victoria,'
   et 'laos,' 'populus,' Grecis nominibus componatur, cumque victor
   mundus de hominum multitudine sine dubitatione triumphet et
   tu victus in mundo maneres quasi victus in populo, de Nicholao
9 Nicholus non incongrue vocabaris. Sed et mundi languentis im-
   mundiciam relinquendo, quasi victor unus ex populo, postquam
   hanc victoriam per dei gratiam habiturus eras, bene in tue nomi-
   nationis initio Nicholi vocabulum meruisti. Melius tamen vitam

by the husks of the pigs.[3] You returned to yourself by the light of 5
divine grace shining for you in the shadows (for without grace we
are not only unable to do good, but cannot even effectively wish to
do good). You left stupidity and the name of stupidity behind, and
you changed your name, along with your state of life: you chose—
not only in word, but in deed—the tranquility of the religious life
instead of secular pursuits, the harshness of your order instead of
worldly delights, the yoke of obedience instead of the arrogance of
your life up to that point (in which, with elated spirits, you were
always longing for higher and higher ranks). You assumed a most
glorious name, so that from then on, instead of *Niccolò*, you were
called *Girolamo*.

Don't argue that you were not stupid, you who were only wise 6
with respect to carnal things and thought only about the temporal.
What were you doing in the secular world but piling up riches,
going crazy for glory, indulging in delights, canvassing for offices,
and avidly seeking honors? But if men wise in the wisdom of this 7
world (a wisdom that God made stupid as the apostle attests)[4]
judge your former occupations as stupidity, what should we call
the things related to the true and ineffable wisdom of God but
stupidity's stupidity, just as you were called *Niccolò* from *Nicholaus*?
But if you should delight more in Greek appellations, you were 8
not inappropriately called *Niccolò* from *Nicholaus*. *Nicholaus* is composed of Greek nouns *nikos* ("victory") and *laos* ("people"). Without a doubt, the world triumphs as victor over a multitude of
people; you, having been conquered in the world, remained as one
conquered among the people. But you also relinquished the impu- 9
rity of the languishing world, and since you were going to have
this victory achieved through God's grace, you were, as it were, a
single victor from among the people. So you well deserved the
name of *Niccolò*, which you had from the beginning. However, you

mutans, stulticiam abiciens, et de mundo religionem sanctissimam eligendo triumphans, ut dicereris amodo Ieronimus elegisti.

10   Omittamus enim quod ex devotione quam semper ad illum sanctissimum doctorem ⟨habuisti⟩ cuius labores illuminaverunt ecclesiam et nobis non humane sed divine potius translationis beneficio veritatem sacrarum litterarum stilo luculentissimo tradiderunt vocamen illud assumpseris: crede michi, te in huius electionem nominis futurorum ordinatrix et prescia dei manus ad designationem etiam vite quam transigis sine dubitatione perduxit.

11   Interpretatur enim Ieronimus 'visio pulcritudinis' vel 'diiudicans locutiones'; 'ieron' autem, unde et Ieronimus dici potest, 'timor' vel 'peregrinatio,' 'timidus' vel 'peregrinus' iuxta sacrarum litterarum

12   interpretem dicitur importare. Videamus ergo, si placet, cum mundum fugiens, prout sepius dictum est et persepe dicendum, ad deum per iter religionis te converteris, an interpretationes iste tibi conveniant. Que namque pulcrior visio quam mentis intuitum de feditate terrena dirigere in celum, pro corruptibilium amore diligere et considerare perpetua, pro gravantibus elevantia proque transitoria creatura creatorem deum totis affectibus contemplari?

13   O visio pulcra, visio speciosa, visio salutaris! Hactenus videbas vitia, nunc virtutes; hactenus vana, nunc solida; hactenus gravantia animam et deprimentia sensum, nunc vivificantia mentem vides.

14   Denique stabas in mundo quasi civis et incola totus in terrenorum amore submersus. Nunc autem te viatorem agnoscens cepisti te gerere peregrinum in terris et de timore servili, si quis in te tunc erat quo peccator dei iudicium metuebas, ad timorem dilectionis

made a better choice when you changed your manner of life, cast off stupidity, triumphed over the world by choosing holy religious life, and chose henceforth to be called *Girolamo*.

Let us not mention that you took that name out of the devo- 10 tion that you always had to that holy scholar, Jerome, whose labors illuminated the church and, by the gift of a translation not human but divine, handed down to us in brilliant style the truth of the sacred scriptures. Believe me, God's prescient hand, the arranger of future events, certainly led you to the choice of this name, even to the designation of the life you are now leading. For *Girolamo* 11 means "vision of beauty" or "discriminating between words." *Girolamo* can also be derived from *ieron*, which is said to signify "fear" or "pilgrimage," "timid" or "pilgrim" according to the interpreter of sacred literature.[5] Let us see, then, if you please, whether these 12 interpretations apply to you, as you are fleeing the world and (as has often been said and must be repeated very often) turning to God along the path of religious life. What is a more beautiful vision than to direct the mind's gaze away from earthly filth up to heaven; to love and ponder the eternal instead of loving the corruptible; to contemplate with all our feeling what edifies instead of what weighs down, and God the Creator instead of his transitory creature? O beautiful vision, handsome vision, vision that brings 13 salvation! You once saw vices, now you see virtues; you once saw empty things, now you see solid; you once saw things that weigh down the soul and oppress the senses, now you see things that enliven the mind. Finally, you stood in the world as a citizen and 14 inhabitant totally immersed in the love of earthly things. But now, recognizing that you are only a traveler, you have begun to behave as a pilgrim on earth. Moving from a servile fear (if there was any fear in you then that made you, a sinner, worry about the judgment of God) to a fear originating in love and reverence, you have

et reverentie, quod declarat religionis electio, te ad deum, crea-
15 torem et redemptorem tuum, laudabiliter convertisti. Unde et
peregrinus et timidus dici non solum condicione nature sed dispositione mentis proculdubio merearis. Et, ne etiam rationem iu-
dicantis locutiones effugias, quis nescit quod, cum mundum se-
quebaris, quasi eunuchus Ethiops thesauris prepositus legens
scripturas non intelligebas vel forsan intelligens (quod est longe
deterius) negligebas? Nunc vero religioni deditus incepisti denique
16 de scripturis salutem nostram evangelizantibus iudicare. Vere Ieronimus, ut ad Grecum veniam, unde et hoc vocabulum derivatur
(dicitur enim hoc nomen a 'iera,' 'sacra,' et 'nomos,' 'lex' vel 'regula,'
quasi 'sacra lex' 'regula'), quod autem vite quam elegisti vocamen
est aptius quam ut sacra lex et sacra regula vocitetur?

17 Ad te igitur, cuius vite progressum et ab initio datum et assumptum denique nomina tam clare tamque perspicue propheta-
runt, libellus iste dirigitur, cuius prima pars mundum quem
18 amabas et tuas stulticias longiuscula disputatione discussit. Nunc
ad id quod eligendum instituisti sermo flectendus est, quod proximo libello perficiam. In quo de deo, quem super omnia sequendum ducis, de beatitudine et de religione tractabo, in qua semina-
tus voluntate tua cecidisti in terram bonam et dabis fructum in
tempore tuo, fructum quidem non trigesimum solum, quem dant
communiter Christiani, neque sexagesimum, qui convenit clericis,
sed centesimum, qui debetur sine dubio religiosis.

19 Unum autem obtestor et tibi et omnibus in quorum manus ista
pervenerint, aperte denuntio me verborum meorum seriem ad
illam proprietatem quam modernorum sophystarum requirit
subtilitas nullatenus astrinxisse. Non itaque de hoc vel invidia vel

laudably turned to God, your Creator and Redeemer—this is what the choice of religious life proclaims. Therefore, you truly 15 deserve to be called both a pilgrim and timid, not only in terms of natural circumstances, but also because of mental disposition. And (lest you escape an explanation of "discriminating between words") who doesn't know that, when you were following the world, like the Ethiopian eunuch in charge of the treasury, you read the scriptures without understanding them?[6] Or perhaps you understood them but disregarded them, which is far worse. Now, however, you have devoted yourself to religious life and begun at last to make judgments about the scriptures that announce the good news of our salvation. To come to the Greek, from which *Girolamo* 16 is also derived: this name comes from *iera* ("holy") and *nomos* ("law" or "rule"), so that the meaning is "holy law" or "rule." And what name is more fitting for your chosen way of life than for it to be called *holy law* or *holy rule*?

This book is directed to you, then, whose life's progress the 17 names—both the one given at birth and the one assumed later in life—so clearly and transparently foretold. In a rather long disputation, the first part dealt with the world you used to love and with your stupidities. Now the discussion must turn to what you 18 determined must be chosen; I will accomplish this in the following book. There I will write about God, whom you believe must be followed above all things, about blessedness and religious life. This is the life in which you have been willingly sown; you have fallen into good soil, and you will bear fruit in your season—indeed, not only thirtyfold (which Christians commonly bear), not sixtyfold (which applies to clerics), but a hundredfold (which certainly belongs to religious).[7]

But there is one thing I testify to before both you and all into 19 whose hands this book comes: I openly declare that in no way have I joined together my string of words to that level of proper usage required by the subtlety of modern sophists. And so neither

altitudo sive potius exquisitio moderna contendat. Pingui quidem, ut aiunt, Minerva agimus gaudens potius rerum veritatem sub improprietate verborum attingere quam sententiarum inops inter

20 illas terminorum angustias laborare. Nec curet lector verba requirere cum quid sentiamus possit facile iudicare. Ad ultimum, quia de deo michi futurus est sermo, qui quidem inenarrabilis est et de quo, ut alicubi Cicero inquit, melius quid non sit quam quid sit dixerim, et rerum et verborum curam simul habere non potui.

21 Velit ille qui rictus et labra rudentis aselle in editionem vocis humane composuit quod ita vere aliquid de rebus tam arduis promam quam devote et religiose ad ista dictanda perveni, quod quidem ipse sua misericordia, quantum spero, perficiet, si tamen tu et alii confratres tui me fueritis devotissimarum orationum favoribus prosecuti.

Explicit prohemium secundi libri
De seculo et religione
Colucii Pyeri de Stignano.
Nunc autem liber secundus incipit feliciter.

: I :

De deo quem diligere debemus.

1 Fugisti, mi Ieronime (tantum in te divina gratia valuit), carnem, mundum, et diabolum, que tria mors sunt, et deum sequeris, pa-
2 trem, filium, et spiritum sanctum, qui tres vita sunt. Et, ut aliquid

envy nor modern heights (or rather, exquisiteness) of eloquence should argue with that. I am acting with fat Minerva, as they say,[8] rejoicing rather to touch on the truth of the subject matter with improper words than to labor, devoid of ideas, amid the narrow confines of terminology. Let the reader not trouble to ask for words when he can easily enough judge what we think. Finally, my disquisition will be about God, who is ineffable; as Cicero says somewhere, it is better that I say what is not true of him than what is.[9] For this reason, I was unable to take pains about both substance and words at the same time. May the One who fashioned the jaws and lips of a braying ass for the production of human speech[10] be willing that I utter something true about matters so difficult to the degree that I have approached my material with devotion and piety. Indeed, he himself will accomplish this by his mercy (as I hope), if you and your confreres attend me with the favor of your most devoted prayers.

Here ends the proem of the second book
On the World and Religious Life
by Coluccio di Piero of Stignano.
Now the second book begins.

: I :

On God, whom we ought to love.

You have fled, dear Girolamo—divine grace has had so much power within you—the flesh, the world, and the devil, which three are death; you are following God, Father, Son, and Holy Spirit, which three are life. And, to communicate something of

de hoc quem decrevisti querere quique finis est omnium referamus, quamvis inenarrabilis sit nichilque possit dignum expres-
sione tante maiestatis mortalitatis nostre viribus cogitari, si essentiam queris, unus est; si personas, trinitas est; si principium, a
nullo est; si existentiam, ante omnia est; si magnitudinem, immen-
sus est; si altitudinem, excelsus est; si circumscriptionem, infinitus
est; si rerum causam, prima et summa causa est; si gubernationem,
3 omnia regens est. Et denique hic solus est sine principio, sine fine,
principium quidem quod a nullo existens in se ipso est, ex quo
omnia sine diminutione substantialitatis, in quo omnia sine de-
fectu simplicitatis, et per quod omnia sunt sine accessione mutabi-
litatis; principium sine principio et finis sine fine, essentiaque tam
eterna tamque vera ut, quod vix extimari potest, nec ordine nec
tempore nec natura nec aliqua alia, que in mentem humanam ca-
dere valeat, ratione possit intelligi, vel etiam cogitari quomodolibet
non fuisse et, quod non sine quadam pugna verborum dicitur, ante
se nec nichil nec aliquid presupponat; actus purissimus formaque
solummodo per se subsistens, nedumque sine materia sed in nullam prorsus introducenda materiam nullique in ratione composi-
tionis permiscenda substantie; cui soli esse sicut essentia simul est.
4 Sed quid conor hoc pauciloquio ineffabilem illam maiestatem ex-
primere quam in hac corporee nostre molis densitate nec intelligere possumus nec videre? Nam postquam intellectu nostro non
capitur, nullis proculdubio inventionis humane vocabulis explica-
5 tur. Non igitur frustra sulcabo litus aratro nec aquam in mortario
conabor atterere. Sufficiat enim tibi et michi de deo scire quod
sit, et quod nichil eorum sit que intelligimus vel videmus, et non
solum aliquid tale quod maius eo nequeat cogitari sed omnino

this One whom you have decided to seek, who is the end to which we refer all things, I will say the following. Although he is ineffable, and nothing could be thought by our mortal powers that would be worthy to express such great majesty, if you seek his essence, he is one; if persons, he is a Trinity; if a beginning, he has none; if his existence, he exists prior to all things; if his magnitude, he is unbounded; if his height, he is most high; if his circumference, he is infinite; if the cause of things, he is the first and supreme cause; if governance, he is the ruler of all. Finally, he 3 alone is without beginning, without end, indeed the beginning that exists in itself from no other; out of which all things are, without diminishing his substance; in which all things are, without taking away from his simplicity; and through which all things are, without giving him mutability. God is the beginning without beginning and the end without end; an essence as eternal as it is true. Consequently (and this can scarcely be reckoned), God can be understood by no order, time, nature, or any other concept that falls within the scope of the human mind. He can't even be thought in any way *not* to have existed:[11] he presupposes neither nothing nor something before himself (this can only be expressed in a kind of struggle against words). God is the purest act and form subsisting only through itself, form not only without matter but not even destined to be introduced into any matter or mixed in any scheme of composition with any substance. He alone has being and essence simultaneously. But why am I trying to express 4 in my brief account that ineffable majesty that we, in this density of our bodily mass, can neither understand nor see? For since it is not grasped by our intellect, it is certainly not explained by any words of human invention. Therefore, I will not fruitlessly plow 5 the beach or try to grind water in a mortar. Let it be enough for you and for me to know that God exists, and that he is none of those things that we understand or see; he is not only of such a kind that something greater than he cannot be conceived,[12] but it

quantum et quale cum hac mortalitatis nostre sarcina cogitari non potest.

6   Nec simus de numero insipientum de quibus propheta ait, 'Dixit insipiens in corde suo, "non est deus."' Nam si creatura est, sicut videmus, proculdubio creator est, licet non videamus. Si motum est, quod cernitur sensu, nemini dubium quin sit et motor, quod solum percipimus intellectu; cumque nichil se ipsum deducat in esse, postquam aliquid esse videmus, nonne aliquid semper per se fuisse necessarium est, a nullo necessitatem habens, necessa-

7   ria cuncta necessitans? Quod si omnia que sunt comparari adinvicem possunt et est de ipsis dicere, 'hoc maius et nobilius isto est,' ergo aliquid omnium maximum est, maxime ens et maxime verum, et cum omnia que sunt sive naturali sive voluntario motu ad finem aliquem dirigantur et appetant illum ultimum omnium voluntatum et motuum et denique finium finem summe desiderabilem quem nos appetere sine dubitatione sentimus, credere nichil fore inanis dementie et dementis inanitatis est. Et quoniam om-

8   nium ratione degentium consensu firma mentibus nostris inhesit opinio necnon ratio ipsa concludit vim aliquam esse que retribuat omnibus secundum iusticie mensuram ne peccata donentur impunitate peccantibus vel bona sine retributione debita dimittantur, cumque hoc nulli prorsus creature competat usurpatione, natura, consuetudine, vel consensu, nonne oportet, nisi desipere voluerimus, confiteri aliquam super omnes creaturas increatam esse substantiam, ministratricem, iusticie, cuncta cernentem ne decipi pos-

9   sit et omnia iustissime iudicantem? Est igitur deus omnium creator et motor manifeste ex eo quod aliquid sit, per se necessarium quiddam, aliunde necessitatem non habens, omnium entium

is even altogether impossible to conceive of his magnitude and nature with the burden of our mortality.

We must not be among the ranks of the foolish about whom 6 the prophet says, "The fool said in his heart, 'There is no God.'"[13] For if there is a creature, as we see, there is beyond a doubt a Creator, even though we do not see him.[14] If there is something moved (this we discern by the senses), no one doubts that there is also a Mover (this we only perceive with the intellect). And since nothing leads itself into being, when we see that something exists, surely it is necessary, is it not, that something always existed through itself, experiencing no constraint from any thing, but constraining all necessary things? And if all things that exist can be 7 compared with one another and it can be said about them that "this is greater and nobler than that," there must be a greatest thing of all, something existing the most and the most true. And since all things that exist are directed to a certain end by either natural or willed motion, and seek that highly desirable final end of all wishes and movements and ends, which doubtless we believe we are seeking, to believe that there is nothing is a mark of inane craziness and crazy inanity. By the consensus of all who live ratio- 8 nally, a firm opinion has established itself in our minds, and reason itself has concluded, that there is a force that repays everyone according to the measure of justice, lest sinners be pardoned with impunity for their sins or good deeds be passed by without due recompense. Absolutely no creature is capable of this, by usurpation, nature, custom, or agreement. We must, then, confess, must we not (unless we want to play the fool), that there is some uncreated substance above all creatures that administers justice, seeing all things so that it is incapable of being deceived, and judging everything with utmost justice? Therefore, God, the Creator and 9 Mover of all things, manifestly exists from the fact that anything exists; he is something necessary per se, not having any necessity

et omnium que vera sint et maxime ens et maxime verum, finis in quem omnia referuntur, quodque omnia regat et iudicet, ut qui hoc ausu sacrilego negare voluerit, si sibi ipsi constiterit, necesse sit eum negando desipere et desipiendo negare.

10   Hic est, mi Ieronime, verus rex et verus dominus, cuius imperium leve est et iugum suave, suave quidem subire volentibus et leve, sicut decet, cupientibus obedire. Hic est qui nos diligit non propter se, qui fons plenitudinis et omnis sufficientie est, sed solum infinita bonitate sua, ut, sicut esse, sic et gloriam suam extendat ad nos, ut in ea ipso summo et beatifico bono in future eternitatis societate fruamur, ut nos hoc modo non diligat nisi propter nos, a nobis tamen diligendus tum maxime propter se, tum etiam propter nos; propter se quidem diligendus quia summum bonum est, propter nos autem ut gratie sue beneficio, qua prevenimur tam in actibus elicitis quam imperatis, perficiamur in lumine vultus sui et, ut Cicero ait, evo sempiterno fruamur et in continua sue essen-
11   tie influentia conservemur. O mens ceca mortalium! Deus qui nostri non indiget (tanta est sua bonitas), nos diligit; homo vero, cum in omnibus deo indigeat (tanta est nostra perversitas), deum non amat.

12   Ille a nobis offensus, ut nos ab hoste liberaret antiquo, tantum nos dilexit quod in persona filii, non personam hominis sed humanitatem accipiens, de sublimi divinitatis gloria ad infimam nostre mortalitatis obscuritatem se inclinavit, et illam summam beatitudinem salva divinitatis maiestate, que mutationi non subest in

imposed from elsewhere. Of all that exists and of all that is true, God is the most fully existing and most true; he is the end to which all things are referred; he is what rules and judges all things. Whoever with sacrilegious rashness wishes to deny this and is consistent in his views must be a fool in his denial or deny it in his foolishness.

He, dear Girolamo, is the true King and true Lord, whose rule 10 is light and yoke sweet—sweet indeed to those willing to submit to it and light, as is fitting, to those desiring to obey. He is the one who loves us not for his own sake (since he is the source of plenitude and of all-sufficiency), but only out of his infinite goodness; just as he extends his being to us, so too he extends his glory, so that in it we may enjoy the highest and beatific good in the communion of the eternity that awaits us. Though God does not love us in this way except for our own sake, yet he must be loved by us as much as possible for his sake, and then also for ourselves. He must be loved for his own sake because he is the highest good, and for our sake in order that we may, by the favor of his grace (which anticipates our acts both elicited and commanded), come to perfection in the light of his countenance, and (as Cicero says) enjoy eternity and be preserved in the continuous influx of his essence.[15] O blind mind of mortals! God, who does not need us, loves us: so 11 great is his goodness. But humankind, although it needs God in everything, does not love God: so great is our perversity.

God, although offended by us, loved us so much that in the 12 Person of his Son, he took on the person not of a man but of humanity, in order to free us from the ancient Enemy. He bent down from the sublime glory of his divinity to the low obscurity of our mortality, and exchanged the pinnacle of beatitude for the misery of our condition, as a result of the fact that the Word was made flesh (the majesty of his divinity, however, remained intact,

unigeniti sui persona, ex eo quod verbum caro factum est, in nos-
13 tre condicionis miseriam commutavit. Et sic creator creatura factus
non solum corporis nostri fastidia sed proditionis osculum, ludi-
bria, flagella, falsas accusationes, et crucis penam ac damnationis
ignominiam passus est; passus quidem innocens pro nocentibus,
dominus pro servis, creator pro creaturis, offensus pro offensori-
14 bus, et iustus pro iniustis. Et in humanitate quam accepit de patria
taliter in exilium venit quod mortis sue misterio ac resurrectionis
beneficio nos ab exilio revocavit in patriam et a iuste indignationis
ira reconciliavit in gratia, necnon clausas inferni portas in glorie
sue potentia frangens sanctorum patrum animas de carceris illius
obscuritate, aditum celorum aperiens, in eterne beatitudinis lu-
15 mine collocavit. At nos miseri mortales, vere vasa iniquitatis et ire,
post tot beneficia creationis, redemptionis, et gratie, in tanta mentis cecitate versamur quod adhuc deum glorie non cognoscimus
sed nostris gaudentes malis eidem in future nostre damnationis
sententiam adversamur.

: II :

De futuri seculi gloria.

1 Nec cogitamus miseri mortales, deum in nostrum exitium offen-
dentes, qualis et quanta futura sit illa glorie beatitudo cum per
creati luminis claritatem purgatis intellectus nostri nebulis et de
statu nostre condicionis mirabiliter elevati, increati et eterni luminis intelligendo facti participes, omnibus eius sine termino et sine

not undergoing change in the Person of his only-begotten Son).
Thus, the Creator, having become a creature, suffered not only the   13
discomforts of our body, but also the kiss of betrayal, mockery,
beatings, false accusations, the punishment of the cross, and the
ignominy of condemnation; indeed, the Harmless suffered for the
harmful, the Master for the slaves, the Creator for the creatures,
the offended One for the offenders, and the just One for the unjust. In the humanity he took on he went from his homeland into   14
exile in such a way that by the mystery of his death and the gift of
his resurrection he called us back from exile into our homeland
and, after the anger of just indignation, reconciled us in his grace.
In the power of his glory he shattered the closed gates of hell and
opened access to heaven, and taking the souls of the holy fathers
out of the darkness of that prison, he set them in the light of eternal blessedness. But we wretched mortals, truly vessels of iniquity   15
and wrath, after so many gifts of creation, redemption, and grace,
wander in such great mental blindness that we do not yet recognize the God of glory, but, rejoicing in our wicked deeds, we oppose him, bringing upon ourselves the sentence of our future
damnation.

: II :

The glory of the future age.

We wretched mortals do not consider, as we offend God to our   1
own destruction, the nature and magnitude of the bliss of that
future glory, when, the clouds of our intellect cleansed by the clarity of created light and ourselves wonderfully raised from the state
of our condition, made participants in the uncreated and eternal
light by our understanding, we will perpetually enjoy everything

2 fine beatifica illa divina essentia perfruemur. O felicem qui in illa recipietur! Videbit enim actualem future eternitatis sue statum nullius rei indigum, non solum necessaria (si qua beatis imminere potest necessitas) ministrantem sed ad satietatem usque voluntatem eius, quocunque se flexerit, repleturum. In quo sempiterna repletus leticia et totis viribus in perfectam caritatem effusus nichil

3 timere valeat vel dolere. Videbit enim quicunque per baptismalis regenerationis donum et in fide viva dei filius factus iuxta meritorum mensuram in illa felicitate receptus erit, opes atque divitias — non istas fragiles et fugaces quas insipientis vulgi nimium admiratur inscitia queve pecunie studium habent, quibus tantum tribuit mortalium error quod eisdem putent divina pariter et humana subesse; non istas que laboriose queruntur, anxie possidentur, et cum dolore perduntur queve congregate cupiditatem non satiant sed accendunt — sed divitias salutis que sunt sapientia et scientia in remissionem peccatorum, et divitias gratie eius que superabundabit in nobis in omni sapientia et prudentia, et illam altitudinem divitiarum, sapientie et scientie dei, cuius incomprehensibilia iudicia et investigabiles vie sunt, divitiasque glorie dei quam ostendet in vasa misericordie que preparavit in gloriam.

4 Illic videbit veram gloriam — non istam que in vana popularis aure celebritate consistit, anxia, fallax, instabilis, et incerta, et que plerumque in decepti vulgi fundatur errore — sed illam que ab omnium rerum infallibili cognitore deo, a cuius prescientia et beneplacito, sicut ex vera causa, omnis rerum et essentia et perfectio pendet, noscitur provenire; gloriam quidem que beatum

that belongs to the light, and that beatific divine essence without limit and without end. Happy the person who will be received in 2 glory! For he will see the real state of his future eternity: a state in need of nothing, not only supplying the necessary (if any necessity can threaten the blessed), but fulfilling his wishes, whithersoever they may turn, to the point of satiety. In this state, filled with everlasting joy and overflowing with all its strength into perfect love, he has nothing to fear or cause him pain. Whoever, through the 3 gift of baptismal regeneration and made a child of God in living faith, will be received according to the measure of his merits in that felicity, will see wealth and riches. I do not mean those fragile and fleeting riches that the ignorance of the senseless mob excessively admires, or riches that involve the pursuit of money (to which the error of mortals attributes so much power that they think divine and human affairs are equally dependent upon it); I do not mean those riches that are laboriously sought, anxiously possessed, and lost with grief, or riches that, once accumulated, do not satisfy but inflame desire. Rather, I mean the riches of salvation, which are wisdom and knowledge in the remission of sins, and the riches of salvation's grace, which will superabound in us in all wisdom and discretion; I mean those heights of riches — of the wisdom and knowledge of God, whose judgments are unsearchable and ways inscrutable — and the riches of God's glory that he will reveal for the vessels of his mercy that he has prepared for glory.

There he will see true glory, not that which consists in the 4 empty celebrity of the popular breeze — anxious, deceitful, unstable, unreliable, and generally founded on the error of the deceived mob — but that which is known to come from God, the infallible Knower of all things, on whose foreknowledge and gracious purpose both the entire essence and perfection of the world depends, as on a true cause. This indeed is glory that makes one blessed,

5 efficit, non que ex hominis inchoata perfectione descendit. Ibi erit
et honor, non iste mundanus qui nichil in honorato ponit, nisi
forsitan si hoc aliquid est quantum inflaverit nisique quod sepius
insulsi vulgi mentibus falsam opinionem meritorum ingerit et virtutis, quique plerumque aut tanto ardore appetitur quod per ambitionem de ardua humilitatis via precipitet in superbiam aut tanta
pertinacia custoditur quod de via salutis deferat in ruinam; sed ille
verus honor qui a benigno iudice deo in acceptatione meritorum
electis suis iuxta gradum beatitudinis exhibetur, secundum quem
fulgebunt iusti ut sidera, et dominus noster, Iesus Christus, accinc-

6 tus ministrabit eis in domo patris sui. Illic comprehendet rationalis creatura, quamvis finita secundum lumen intellectus, illam infinitam et incommutabilem potestatem qua deus optimus cuncta
bona disponit et regit, cui subesse atque obtemperare summa et
vera libertas est; non istas potestates terrenas que, quamvis date
sint desuper, sollicitas tamen mentes efficiunt et meticulosas, que
lictorum apparatu et circumlatis securibus formidantur et quarum
usus beatitudo non est, sed que potius per virtutem ad beatitudinem ordinantur; queve malis obvenientes nedum non beatos faciunt sed nec bonos, imo plerumque solent de bonis malos efficere
et malos in pessimos depravare.

7 Illic voluptates, non iste corporee quas communes habemus
cum beluis, que in concupiscentia carnis et oculorum delectatione
versantur, de quibus scriptum est, 'Adolescentia et voluptas vana
sunt,' et quas sibi Epycureorum grex summum bonum et omnium
humanorum actuum finem ultimum proponebat (que quidem vox,

not that which derives from the incomplete perfection of human-kind. Honor too will be there, and not that mundane kind that 5 does not put much stock in what is honored (unless perchance this is something as great as it has been puffed up to be, and un-less it is something that has often foisted a false opinion of merits and of virtue onto the minds of the tasteless mob) and that is usu-ally sought with such great ardor that on account of ambition it falls headlong from humility's steep path into arrogance or is guarded with stubbornness so great that it leads from the way of salvation, to ruin. Rather, true honor will be there, which is shown by God, the kindly Judge, to his elect, in the acceptance of their merits, according to the degree of their beatitude, in accord with which the just will shine like stars, and our Lord Jesus Christ will gird himself and minister to them in his Father's house. There the 6 rational creature will comprehend (although he is finite with re-spect to the light of the intellect) that infinite and unchanging power by which our excellent God disposes and rules all good things; and that the highest liberty, true liberty, is to submit to and obey this power — not those earthly powers which, although granted from above, nevertheless make minds harried and timid, which are feared, with their display of lictors and axes carried round about, and the holding of which is no blessing. Rather, I am speaking of the powers that are directed, through virtue, to beati-tude. The powers that fall to bad people not only fail to make them blessed — they do not even make them good. Rather, these powers tend to make bad out of good and degrade bad to worse.

Pleasures are there, not those physical pleasures that we have in 7 common with beasts, pleasures that have to do with concupiscence of the flesh and delight of the eyes. About these it is written, "Youth and pleasure are empty";[16] the Epicurean herd used to set these pleasures for itself as the highest good and the final end of

ut inquit Cicero, pecudum videtur esse, non hominum) sed tor-
rens voluptatis domini, qui ab illa summi boni infinitate et infinita
bonitate derivans in alveum voluptatum nostrarum cursum faciet
et irrumpet talique nos immutabilitate firmabit ut in illo solo
fruendo solum id velimus quod ille vult et eius voluntatem solum-
8 modo faciamus. O felicem creaturam que nichil volet nisi quod
deus vult nichilque plus quam deus dederit exoptabit, queve tantum delectabitur in iusticia et bonitate dei quod suo gradu contenta
in proximorum quamvis eminentiori beatitudinis statu non minus
9 quam in propria felicitate gaudebit! Cui dabit se videndam facie ad
faciem inenarrabilis illa personarum trinitas in unitate substantie
et illa substantie simplex unitas in trinitate persone, ultra quam
nichil desiderari potest, in qua cuncta apud nos tribus distincta
temporibus in unius eternitatis indivisa presentialitate cernuntur,
in qua veritas per se ipsam sine laboriose ratiocinationis discur-
sione fulgebit, in qua quicquid est iocundum est, bonum est, eternum est; extra quam nichil videri potest, nichil etiam cogitari, cum
ipsa sit implens omnia et continens omnia, implens quidem exis-
tentie munere, continens vero providentie dispositione; in qua denique beatis nichil triste, nichil molestum, nichil formidabile vel
incertum, sed omnia leta, omnia grata, omnia secura, et cuncta
sunt fixa.

10   Adde qualis erit electorum corporalis in illa generali resurrec-
tione condicio. Erunt enim corpora defecata, splendida, incorrup-
tibilia, levia, et taliter in agilitate sua obedientia voluntati quod,
quantacunque possit intercapedo mente concipi aut etiam ultimi
continentis spaciis designari, in instantis eiusdem articulo volun-
11 tate pene tardius quam corporibus transigatur. Erunt etiam sine
lassationis debilitate fortia, sine morborum concursione salubria,

all human activity (this indeed seems to be, as Cicero says, the voice of cattle, not of humans).[17] No, I am speaking of the torrent of the Lord's pleasure that, flowing down from the infinity of the highest good and from infinite goodness, will make its course into the riverbed of our pleasures; it will break forth and strengthen us with such immutability that, enjoying him alone, we want only what he wants and we do only his will. O happy creature who 8 wants nothing but what God wants, and who wishes for nothing more than God has given; who delights so much in God's justice and goodness that, satisfied with his station, he will rejoice in his neighbors' state of blessedness, although more eminent, no less than in his own felicity! To this person that ineffable Trinity of 9 Persons will give itself to be seen face to face in unity of being— the simple unity of being in the Trinity of Persons, than which nothing more can be desired; in which all things distinguished by us into three times[18] are discerned in the undivided presence of one eternity; in which the truth will shine forth by itself without discursive and laborious ratiocination; in which whatever is, is pleasant, good, and eternal; outside of which nothing can be seen, nothing can even be thought, since the Trinity itself fills and contains all things, filling by the gift of existence, containing by the ordering of providence; in which, finally, the blessed ones experience nothing sad, nothing irksome, nothing frightening or uncertain, but all is happy, pleasing, carefree, and fixed.

Moreover, consider what the physical condition of the elect will 10 be like in the general resurrection. There will be cleansed bodies, splendid, incorruptible, light, and in their agility so obedient to the will that, however big an interval can be conceived by the mind or traced by the spaces of the furthest continent, it is crossed in an instant by the will almost more slowly than by those bodies. The bodies will also be strong, without debilitating exhaus- 11 tion; healthy, without the affliction of disease; destined to endure

et absque mortis formidine perpetuo duratura. In illis erit color vividus, vigor inexhaustus, robur firmissimum, consortiumque
12 nullatenus onerosum. O felicem animam que non sentiet legem in membris corporeis legi sue, sicut hic percipimus, repugnantem, sed beatitudinis capacissimum corpus in immortalitatis contubernio totius mansure eternitatis die per seculorum secula possidebit! Quid illa societate iocundius, quid in creaturis tali connexione formosius, quid illa conversatione suavius?

13   Accedat et lumen illud intellectus quo nos ipsos et creaturas et, quod summe beatificum est, creatorem nostrum non fantasmate mentium, non discursu rationum, sed in se ipsis realiter cognosce-
14 mus. Adiciatur et illud, si placet, fixum et indissolubile vere ferventisque vinculum caritatis taliter incommutabili dei gratia confirmate quod, cum impeccabiles facti fuerimus, nedum non poterit in odium commutari sed nec etiam minimo tepefactionis gradu ab
15 intensionis sue culmine dimoveri. In illa deo, in illa nobis, in illa proximis perfruemur in tali tantaque concordia ut, quod in hoc corruptibili mundo non datur, nobiscum et cum reliquis nullam prorsus discordiam habeamus, tanto repleti cum firma securitate perpetue beatitudinis gaudio quod nulla prorsus miserie suspicione vel tristicia contingamur.

16   Pone nunc tibi, mi Ieronime et quisquis hec nostra perlegeris, ante mentis oculos mundum istum cum immundiciis et corruptionibus suis; deinde quantum potes mente convertere ad creatorem tuum et illam perfectissimam beatitudinem de qua, quia imperfecti sumus, aut perfecte loqui aut eius perfectionem mente concipere non valemus: nonne videbis ea nedum diversa sed adversa?
17 Nonne tantam contradictionem aspiciens minus miraberis apostolum dixisse, 'Adulteri, nescitis quia amicicia huius mundi inimica est deo?' Nonne videbis quod quicunque voluerit amicus esse

without the perpetual fear of death. Their color will be vivid, their vigor inexhaustible, their strength solid, and their company in no way burdensome. O happy soul that will not feel the law in the 12 physical members rebelling against its own law (as we experience here), but that will possess a body most capable of beatitude in the shared lot of the immortality of full eternity destined to last forever and ever! What is more pleasant than that society, what among creatures is more attractive than such a connection, what sweeter than that association?

In addition, there is that light of the understanding by which 13 we come to know ourselves, creatures, and (the ultimate blessing) our Creator, not in our minds' fantasy, not by discursive arguments, but in themselves as they really are. We can add, if you 14 like, the firm and indissoluble chain of truly fervent charity that is made so strong by God's unchangeable grace that, when we will have been made incapable of sin, it not only cannot turn into hatred, but cannot even be moved from the peak of its intensity by the least degree of cooling off. In that charity we will delight in 15 God, ourselves, and our neighbors so harmoniously that we will have absolutely no discord with ourselves and others (something not granted in this corruptible world). We will be filled with such great joy, along with the firm security of perpetual beatitude, that we will not at all be affected by sadness or worry about misery.

Now, dear Girolamo (and readers of my work, whoever you 16 are), imagine for yourself this world in its impurity and corruption; then, as much as you can, turn mentally to your Creator and to that perfect beatitude, about which, because we are imperfect, we can neither speak perfectly nor conceive its perfection with our mind. Will you not see that these two states are not only different, but opposed? In view of such a great contradiction, 17 will you not be amazed that the apostle said, "Adulterers, do you not know that friendship with this world is inimical to God?"[19] Won't you see that whoever wants to be the friend of this

18   mundi huius inimicus dei constituetur? Et ista considerans nonne gaudebis fugisse mundum et deo per religionis vinculum adhesisse? Fugisse profecto gaudebis, mi Ieronime, et, quanto magis hec cogitaveris, tanto magis te reliquisse mundum tota mente letabere.

19   Cavendum tamen diligenter, cum spiritus promptus sit, caro vero infirma, ne suggestione diabolica aut fragilitate carnali inter orationum tuarum honestissima vota, inter contemplationis altissimas cogitationes et optime spei sanctissima desideria, tibi mundi blandientis hostiles occurrant facies et carnalium delectationum faces irrumpant, ut quandocunque, quicquid sit, illud subeat vel obrepat, tu confestim in te reductus stupeas, horreas, teque in virtutis et religionis arcem colligas conerisque quidnam sit illud agnoscere. Insidiantur quidem vitia sub facie et forma virtutum falluntque sub specie recti, nisique peracutissimo discutiantur examine, nedum peccatores coinquinant sed etiam perfectos excecant.

20   Vidisti autem quid mundus est quem fugiendum optimo consilio decrevisti. Quicquid te ad ipsum revocat malum est; quicquid ad corruptibilia mentem allicit mundus est; quicquid te aliquid citra deum desiderare facit diabolus est. Non putes enim ex deo esse quod temptat. Intemptator enim, ut inquit apostolus, deus est. Equidem unus quisque temptatur a concupiscentia sua abstractus

21   et illectus. Pudeat igitur, pudeat, cum mortalis et immortalis sis, mortali immortale subicere, cedere carni, et non credere rationi. Pudeat quidem quia bestiarum est sensibus trahi, hominis vero, cuius facies in celum erecta conspicitur, proprium est vincere

22   sensus, dimittere mundum, petere celum. 'Arbor conversa' Greco vocabulo dictus est homo, cuius radices circa caput sunt, quo

world will be positioned as God's enemy? Considering these   18
things, won't you rejoice that you have fled the world and attached
yourself to God by the chain of the religious life? You will absolutely rejoice that you have fled, dear Girolamo, and the more you
reflect on these matters, the more you will be happy that you have
left the world with your whole mind.

Yet you must be diligently on your guard, since the spirit is will-   19
ing but the flesh is weak,[20] lest by diabolical suggestion or carnal
fragility inimical images of the caressing world accost you and the
torches of carnal delights break in on you in the midst of the honorable vows of your prayers, your lofty ruminations, and your holy
desires for the best hope. Whenever it — whatever it is — sneaks in
or surprises you, quickly return to yourself in amazement, shudder in horror, and gather yourself into the fortress of virtue and
religion, trying to recognize what that disturbance is. Vices ambush people under the mask and shape of virtues, and they deceive
under a righteous appearance. Unless they are dispelled by sharp
examination, not only do they taint sinners but even blind the
perfect. You have seen what the world is and have decided with   20
excellent counsel that it is to be fled. Whatever calls you back to it
is evil; whatever entices the mind to corruptible things is the
world; whatever makes you desire anything short of God is the
devil. For you must not think that what tempts you comes from
God. God tempts no one, as the apostle says.[21] Indeed, every individual is tempted, distracted and seduced by his own concupiscence. You should, therefore, be ashamed — ashamed! — being   21
mortal and immortal, to subordinate the immortal to the mortal,
to yield to the flesh, and not to trust reason. You should be
ashamed, since it is characteristic of beasts to be led by the senses,
but to humankind — whose face is seen to be lifted to the sky —
belongs conquering the senses, dismissing the world, and seeking
heaven. Humankind is called in Greek the *upside-down tree*,[22] since   22
its roots are around the head, with which it stretches toward

protenditur in celestia ut iam non mundo sed celo debeat coalescere; pedes autem ad peragrandam terram dati sunt. Nos contra naturam ipsos in celum convertimus, quibus superna fugientes caput defigimus in terrenis.

23 Habuisti longiore forsan disputatione quam oportuerit quid sit mundus iste quem fugis. Deinde de deo et illa incorruptibili beatitudine raptim aliquid audivisti. Nunc autem iuxta promissorum ordinem debeo te ad incepta breviter exhortari. Quod ut fiat de religione paucula disseremus.

: III :

Quam commendabilis sit religio et que vota contineat.

1 Igitur relicto mundo deum et deo frui, in quibus consistit omnis futura mortalium immortalis beatitudo, desiderans te religioni maximo atque optimo consilio (et vinculo pene necessario dixe-
2 rim) tradidisti. Cathena quidem est non illa aurea quam fabulosus Homerus de celo in terram nescio quem Iovem memorat dimisisse, sed quam rationalis creatura suo creatori desiderosa coniungi devota solennitate sue libertati et motibus ingerit voluntatis, ut se mundo subtrahat statumque perfectionis religionis dignitate professus in diesque magis atque magis proficiens in illam perfectionem redigatur per gratiam, qua illi summo et ineffabili bono in quod omnia tendunt, immarcescibilis et eterne glorie particeps

heavenly things, so that it ought to grow, not in the world, but in the sky, whereas the feet have been given for walking the earth. Against nature, we turn our feet to the sky, thereby fleeing the supernal, and plant our head firmly in the terrestrial.

There you have, in what is perhaps an overlong disputation, an account of the world that you are fleeing. Next, you heard a succinct account of God and his incorruptible beatitude. Now, according to my promised order of topics, I should briefly encourage you in your new undertaking. In order to do this, I will discuss a few points concerning religious life. 23

: III :

How commendable the religious life is and the vows it entails.

You have left the world, then, in your desire for God and to enjoy him (the two things in which the whole immortal beatitude awaiting mortals consists); in your excellent and superior counsel, you have given yourself over to religious life (and to a bond I would almost call compulsory). The chain is not that golden one that Homer the storyteller relates some Jupiter or other to have let down from heaven to earth,[23] but the one that the rational creature, desirous of being joined to his Creator, with devout ceremony puts on the liberty and movements of his own will. Hence he withdraws from the world and, having professed with dignity the state of perfection of the religious life and making more and more progress daily toward that perfection, by the grace by which he is bound to that highest and inexpressible good to which all things tend, he is made a participant in unfading and eternal glory. 1

2

religetur. A qua religatione (id est perfecta, non solum iterata liga-
tione) vocabulum illud credi potest non irrationabiliter descen-
3   disse. O felix vinculum! O preciosa cathena! O salutare ligamen!
O funicule triplex per mare, per terras, inter ignes et gladios et
quecunque pericula cogitari valeant expetende! Tu vere funiculus
es hereditatis predestinate, Iacob, quem deus sub terre repromissionis involucro priscis sanctissimis patriarchis in revelatione sancti
spiritus nuntians demum per unigenitum filium suum, Iesum
Christum, salvatorem nostrum, fidelibus declaravit.

4   Servitus etenim Israel in Egipto quid aliud commode nobis significat nisi statum, imo cecitatem gentium, que diis suis turpissime
serviebat? Quid postea transitus per desertum, ubi carnalis ille
populus in deum suum totiens murmurabat et ab eodem tanta
vanitate discessit quod taurum manu factum sibi proposuit ado-
randum, quid, inquam, transitus ille signavit nisi sinagogam cir-
5   cumcisionis, que semper idoloticis fuit permixta? Quid autem ultra Iordanem sex gentium et treginta duorum regum expugnatio
figuravit, ubi postea sancta Ierusalem et ipsum dei templum con-
structum est, apud quam demum crucis erecto vexillo mediator
dei et hominum, Christus Iesus, morte sua mortem perdens adi-
6   tum celorum aperuit, nisi Christianam religionem? Primo quidem
ibi fuit transitus per Iordanem, et hec nostra religio in baptismate
capit initium. Ibi fuit pugna cum regibus, hic vero cum vitiis decertamus et in lumine fidei fervoreque caritatis accipientes quilibet
crucem suam Christum secuti nos mundo crucifigimus, ut edifi-
cata vera Ierusalem offeramus acceptum deo sacrificium iusticie et
7   super eius altare vitulos immolemus. In hac autem Christiana religione, per funiculum terre repromissionis sicut diximus figurata,

We can believe quite reasonably that the word *religion* [*religio*] came from this "binding together" (*religatio*) — that is, the perfect, not merely the repeated binding. O happy bond! O precious chain! O tie of salvation! O triple cord, to be sought out by sea, by land, amid fire and sword and every conceivable danger! You are truly the cord of predestined heredity, Jacob, that God announced to the ancient holy patriarchs in the figure of the Promised Land by the revelation of the Holy Spirit, and finally made known to the faithful through his only-begotten Son, Jesus Christ, our Savior.

Indeed, what does the slavery of Israel in Egypt more aptly signify for us than the state — rather, the blindness — of the peoples that used to serve their own gods most disgracefully? What about the journey through the desert that followed, where that carnal people murmured so often against their God, and departed from him with a fickleness so great that it set up for itself a handmade calf to adore? What, I say, did that journey signify but the synagogue of circumcision, which was always mixed up with idols? And what did the storming of six peoples and thirty-two kings beyond the Jordan allude to, where afterward holy Jerusalem and the Temple of God itself were built; where, finally, the banner of the cross was raised and the mediator between God and humankind, Jesus Christ, by his death destroying death, opened the entrance to heaven? What, but our Christian religious life? First, there was that crossing of the Jordan; our religious life begins with baptism. There, battle was waged with kings. Here, we contend with vices, and in the light of faith and the fervor of charity, each one takes up his cross; following Christ, we crucify ourselves to the world, so that, with the true Jerusalem built, we offer a sacrifice of justice acceptable to God and slay calves on his altar. In this Christian religion, figured, as we have said, by the cord of the Promised Land, many go (according to the words of the holy

3

4

5

6

7

multi iuxta sanctorum Evangeliorum oracula eunt in villam aut negociationem suam pergentes post concupiscentiam oculorum; aliqui, quos concupiscentia carnis trahit, uxorem accipiunt; aliqui vero in superbie spiritu vocantis ad cenam servos afficiunt et occi-

8 dunt. Ex quo in hac Christiana religione aliqui religiosiores effecti quam carnalis ecclesie multitudo que deum professa mundo militat atque servit, triplici funiculo se constringunt. Videamus, si placet, an vere funiculus triplex sit hec de qua loquimur quamve sequeris mundi contagione modis omnibus expiata religio.

9 Triplicis, ni fallor, consecratione voti totius religionis perfectio continetur, sicut, iuxta dictum apostoli, quicquid in mundo est tria est: concupiscentie quidem carnis continentie votum opponitur; concupiscentie vero oculorum, que profecto pallentis avaricie est, illa felix et locuplex electio paupertatis, qua propter deum cuncta dimittimus queve sic nos in via vacuos reddit quod pleniores veniamus in patriam, sic temporalibus exuit quod induat nos eternis, noscitur contraponi; superbie autem vite quis nescit obici abdicationem proprie voluntatis et illam difficilis obedientie sponsionem?

10 O felicem qui te cognoscit, religio, qui cognitam amplectitur et amplexam constanter prosequitur usque in finem! O via nedum parum nota sed paucis, via quidem arcta, ardua, et laboriosa, deducens tamen in patriam, via quidem difficilis sed virtutis, via mortalium sed ad immortalia, via sollicitudinis sed ad metam tranquillitatis, et, quod dulcissimum est, via preter abrupta seculi

11 dirigens ad amena spacia paradisi! Tu status perfectionis, licet non semper collectio perfectorum. Tu scola veritatis, vitiorum expultrix, regula morum, cultura virtutum. Tu custos pudicicie,

Gospels) to their estate or to their business, making their way after concupiscence of the eyes; others, drawn by concupiscence of
the flesh, take a wife; and others in a spirit of arrogance torture
and kill the servants of the one inviting them to the banquet. From 8
this we conclude that in this Christian religion, some people are
made more religious than the multitude of the carnal church that
professes God, fights, and serves in the world, and that such people bind themselves with a triple cord. Let us see, if you will,
whether this religious life that we are speaking of and you are following, religion purified in all ways from the world's contagion, is
truly a triple cord.

Unless I am mistaken, the perfection of the entire religious life 9
is contained in the consecration of the triple vow, just as, according
to the saying of the apostle, the world consists of three things.[24]
To the concupiscence of the flesh is opposed the vow of chastity.
To the concupiscence of the eyes (which is really pale avarice), that
fruitful and rich choice of poverty is known to be in opposition:
by this means we leave all for the sake of God; poverty renders us
empty on the way so that we arrive fuller in our homeland, and
so divests us of temporal things that it endues us with eternal.
To arrogance of life, who does not know that the abdication of
one's own will and the promise of difficult obedience is opposed?
Happy the person who knows you, O religious life, who embraces 10
you once known, and with constancy pursues you, once embraced,
right up to the end! O way not only little known, but known to
few; way narrow, steep, and toilsome, yet leading to the homeland;
way difficult but way of virtue, way of mortals yet to immortality,
way of worry yet to the goal of tranquility, and — this is the sweetest thing — way pointing beyond the jaggedness of this age to the
pleasant spaces of paradise! You are the state of perfection, al- 11
though not always a collection of perfect people. You are the
school of truth, the expeller of vice, the standard of morals, the
cultivation of virtues. You are the guardian of chastity, the teaching

doctrina obedientie, mater honestatis, magistra sobrietatis. Tu victrix insolentie, superatrix inanis glorie, fugatrix elationis, sedatrix contentionis. Tu precepta iubes, ad consilia obligas, auges merita, aggravas delicta, et, quod super omnia maximum est, tu sola cum caritate vinculum es quo deo coniungimur et unimur.

: IV :

*Quod ad religionem confugiendum sit
et quid maxime religiosi devoveant.*

1 Ad religionem igitur confugiendum est miseris mortalibus, qui post mundi corrumpentis illecebras incedentes abierunt accepta carnali portione substantie in regionem longinquam, et a deo longe factus est incolatus eorum. Cogita quod immolavit in cruce se Christus ut redemptos suo precioso sanguine morte suscepta sal-
2 varet. Immolemus Christo nos ipsos ut salvemur in religione. Ara quidem maxima et sanctissima est hec semper cum veneratione nominanda religio, in qua non terrenas fruges sicut agricola reprobatusque, Cayn, offerimus sed sicut pastor ovium, electus Abel, primogenita gregum et de ipsorum adipibus immolamus.
3 Quid est autem agricolam esse nisi terram colere? Quid terre fruges offerre nisi deo terrenis operibus velle placere? Quid est pastorem ovium esse nisi sensus nostros, quos cum bestiis communes habemus, pastoralem curam assumentes regere et, ne vagentur bestialiter, cohibere? Quid sunt ovium primogenita nisi
4 mentium nostrarum primi motus, quos tunc deo offerimus cum,

of obedience, the mother of integrity, the teacher of sobriety. You are the victor over insolence, the conqueror of vainglory, the router of pride, the queller of contention. You command the fulfilling of precepts; you oblige people to follow counsels; you augment merits; you give weight to wrongs; and, what is greatest of all, you alone are the bond by which we are with charity conjoined and united to God.

: IV :

One must escape to the religious life.
What the religious vow most of all.

Wretched mortals must take refuge in the religious life, mortals 1 who, marching after the corrupting world's enticements and having welcomed the carnal portion of their being, have departed to a faraway land and made their dwelling far from God. Reflect that Christ sacrificed himself on the cross to save with his willing death those redeemed by his precious blood. Let us sacrifice ourselves for Christ in order to be saved in religious life. The greatest and 2 most holy altar is religion (always to be named with veneration), in which we do not offer the fruits of the earth like the rejected farmer Cain, but like the shepherd Abel, the chosen one, we sacrifice the firstborn of the flocks and some of their fat. What is it to 3 be a farmer but to cultivate the earth? What is it to offer the fruits of the earth but to wish to please God with earthly works? What is it to be a shepherd but to rule our senses (which we have in common with the beasts), assuming pastoral care of them, and to hold them in lest they wander in beastly fashion? What are the 4 firstborn of the sheep but the first movements of our mind, which

ne bestialiter efferantur, rationis moderamine continemus? Quid sunt primogenitorum adipes nisi primorum motuum sequaces actus, quos per sancte religionis ministerium consecramus?

5 Non igitur respexit deus ad munera Cayn qui terrena solum operabatur. Nam has terrenas et mundanas operas deus ad meritum non acceptat. Respicit autem dominus ad Abel et munera sua quia rationis operas, primos illos motus et ipsorum motuum opera

6 comprimentes, in acceptationem meriti deus admittit. Unde dominus increpans fratricidam quia conciderat vultus suus non dixit 'quia non placet michi oblatio frugum,' sed ait, 'Non si bene egeris recipies; si autem male, statim in foribus peccatum aderit.' Et exprimens id quod sibi vult offerri subiunxit, 'Sed sub te erit appeti-

7 tus eius, et tu dominaberis illius.' Non putemus igitur deum incorporeum percepto naribus et olfactu nidore carnium per sacrificium Abel in illa odoris suavitate delectatum, de quo teste propheta scriptum est, 'Utique sacrificiis non delectaberis: nam sacrificium deo spiritus contribulatus; cor autem contritum et humiliatum,

8 deus, non despicies.' Placuit ergo sibi pastorem Abel voluntatem et appetitum in sacrificio illo dilecto, discedendo ab omni iniquitate, quod precipuum religionis est munus, sub rationis regula compres-

9 sisse. Sacrificium quidem Abel figura religionis est. Nam sicut in illo rerum omnium principe, deo, ex primogenitis ovium et ipsorum adipibus immolatur, hoc est, ut sepius dixi, primi mentium motus et sensibiles opere consecrantur, ita sacram religionem professi deo primos mentis et ulteriores sensuum suorum affectus voluntatem abdicantes offerunt et submittunt, ut maxima vobis sit

we offer to God when we contain them by the controlling force of reason so that they do not go wild like beasts? What is the fat of the firstborn but the acts that follow the first movements and which we consecrate through the ministry of holy religion?

Therefore, God did not look favorably upon the gifts of Cain, 5 whose work was only of the earth. For God does not accept these earthly and mundane works for merit. God looks favorably on Abel and his gifts, since God allows works of reason, which restrain those first movements and their resulting works, to increase merit. Whence the Lord, chastising the fratricide for his fallen 6 countenance, did not say "since an offering of fruits does not please me," but says, "If you act well, will you not be accepted? But if you act badly, at once sin will be at your door." Expressing what he wishes as an offering for himself, God adds, "But sin's desire will be under you, and you will rule over it."[25] Let us not think, there- 7 fore, that God, who is incorporeal, perceived with nostrils and sense of smell the aroma of meat emitted by Abel's sacrifice and took pleasure in its savoriness. For about God it is written with the prophet's testimony that "You will take no pleasure in sacrifices, for a sacrifice to God is a contrite spirit; a humble and contrite heart, O God, you will not spurn."[26] Therefore, it pleased 8 God that Abel the shepherd constrained his will and appetite under the rule of reason in a pleasing sacrifice by departing from all iniquity: this is the special gift of religious life. Indeed, Abel's sacrifice is a figure of religious life. Just as for the Ruler of all, God, 9 the firstborn of the sheep and some of their fat is sacrificed (that is, as I have often said, the first movements of the mind and their tangible works are consecrated), so professed religious, giving up their own will, offer and submit to God the first impulses of their mind and the consequent impulses of their senses. As a result, the

iniuncta necessitas, cum ad aliquid movemini, non solum rationem consulere sed etiam ne deo mentiamini cautissime precavere.

10   Et quoniam non qui inceperit sed qui perseveraverit coronam accipiet, cavendum est ne post inviolande religionis ingressum, ne post illam obligatoriam sanctissimi voti emissionem, egrediamur foras in agrum, hoc est ad secularia redeamus, ne insurgat in nos

11 diaboli figura, Cayn, et interficiat nos. Qui enim in agro fuerit, id est mundi negociis deditus, gladio iuxta propheticum oraculum morietur. Nam religio munda et immaculata apud deum hec est, immaculatum se custodire ab hoc seculo. Quis autem infecto mundo poterit inherere quod mundus et sine macula conservetur?

12 Nec te seducat hostis mundus, hostis diabolus, hostis caro. Hactenus enim sic dei fueras quod tue voluntatis dominus esses. Nunc autem tue voluntatis dominium amisisti, imo apud deum abdicatione voluntaria recondisti. Cave quia, quotiens illam sine deo

13 flexeris, furti reus constitueris. Tunc autem sine deo voluntatem flectimus cum eam movendo, cum deo deficientes, ad illicita declinamus, et si contra voti limites nobis aliquid indulgemus. Noli nos, imo noli te decipere. Si mundum et immaculatum intra cordis penetralia te non servas, cum albas, nitidas, et sine sordibus vestes

14 indutus sis, ypocrita quidem es. Si ad mundum reverteris, immundus es; si extra claustrum post temporalia etiam sola mente suspiras, apostata es; si extra obedientiam dei vel regule vel prelati quomodocunque versaris, transgressor es; etiam bonum si non bene feceris, hoc est contra obedientiam, reus eris.

greatest necessity is enjoined upon you, when you are moved to do anything, not only to consult reason, but also, with utmost caution, to see to it that you do not lie to God.

The crown is awarded not to the one who has begun, but to the 10 one who has persevered. Therefore, after our entry into a religious life that must not be violated, after our utterance of holy vows, we must be careful not to go out into the field (that is, to return to secular life), lest the figure of the devil, Cain, attack and kill us. For whoever is in the field (that is, devoted to the affairs of the 11 world) will die by the sword, according to the prophecy. Religion that is pure and untarnished before God consists in keeping oneself untarnished by the secular. Who could adhere to the infected world and yet remain pure and without spot? Don't allow yourself to be seduced by your enemies, namely the world, the devil, and the flesh. Until you entered religious life, you were God's master, 12 in the sense that you were master of your own will. Now you have lost dominion over your will; better, you have buried your will with God by voluntary abdication. Watch out that you don't commit theft by directing your will apart from God. We direct our 13 will apart from God when we set it in motion while forsaking him: we incline to illicit things, and we indulge ourselves in something contrary to the limits of our vows. Don't deceive us — rather, don't deceive yourself. If you don't keep yourself pure and untainted in the inner chambers of the heart, when you have put on splendid, white, clean clothes, you are a hypocrite indeed. If you return to 14 the world, you are impure; if you sigh, even if only in your mind, for temporal things outside the cloister, you are an apostate; if you act in some way outside of obedience to God, the rule, or your superior, you are a transgressor; even if you do something good but not well (that is, you do it against obedience), you will be in the wrong.

: V :

Quanta puritas religiosos deceat et quid
varie religionum vestes significent.

1 Considera sepius, mi Ieronime, vestes quibus circumdatus es: albe
sunt et munde et in quibus vel levissima macula facile possit omni-
2 bus apparere. Talis est conspicuus gloriose religionis status. Vos
enim quodam modo in maxima luce positi et vos et maculas
vestras abscondere non potestis. Cum enim magni sitis et in arduo
constituti super alios eminetis — magni quidem quia maximi principis servi, super alios autem quia, sicut de domo domini, sic familiares eidem, et, sicut familiares, sic et super alios dispensatores
3 estis. Ex quo, quoniam omne animi vitium tanto conspectius in se
crimen habet quanto qui peccat maior habetur, notabiliora in
4 vobis delicta sunt. Scio te curiosum esse ut candorem illum et
mundiciam vestium immaculatam et sine labe conserves in oculis
omnium. Fac quod saltem non minorem curam adhibeas ut te
candidum, mundum, et immaculatum in secreto tacite mentis tue
recessu deo, quem latere non potes, et tibi ipsi cunctis temporibus
5 prebeas. Noli magis esse de perituris vestibus quam de immortali
mente sollicitus. Veterascent enim ille et una cum corpore cor-
rumpentur. Tu autem nudus hinc exiens ante tribunal infallibile
statueris, maculatus tamen tetra labe vitiorum si qua deficiendo
contraxeris, candidus vero suffragio meritorum si qua bona dei
6 gratia concomitante perfeceris. Coneris igitur tibi salubriter, imo
taliter consulere quod illuc procedas sine corrupte deficientisque

: V :

The great purity that is proper for religious.
What the various garments of religious signify.

Consider often, dear Girolamo, the garments that envelop you: 1
they are white and pure, and even the slightest spot on them is
obvious to all. Such is the conspicuous state of glorious religious
life. For you are, so to speak, positioned in the brightest light, and 2
you are unable to conceal your stains. You are great, and, set upon
a steep path, you tower over others — great because you are servants of the most powerful Prince, and preeminent because you
are part of the Lord's household, and, as such, you are his friends
and, as friends, so you are also set over others as managers of his
goods. Consequently, since every vice of character is more con- 3
spicuously criminal the greater the sinner is held to be, offenses are
all the more obvious in you. I know that you are careful to keep 4
the brightness and purity of your clothing immaculate and without spot for all to see. You should, at least, apply no less care to
presenting yourself at all times as bright, pure, and immaculate in
the secret recesses of your quiet mind, for God (from whom you
cannot hide) and your own self to see. Don't be more concerned 5
about perishable clothing than about your immortal mind. Clothing ages and is corrupted along with the body. You, however, will
depart this world naked and stand before the infallible tribunal:
you will be stained by the dark spot of vice if you have acquired
it by falling short in any way; but you will shine by the support
of your merits if — with the cooperation of God's grace — you
have done any good. Try to take thought for yourself in a whole- 6
some way, I mean in such a way that you go there without stain

voluntatis macula sive nevo, virtutum vivificantium operibus exor-
natus, et, quicquid feceris atque cogitaveris, ante omnia recordare
quod adducet te deus in iudicium pro omni errato, sive bonum
sive malum sit, ut non quod nunc tibi carnaliter in manibus tuis
versatur sed potius quid tibi spiritualiter futurum sit, cum ponet
tecum dominus calculum, et rationem reddes villicationis tue,
7   mentis indagine metiaris. Et cogita tecum has puras vestes magno
te astringere vinculo puritati. Quas mecum sepe considerans minus admiror sanctissimum illum patrem virginisque Marie devo-
tum, sanctum Bernardum, necnon sanctum Romualdum tuum
divina revelatione vidisse albis indutos vestibus scalas ascendere
8   paradisi. Aptissimus quidem iudicio meo religioni color qui semper admoneat quam immaculate sint vite nostre tempora transigenda. Significet enim licet color niger penitentie luctum et nostri
merorem exilii, sint ille permixtorum colorum et nativis intexte
lanis vestes humilitatis et abiectionis indicium, magis tamen propriam vim religionis amplectitur color albus, qui presentis vite curam et future statum magno misterio representat.

∶ VI ∶

Semper habenda professionis sue memoria
et quod maius sit meritum religiosorum quam eorum
qui citra voti vinculum operantur.

1   Sed tibi semper, mi Ieronime, versetur ante mentis oculos dies
illa meliori numeranda lapillo qua te mundo occidens ante altare
quasi mortuum protendisti. Recordare iugiter obligationis tue

or spot of a corrupt and deficient will, decked out in the works of life-giving virtues, and, whatever you do and think about, above all remember that God will bring you to judgment for every error, whether good or bad. So don't measure with mental investigation what is now happening in front of you carnally, but rather what your future will be spiritually, when the Lord will come for a reckoning with you, and you will render an account of your stewardship. Reflect that these pure garments bind you to purity by a great chain. I often muse about these clothes and wonder the less that Saint Bernard, the very holy father and devotee of the Virgin Mary, and also your Saint Romuald saw in divine revelation people dressed in white clothing ascending the ladder to paradise. In my opinion, most fitting indeed for religious life is the color that always reminds one how spotlessly the times of our life ought to be spent. Although the color black may signify the mourning of penance and the sorrow of our exile, and clothes of mixed colors embroidered with native yarn are a sign of humility and abjection, nevertheless the color white encompasses the particular force of religious life, since it represents, with great mystery, your care of the present, and the state of your future life.

7

8

: VI :

One must always remember one's profession.
The merit of the religious is greater than that
of those who act outside the bond of a vow.

Before the eyes of your mind, dear Girolamo, should always be that auspicious day on which, dying to the world, you prostrated yourself before the altar like a dead man. Constantly call to mind the contract of your obligation and the set form of words with

1

cyrographum et verba illa formata quibus te omnipotenti deo so-
2 lenni voto pie atque humiliter dedicasti. Illa quidem dies te, prius
Christianum, deinde vero clericum et sacerdotem, illa quidem dies
te deo propioribus vinculis religavit; illa, illa dies cunctos actus
tuos direxit et ordinavit in deum; illa te in bonarum actionum
proposito confirmavit; illa te in illam perfectionem evexit quam
3 humanis possumus viribus adipisci. O te felicem, mi Ieronime, si
corrumpentis mundi non revertaris ad vomitum, si, postquam ad
aratrum manum posuisti, te non converteris retro, si salutem
anime tue, imo ipsam animam, in dei obedientia continebis, si eam
4 inter hec terrena respicere non optabis. Hactenus enim ipsa in
terrenarum rerum inferno demersa tam dulci modulatione, sicut
de Orpheo fabule referunt, hoc est illa eterni dei et divine eternitatis armonia secundum quam misterio sacri baptismatis et ordinis
carathere clericalis demumque funiculo religionis deum flectimus,
apud inferos cecinisti quod ipsam inferorum duricia superata dono
recipere meruisti, lege tamen accepta quod, donec eam ab infe-
5 ris extraxeris, illam apud inferos respicere non deberes. Si enim
ipsam, ut de illo summo poeta non incongrue fictum est, aliquando apud inferos aspicere voles, tam carum donum amittes,
6 forte frustra cunctis tue vite temporibus concenturus. Recordare
igitur diem illam in qua de profundis clamasti ad dominum et
animam tuam apud terrena retentam in salutis eterne premium ad
superos revocasti. Fac quod eam taliter in celestia dirigas quod, licet retro te flexeris, ipsam adhuc non videas in inferno, et si forte
7 videris, non eam ibi videre gaudeas et amittas. Semel deo conse-
cratus es. Sacrilegium erit si te iterum converteris ad terrena. Time

which you piously and humbly dedicated yourself to all-powerful
God in a solemn vow. That day bound you, first a Christian, then 2
a cleric and priest—indeed, that day bound you to God by tighter
chains; that day directed all your actions and ordered them toward
God; that day strengthened you in your intention to act well; that
day carried you up to the perfection that we can gain by means of
human effort. How you are blessed, dear Girolamo, if you do not 3
return to the vomit of the corrupting world; if, after you have put
your hand to the plow, you do not turn back; if you hold the
health of your soul—better, your soul itself—within the bounds
of obedience to God; if you do not opt to regard your soul among
the things of the earth. Up until your profession, your soul was 4
submerged in the inferno of earthly affairs. As they tell of the
mythical Orpheus,[27] you sang a sweet song in the netherworld,
that is, with the harmony of eternal God and of divine eternity by
which we move God with the mystery of holy baptism and the
mark of clerical orders and finally by the cord of religious life.
Thus, the harshness of the shades overcome, you merited to receive your soul as a gift. But you accepted the stipulation that until
you have extracted your soul from the underworld, you may not
look back at it among the shades. And if you wish sometime to 5
look back at your soul in the underworld (as was aptly invented
concerning that best of poets), you will lose so dear a gift, and
perhaps be destined to sing in vain all the days of your life. Re- 6
member, therefore, that day on which you cried out of the depths
to the Lord and recalled your soul, held among earthly things, to
the reward of eternal salvation on high. See to it that you orient
your soul to the celestial in such a way that, although you may
turn back, you do not see it still in the underworld; and if by
chance you do see it, that you don't rejoice to see it there, and lose
it. You have been consecrated to God once and for all: it would be 7
sacrilege if you were to turn again to earthly things. Fear the

creditorem cui te indissolubiliter obligasti. Time dominum cui voluntatis tue dominium tradidisti. Time quidem eum nec sis incredibilis verbo eius. Time dominum et inquire que beneplacita sunt

8 illi. Quid autem sibi placeat sapiens admonet et propheta confirmat. Inquit enim ille, 'Si quid vovisti deo non moreris reddere; displicet enim ei infidelis et stulta promissio.' Hic autem ad votum exhortans ait, 'Vovete et reddite domino deo vestro, omnes qui in circuitu eius affertis munera.' Reddat enim, ut iubet apostolus, 'unusquisque prout destinavit in corde suo, non ex tristicia aut necessitate; hilarem enim datorem diligit deus.'

9   Quod si dederit tibi dominus (dabit enim si voles) ut voti non peniteat tui, si non in necessitatis tristicia sed in leticia voluntatis promissa persolves, non trigesimum de tui seminis, hoc est voti, largitate fructum, non sexagesimum solum, quorum ille simpliciter Christianis, ut supra commemini, iste vero clericis reservatur, sed centesimum altissime perfectionis fructum accipies, qui consuma-

10 tissimis competit religiosis. Tu enim te ipsum, voluntatem et opera tua deo religionem ingrediens dedicasti. Hoc est vere sacrificium iusticie, quod edificatis muris Ierusalem dominus acceptat cum totus homo totius redditur creatori. Hoc est vere holocaustum, id est totum exustum et incensum, in quo totum quod sumus et possumus deo committimus, et nichil in nostra relinquimus po-

11 testate. Hoc non faciunt qui sine voto solum operas offerunt, et ob id apud dei benignitatem non est dignum ipsos tantundem quantum votis obnoxios promereri. Quis enim plus gratie meretur, an qui solum fructus arboris sic superiori donaret quod ad illorum

Creditor to whom you have indissolubly obliged yourself. Fear the Lord to whom you have handed dominion over your will. Fear him, and don't mistrust his word. Fear the Lord, and seek the things by which he is well pleased. The wise man counsels and the 8 prophet confirms what is pleasing to God. The wise man says, "If you have promised anything to God, don't delay in fulfilling it; for displeasing to him is a faithless and foolish promise."[28] And the prophet, encouraging us to make a vow, says, "Vow and render to the Lord your God, all you who surround him, bringing gifts."[29] Let each one render, as the apostle commands, "according as he has determined in his heart, not out of sadness or necessity; for God loves a cheerful giver."[30]

But if the Lord has granted to you (for he will grant it if you 9 wish it) that you not regret your vow; if you fulfill your promises not in the sadness of necessity but in the happiness of willingness; then you will receive not thirtyfold fruit from the generosity of your seed (that is, of your vow), and not only sixtyfold. As I explained above, the former is for those who are simply Christians, while the latter is reserved for clerics. No, you will receive a hundredfold fruit of your highest perfection, which properly belongs to the consummate religious.[31] Entering religious life, you dedi- 10 cated yourself, your will, and your works to God. This is truly a sacrifice of justice, which, the walls of Jerusalem having been built, the Lord receives when the whole person is wholly rendered to his Creator. This is truly a holocaust (that is, the whole set aflame and burned up), in which we commit to God all of what we are and can do, and we leave nothing to our own power. Those who offer 11 only works without a vow do not do this, and on that account it is not proper that they merit as much from God's benevolence as those who are obligated by vows. For who merits more grace: the one who gives only the fruits of the tree to his superior in such a

prestationem nisi quantum sibi placuerit non teneatur, an qui et arborem donat et fructus tali condicione quod etiam post donatio-
12 nem nequeat revocare? Nemini dubium illum qui plus donaverit plus mereri; plus autem largitur qui fructus et arborem quam qui solum fructus exhibeat, longeque plus qui taliter in perpetuum donat quod retractare non possit quam qui taliter prestat quod
13 ulterius, si non velit, impune valeat non prestare. Etenim qui bonum libera voluntate facit, sicut evenit in solutis a voto, unicum bonum facit; qui vero vovet et facit, dum voto se obligat, meretur et bonum facit. Dum autem vota reddit, licet faciat debitum, nichilominus bonum facit.

14   Non enim audiendi sunt qui delirantes conantur asserere bona que sine voto fiunt his que ex obedientia voti facimus esse maiora, adducentes quod plus obligamur libera voluntate donanti quam debitum persolventi, quasi quod vovens debitor factus sit, non ex libera processerit voluntate, et quod aliquid libere promittenti nichil eo quod promiserit debeamus, et ipsum promisisse cum prestatione polliciti minus sit quam simpliciter exhibere. Errant hi profecto. Nam longe maiore caritate, que finis est precepti, vovetur
15 atque perficitur quam si simpliciter aliquid prebeamus. Cum enim consilia non nisi ex bono meliore tradantur, et per prophetam consulendo dictum sit, 'Vovete et reddite domino deo vestro,' quis audebit dicere emissionem voti, quod cunctis que postea reddimus, ac velut singulare divini cultus officium, quod latriam vocant, formaliter coexistit, quodque nostros actus, quos ad aliud non illaudabiliter secundum politicam societatem referre possemus, in

way that he is not obliged to offer those except insofar as he pleases; or the one who gives both the tree and its fruits on the condition that he cannot revoke them after the giving? No one 12 doubts that the one who gives more merits more; and the one who offers the fruits and the tree gives more than the one who only offers the fruits. The one who gives in perpetuity what he is not able to retract gives more by far than the one who offers in such a way that he can with impunity offer nothing further, if he does not wish it. Indeed, the one who does good of his own free will, as 13 happens in the case of those not bound by a vow, does a unique good; but the one who vows and acts accordingly, since he obligates himself by the vow, earns merit and does good. And when he fulfills his vow, although he is doing what he owes, nevertheless he does good.

We must not listen to those who crazily try to assert that the 14 good things that happen without a vow are greater than the things that we do out of obedience to a vow. Such people argue that we are more obliged to a person who gives of his own free will than to one repaying a debt. As if the one making a vow did not become a debtor of his own free will; as if we owed nothing to a person who promised freely for the very reason that he promised; as if the fact that a person promised, along with the offering of the thing promised, were less than simply to donate something. These people are utterly mistaken. For one vows and fulfills the vow with a far greater love — which is the goal of the teaching — than if one simply offers something. Counsels are not handed down unless it 15 be for our greater good, and the prophet counseled, "Vow and render to the Lord your God."[32] A vow formally coexists with everything that we render afterward, analogously to the singular office of divine worship that they call *service*. Moreover, a vow directs and orders our activity toward God alone (although, with regard to political society, we could render a vow to something

deum solummodo dirigit atque ordinat, nostrarum diminuat meritum actionum, precipue cum proprium voti sit voluntatem ad exhibitionem bonorum operum confirmare, quod non aliter bonum auget quam aggravetur culpa obstinata voluntate peccandi?

16   Quid autem dicent hi latratores si forte respondeam, 'Stulte, putasne tibi deum facere debitorem ex his que vel libera voluntate feceris vel ex voti necessitate persolveris, sicut obligamus nobis homines quibus aliquid condonamus? Possumus enim iuxta legis statute seriem forte ius aliquod, postquam in gratia fuerimus, nobis acquirere, simpliciter autem nullo modo nobis deum efficere debitorem, a quo sumus quicquid sumus. Quam igitur doni vel debiti similitudinem adducis cum nichil deo tantum facere possis

17   quin semper ad maiora remaneas obligatus?' Nichil deo donare possumus cuius est celum et terra atque plenitudo eius. Scriptum est enim, 'Cum omnia que precepta sunt feceritis, dicite: "Servi inutiles sumus; que debuimus facere fecimus."' Ut iam patere debeat

18   nos deum nobis non posse ex nostris operibus obligare. Si enim, ut illi volunt, deum nobis obligaremus, non iam benignitate gratie sed necessitate iusticie salvaremur. Quod quam sit absurdum non putem etiam illos garrulos denegare. Denique que cecitas est credere quod nobis deus bonis que facimus, imo que ipse per nos fa-

19   cit, sicut illi sentiunt, obligetur! Possumus per nos in actibus nostris, qui in eo quod aliquid sunt boni et ab efficiente deo sunt, agendo deficere, et deficiendo labem delicti peccatique turpitudinem contractare, quo deformes effecti deum offendimus nosque,

else and still find praise). Who, then, will dare to say that the utterance of a vow diminishes the merit of our actions, especially when it is proper to a vow to strengthen the will for the carrying out of good deeds? Since the good increases in no other way than that the guilt of sinning with stubborn will is made more serious.

What will those barking dogs say if I should reply, "You fool, do you think that you are making God your debtor on account of those things that you did either of your own free will or that you did out of the necessity of fulfilling a vow, in the way that we oblige people to ourselves when we grant them something? We are able to acquire for ourselves, according to the series of established law, a certain right after we have incurred gratitude, but in no way can we simply make God, from whom we are whatever we are, our debtor. What likeness, therefore, of gift or debt do you adduce when you can do nothing so great for God that you will not always remain obliged to do greater things?" We can grant nothing to God; to him belongs the sky, and the earth with its plenitude. For it is written, "When you have done all that was commanded, say, 'We are useless servants; we did what we had to do.'"[33] Now it should be clear that we are unable to put God under obligation to ourselves as a result of our works. For if, as those people hold, we put God under obligation to ourselves, then we would no longer be saved by the generosity of grace, but by the necessity of justice. I should think that even those garrulous persons would admit what an absurd idea that is. Finally, what blindness it is to believe, as those people do, that God is obliged to us for the good things that we do — better, that he himself does through us! We can, by acting, fall short by ourselves in our acts, which are good and a result of God's work; by falling short we can contract the turpitude of crime and sin, deformed by which, we offend God and oblige ourselves to perpetual punishment, unless we are liberated

nisi liberemur per gratiam, cruciatibus perpetuis obligamus. Bona vero non possumus, nisi divina gratia nos preveniat, preventos adiuvet, et cum adiutis usque in exitum operetur, nedum efficaciter perficere sed nec velle, ut fateri oporteat apostolicum verbum illud, quicquid sumus dei gratia sumus et quicquid ab essendo deficimus malicia nostra deficimus.

20 Habemus itaque liberum nostre voluntatis arbitrium, quo mala per nos solos in damnationem nostram agimus, bona vero nisi divine gratie auxilio freti perficere non valemus. Subiugemus igitur religione voluntatis arbitrium deo ut obedientes eidem quicquid facimus operemur ac ut bonitate sua nobis legem quam tulit observet et ad preparatum celorum regnum nos, non actores sed sola instrumenta bonorum que facere dicimur acceptando, sicut decrevit bonam electionem nostram quam sine ipso non facimus, nos 21 gratuite perducat. O felicem contractum! O vere lucrose permutationis auctionem! Religione voluntates nostras, quibus soli mortalia possumus, deo concedimus ut coexistente nobis deo vitalia faciamus. Ex hoc enim, quantum nobis minui videtur arbitrii, tantum nostris operibus vite cumulatur et meriti.

through grace. But we are unable to carry out good deeds effectively—we are unable even to wish to carry them out—unless divine grace anticipates us, assists us once anticipated, and works with us through to the end once assisted. Consequently, it behooves us to utter that apostolic dictum that whatever we are, we are by God's grace,[34] and whatever defects we have in our being, we have as a result of our own badness.

And so we have free control over our will, and by this means we   20
do ill by ourselves alone to our own damnation; but we are unable to carry out good except by relying upon the support of divine grace. Therefore, let us subjugate the control of the will to God by means of religion, so that we do whatever we do in obedience to him; and so that God may fulfill the law he decreed for us out of his own goodness, and lead us by his grace to the kingdom of heaven prepared for us—we who are not agents, but only instruments of the good things that we are said to do in accepting the grace—just as he determined our good choice, which we do not make without him. O happy contract! O gain of a truly profitable   21
transformation! By means of religious life we yield our wills (by which we, on our own, are capable of the deeds of death) to God, so that we, accompanied by God, may do deeds of life. As a result, as much as our freedom of choice is seen to diminish, so much life and merit are added to our deeds.

: VII :

Quod religiosi debeant resistere temptationibus,
quibus eos diabolus conatur a proposito revocare.

1 Sed temptabit diabolus, 'Ieronime, quid fecisti? Quid te his laboribus implicasti? Quid tue perfectionis statui per religionis vinculum addidisti? Nonne clericus, sacerdos, et prelatus eras, deo sicut et nunc etiam voto solenniter obligatus? Nolo te ad opulentiam quam dimisisti retrahere, cuius si fuisses fidelis, ut iura statuunt, dispensator, quot pauperibus profuisses, quantum placuisses deo, quantis denique incommodis caruisses! Nunc autem in simplicitate tua, vota votis inculcans, nonne ad id devenisti, ut non solum proximo, si quem sentias indigere, subvenire non possis, sed etiam, quo nichil miserius est, te pro tuis oporteat necessitatibus mendi-

2 care?' He si quando subierint animum tuum cogitationes, gaudeas diabolum electioni tue detrahere, dummodo tam sancti propositi in animum non induxeris penitere. Id enim esset post tergum respicere et ad iam salubriter dimissa, mutata in malum mente, re-

3 dire. Quid enim iuvat continere corpus in claustro si mente vagaris in mundo; quid prodest anachorite fugiendo mundi contagia, deserta petisse si subeunte illecebris mundi recordatione ad illum

4 mente redit quem corpore dereliquit? Mundum expertus mundum dimittere decrevisti. Scio te hoc non potuisse nisi quia ipsum nedum non amandum sed odiendum iudicasti. Si ergo revertatur in animum mortifera mundi dilectio recordare cur eum reliqueris,

: VII :

The religious should resist temptation, by which the
devil tries to call them back from their intention.

But the devil will tempt you: "Girolamo, what have you done? 1
Why have you entangled yourself in these toils? Why have you
added to the status of your perfection through religion's chain?
Were you not a cleric, priest, and prelate, then as now also solemnly obliged to God by a vow? I do not wish to draw you back
to the opulence you have let go; if you had been the faithful dispenser of this, as the laws prescribe, how many poor people you
would have helped, how much you would have pleased God, finally, what great inconveniences you would have lacked! Now,
however, in your simplicity, forcing vow upon vow, have you not
only reached the point that you cannot help your neighbor, if
you sense that anyone is in need, but even — the most miserable
thing there is — must beg for your necessities yourself?" If these 2
thoughts ever steal into your mind, rejoice that the devil is deni-
grating your choice, as long as you are not induced to regret your
sacred plan. That would be to look back and return, with mind
turned to evil, to the things you have already wholesomely dismissed. What does it help to confine the body in the cloister if 3
you are wandering the world in your mind? What good is it for an
anchorite, in fleeing the world's infection, to have sought deserted
places, if, with the memory sneaking into the world's enticements,
he mentally returns to that which he has corporally abandoned?
Having experienced the world, you decided to abandon the world. 4
I know that you could not have done this unless you judged it not
merely unlovable, but hateful. If, then, that death-dealing love of
the world returns to your mind, remember why you left, why you

cur ipsum odio habueris; recordare, si placet, que supra, dum in mundum inveherer, pertractavi.

5   Facile, ni fallor, ad idem relinquendi consilium reverteris diaboloque, sicut proxime diximus, instiganti tecum ipse respondeas, 'Clericus, sacerdos, et prelatus eram, fateor, et deo per votum solenniter obligatus, secularis tamen et non religiosus, ut, si respiciamus ad statum, religionem secutus, longe perfectiorem elegerim; si gradum, non ipsum religione minuerim; si votum, cum potuerim inde discedere ut huc venirem, unde separari ut ad primum redeam amodo nulla datur de iure facultas, quis hanc ultimam voti emissionem illa dicat, a qua discedere licuit, esse minorem? Vade igitur retro, Sathanas, meque perpetuo deo con-

6 iunctum sine ulteriori vexatione relinque. Nec iam paupertatem obicias, quam propter deum leta dispositione mentis elegi. Non abstuli quidem illa pauperibus sed reliqui, maloque divitias illas alium bene dispensare quam ipsas fore mecum in perditione. Nunquam enim tantum habui quantum volebam; nunquam tantum

7 dispensavi quantum debebam. Sit alius illarum arbiter. Ego autem voluntaria paupertate contentus, si proximo pecunia non prodero, ipsum tamen quantum potero devotis orationibus adiuvabo.' Hec tecum et alia plura que sancti spiritus gratia suggeret contra temptationes diabolicas pertractabis.

8   Ego autem tecum aliter agam teque ad clericatus initium et ad electe religionis principia revocabo. Responde michi, Ieronime, quando clericalem caratherem assumpsisti, fare, precor, quid

9 tecum tacitus meditabare? Quas tecum deputabas rationes? Certe noli te fallere, noli ad contegendam turpitudinem cogitationum

held the world as an object of hatred; remember, if you please, the things I discussed above, when I was inveighing against the world.

You will, I believe, easily return to the same plan of departure, 5 and you yourself will silently reply to the devil when he goads you as I have just described: "Cleric, priest, and prelate I was, I acknowledge, and under solemn obligation to God through a vow. However, I was secular, not religious, so that, with respect to my state in life, I chose a far more perfect one when I followed religious life. With respect to my rank, I did not diminish it by religious life. With respect to my vow, I was able to depart from it to come here, yet from now on, no legal means are granted to be separated from here so that I may return to the first vow: who would say that this last utterance of a vow is lesser than that from which it was permitted to depart? Therefore, get thee behind me, Satan, and leave me joined to God perpetually without any further vexation. And stop raising the objection of poverty, which I chose 6 on account of God with a happy frame of mind. I did not take those things away from the poor, but I left them to the poor, and I would rather that another dispense those riches well than that the riches be with me in perdition. For I never had as much as I wanted; I never dispensed as much as I ought. Let another be 7 their manager. I am content with voluntary poverty, and if I will be of no use to my neighbor monetarily, I will nevertheless help him as much as I can with devoted prayers." You will run through these arguments in your mind and several others that will occur to you, by the grace of the Holy Spirit, against diabolical temptations.

I, however, will deal with you differently and call you back to 8 the beginning of your clerical office and the initial stages of the religious life you have chosen. Answer me, Girolamo, tell me, I pray: when you assumed the mark of a cleric, what did you silently ponder? What arguments did you revolve in your mind? Don't 9 deceive yourself, don't use lies to cover the turpitude of your

tuarum mendaciis uti: non deo famulatum sed prebendas, beneficia, prelaturas, et episcopales infulas tibi ante mentis oculos pro-
ponebas. Nec te fefellit opinio. Obventionibus equidem pene epi-
scopus ad gradum et ordinem pontificio proximum pervenisti.

10 Fundasti itaque tue mentis propositum non in deo sed in Mamona, in divitiis, in ambitione, opulentiam temporalem carnali,
non spirituali studio, et superexcellentiam in domo domini et in

11 eius ecclesia cupiendo. Cum vero de religione cepisti tecum meliori
consilio cogitare, quid occurrebat animo, quid tuis desideriis inge-
rebatur? Certe non opes, qui dimissis omnibus que habebas paupertatem eras solenniter promissurus; non splendida et lauta
convivia, qui de copiosis mensis eras ad mendicandi victus non
frugalitatem sed inopiam transiturus; non, ut arbitror, prelaturas.
Non enim adeo futilis te puto fore consilii quod de tuorum bene-
ficiorum prelationibus, quas certissime possidebas, ad incertam
spem minoris presulatus per transigenda religionis munera te

12 transferres. Non igitur in hoc sancto tue professionis auspicio occurrit tibi nisi deus, nisi Christus crucifixus, nisi desideranda
cunctis, si non relaxate fuissent habene deliciis, egestatis militia,
continentie frenum, et obedientie iugum, ut sic, deo conciliatus
Christoque coniunctus in perfectione caritatis, non opera mortalia
sicut hactenus sed vitalia, non damnantia sed meritoria, non of-
fendentia sed deum placantia consumares.

13 O felix vite commutatio! Que cum fundata fuisset in diabolo,
radices haberet in mundo, queve carnis fimo circumdata pedes
posuisset in lubrico, fundamentum iecit in Christo, radices de-
fixit in celo, et carnis purgato contagio pedes firmavit in solido.

thoughts: you did not hold before the mind's eye service to God, but prebends, benefices, prelatures, and episcopal miters. Nor did your idea miss the mark. To be sure, almost a bishop in terms of income, you reached the rank and order nearest to the episcopate. And so you founded your plan not on God but on mammon, on 10 riches, on ambition, as you desired temporal opulence along with preeminence in the house of the Lord and in his church with carnal, not spiritual zeal. But when, with better judgment, you began 11 to think about religious life, what occurred to your mind, what was the object of your desires? Certainly not wealth, since after ridding yourself of all possessions you were about to solemnly profess poverty; not splendid and elegant parties, since you were about to pass from overflowing tables not to frugality but dearth of food, and such that you would have to beg for; not, I believe, prelatures. For I do not think that you are so devoid of sense that you would transfer yourself from the prelacies of your benefices (which you possessed with certainty) to the uncertain hope of a lesser office of abbot through carrying out the duties of religious life. Nothing, then, crossed your mind at the holy beginning of 12 your profession but God, but Christ crucified, but the military service of poverty that ought to be desired by everyone (if only the reins had not become slack through pleasure-seeking), the bridle of continence, and the yoke of obedience. Thus, reconciled to God and joined to Christ in the perfection of charity, you would bring to completion not mortal (as you had been doing) but life-giving works, not damning but meritorious works that do not offend God but appease him.

Happy transmutation of life! Your life had been founded on the 13 devil; it had its roots in the world; surrounded by the filth of the flesh, it had placed its feet on slippery ground. But now it has laid its foundation in Christ, fixed its roots in heaven, and, purified of the infection of the flesh, it has planted its feet on solid ground.

14 Quicquid igitur suggerat diabolus, cum optimo principio saluberrimam viam fueris ingressus, non peniteat propiorem deo te per religionis fecisse ministerium, imo ad promissam observantiam in dies alacriorem te reddas et ad vota complenda fideliorem. Amat enim deus alacrem solutorem.

: VIII :

De voto continentie.

1 Et quoniam inter alia continentie votum emisisti, de cuius observatione tu solus tibi plenissimus testis eris, fac, obsecro, mi Ieronime, ut ad illud implendum te tota mente disponas, nec tantum custodias ne corpus tuum aliquo nefando concubitu polluas (omnis enim libidinosus effluxus tibi et reliquis castitatis professoribus nefandus est), sed etiam diligenter attendas ne vel sola mentis in-
2 clinatione federis. Nam quid tibi proderit si, ut inquit poeta, vix inter hec honesta colloquia nominandus,

> licet omnia claudas,
> omnibus exclusis intus adulter erit?

3 Sed quid ego poetas in testes adduco? Audi veritatem, Christum benedictum, redemptorem nostrum, quem sequendum optimo consilio censuisti: 'Ego autem,' inquit ille, 'dico vobis quoniam omnis qui viderit mulierem ad concupiscendum eam iam mechatus est eam in corde suo.' Periculosum quidem est hoc et quod pene

Whatever the devil suggests, since in an excellent beginning you   14
have entered upon a most wholesome path, do not regret that you
have made yourself nearer to God through religious ministry.
Rather, make yourself keener day by day for your promised observance, and more faithful in the fulfillment of your vows. For God
loves a keen repayer.

: VIII :

On the vow of chastity.

Among other vows you took a vow of chastity. You alone will be   1
your own best witness as to your observance of it. I pray, dear
Girolamo, see to it that you dispose yourself with all your mind
to its fulfillment. Don't limit yourself to guarding against pollut-
ing your body by some illicit act of intercourse (for every libidinous act is illicit for you and all others who have made a profession of chastity), but also take diligent care lest you be soiled by
mental inclination alone. For what will it benefit you if (as the   2
poet, scarcely to be mentioned by name in this respectable discussion, says),

> though you close all gateways,
> with all shut out, there will be an adulterer within?[35]

But why am I bringing in poets as witnesses? Listen to the Truth,   3
blessed Christ, our Redeemer, whom, with excellent counsel, you
decided ought to be followed: "But I say to you," he said, "that
anyone who looks at a woman with lust has already committed
adultery with her in his heart."[36] This is perilous indeed, and
something one is scarcely able to avoid. For this reason, it is all the

vitari queat, eoque cautius et diligentius, imo fortius superandum
4 aut, si id minus successerit, fugiendum. Scio enim et multos ipse
cognosco qui, cum humiles sint, iusti, deum timentes, et, ut omnia
simul colligam, boni, boni, inquam, non illa bonitate perfecta ad
quam paucissimi pervenerunt, sed ita boni sicut in communi usu
locutionis habetur, adeo tamen violenter impetu libidinis rapiun-
tur, adeo venereis concutiuntur illecebris quod ferme se continent
5 quin labantur. Audivique multorum sanctorum patrum, quos castitatis et pudicicie creditum est fuisse cultores, frequentes extitisse
sermones, 'Non audeo me virginem dicere cum tamen nesciam cur
6 id non debeam affirmare.' Et certe nedum modeste sed circum-
spectissime dictum est illud. Nichil enim mundius, nichil delicatius virginitate, nichilque custodiri difficilius; unica quidem etiam
levi impressione violatur.

7   Nulla autem temptatio libidine blandior, nulla frequentior, nullaque nobis intestinior. Nam, ut inquit apostolus, 'Omne peccatum, quodcunque fecerit homo, extra corpus est. Qui autem forni-
catur in corpus suum peccat.' Nulla etiam temptatio maior aut
infestior, qua spiritu sancto plenus et raptus usque ad tertium celum apostolus ipse non caruit. Adest enim semper stimulus carnis
8 nobis. Cum reficimur, alitur; cum quiescimus, excitatur; somnis
admiscetur, inter orationes irrumpit, contemplationibus se ingerit,
solis adest, sociatos invadit, per oculos intrat, auditu concitatur,
odoratu fovetur, gustu gignitur, tactu consumatur, et pravarum
delectationum recordatione adeo violenter plerumque movetur
quod multorum annorum castimoniam uno momento pervertit.

more carefully and diligently — better, all the more strongly — to be overcome, or, if one is not so successful, to be fled. I know of, and have made personal acquaintance of many who, although they are humble, just, God-fearing, and, in sum, good — good, I say, not with that perfect goodness that only a very few attain, but good in the usual sense of the word[37] — nevertheless are so violently seized by attacks of desire, so shaken by sexual enticements that they can hardly prevent themselves from succumbing. And I have heard that many holy fathers, who are believed to have been cultivators of chastity and modesty, frequently said, "I don't dare to call myself a virgin, though I don't know why I ought not to make that assertion." And certainly they say that not only with modesty, but also with great circumspection. Nothing is purer, nothing more delicate than virginity, and nothing more difficult to protect; indeed, it is violated by even a single slight mark.

There is no temptation more wheedling than lust, none more persistent, none more internal to us. For, as the apostle says, "Every sin that a person commits is outside the body. But the fornicator sins against his own body."[38] No temptation is greater or more threatening than the one of which the apostle himself, filled with the Holy Spirit and borne up all the way to the third heaven, was not free. The goad of the flesh is always with us. When we are refreshed, it is nourished; when we rest, it is excited; it is mixed into our dreams; it barges in on our prayers; it obtrudes itself upon our contemplation; it is present when we are alone and attacks us when we are in company; it enters by the eyes, is roused by the hearing, is fostered by smell, is generated by taste, and is consummated by touch; it is generally set in motion so violently by the recollection of base pleasures that in one moment it overturns the chastity of many years.

9   Hunc igitur continuum hostem, imo carnis inimice blandum et continuum telum, fac expugnes, fac superes, fac saltem quod fugiendo devites. In reliquis pugnationibus ignominiosum est fugere; in hac vero, quam cum libidine pugnam conserimus, cum periculosum sit resistere, amplissimus et certus triumphus est incolu-

10   mem invictumque fugisse. Pessundanda superbia est, comprimenda ira, extinguendus ignis invidie, eludenda gula, exagitanda accidia, spolianda avaricia; luxuria vero aut expugnanda, quod periculosum est et pene per omnes aliorum vitiorum victorias obtinendum, aut, quod tutius est, etiam timide fugienda.

11   Hec est enim illa membrorum inobedientium lex que rationi repugnat, in carne nostra militat, et adeo ferociter mentes nostras invadit quod maximo cum ipsa periculo dimicetur. Hec est illa pestis que filiis dei prima etate cum filiabus hominum concumbentibus in maximam divine maiestatis offensam, paucis servatis in

12   arca, diluvio maximo carnem omnem extinxit. Hec ex opulentia nascens Pentapolim celestis ignis imbre succendit. Hec ex ebrietate proveniens permixtum filiabus Loth corrupit, quique mundus perseveravit in Sodomis pollutus est incestuoso concubitu tam turpi-

13   ter in montanis. Hec pulcritudine Dyne conflata regem Hemor, Sichen, filium eius, et omnem suam familiam atque credulam et infelicissimam civitatem iam die tertio circumcisam in gladiis Simeontis et Levi, filiorum Iacob, crudeli cede vastavit. Hec temulentie permixta ferocissimum Holofernem sancte Iudith victimam

14   prebuit. Hec fraterna periturum cede Amon, David filium, Thamar sorori permiscuit. Hec Bethsabee, Urie coniugem, in solario visam ad pulvinaria regis non absque scelerata sequentis prodi-

15   tionis et homicidii cumulatione perduxit. Hec sapientissimum

See to it, therefore, that you rout and overcome this perpetual 9
enemy (more precisely, this blandishing and perpetual weapon of
the inimical flesh); at the very least, see to it that you avoid it by
flight. In other battles it is ignominious to flee. In this one, however, that we engage in against lust, it is a very splendid and certain
triumph to have escaped unscathed and unconquered, since resis-
tance is dangerous. Arrogance must be crushed, wrath suppressed, 10
envy's fire extinguished, gluttony foiled, sloth stirred into action,
avarice despoiled; but as for sensual excess, you must either conquer it (which is dangerous and barely attainable through victory
over the other vices) or (the safer course) run from it in fear.

For this is the law of the disobedient members that resists rea- 11
son, wages war in the flesh, and invades our minds so fiercely that
we are in extreme danger when we struggle with it. This is the
pestilence that extinguished all flesh by a great flood (though a few
were saved in the ark), when in the first age the sons of God were
sleeping with the daughters of men, causing great offense to the
divine majesty. This, born of opulence, inflamed the Pentapolis 12
with a shower of celestial fire.[39] This, arising out of drunkenness,
corrupted Lot when he slept with his daughters; he who persevered in purity among the Sodomites was polluted by incestuous
intercourse so vilely among the people of the hills. This was fo- 13
mented by Dinah's beauty; by the swords of Simeon and Levi, the
sons of Jacob; it laid waste King Hamor in cruel slaughter, along
with Schechem his son, his entire family, and his faithful, most
unlucky city, two days after its men had been circumcised. This,
mixed with intoxication, made fierce Holofernes a victim of holy
Judith. This made Amnon, son of David, have sex with his sister 14
Tamar — an act that was to bring about his death by his brother's
hand. This led Bathsheba, the wife of Uriah, seen on the roof,
to the king's couch — an event that occasioned a criminal heap-
ing up of betrayal and homicide. This made the extremely wise 15

Salomonem a dei sui cultura et a mirabilis templi quod construxe-
rat sanctimonia, sue sapientie oblitum, ad sacrificia gentium in
16 excelsis exhibenda mutis idolis inclinavit. Hec in Beniamin reliquas tribus armavit et triduano congressu hinc quadraginta, inde
vero viginti quinque milia virorum infelici victoria et consanguinea
17 cede delevit. Hec fortissimum Sansona, cuius mirabile robur mira-
biliori dei dispositione crinibus continebatur, infideli puelle
tondendum tradidit et in hostium potestatem multo venditum
argento coniecit, a quibus effossis oculis in ludum a carcere duce-
18 retur. Hec Susannam polluendam senibus prebuit aut iniusti iudicii sub attestatione falsissima condemnandam. Hec iustissimum
pudicumque Iosep, dum libidini domine sue fugiendo resistit, in
19 carcerem falsa vinctum accusatione conclusit. Sed quid per cuncta
trahor? Hec est illa bestia ferox que inobedientia membra colens
adolescentiam commovet, iuventutem enervat, et ipsam attaminat
ac polluit senectutem. Hec enim, quasi naturale tributum expos-
cat, sua contra rationis imperium membra movet.

20   Fuge igitur, mi Ieronime, monstrum istud beluamque multicipi-
tem, que potentissima est etiam constantissimos ad mundi fallacis
et blandientis carnis illecebras revocare. Fuge igitur eam, fuge,
precor. Cum qua pugnans tecum pugnas; in quo certamine tu ipse
21 triumphator eris et triumphatus. Et, ut ipsam fugias aut superes,
fuge quecunque possunt in te furoris illius impetum excitare. Sub-
trahe carni ieiunando cibum et Bacum sine quibus, ut in Teren-
tiano proverbio legitur, 'friget Venus.' Nunquam enim libidinem
fugies nisi simul abieceris satietatem. Quanto quidem magis epulis

Solomon forget his wisdom and turn away from worshipping his God and from the sanctity of the marvelous temple he had constructed, to the sacrifices of the gentiles, which were to be exhibited to mute idols on mountain tops. This armed the other tribes against Benjamin, and in a three-day-long engagement destroyed forty Israelites on one side and twenty-five thousand Benjaminites on the other, in an unhappy victory, a bloody slaughter among kinsmen.[40] This delivered mighty Samson (whose miraculous strength was, by God's even more miraculous plan, contained in his hair) to a treacherous girl for a haircut, and flung him, sold for much silver, into the power of his enemies, by whom he was led out of prison, his eyes gouged out, as entertainment. This presented Susanna with the choice of being polluted by the elders or condemned under false testimony in an unjust tribunal. This shut the righteous and chaste Joseph in prison, bound by a false accusation, when he resisted his mistress' desire by flight. But why am I getting carried away, going through every example? This is that ferocious beast that, fostering disobedient members, stirs up youth, enervates the prime of life, and dishonors and pollutes old age itself. For this beast, as if it demanded a natural tribute, stirs its members against the rule of reason.

Flee, then, dear Girolamo, that monster and many-headed beast that is powerful enough to call even the most steadfast people back to the allurements of the deceiving world and the blandishing flesh. Flee it, then, flee, I pray. When you fight against it, you are fighting against yourself; in this struggle you yourself will be the one triumphing and the one triumphed over. And, in order to either flee it or conquer it, flee whatever has the ability to incite an attack of its fury against you. Remove food and wine from the flesh by fasting, for without these (as we read in Terence's proverb) "Venus cools off."[41] You will never escape lust if you don't reject satiation at the same time. The more the stomach is filled by

22 venter reficitur, tanto magis furor libidinis excitatur. Fuge igitur hostiles facies, fuge mulierum aspectum, fuge quicquid visum potest illo furore mentem accendere aut in exactarum voluptatum memoriam revocare. Fuge mulierum etiam honesta etiamque confessionum secreta colloquia. Heu quotiens ornata mulier peccatorum sarcinam depositura pontificem adiens suis sacerdotem illece-

23 bris irretivit! Habent mulierum verba nescio quos voluptatis stimulos, ut, sive cum honestate proferant seria sive narrent cum iocunditate lasciva, cordibus audientium infigantur et, tanquam appositus ignis ad stipulam, soleant infectum humanis mentibus afflare calorem ingensque contra rationem incendium concitare.

24 Fuge igitur mulieres,

> carpit enim vires paulatim uritque videndo
> femina,

ut ille ait. Cave ne oculos homicidas et vagos oculis imprimat tuis. Est enim muliebris intuitus sub ciliorum arcu preparata sagitta. Eodem namque momento videt et ferit. O quot et quanti post muliebres aspectus cum poeta flentes dicunt,

> ut vidi, ut perii, ut me malus abstulit error!

25 Non solum igitur continentie voto sed abstinentia visus, auditus, et victus contra hanc venenosam venerem muniaris, ut in temptationis die aut viriliter vincendo triumphes aut saltem invictus gloriosissime fugiendo te miserrime surripias servituti.

feasts, the more the frenzy of lust is excited. Flee, then, hostile   22
faces, flee the sight of women, flee whatever, once seen, has the
capacity to inflame your mind with raving madness or evoke the
memory of pleasures enjoyed. Flee conversations with women,
even if the talk is respectable, and even if it involves the secrets of
confessions. Alas, how many times has a nicely adorned woman,
approaching the bishop to lay down the burden of her sins, ensnared the priest in her charms! Women's words contain unfath-   23
omable spurs to pleasure: whether they bring forth serious matters
righteously or tell lascivious tales humorously, these words lodge
in the hearts of their hearers; like fire placed next to hay, they have
a way of blowing an infected heat at human minds and stirring up
a huge conflagration against reason. So, flee women,   24

> for woman wears down strength little by little and burns
> by the seeing,

as the poet says.[42] Take care that she does not fix her homicidal
and wandering eyes on your eyes. The female gaze is an arrow
drawn under the bow of the eyelids. In the selfsame moment it
sees and strikes. O how many and what great men, after being afflicted by the sight of women, cry with the poet, saying,

> how I saw, how I perished, how wicked error carried me
> away![43]

Therefore, fortify yourself against this venomous desire not only   25
by your vow of chastity, but also by abstinence from sight, hearing,
and food, so that on the day of temptation you will either triumph
by conquering manfully, or at least snatch yourself away from
wretched slavery by fleeing, gloriously unconquered.

: XIX :

De voto paupertatis.

1 Exuta igitur per continentie votum carnis venenosa libidine, propter quod uxorem relinquimus, que vinculum est in hac humana conversatione validissimum atque primum, quis non videt talia vota professos relinquere patrem et matrem, quos propter uxorem primi parentis oraculo novimus dimittendos, ut sic carnalibus his 2 necessitudinibus absoluti viam domini facilius prosequamur? Verum, quia nos etiam detinent ne deo propiores efficiamur onerose divitie, ut expeditior per inceptum iter possis incedere, paupertatem voluntariam elegisti; paupertatem, inquam, que, nisi consuetudo mortalium hanc rerum temporalium inanitatem atque carentiam per paupertatis appellare vocabulum usurpasset, verius 3 deberet divitie nominari. Nam, si indigentiam volumus esse paupertatem, pluribus videmus divites egere pluraque parare quam pauperes appetant; si vero cupiditatem, cum

> crescat amor nummi quantum pecunia crescit,

ut ille ait, quis nescit divitiis opulentos cupidiosiores esse quam 4 pauperes? Sed cedamus consuetudini et hanc rerum temporalium absentiam pauperiem appellemus, quam tu perfectionis viam post Christum ingressus consultissime devovisti. Quo quid melius fieri 5 potuit? Non enim es de illorum numero qui, cum vocarentur ad nuptias, abierunt, alius in villam suam, alius in negociationem suam, sed villas et negocia tua dimittens accepisti, quod solum perfectionis est, crucem tuam et secutus es eum qui crucis subire

: IX :

On the vow of poverty.

Through the vow of chastity, venomous lust of the flesh has been 1
cast off; accordingly, we leave behind our wife, who is the first and
strongest tie in human interaction. Who does not see, then, that
people who have professed such vows leave behind father and
mother (whom we know from the words of our first parent are to
be left behind on account of our wife),⁴⁴ so that freed from these
carnal relationships we may more easily follow the way of the
Lord? But, since burdensome riches also detain us so that we can- 2
not become closer to God, you have chosen voluntary poverty, so
that you may proceed more unencumbered on the journey you
have undertaken—poverty, I say, which, should have more truly
been called *wealth*, except that the convention of mortals used the
word *poverty* to designate this emptiness and lack of temporal
goods. For, if we hold that need is poverty, we see that rich people 3
need more things and seek to acquire more things than poor people do. If we hold covetousness to be poverty, who doesn't know
that the wealthy are more covetous of riches than the poor, since

love of money increases as money increases,

as the poet says.⁴⁵ But let us yield to convention and call this ab- 4
sence of temporal things *poverty*, which you most wisely vowed to
practice when you entered on the way of perfection in the steps of
Christ. What better thing could have happened? You are not 5
among the number of those who turned away when they were
summoned to the wedding banquet, one to his farm, the other
to his business. Rather, you renounced your farms and busi-
nesses and accepted your cross (this alone belongs to perfection) and followed him who by no means refused to undergo the

supplicium pro nostris peccatis minime recusavit. Sciebas enim difficillimum fore possidendo divitias esse perfectum.

6   Paucissimis enim dictum est id quod illi patri multarum gentium, qui possedit divitias multas et dimisit Ysaac, filio suo, 'Ambula scilicet coram me et esto perfectus.' 'Beatus est enim dives qui inventus est sine macula et qui post aurum non abiit nec speravit in pecunia et thesauris.' Et, quoniam tales admodum rari sunt, subditur, 'Quis est hic, et laudabimus eum? Fecit enim mirabilia in

7 vita sua.' Ut, cum ferme sit impossibile in incerto divitiarum divitem non sperare et pauperes ipsos divitias non appetere, non immerito valde mirarentur discipuli postquam dixisset Iesus, 'Facilius est camelum per foramen acus transire quam divitem intrare in regnum celorum,' et dixerint, 'Quis ergo poterit salvus esse?' Nam si illud de divitibus solum intelligendum esset et non de illis qui vel appetunt vel sperant in divitiis, cum pauci sint isti divites, pau-

8 peres vero multi, non dixissent illi, 'Quis ergo salvus erit?' Non igitur te solum divitiis spoliasti sed, ut decet viam perfectionis ingressos, illas mente et affectibus reliquisti, elevansque in superos animum et Christum nostrum crucifixum sequendo pedibus hec inferiora conculcans illarum vincula dissolvisti, ut merito cum psalmilogo dicere possis, 'Anima mea sicut passer erepta est de laqueo venantium. Laqueus contritus est et nos liberati sumus.'

9 Ceterum iste quas tantopere miramur divitie quasque relinquere tam arduum reputamus nullam permittunt mortales habere quietem. Si absunt, desiderantur; si possidentur, cum amitti possint, metu continuo nos excruciant; si vero perduntur, in miseria-

10 rum infimum nos demergunt. Adde, cum divitias querimus, quot

punishment of the cross for our sins. For you were aware that it would be extremely difficult for the possessor of riches to be perfect.

To very few has been said what was said to that father of many 6 peoples, who possessed great wealth and gave it to Isaac, his son: "Walk before me and be perfect."[46] "Blessed is the rich man who was found to be blameless and who did not go after gold or place his hope in money or treasure." And, since such individuals are rare, it is added, "Who is this man, and shall we praise him? For he has done marvelous things in his life."[47] Since it is almost im- 7 possible for a rich man not to place his hope in riches (however unreliable) and for poor men themselves not to seek them, not without cause did the disciples marvel greatly after Jesus had said, "It is easier for a camel to pass through the eye of a needle than for a rich man to enter the kingdom of heaven." To which they responded, "Who, then, can be saved?"[48] For if that saying is to be understood as pertaining only to the wealthy and not to those who seek after or aspire to riches, since the rich are few, the poor many, they would not have asked, "Who, then, can be saved?" You have, 8 therefore, not only despoiled yourself of riches, but (as befits those who have entered on the way of perfection) you have left them behind mentally and emotionally. Raising your soul on high and trampling these lower things under foot by following our crucified Christ, you have dissolved the chains of riches, so that you deserve to be able to say with the psalmist, "My soul has been snatched away like a sparrow from the hunters' snare. The snare has been crushed, and we have been freed."[49]

Besides, those riches that we so greatly admire and that we find 9 so difficult to relinquish allow mortals to have no peace. If they are absent, they are desired; if they are possessed, they torture us with continual fear, because they can be lost; and if they are lost, they plunge us into the depths of misery. Moreover, when we seek 10

nos laboribus implicamus? Quid recusamus? Cui parcimus hominum? Nonne blandimur, assentamur, decipimus, prodimus, occidimus, et mentimur? Nec illas cum impurissime cumulamus, possumus sine macula possidere aut sine vitiorum contagio perdidisse.

11 Nec cogitamus miseri mortales contra naturam esse quod illas ad
usum omnium procreatas per avariciam in nostre proprietatis dominium vendicemus, cumque vite nostre debeant deservire, facimus illas nobis flagitiorum, voluptatum, et cunctorum scelerum

12 instrumenta. Quo magis admiror deceptos homines tanta divitiarum cupidine detineri cum, quanto magis congregate fuerint, tanto
magis impediant atque gravent, precipue quia si naturam con-
suleremus, cum ille nec nobiscum nascantur nec sint morituros
post interitum secuture, perpendere debeamus eas omnino nostras

13 non fore. Unde sapientissimus ille Grecorum, Hyantes quidem, ut
arbitratur Cicero, sed ut alii putant Bias, cum patria sua ab hostibus capta foret omnesque cum quibus poterant rebus effugerent,
consulenti cuidam quod et ipse de suis aliquid preciosius secum
ferret, cum tamen vacuus hostibus cederet, inquit, 'Ego vero id
quod suades optime facio; omnia quidem mecum porto mea,'
volens intelligi quod illa quibus onusti cives sui cladem patrie fu-
giebant eorum omnino non erant, cum ea, sicut docebat imminens
casus, facile possent amitti.

14   Deinde cur tam ardenter pecunias ludibriaque fortune concupiscimus? An quia bona sunt? Bona quidem sunt, fateor, in eo
quod sunt, sed media, et ita tantum bona si illis utamur bene.

15 Nam male utentibus mala sunt. Quis autem, cum accepit magnam
pecuniam, non simul accepit et superbiam, caput, et avariciam,
radicem omnium peccatorum? Nam et ille qui interrogavit Iesum,
'Magister bone, quid faciam ut vitam eternam possideam?' cum

riches, in how many toils do we entangle ourselves? From what do we refrain? Whom do we spare? Don't we wheedle, flatter, deceive, betray, kill, and lie? When we accumulate riches by impure means, we cannot possess them without blot or lose them without infection by vice. We wretched mortals do not think it against nature 11 that through avarice we claim those riches, which have been created for everyone's use, as our own property; while they ought to serve our life, we make them our instruments of offenses, pleasures, and all crimes. So I am all the more amazed that people are 12 deceived and held by such great desire for riches, when the more wealth has been accumulated, the more this wealth impedes and burdens—especially since if we look to nature, we should ponder the fact that riches are really not our own, as they are neither born with us nor will they follow us (who are bound to die) after we pass away. Hence that wisest of Greeks, Hyantes (as Cicero believes, though Bias, as others think), when his homeland was captured by enemies and all were fleeing with whatever things they could, said to someone who advised him that he too should take with him one of his precious possessions, "But I am doing excellently what you advise; indeed, all that I have I am taking with me."[50] He wanted it to be understood that those things with which his fellow citizens were burdened as they fled the disaster of their homeland did not really belong to them, since those things, as the imminent calamity illustrated, could easily be lost.

Then why do we so ardently desire money and fortune's play- 14 things? Because they are good? Good they are, I acknowledge, for what they are—means—and they are only good if we use them well; they are bad for those who use them badly. Who, when he 15 has received a lot of money, has not at the same time received arrogance and avarice, respectively the head and root of all sins? For even the man who asked Jesus, "Good teacher, what should I do to have eternal life?" was saddened and went away upset at the

audisset, 'Unum tibi deest: vade, quecunque habes vende, et da pauperibus et habebis thesaurum in celo, et veni, sequere me,' contristatus in verbo abiit merens.'Erat enim,' ut subditur,'habens possessiones multas.' Unde Iesus ipse subintulit: 'Quam difficile qui pecunias habent in regnum dei introibunt!' Ut manifeste videa-

16 mus divitiarum comitem avariciam fore. Et videns apostolus su-perbiam a divitibus non abesse discipulo Timotheo iubet: 'Diviti-bus huius seculi precipe non sublime sapere.' Unde et post Salomonem sapiens inquit, 'Avaro autem nichil est scelestius,' et subdit, 'Quid superbit caro et cinis?' et sequitur, 'Nichil est ini-

17 quius quam amare pecuniam.' Sed tanta cecitas est humanarum mentium tantaque perverse consuetudinis violentia tantusque in institucione vite tamque continuus error quod cum sensibus ac-quiescimus et volumus posse preclaris vestibus indui, lautis dapi-bus epulari, plusque posse ceteris aut pluris quam proximi reputari vel, ut nostris, imo incertis (nescimus enim quid in crastinum sit futurum), maximos census relinquamus heredibus, studere divitiis

18 non cessamus. Cum legimus ista vel de monitoris ore percipimus, laudamus, acquiescimus, eaque verissima fore refellere non vale-mus, sed cum oculus a legendo divertitur, cum cessat admonitor auribus insonare, in contrarium repente dilabimur et cumulanda-rum divitiarum effectibus implicamur.

19   Quod si cogitaremus duas omnino fuisse et esse debitas morta-libus civitates, unam spiritualem quam dei dicimus, alteram vero carnalem quam mundi possumus appellare, et ad alterutram ipsa-rum affectus nostros et finem nostrorum operum statueremus, occurreret nobis utramque civitatem a pauperibus institutam, a divitibus vero dirutam et corruptam. Et prius, si placet, de hac

answer when he heard, "One thing you lack: go and sell whatever you have and give it to the poor, and you will have treasure in heaven, and come, follow me." "For he had," the text continues, "many possessions." Hence Jesus himself commented, "With what difficulty those who have money will enter the kingdom of God!"[51] So we clearly see that avarice is the companion of riches. And the apostle, seeing that arrogance was not absent from the rich, ordered his disciple Timothy, "Instruct the rich of this world not to think lofty thoughts."[52] Hence after Solomon the wise man says, "Nothing is more wicked than a miser," and adds, "Why is flesh and dust haughty?," he continues, "Nothing is more injurious than to love money."[53] But the blindness of human minds is so great, so great is the impetuosity of perverse habit, and so great and continual is our error in planning our lives that when we give in to our senses and want to be able to put on fancy clothes, dine at sumptuous feasts, and be reckoned as more influential than others or of more worth than our neighbors; or in order to leave great wealth to our heirs (uncertain though these be, for we do not know what will happen tomorrow); we do not cease from the pursuit of riches. When we read those words or take them from the lips of an advisor, we praise them, we give our assent, and we are unable to refute their truth; but when the eye is diverted from reading, when the advisor ceases to sound in our ears, we suddenly slip into the opposite mode and are entangled in efforts to accumulate riches.

But if we reflected that there were and were owed to mortals altogether two cities — one spiritual, which we call the city of God, the other carnal, which we can call the city of the world — and if we were to set our emotions and the goal of our works in relation to one or the other of these, it would occur to us that each city has been established by the poor, but destroyed and corrupted by the

16

17

18

19

20 mundana civitate quos autores habuerit speculemur. Nolo, licet facile possem per cuncta regna discurrere, sed illud quod omnium maximum et fortissimum fuit et quod adhuc saltem nominis obtinet principatum, Romanorum videlicet, perquiramus. Romulus, ut antiquiora dimittam et Evandrum regem preteream, pauper fuit, nec ipsum credamus augustum edificasse Palatium, cum usque ad tempora Gallorum Senonum, qui urbem incenderunt, remansisse

21 sue paupertatis vestigia referantur. Unde et nobilis epithomator hystorie Romane, Florus, illud incendium urbisque captivitatem, Capitolii defensionem, et cetera breviloquio prosecutus hec verba subintulit: 'Agere gratias diis immortalibus ipso tante cladis nomine libet. Pastorum casas ignis ille et flama et paupertatem Ro-

22 muli abscondit.' Hec ille. Quid autem de Numa Pompilio dicam, qui, cum Romanorum superstitionum callidus atque religionificus autor fuerit, non habuit unde diis suis vasa conflaret sed, quod maxime paupertatis argumentum est, consecravit cedendo necessitati fictilia?

23 Nec de reliquis regibus multa subnectam. Sufficiat enim ultimum illum superbum Tarquinium, in cuius dicionem venit quicquid antecendentium principum parsimonia iam per ducentorum annorum curricula reservaverat. Nonne in fundatione templi Capi-

24 tolini Iovis exhaustus est? Nonne etiam idem patris Lucomonis (sic enim appellatum Priscum Tarquinium commemorant) opes et predam Suessanam et templo et aliis publicis operibus que pro qualitate temporum magnificentissima instituerat absumpsit?

25 Nonne ea res inferendi bellum contra Ardeam, tunc opulentissimam civitatem, causa fuit, et, ut inde ditaretur ac preda infestos

rich. Let us first, if you please, observe this worldly city, and what
founders it has. Although I could easily canvass all the kingdoms,   20
I do not wish to do so. Let us investigate that one which was the
greatest and bravest of all and which to this day keeps its sover-
eignty at least in name,[54] that of the Romans. To omit more ancient times and pass over King Evander, Romulus was a poor man;
let us not believe that he built the august Palatine, since the ves-
tiges of his poverty are said to have remained up until the time of
the Gallic Senones, who set fire to the city. Hence even that noble   21
epitomizer of Roman history, Florus, having succinctly told the
story of that fire and the captivity of the city, the defense of the
Capitolium, and the rest, added these words: "It is pleasing to give
thanks to the immortal gods on account of such great disaster.
That fire and flame made away with the huts of the shepherds and
the poverty of Romulus."[55] Why should I speak of Numa Pom-   22
pilius? When he, a clever and religious innovator of Romans' su-
perstitions, did not have the materials from which to make vases
for the gods, yielding to necessity, he consecrated earthenware vessels (the greatest evidence of poverty).[56]

I will not add many things concerning the remaining kings. Let   23
it suffice to mention the last one, Tarquin the Proud, into whose
power came whatever the parsimony of the preceding rulers had
preserved over the course of two hundred years. Was he not exhausted by the founding of the temple of Capitoline Jupiter? Did   24
the same king not use the wealth of his father Luco (for they relate
that Tarquinius Priscus was so named) and the booty of Suessa
both for the temple and for other public works that he had instituted, most magnificent according to the standards of the times?
Wasn't that the cause of waging war against Ardea, then a most   25
opulent city? Didn't Tarquin take up arms in order to enrich

sibi Romanos, quos ad opera servilia edificando compulerat, miti-
garet, arma movit? Ut satis aperte possit intelligi non parvam tunc
fuisse pauperiem Romanorum, ob quam bella movere finitimis
cogebantur.

26   Age vero, urbe regibus liberata, nonne P. Valerius, qui postea
Publicola dictus est quod domum, quam alto et munito loco in
summa Velia construebat, unde affectati regni suspicio fuit exorta,
diruit et infimo loco constituit, iam quater consul moriens, 'Omnium consensu,' ut inquit Livius, 'princeps belli pacisque artibus,'
licet ingenti gloria, utpote qui de superato Tarquinio triumphum
primum libere civitatis egerit et Porsene restiterit et alia plura
laude digna perfecerit, adeo pauper inventus est ut mortuo defice-
ret sumptus necessarius sepulture et opus esset eum impensa facta
27   de publico sepeliri? Quid Lucium Quintium Cincinnatum referam, qui paupertate ad ligones et aratra compulsus est, quemve
non puduit iam tunc florentem rem publicam Romanorum medie
sementis tempore ab stiva ad scipionem dictatorium et pompam
timendorum fascium circumventis in Algido monte legionibus re-
28   vocare? An pauperi liberatis exercitibus, victis hostibus atque sub
iugum missis, de solenni splendidoque triumpho turpe aut inglo-
rium visum est resignato summo magistratu, quem pro sex mensibus acceperat, ad opera dimissa redire? O virum fortem! O virum
dignum qui ad Christi tempora deveniret! Erat enim non tantum

himself from that source and to mollify the Romans with booty (for they hated the king, who had forced them into slave labor by his building program)?[57] Thus, it is patently clear that the poverty of the Romans at that time was not negligible; on account of poverty, they were compelled to wage war on their neighbors.

After Rome had been liberated from its kings, take the case of 26 Publius Valerius, who was later was called *Publicola* because he destroyed and reestablished in a low place the house he had been building in a high and walled location on top of the Velian hill (hence the suspicion had arisen that he was aiming at kingship). With great glory Valerius had held the first triumph of the free city over the conquered Tarquin,[58] had resisted Porsena, and had accomplished many other things worthy of praise. Was it nonetheless not the case that, dying as consul now for the fourth time — as Livy says, "by common consent, prince in the arts of war and peace"[59] — he was found to be so poor that the expenses necessary for his burial were lacking and he had to be buried at public expense? Why should I mention Lucius Quintius[60] Cincinnatus, 27 who was compelled by poverty to hoe and plow, whom the Roman republic (which was already flourishing at that time) was not ashamed to call back, in the middle of the planting season, from the plow handle to the dictatorial staff and the pomp of the fear-inspiring fasces when the legions were surrounded on Mount Algidus? When the armies had been freed, the enemy conquered and 28 sent under the yoke, did it seem base or inglorious to the pauper, after celebrating a solemn and splendid triumph, to resign from the highest office,[61] which he had accepted for six months, and return to the work he had abandoned?[62] O brave man! O man, worthy to live in Christian times! For he was not only a tolerator

29 patiens paupertatis sed amator et cultor. Et, ne per singula Romane virtutis lumina ferar, qui se ad huius rei publice fundatores, defensores, aut augmentatores converterit inveniet famose paupertatis Fabricium Lucilium, qui cum pauperrimus esset et Samniticum aurum ac regis Pyrrhi munera sprevit nec unquam potuit a suarum virtutum proposito, hoc eodem rege testante, magis quam

30 sol a suis cursibus dimoveri. Inveniet et huius Fabricii coetaneum et aliquando collegam, Marcum Curium Dentatum, bis uno magistratu, de Sabinis semel semelque de Samnitibus, triumphantem, qui etiam magnum Samnitum auri pondus pariter ut sibi supervacuum respuit et irrisit, aiens se gloriosum ducere non aurum

31 habere sed aurum habentibus imperare. Nec inter paupertatis eloquia reticendus est ille patrum et plebis conciliator, Menenius Agrippa, qui virtutibus dives nec vivens habuit quid referret in censum nec unde posset moriens habere sepulcrum.

32 Et, quoniam non facile possem per cuncta discurrere, omittam Emilium Papum, Atilios, Elios, Scipiones, Catones, Scauros, et alia Romane rei publice sidera, de quorum paupertate, cum multa legantur, de virtutibus plurima dici possunt, cum ex modo dotium

33 universorum patrimonia iudicari queant. Nam usque in tempora Africani superioris, quo non habuit illa inclita Roma et belli gloria et pacis artibus digniorem, dotes parvissime fuerunt, cum legamus Cesonis filiam dotis maxime nomine decem milia eris in penates

34 coniugis ingessisse. Et senatus munificentia pro Gn. Scipionis filia, quam ut nuptui traderet, cum bellum in Hyspania contra Penos gereret una cum P. Scipione, germano suo atque collega, successorem cum instantia postulabat, quadraginta milia eris persolvit. Es

of poverty, but its lover and cultivator. And (lest I get carried away   29
through each and every bright light of Roman virtue) whoever
turns his attention to the founders, defenders, or builders of this
republic will come upon Fabricius Lucilius[63] of famed poverty,
who although he was extremely poor, spurned Samnite gold[64] and
the gifts of King Pyrrhus; he could never be moved from his virtuous goal (as this same king attests), any more than the sun could
be moved from its course. He will also come upon the contempo-   30
rary and sometime colleague of this Fabricius, Marcus[65] Curius
Dentatus, who triumphed twice in one consulship (once over the
Sabines and once over the Samnites):[66] he even rejected and ridi-
culed a great weight of Samnite gold as if it was something superfluous to him, saying that he considered it glorious not to have
gold, but to rule those who have it.[67] When speaking of poverty,   31
one must not neglect to mention that conciliator of patricians and
plebs, Menenius Agrippa, who, rich in virtues, when alive did not
have anything to report in the census, and in death did not have
the means for a grave.[68]

And since I could not easily survey everything, I will omit Ae-   32
milus Papus,[69] the Atilii, Aelii, Scipios, Catos, Scauri, and other
stars of the Roman republic. Much is read concerning their poverty, but a great many things can be said about their virtues, although the patrimonies of one and all can be judged from the
measure of their dowries. For up until the times of the elder Afri-   33
canus (and famous Rome had no one worthier in the glory of war
and arts of peace than he), dowries were extremely meager. We
read that the daughter of Caeso, by way of a very great dowry,
brought ten thousand *asses* to her husband's home.[70] And the mu-   34
nificence of the senate paid forty thousand *asses* for the daughter of
Gnaeus Scipio, when he was waging war against the Carthaginians
in Spain together with Publius Scipio, his brother and colleague,
and was insistently demanding a successor, so that he might give
her in marriage.[71] The *as* (if one understands it correctly) was the

autem, si quis recte respiciat, prima et vilissima Romanorum moneta fuit, ut quasi quodam modo dici possint quadraginta milia
35 denariorum. Quid plura, cum pleni sint omnium hystoriarum libri de paupertate, moderatione, et abstinentia Romanorum? Hi pauperes tantum imperium fundaverunt quod, 'postea quam,' ut nobilis et veritate insignis hystoricus ait, 'divitie honori esse ceperunt et eas gloria, imperium, et potentia sequebatur, hebescere virtus,
36 paupertas probro haberi cepit,' successores divites everterunt. Et, ut paulo superius eiusdem autoris verba referam, 'ubi labore atque iusticia res publica crevit, reges magni bello domiti, gnationes fere et populi ingentes vi subacti sunt, Carthago emula Romani imperii ab stirpe interiit, cuncta maria terreque patebant, sevire fortuna ac miscere omnia cepit.' Et, ne cuncta subtexam, infra subiungit: 'Igitur primo pecunie, deinde imperii cupido crevit. Ea quasi mate-
37 ries omnium malorum fuerunt.' Hec ille. Nec minus hec vera quam reliqua. Rem enim publicam Romanorum, quam pauper fundavit Romulus et pauperrimi principes ad tantam magnitudinem evexerunt ut imperium occeano, astris vero gloriam terminaret et eis ad occasum ab ortu solis omnia domita armis parerent, divites, L. Silla crudelis, Cinna ferox, ambitiosusque Marius, labefactaverunt, et ditiores, M. Crassus, Gn. Pompeius Magnus, ac
38 Gaius Cesar, Lucii Cesaris filius, funditus destruxerunt. Ut in hac rerum gestarum memoria quasi quodam in speculo videre possit mortalium genus ad hanc terrenam civitatem instituendam, augendam, atque conservandam pauperes divitibus prestitisse. Nam, ut sepefatus testatur hystoricus, 'Ex divitiis iuventutem luxuria atque avaricia cum superbia invasere, rapere, consumere, sua parvipendere, aliena cupere, pudorem, pudiciciam, divina atque humana promiscua, nichil pensi neque moderati habere.'

first and least valuable Roman coin, so that the sum could be said to be roughly forty thousand denarii.[72] Why should I say more, when books are full of all sorts of stories about the poverty, moderation, and self-restraint of the Romans? These paupers founded such a great empire, which their rich successors subverted. As a noble historian distinguished for truth says, "after riches began to be an honor and glory, sovereign rule, and power followed them, virtue began to grow dull, poverty to be held a disgrace."[73] And (to use the words of the same author quoted above) "when the republic grew by labor and justice; when great kings were tamed by war, wild nations and huge populations subjected by force; when Carthage, emulous of the Roman empire, perished root and branch; when all the seas and lands lay open; then fortune began to rage and throw everything into confusion."[74] And (so as not to quote everything) he adds below: "Therefore, first money grew, then the desire to rule. Those two were, so to speak, the fuel of all evils."[75] These words are no less true than the rest. The Roman state was founded by Romulus the pauper and leaders living in utter poverty and raised up to such greatness that its rule was bounded by the ocean and its glory by the stars,[76] and all the world, tamed by its arms alone, from the rising to the setting sun, obeyed it. But rich men — cruel Lucius Sulla, fierce Cinna, and ambitious Marius — weakened it, and richer men — Marcus Crassus, Gnaeus Pompeius Magnus, and Gaius Caesar (son of Lucius Caesar) — destroyed it completely. Consequently, in this historical account, the race of mortals can see, as if in a mirror, that the poor surpass the rich in establishing, augmenting, and preserving this earthly city. For (as the oft-mentioned historian attests) "as a result of wealth, luxury and avarice along with arrogance attacked, seized, consumed men in their prime; they held their own possessions to be of no account, coveted those of others; shame and modesty, divine and human affairs were jumbled together; they had no thought, no restraint."[77]

35

36

37

38

39   Quid autem de illa civitate que ad supernam spectat Ierusalem dicam? Nonne fundator eius et caput, Christus, dei filius, ex intemerati virginalis thalami penetralibus sine labe concubitus, de spiritu sancto conceptus et genitus, paupertatem predicavit et iussit? Nonne etiam pauper fuit qui, cum proficisceretur in Ierusalem, de se dixit, 'Vulpes foveas habent et volucres celi nidos; filius autem

40   hominis non habet ubi caput reclinet'? Quid Cephas, apostolorum princeps et petre fundamentalis ecclesie vicem gerens, an dives erat, qui, cum ascenderet in templum una cum Iohanne, roganti claudo a nativitate ut ab eis reciperet elemosinam, ait, 'Argentum et aurum non est michi; quod autem habeo, hoc tibi do. In nomine

41   Iesu Christi Nazareni surge et ambula'? Quid Paulus, vas electionis, doctor gentium ac veritatis et fidei predicator? Nonne tante paupertatis fuit quod, sicut ipse scribens ad Macedonas inquit,

42   fatigaretur nocte ac die operans ne quem ipsorum gravaret? Sed quid in re clarissima per multa trahor? Nonne, si respiciamus morem et institutionem ecclesie primitive, cuncti possessores agrorum atque domorum ea vendentes afferebant precia eorum que vendebant et ponebant ante pedes apostolorum, et, cum Ananias mentiens deo et hominibus cum Saphyra, uxore sua, attulissent partem precii ex agro quem vendiderant et partem sibi reservassent, increpiti a Petro subito ceciderunt expirantes et sepulti sunt?

43   Ut manifeste cunctis appareat illos primos in renovatione temporum celestis civitatis et ecclesie catholice fundatores aut pauperes extitisse aut venditis omnibus que habebant et in communi

But what should I say about that city that points to the heav- 39
enly Jerusalem? Did not its founder and head, Christ, Son of
God, born out of the inner chambers of an undefiled virginal
bedroom without the disgrace of sexual intercourse, conceived
and begotten by the Holy Spirit, preach and command poverty?
Wasn't he also a pauper, who when setting out for Jerusalem said
of himself, "Foxes have holes and birds have their nests; but the
Son of Man has nowhere to lay his head"?[78] What about Cephas, 40
first of apostles, serving as the foundation stone of the church? Do
you think he was rich, the man who, when he was going up to the
temple together with John, said to the man lame from birth and
asking to receive alms from them, "Silver and gold have I none; but
what I have, I give to you. In the name of Jesus Christ of Naza-
reth, get up and walk"?[79] What of Paul, chosen vessel, teacher of 41
the gentiles and preacher of truth and of the faith? Was he not a
man of such great poverty that, as he himself says when writing to
the Macedonians, he was exhausting himself night and day, working in order not to be a burden to any of them?[80] But why am I 42
being drawn through many examples in a matter that is crystal
clear? Surely, if we examine the custom and institution of the early
church, we see that all owners of farms and homes were selling
them and bringing the price received from the sale and placing it at
the apostles' feet; and, when Ananias together with his wife Sap-
phira, lying to God and men, brought part of the price they had
received for the farm they had sold and reserved part for themselves, they were chastised by Peter, whereupon they suddenly fell
down dead, and were buried.[81]

It should be manifestly clear to all, then, that those first found- 43
ers of the celestial city and the Catholic Church in the renewal of

44 collatis paupertatem voluntariam elegisse. Hi fuerunt qui non in
secularis potentatus brachio, non in fugacium divitiarum falso
splendore, sed in humilitatis altitudine et abiecte paupertatis solida
firmitate adeo vite integritate et innocentia miraculisque in fidei
perfectione confectis et imperterrita constantia claruerunt quod in
omnem terram exivit sonus eorum et in fines orbis terre verba eo-

45 rum. Hi pauperes et humiles infinitis martiriis per ducentos treginta et amplius annos ab Nerone, primo Christianorum persecu-
tore, usque in Dyoclitianum et Maximum imperatores, quorum
tempore decima plaga Christiane persecutionis efferbuit, ecclesiam

46 catholicam fundaverunt. Quam post Constantinum, qui non dotavit sed ditavit ecclesiam et superba sibi tradidit imperialis apicis
ornamenta (pace cunctorum dictum sit), hi nostri presules, quibus
sicut aliis illis ducibus terrene civitatis primo pecunie, deinde imperii cupido crevit, postquam simulam, mel, et oleum comederunt
et ornati sunt auro et argento et vestiti sunt bysso et pollimito et
multicoloribus et decori facti sunt vehementer nimis et demum
profecerunt in regnum, illam civitatem gloriosam abominabilem

47 reddiderunt. Nunc, quod summe deflendum est, cum videant
Christianam fidem olim toto orbe diffusam abominatione Sarace-
nica tot terrarum spacia perdidisse, cum videant antiquum Grecu-
lorum scisma tot populos, tot urbes, totque quondam opulentis-
sima regna ab unitate sancte matris ecclesie separasse, quasi adhuc
nimia moles esset nimiaque fidelium multitudo, duos summos
pontifices variis temporibus eligendo, si tamen electiones censende
sunt quas vel odium vel ambitio vel alie mentium humanarum

the times either were paupers or chose voluntary poverty, selling
all that they had and pooling their resources. These were people   44
who were distinguished not with the strength of secular power,
not with the false splendor of fleeting riches, but with depth of
humility and the solid firmness of abject poverty, integrity of life,
innocence, miracles performed in perfection of faith, and fearless
constancy, so that their sound went out through all the earth, their
words to the ends of the world.[82] These paupers and humble   45
people founded the Catholic Church, suffering countless martyr-
doms over the course of 230 and more years, from the reign of
Nero (the first persecutor of Christians) up until the emperors
Diocletian and Maximus, under whom the tenth plague of Christian persecution seethed. After Constantine, who did not endow,   46
but enriched the church,[83] transferred the haughty ornaments of
the imperial crown to himself, first a desire for money, then a desire for power (let it be said with the permission of all) grew in
these bishops of ours, just as in those other leaders of the earthly
city. They ate the finest wheat flour, honey, and oil; they were
adorned with gold and silver; they were clothed in linen and deco-
rated with many-colored embroidery. Finally they proceeded with
excessive violence to kingship, and rendered that glorious city
abominable. Now (and this is utterly lamentable) they see that the   47
Christian faith, once spread throughout the whole world, has lost
so much territory to the Saracen abomination; they see that the
ancient schism of the Greeks has separated so many peoples, so
many cities, and so many once opulent kingdoms from the unity
of holy mother church. Regardless (as if up until now the mass
and multitude of the faithful were excessive), they have given birth
to the most pernicious schism by electing two popes at different
times — if we are to consider as elections proceedings distorted by
hatred, ambition, and other turbulent passions of human minds,

turbide passiones extorquent, non que in zelo fidei et in edificatio-
nem celestis Ierusalem celebrantur, scisma perniciosissimum pepe-
rerunt.

48   Ut, sicut illi utriusque civitatis principes et autores, dum paupertatem dilexerunt, nedum fundamenta duarum illarum urbium
iacientes in ingens maxime molis opificium profecerunt sed incre-
mentis mirabilibus inter labores et sanguinem aucti sunt, ita isti
divites corrumpente pecunia mentes et bonos mores pene cuncta
49   cum sua gloriosa rerum omnium opulentia destruxerunt. Que
cum ita sint, nisi desipere gaudeamus, si celesti vel terrene civitati
servire, si nos utrique vel alterutri volumus utiles exhibere, quis
non videt dimittendas esse divitias, que suos adeo corrumpant et
attaminent possessores?

50   Gaude igitur te illarum absolutum esse consortio, nec ad ipsas
te quoquo modo vel sola mentis inclinatione convertas, que non
solum profectionem in patriam retardant sed impediunt, non solum impediunt sed prohibent, nec solum prohibent sed in Tartara
51   retrahunt et submergunt. Unde non incongrue Tiberianus ait:
'Aurum quo precio reserantur limina Ditis.' Denique, si quando
forsan ad illarum illecebrosam dulcedinem animus revertatur tuus,
recordare, precor, apostolici documenti. Inquit enim: 'Nam qui
volunt divites fieri incidunt in temptationem et in laqueum diaboli
et desideria multa inutilia et nociva, que mergunt hominem in interitum et perditionem.' Ut facile possis, cum hec sepius tecum
reputaveris, illarum amorem dimittere tecumqe debeas, quod illas
aliquando reliqueris, exultare.

instead of being celebrated in the zeal of the faith and for the purpose of building the heavenly Jerusalem.[84]

As a result, just as the leaders and founders of each of the two 48
cities, as long as they loved poverty, not only laid the foundations of those cities and thus progressed to a huge work of great scope, but were also, by miraculous increments, themselves magnified amid toil and blood; just so, those rich men, with money corrupting their minds and good morals, destroyed almost everything with their own glorious, all-encompassing opulence. Since this is 49
so, if we wish to serve the heavenly or the earthly city, if we want to show ourselves useful to both or either of the two, who doesn't see (unless we enjoy being fools) that riches must be renounced, since they so corrupt and contaminate their possessors?

Rejoice, then, that you have been freed from association with 50
riches. Don't turn to them in any way, even solely by mental inclination. Riches not only delay, but also impede, your progress to your homeland; they not only impede, but prevent; they not only prevent, but drag you down to Tartarus and engulf you. Hence 51
Tiberianus aptly said, "Gold — by its price the threshold of Dis is unlocked."[85] Finally, if your spirit should ever revert to the seductive sweetness of riches, remember, I pray, the apostolic example. For he says, "Those who wish to become rich fall into temptation, the devil's snare, and many useless and harmful desires that plunge a person into ruin and perdition."[86] Hence, when one reflects on this often, one could easily renounce the love of riches, and you ought to exult that you at long last have left them behind.

: X :

De obedientie voto.

1 Spopondisti et, mi Ieronime, contra vite superbiam saluberrimam
obedientiam, per quam, voluntati proprie libera voluntate renun-
tians, te voluntati dei, voluntati prelati, et preceptis religionis et
2 ordinis obligasti. Que tanto gloriosior est quanto humilior, tanto
magis levis et facilis quanto maioris caritatis affectibus exhibetur,
tantoque maioris meriti quanto minus habuerit extranei. Nam si
bonum facis quia bonum illud placet et ad illud non sola illius
boni sed etiam dei firma dilectione deflecteris, bonum quidem fa-
3 cis et id faciendo mereris. Sed si bene faciens ante oculos tibi po-
nes dei prelatique preceptum, illud religiose, hoc vero in observan-
tia regulari perficiens, ita quod non minus ex dilectione obedientie
quam ex boni quod acturus es beneplacito movearis, bona cumu-
las, meritum auges, tantoque plus remunerationis accipies quanto
plus ad preceptum fervoris habueris cum illud bonum faciens
4 obedisti. Unde fit, quantum ad hanc spectat, quod plus nobis
mercedis proponatur si iubeamur que secundum se nature quodam horrore fugere debeamus quam si detur de re nobis accepta
preceptum.

Iussit dominus deus Abrahe: 'Egredere de terra tua et cogna-
tione tua et de domo patris tui et veni in terram quam monstrabo
5 tibi.' Durus profecto sermo, dimittere dulcedinem patrie, suavitatem cognatorum, et consuetudinem paterne domus. Quod

: X :

On the vow of obedience.

You have also vowed, dear Girolamo, a most wholesome obedience   1
in opposition to the arrogance of life. Through obedience, you renounced your own will of your own free will; you have obliged
yourself to the will of God, to the will of your superior, and to the
precepts of religious life and of your order. Obedience is the more   2
glorious the more humble it is; lighter and easier, to the degree
that it is performed with a disposition of greater charity; of greater
merit, the less it involves external stimulus. For if you do good
because that good pleases you, and if you incline toward it with a
firm love both of that good and of God, you are indeed doing
good and earn merit by doing it. But if in doing well you put be-   3
fore your eyes the precept of God and your superior, and you do
the former religiously, the latter in observance of the rule, so that
you are moved no less by the love of obedience than by pleasure
taken in the good you are about to do, you accumulate good
things, increase merit, and you will receive more remuneration the
more fervor you had for the precept when you did that good deed
in obedience. Consequently, as far as obedience is concerned, a   4
greater reward is available to us if we are ordered to do things that
in themselves we ought to flee by a certain revulsion of our nature
than if a precept is given involving something that is agreeable
to us.

The Lord God ordered Abraham, "Go out from your own land
and your family and from your father's house and come into the
land that I will show to you."[87] A hard saying, certainly, to leave   5
the pleasantness of homeland, the sweetness of relatives, and
the familiarity of the paternal home. Although he did this in

quamvis obeditione precepti fecerit, potuit tamen et illud quod iubebatur egisse spe divine promissionis, qui dixerat: 'Faciam te in gentem magnam, benedicam tibi et magnificabo nomen tuum, atque in te benedicentur omnes cognationes terre.' Magna quidem promissio, cui voci taliter obedivit ut etiam filium suum redire in
6 sue cognationis patriam prohiberet. Sed mira obedientia fuit cum audivit vocem dei vocantis eum et dicentis, 'Tolle filium tuum unigenitum quem diligis, Ysaac, et vade in terram Visionis atque offer eum ibi holocaustum super unum montium quem monstravero tibi,' et hoc facere sine trepidatione paravit. Ista fuit obedientia que profecto nichil extra se habuit, sed tota fuit in consumatione precepti, nisi forte putemus citra divine iussionis imperium, quo voluit deus obedientiam electissimi patriarche non videre, quam etiam si futuram noluisset ab eterno cognoverat, sed nobis admirandam proponere et complendam in unigeniti sui persona, quem pro nobis in ara crucis immolavit, ante per tot secula figurare ipsum Abraham, virum perfectum, coram domino suum fi-
8 lium placenter occidere potuisse. Non ergo mirum si deus per angelum suum vocavit Abraham de celo dicens, 'Per memet ipsum iuravi quia fecisti rem hanc et non pepercisti filio tuo unigenito propter me. Benedicam tibi et multiplicabo semen tuum sicut stellas celi et velut arenam que est in litore maris. Possidebit semen tuum portas inimicorum suorum. Et benedicentur in semine tuo omnes gentes terre quia obedisti voci mee.'
9   O gloriosa obedientia! O virtus plena gratie! O sola que genus humanum ab inimici manibus liberasti! Nam sicut per inobedientiam unius hominis peccatores constituti sunt multi, ita et per

obedience to the precept, he could have done what he was ordered out of hope in the divine promise, for the Lord had said, "I will make you into a great nation, I will bless you and glorify your name, and in you all peoples of the world will be blessed."[88] A great promise indeed, an utterance that Abraham obeyed so strictly that he even forbade his son to return to his family's homeland. But it was wonderful obedience when he heard the voice of God calling him and saying, "Take your only-begotten son, whom you love, Isaac, and go into the land of Vision and offer him there as a burned offering on one of the mountains, which I will show to you."[89] Without trepidation, he prepared to do this. This was obedience that contained absolutely nothing extraneous, but existed completely in the fulfilling of the precept — unless, that is, we hold that Abraham could have taken pleasure in killing his own son before the Lord apart from the power of the divine command. By means of this command, God wanted not to see the obedience of the chosen patriarch (God had recognized his obedience from eternity, even if he had not wanted the act to be fulfilled); rather, he wanted to hold before us this obedience as worthy of admiration, an obedience to be fulfilled in the Person of his only-begotten Son, whom he sacrificed for us on the altar of the Cross, and whom he wanted Abraham himself, the perfect man, to prefigure so many centuries earlier. It is no wonder, then, that God, by means of his angel, called to Abraham from the sky, saying, "By myself I have sworn that you have done this thing and, for my sake, have not spared your only-begotten son. I will bless you and multiply your seed like the stars of the sky and like the sand on the shore of the sea. Your seed will possess the gates of its enemies. And all peoples of the world will be blessed in your seed because you obeyed my voice."[90]

O glorious obedience! O virtue full of grace! Only you have liberated the human race from the hands of the Enemy! For just as through the disobedience of one man many were made sinners, so

10   unius obedientiam iusti constituuntur et multi. Quid enim convenientius, quoniam voluntate libera nostri primi parentes se posteritatemque suam omnem inimicos deo statuerunt, ut hac infirmitate nature nec bonum efficaciter elicere valeamus nec nobis in voluntate et arbitrii libertate per rationem ut ad exitum veniat imperare, mala vero possimus, quid profecto convenientius quam hanc voluntatem deo obligare ita quod ipsam sine maxima consideratione, si nobis constare voluerimus ne deum offendamus, ulte-

11   rius flectere non possimus? Ut sicut illa libertas, rupta armonia originalis iusticie, qua privati quadam corruptione nature facti sumus concupiscibiles et ad mala proclives, nos vasa fecerat ire, sic ista salubris servitus regeneratos in Christo Iesu sublata saltem

12   egritudine culpe in adoptionis filios nos commutet et gratie. Nec mirum. Postquam enim cum benignissimo patre nobis negocium est, quis non speret de salvatoris nostri manu gratiam, qui dignatus fuerit primorum parentum inobedientiam, factus obediens usque ad mortem, in arduo crucis per suum preciosissimum sanguinem abolere?

13   Nec solitaria virtus est obedientia, sed plane cunctis est admixta virtutibus. Nam, sicut inquit expolitissimus antistes Gregorius, 'Obedientia sola virtus est que virtutes ceteras menti inserit in-

14   sertasque custodit.' Quod quidem et ille Libicus fidei nostre illuminator, divus Aurelius Augustinus, ex eiusdem sancti spiritus inspiratione predixerat, inquiens, 'Obedientia commendata est in precepto, que virtus in creatura rationali mater quodam modo est

15   omnium custosque virtutum.' Hec illi. Nec sit quod de hoc dubitationem aliquam faciamus. Nam cum duo nobis precepta caritatis data sint, ut deum scilicet et proximum diligamus, et in istis contineatur integritas omnis atque plenitudo virtutum, imperate sunt

through one man's obedience many were also made just. What is   10
more fitting? By their free will, our first parents set themselves and
their entire posterity as enemies to God. As a result of this natural
infirmity, we can neither effectively elicit good nor command ourselves through reason, with our will and freedom of judgment, for
the good to come to fruition; yet we can do bad deeds. What indeed is more fitting than to oblige this will to God in such a way
that we cannot bend it further without the greatest premeditation,
if we wish consistently to avoid offending God? Thus, once the   11
harmony of the original justice had been broken, deprived of liberty, by a certain corruption of our nature, we became capable of
concupiscence and inclined to evil; just as liberty made us into
vessels of wrath, so may that healthy servitude transform us, born
again in Christ Jesus — sin's sickness, at least, taken away — into
children of adoption and of grace. Nor is that remarkable. For   12
when we are dealing with our most generous Father, who would
not hope for grace from the hand of our Savior, who, made obedient unto death, deigned to abolish the disobedience of our first
parents through his own most precious blood, in the rigors of the
Cross?

Obedience is not a solitary virtue, but one that is clearly mixed   13
with all the virtues. As the most eloquent bishop Gregory says,
"Obedience is the only virtue that plants the other virtues in the
mind, and guards them once they have been planted."[91] Indeed,   14
that Libyan illuminator of our faith, the divine Aurelius Augustine, also proclaimed that thought, by the inspiration of the same
Holy Spirit: "Obedience was commended in the precept; this virtue in a rational creature is, in a manner of speaking, the mother
and guardian of all the virtues."[92] Let us have no doubt about this.   15
For two precepts concerning charity have been given to us, namely
that we love God and neighbor; all integrity and plenitude of

cuncte sine dubitatione virtutes, ut etiam bona facientes oporteat cogitare nos consumate virtuose non agere nisi simul et preceptis
16 dilexerimus obedire. Quo fit, amantissime mi Ieronime, ut cuncta que facimus, si comes sit, ut decet, obediendi propositum, ⟨et⟩ precipientis memores in deum quicquid boni facimus dirigamus, nec malum possimus aliquid agere quin cognoscamus nos divino
17 per inobedientiam imperio contraire. Et quoniam Christiane perfectionis est, sicut testatur veritas, servare precepta atque vendere omnia que habemus dareque pauperibus et sequi Christum, moniti meliora sequamur, non quidem in metu pene sed in dilectione iusticie, non coactione tristes sed dicto pareamus ovantes, certi de retributione, tanto maioris meriti quanto promptiores fuerimus in executione precepti.

18   Nescio si verum dicam, devotissime tamen ausim asserere cunctos qui citra divine maiestatis obedientiam virtuosum aliquid operantur, nedum non mereri sed improbe facere, et omnes qui agunt verbi gratia frequentes actus fortitudinis vel temperantie ob hoc solum, ut fortes vel temperati sint, non etiam ut videantur, nedum carnaliter sapere sed etiam a gentilium philosophis non differre.
19 Omittamus enim Romanos, qui cunctarum actionum suarum finem sibi mundanam gloriam proponebant. Nonne illi philosophi qui terminum bonorum omnium virtutem, ut ceteros vanioris sententie dimittam, esse volebant, que maxime Stoycorum opinio fuit, se ipsis, ut aiebant, contenti nichil ulterius de suis actionibus requirebant nisi conscientie secretum et ut virtuosi possent evadere
20 secumque de virtutum acquisitione gaudere? Quid igitur ab istis differre dixerimus Christianum qui dei iubentis oblitus et huius

virtues is contained in these. Therefore, without a doubt, all virtues have been commanded in order that even when we are doing
good, we should think that we are not acting with consummate
virtue unless at the same time we love to obey the precepts as well.
So that it happens, my most beloved Girolamo, that if the inten-   16
tion of obeying accompanies all we do (as it should), and we,
mindful of the Preceptor, direct to God whatever good we do, we
cannot do any evil without acknowledging that through our disobedience we are contravening the divine command. And since it   17
is inherent in Christian perfection (as the Truth attests) to keep
the precepts, to sell all we have and give it to the poor, and to follow Christ, let us, who have been warned, pursue better things,
not in fear of punishment but in love of justice; let us obey the
teaching, not sadly out of compulsion, but rejoicing, certain of
recompense that will contain greater merit, the more prompt we
are in the execution of the precept.

I don't know whether I speak a truth, yet I would most de-   18
voutly dare to assert that all who do some virtuous act short of
obedience to the divine majesty not only do not earn merit, but
even act wrongly; and that all who, for example, accomplish fre-
quent acts of fortitude or temperance only in order to be strong or
temperate (and not even just to seem so) are not only thinking
carnally, but are not even different from the pagan philosophers.
Let us pass over the Romans, who proposed worldly glory as the   19
end of all their actions. Did not those philosophers who claimed
that virtue is the end of all goods — and this was especially the
view of the Stoics (to leave others of less sound opinion aside) —
contented with themselves (as they said), require nothing more
from their actions than the secret of their conscience and that
they, the virtuous, might go away and rejoice over their acquisition
of virtue? Why, then, should we say that a Christian is different   20
from those people, if he, forgetting the God who commands him

virtutis habitum derelinquens, non ut deo placeat vel obediat, sed
solum ut bonum aliquod faciat operatur? Certe secure dixerim
tanto deteriorem quanto constitutus per baptismi regenerationem
in gratia et in evangelio veritatem edoctus nec sic agit ut debet nec
ipsis virtutibus utitur ut deceret, imo virtutibus contra rationem
21 nititur frui, quibus sic fruendo verius dicatur abuti. Non igitur
terrena sapiamus sed, cum ad nichil cogamur necessitate nature,
deo, cui fidem promisimus in libertate nobis de nostra voluntate
22 concessa, fideliter pareamus. Pareamus quidem alacriter et in caritate, sine qua, sicut sentit apostolus, cuncta virtutis operatio nichil
est. Parendum itaque illi principi rerum omnium, deo, cuius voluntas semper est recta, semper una, semper immobilis, semper
bona, semper et necessario bonitatem suam volens, qua sola ple-
nissime satiatur, semperque volens quod ab eterno vult, et que una
quidem est regula cunctorum actuum humanorum.

23   O felicissimum humanum genus si voluntate sua proximum
fieret institutioni divine, sique solum ea vellemus que se velle docuit, et illi sicut precipimur audiremus! Non solum autem deo sed
omnes debemus in domino parentibus obedire. Scriptum est enim,
24 'Iudicium patris audite, filii dilecti, et sic facite ut salvi sitis.' Obediamus et potestatibus, nam cum omnis potestas a deo sit, 'qui
potestati resistit,' ut inquit apostolus, 'dei ordinationi resistit.' 'Obe-
dite et prepositis vestris et subiacete eis'; ipsi enim, ut testatur
doctor gentium, 'pervigilant quasi rationem pro animabus vestris
25 reddituri.' Quin etiam subditi simus omni creature propter deum,
sed, ne forte decipiamur, obedire oportet deo magis quam hominibus. Stulta quidem est obedientia et non sine divine maiestatis

and abandoning his practice of this virtue, acts not to please or obey God, but only to do something good? I would certainly say with confidence that a person is all the worse, the more that, put in a state of grace through the regeneration of baptism and taught the truth of the gospel, he does not act as he ought or employ virtues as is fitting, but rather strives against reason to enjoy virtues, which, in thus enjoying them, he may more truly be said to abuse them.[93] Let us not, therefore, be wise in earthly matters, 21 but, although we are not compelled to do anything by necessity of nature, let us faithfully obey God, to whom we promised faith in the freedom granted to us by our own will. Let us obey with en- 22 thusiasm and in love, without which, as the apostle holds, all virtuous action is nothing.[94] And so we must obey God, the Ruler of all things, God, whose will is always right, always one, always immovable, always good; always and necessarily willing its own goodness, by which alone it is most fully satisfied; always willing what it wills eternally; and which is the one standard of all human actions.

O human race, most happy if by its own will it is near the di- 23 vine instruction, and if we only want those things that this instruction taught it to want, and if we heed the instruction as we are commanded! Yet all of us should obey not only God, but also our parents in the Lord. For it is written: "Listen to the judgment of your father, beloved sons, and act accordingly that you may be saved."[95] Let us obey the authorities also, for, since all power is 24 from God, "whoever resists authority," as the apostle says, "resists God's order." "Obey your superiors and subject yourselves to them"; for they (as the teacher of the gentiles attests) "watch over you as if they will one day render an account for your souls."[96] Indeed, let us be subject to every creature for God's sake, but, lest 25 we be deceived, we should obey God more than human beings. Obedience is stupid and not without offense to the divine majesty

iniuria quam relicto deo creatore creaturis et hominibus exhibe-
26 mus. Parendum est et legi potius quam prepositis atque regi. Sic
enim subditi potestatibus esse debemus sicque iussionibus obedire
quod non ad prevaricationem legis sed ad omne bonum opus inve-
27 niat obedientie sedulitas nos paratos. Non sit obedientia nostra
cum murmure sed cum gaudio, nec obediamus labiis iniquis lin-
gueque mendaci. Non obediamus concupiscientiis nostris, nec
propter obediendi propositum precepte dilectionis obedientiam
relinquamus. Impia quidem est obedientia que sine scelere non
impletur. Si quid homini paremus, deum nobis, in cuius oculis
agimus, ante nostre mentis oculos proponamus caveamusque ne
28 nos contingat illum offendere cum alteri voluerimus obedire. Sit
tanta propter deum nostre obedientie promptitudo quod non solum expectemus imperium sed preveniamus cum alacritate preceptum persuadeamusque nobis tanto laudabiliorem ceteris moralibus
virtutibus obedientiam fore quanto maius est anime bonum quod
obediendo spernimus quam alia que propter virtutes reliquas post-
29 ergamus. Parendo quidem nostram contemnimus voluntatem, qua
sola naturalis necessitatis inclinatione beatitudinem exoptamus
quaque deum diligimus, quod longe nobis melius est quam intelligere, quoniam per ipsam dei gratia possumus et non aliter beatitudinem promereri. Hanc igitur parendo contemnimus et alienam
30 induimus voluntatem. Nam, ut inquit apostolus, 'Ego carnalis
sum, venundatus sub peccato. Quod enim operor non intelligo.
Non enim quod ego volo hoc ago, sed quod odio illud facio.' Et
subdit, 'Si autem quod nolo illud facio, consentio legi quoniam
31 bona est.' Ut hec consideranti facile detur intelligi politicis virtutibus obedientiam esse maiorem, quo maius est et intestinius quod
per ipsam contemnimus quam id quod per alias virtutes huiusmodi postponimus vel calcamus.

when we abandon God, our Creator, and show it to his creatures and to men. The law also must be obeyed, more than our superi- 26 ors and the king. For we ought to be subject to authority and obey orders in such a way that earnestness of obedience finds us ready not for the law's prevarication, but for every good work. Let our 27 obedience be accompanied by joy, not grumbling; let us not obey with unjust lips and a lying tongue. Let us not obey our desires; let us not, on account of our resolution to obey, lose our obedience to the command to love. Impious indeed is the obedience that is fulfilled with wrongdoing. If we obey a man in something, let us place God, in whose eyes we are acting, before our mind's eye, taking care not to offend him when we want to obey another. We 28 should be so ready to obey for God's sake that we are not only waiting for a command, but anticipate the order with alacrity. Let us persuade ourselves that obedience is more laudable than the other moral virtues, to the degree that the good of the soul we spurn by obeying is greater than other things we give up on account of the rest of the virtues. By obeying we contemn our own 29 will. With our will alone, by a tendency of natural necessity, we long for beatitude and love God. This is far better for us than to understand him, since there is no other way to merit blessedness than through our will, by God's grace. When we obey, then, we contemn our will and put on the will of another. For, as the 30 apostle says, "I am carnal, put up for sale under sin. For I do not understand what I do. I do not do what I want, but what I hate." And he adds, "If, however, I do what I don't want to do, I give my assent to the law, that it is good."[97] Thus, to one considering these 31 things, it is easily understandable that obedience is greater than the political virtues, in that what we contemn through obedience is a greater and more internal thing than what we disdain as inferior or trample upon through the other virtues.[98]

32   Liberemus igitur voluntatem nostram legi peccati captivatam per obedientie votum et ipsam in deum dedicatione voluntaria dirigamus, condelectemurque legi dei secundum interiorem hominem, ut liberet nos de corpore mortis huius gratia dei per Iesum Christum, dominum nostrum, quem tu et religiosi ceteri decrevistis salubriter imitari.

: XI :

De oratione.

1 Iam finis aderat, karissime mi Ieronime, nisi reputarem indignum te inter confertos hostes in acie positum inermem relinquere, cum videam tibi necessarium fore continua dimicatione certare. In arcem te religionis, quod iam sepe laudavi, magna providentia retu-

2 listi. Cave tamen ne vel parietes istos spiritualis hostis irrumpat teque munitum, quacunque temptaverit, exhibeto. Quod autem venienti temptatori telum obicies? Quo denique contra furentem clipeo protegeris? Quid michi cuncta rimanti tradendum occurrit nisi illud religiose militie validum armamentum quo simul et te protegas et hostem exhaurias, devota quidem et fervens oratio?

3 Hec venientem temptatorem prevenit, postquam venerit, arcet, et, si forsan intraverit, eicit et expellit. Hoc forte michi non credis; audi igitur veritatem: 'Vigilate itaque,' dicit, 'et orate ut non intretis in temptationem. Spiritus quidem promptus, caro vero infirma.'

Therefore, through the vow of obedience let us liberate our will   32
that has been made captive to the law of sin; let us direct it to God
with voluntary dedication. Let us inwardly delight in the law of
God, in order that it may liberate us from the body of this death
by God's grace through Jesus Christ our Lord, whom you and
other religious have soundly decided to imitate.

: XI :

On prayer.

The end of the work would now be at hand, dearest Girolamo, if   1
I did not judge it unfitting to leave you unarmed among enemies
drawn up in battle array, when I see that it will be necessary for
you to fight a continual struggle. With great foresight you have
betaken yourself to the stronghold of religious life; I have already
praised this often. Yet beware that the spiritual Enemy does not   2
break even through those walls. Show yourself to be well fortified,
wherever he attacks. What missile will you hurl against the approaching tempter? Finally, what shield will protect you against
the raging one? What occurs to me to pass on to you, as I investigate everything, but that powerful equipment of the military service of religion—the equipment with which you at the same time
protect yourself and exhaust the Enemy, namely devout and fervent prayer? Prayer forestalls the approaching tempter; fends him   3
off after he has come; and, if by chance he has entered, casts him
out and expels him. You may not believe me in this matter, so listen to the Truth: "Watch, therefore," he says, "and pray that you
not enter into temptation. The spirit is ready, but the flesh is

Nec minus alibi testatus est, 'Hoc genus demonii non eicitur nisi in oratione et ieiunio.' Si enim cunctis virtutibus contra omnia vitia dimicandum est, eligenda sunt arma in quibus cuncte possint

4 convenire virtutes. Quod si tecum volueris clara ratione discutere, nusquam plenius quam in oratione poteris reperire. Nam sicut ad tecti meditullium undique tigillorum omnium capitella conveniunt, sic ad orationem cunctarum virtutum integritas aggregatur.

5 Primo quidem, ut ad virtutum reginam et principem veniamus, orantem oportet caritatem habere. Quomodo enim rogare poterit quem non amat? Et, quia novit dominus cogitationes nostras (scrutatur enim renes et corda), quomodo, si deum non dilexeris, eum orabis? An ut audias, 'Homo iste labiis me honorat; cor au-

6 tem eius longe est a me'? Non possumus deum decipere sicut homines. In huius etenim mortalitatis cecitate diligere simulantes etiam quos habemus odio rogitamus, dumque illi se cupiunt vel arbitrantur amari, deflectimus ad nostra rogamina, quoniam omnis vite nostre conversatio ignorantia et vanitas est.

7 Verum quia triplici gradu status dilectionis humane procedit (amamus enim deum, amamus nos, et amamus proximum), et rationis sit, cuius oratio actus est, cum ad ea obtinenda que recte desideramus ordinetur, secundum caritatem operationes nostras disponere, non sufficit orare deum pro nobis nisi etiam pro proximis exoremus, quos veluti nos ipsos diligere divine legis iussioni-

8 bus imperamur. Diligamus igitur oportet deum ut exaudiat iuxta illud, 'Diligam te, domine, fortitudo mea, dominus fundamentum meum et refugium meum et liberator meus. Laudans invocabo dominum et ab inimicis meis salvus ero.' Nam custodit dominus

9 omnes diligentes se. Diligendus itaque deus non nudis affectibus

weak."[99] No less did he attest elsewhere, "This kind of demon is not cast out except by prayer and fasting."[100] If all the virtues must fight against all the vices, we must select weapons in which all the virtues can come together. But if you want to sort this out for 4 yourself with clarity of reason, nowhere will you be able to find a more complete weapon than prayer. For just as the tops of all the beams from all directions meet in the middle of the roof, so the integrity of all the virtues is combined in prayer. First (to come to 5 the queen and ruler of virtues),[101] the one who prays should have charity. How will he be able to beg of one whom he does not love? And, since the Lord knows our thoughts (for he examines kidneys and hearts),[102] how will you pray to God if you do not love him? Will you do so in order to hear, "That man honors me with his lips; but his heart is far from me"?[103] We can't deceive God as we 6 do human beings. And indeed, we keep begging in the blindness of this mortality, pretending to love even those whom we hate; and while they desire to be loved or believe that they are loved, we turn them to the objects of our prayers, since all the experience of our life is ignorance and vanity.

But the condition of human love proceeds with a triple step 7 (for we love God, ourselves, and our neighbor), and it belongs to reason — and prayer is an act of reason — to dispose our works according to charity — when prayer is ordered to obtaining those things that we rightly desire. Therefore, it is not enough to pray to God for ourselves unless we also pray for our neighbors, whom we are commanded by the orders of divine law to love as ourselves. We must love God, then, in order that he may hear us, according 8 to the verse "I will love you, Lord, my strength, Lord, my foundation, and my refuge, and my liberator. I will call upon the Lord in praise, and from my enemies I will be safe."[104] For the Lord guards all who love him. And so we should love God not with mere 9

mentis sed in effectibus operis. Tunc enim deum vere diligimus cum eius precepta non in metu pene ac servitute timoris sed in dilectionis ardore ac libertate caritatis devotis mentibus observamus. Memento quod, si quis dixerit quia 'deum amo,' precepta autem eius non observet, mendax est.

10 Diligere debemus et nos ipsos, quod quidem implicite preceptum est nobis. Si enim non amaverimus salutem nostram, qui quidem amor, imago, et forma est proximi diligendi, quomodo preceptum implebimus dilectionis ad proximum quem sicut nos ipsos

11 iubemur amare? Simul itaque nobis preceptum est ut nos et proximum diligamus, nec, quantum ad nos attinet, frustra fuit, licet naturaliter insit nobis nostre salutis affectio. Nimia quidem est sensuum nostrorum violentia, nam adeo nos corporee sanitatis, imo suavitatis, efficiunt amatores quod spiritualis salvationis faciant oblivisci. O utinam tanta saltem, postquam maior non est, nobis cura foret anime beatificande quantam inesse videmus cor-

12 poris conservandi! Pro corpore quidem agros colimus, edificamus domos, facimus civitates, congregamus divitias, supellectiliumque procuramus maximum apparatum, lanificium invenimus nendi texendique parta sollertia. Denique tot artes, tot artificum manus, tot et tanta granaria, tot cellaria, tot macella, tot coquinarum pulmenta, tantus mensarum splendor, tot preciosa vasa, tante cubiculorum delicie, tot varietates armorum et vestium et pene quecunque manu facimus inventa sunt (utinam ad necessitatem, non etiam ad voluptatem!) corruptibilibus atque fetidis nostris corpori-

13 bus inservire. Et ut modico tempore (scimus enim diuturniora esse non posse corpora nostra tandem corrumpenda vermesque de se gignendos pascitura) serventur, tot nos laboribus implicamus! Anime vero salutem, que perpetuo sit mansura, tanta mentis

impulses of our mind but in the results of our work. For we truly love God when with devoted minds we observe his precepts, not in fear of punishment and in the slavery of fear, but in the ardor of love and the freedom of charity. Remember that if anyone says "I love God" but does not observe his precepts, that person is a liar.

We ought to love ourselves also; this is an implicit command 10 for us. For if we don't love our salvation, what love, image, and form do we have for loving our neighbor? How will we fulfill the precept of love of neighbor, whom we are commanded to love as ourselves? We are instructed to love ourselves and our neighbor at 11 the same time, then, and, as far as pertains to ourselves, it was not in vain, although there dwells in us by nature a disposition toward our own salvation. The violence of our senses goes to extremes, for they make us lovers of bodily health (better, of bodily pleasure) to such an extent that they make us forget our spiritual salvation. Would that we had at least as much if not greater concern to be-atify the soul as we see we have for preserving the body! For the 12 body we cultivate fields; we build houses, we build cities; we ac-cumulate wealth and procure a lot of ostentatious furniture; we discover wool working, having gained skill in sewing and weaving. In sum, so many arts, so many handicrafts, so many and such great granaries, so many pantries, so many markets, so many culi-nary sauces, such great splendor of tables, so many precious vases, such great charms of bedrooms, so many varieties of weapons and of clothing, and almost anything we make by hand have been in-vented (would that it were just out of necessity, and not also for pleasure!) to serve our corruptible and fetid bodies. And in order 13 that our bodies may be maintained for a brief time (for we know that they cannot exist for longer than this, destined as they finally are for corruption and to feed the worms born from them), we involve ourselves in so many labors! Yet we neglect the salvation of the soul, which will remain forever, with such great mental

cecitate negligimus quod ipsam de preparata gloria in supplicia detrudamus eterna.

14   Diligimus itaque nos sed carnaliter, sed secundum corpus, spiritualiter autem non, sed ipsam animam, tanquam nostri pars non sit, penitus non curamus. Si levissimus etiam languor corpus nostrum invadat, vocamus medicos, paramus medicinas, cibum nobis subtrahimus, et flebiles ac queruli, quicunque dolor immineat, lamentamur, et non minore cum sensuum nostrorum molestia medicamina sumimus quam morbis ipsis, licet gravissimis, laboramus.

15   Cum autem quotidie non levi sed mortali prorsus egritudine mortalium anime teneantur, nulli sentire videntur morbum, nulli medicum petunt, sed compunctionis confessionisque medelam veluti

16   rem amarissimam abhorremus. Cavendum itaque, mi Ieronime, ne nostras animas inter corporalia diligamus. Qui enim amat animam suam perdet eam. Occidamus igitur animas nostras mundo et ipsas secundum carnem odio pertinaciter habeamus. Quantum enim illas oderimus mundo, tantum deo sumus ipsas, si recte sentire voluerimus, amaturi. Hac igitur ratione nos ipsos amare debemus nec sic amando decipi quod aliter nos amemus, dumque oramus

17   nostri solum ad salutem, non ad hec temporalia reminisci. Unica vero debet orantibus sola et determinata fore petitio, ut id videlicet quod nobis diligere debemus devotione supplici postulemus. Hoc autem, postquam cuncta discusseris, quid aliud est quam eterne glorie immutabilis beatitudo? Hanc enim, sicut habemus diligere, ita conari debemus orationibus impetrare.

18   Amandus est etiam, ut dixi, proximus ad eandem salutem quam nobis desiderare debemus in tanta plenitudine caritatis quod non solum dilectionis nostre fervor complectatur amicos sed etiam ad nostros perveniat inimicos. Qua fronte quidem petere deum audemus quod offensus dominus remittat nobis nisi iubente domino

blindness that we thrust it down from the glory prepared for it into eternal punishment.

So we love ourselves, but carnally, according to the flesh, not 14 spiritually; we do not care at all for our very soul, as if it were not part of us. If even a mild weakness attacks our body, we call doctors, we prepare medicines, we go off our food; blubbering and querulous, we groan over whatever ailment threatens us, and we take our medicines with no less irritation of our senses than we labor under from the diseases themselves, even very serious ones. However, although daily the souls of mortals are held by an illness 15 not light but absolutely mortal, nobody seems to sense the disease, nobody seeks a doctor, but we abhor the remedy of compunction and confession as if it were extremely bitter. We must take care, 16 then, dear Girolamo, not to love our souls among the corporeal things. For whoever loves his own soul will lose it. Therefore let us kill our souls to the world and hate them tenaciously according to the flesh. For as much as we hate them as pertains to the world, so much will we love them (if we want to hold the correct belief) for God. Let us, therefore, love ourselves in this manner, and not be so deceived in our loving that we love ourselves otherwise, and, when we pray, we ought to think of ourselves only in relation to salvation, not these temporal things. Those who pray ought to 17 make a single, sole, and determined petition, namely that with suppliant devotion we ask for what we should love. After you have considered everything, what is this thing but the blessedness of immutable glory? Just as we have to love blessedness, so we should try to obtain it by our prayers.

As I said, we must love our neighbor with a view to the same 18 salvation that we ought to desire for ourselves, in such great fullness of charity that the fervor of our love not only embraces friends but also reaches our enemies. Indeed, with what boldness do we dare to ask God that our offended Lord forgive us, if

nostris offensoribus remittamus? Non est enim exaudiri dignus
19 qui quod ab alio postulat non sit alteri concessurus. Quis autem
non videt quod, si in forma data nobis a Christo deum oramus,
penam nobis infligendam concludimus nisi nostris inimicis offen-
siones acceptas et illatas nobis iniurias dimittamus? Omnibus
orare volentibus sed maxime sacerdotibus est iniuncta necessitas
parcendi cunctis qui peccaverunt in ipsos, ut securi possint intra
missarum solennia vel inter orationum secreta colloquia cum
Christo dicere, 'Dimitte nobis debita nostra sicut et nos dimitti-
20 mus debitoribus nostris.' Qua conscientia quidem vadit presbiter
ad altare qui proximum odit? Qua intentione Christum orant qui
mala proximis suis exoptant?

Nec nos moveat quod in psalmorum divinis obsecrationibus
21 videatur prophetes penas diversas hostibus imprecari. Sic enim
confusionem ipsorum et exterminium petit quod in sue mentis
arcano desideret non hostes mori sed potius iniquitatibus deposi-
tis in amicos et benivolos commutari, vel quod in eis ad aliorum
exemplum et confirmationem bonorum divine iusticie severitas
ostendatur, vel ut sublata peccatorum servitute a viis suis pessimis
declinent et abstinentes ab iniquitatibus corrigantur, ut quicquid
execrationis sparsum inter divinarum scripturarum oracula reperitur aliquo sane expositionis misterio ad vere caritatis regulam aut
divine iusticie desiderium referri debeat vel alicuius altioris sensus
lumine sit taliter exponendum quod caritati dei et proximi nullatenus contradicat, cum maxime lata via expositoribus pateat eo
quod in sacris litteris tum multa sepe futura quasi iam facta

we do not forgive those who offend us, as the Lord commands? For whoever will not concede to another what he demands from someone else does not deserve to be listened to. Who does not see that if we pray to God in the form given to us by Christ, we end with the infliction of punishment on ourselves unless we forgive our enemies for the offenses we have suffered and injuries that have been inflicted on us? All wanting to pray, but especially priests, bear the necessity of sparing all who have sinned against them, so that they may be at peace when they say during Mass or in prayer's secret colloquy with Christ, "Forgive us our debts, as we forgive our debtors."[105] With what kind of a conscience does the priest who hates his neighbor go to the altar? With what intention do people who desire evil for their neighbors pray to Christ?

We should not be influenced by the fact that in the divine curses of the Psalms the prophet seems to invoke diverse punishments upon enemies. For the psalmist seeks their confusion and extermination in such a way that in a secret corner of his mind he desires not that his enemies die, but rather that they cast off their iniquities and turn into friendly, benevolent people; or that the severity of divine justice may be shown in them as an example to others and for strengthening the good people; or in order that, their slavery to sin eliminated, they may turn aside from their wicked ways and, abstaining from wrongdoing, be corrected. Hence, whatever element of execration is found scattered in the sayings of divine scripture should be referred, by a mystery of sound exposition, to the rule of true charity or the desire for divine justice; or it should be explained in the light of some higher sense in such a way that it in no way contradicts love of God and neighbor. Great scope is available to expositors, since in sacred literature, on the one hand, future events are often written of as if

19

20

21

scribantur, tum quedam videamus sicut desiderata rogari que desi-
22 derari nefas est credere. Sed dicendum est potius raptos in spiritu
prophetare.

Quid enim? Putandumne est, cum propheta dixit, 'Appone iniquitatem super iniquitatem eorum et non intrent in iusticia tua;
deleantur de libro viventium et cum iustis non scribantur,' licet
contra illos orare videatur qui Christum erant post tot annorum
secula crudeliter occisuri, quod ipsorum damnationem perpetuam
23 exoptarit? Absit a viro sancto de quo dixit deus, 'Inveni hominem
iuxta cor meum,' quemve, licet in Bethsabee et servum Uriam pre-
viderit peccaturum, quod infirmitatis humane fuit, simul tamen et
vidit eundem, quod fuit perfectionis et gratie, se lacrimis et vere
24 penitentie lavacro mundaturum, tam profana suspicio. Sed vidit
ille per spiritum quod futurum erat et in ardore divine iusticie desiderans protulit quod tot seculis ante previdit, licet non inepte
posset pars secundi versiculi salva lege caritatis ut oratio petentis
exponi. Nam cum previdens David peccatum Iudeorum dixisset,
'Appone iniquitatem super iniquitatem eorum,' non id intellexit,
25 quod deus futurus esset autor iniquitatis. Absit enim ut de illo
summo et infinito bono credamus quod aliquando sit causa peccati. Nam licet ad actum efficiendum concurrat in quo peccatum a
nobis mala et corrupta voluntate deficiendo committitur, pro-
26 culdubio tamen in peccando deus nichilum operatur. Sed licet
deus non sit malorum effector, ipsorum tamen est iustissimus or-
dinator. Unde inquit propheta, 'Appone iniquitatem super iniquitatem eorum,' quod quidem ordinantis est, non efficientis. Tunc

they had already happened, while, on the other hand, we see some things being asked for as desired that it is impious to believe are desired. But it must be said, rather, that those taken up by the   22
Spirit are prophesying.

Tell me: must we think, when the prophet said, "Add iniquity upon their iniquity and let them not enter into your righteousness; may they be erased from the book of the living and their names not be inscribed with those of the just,"[106] that he longed for their perpetual damnation, even though he seems to be praying against those who were to kill Christ cruelly after so many centuries? Far   23
be such a profane suspicion from the holy man concerning whom God said, "I have found a man according to my heart,"[107] and whom, although God foresaw that he would sin against Bathsheba and his servant Uriah (which was part of his human weakness), he nonetheless saw simultaneously that the same man would cleanse himself with tears and a bath of true penitence (which belongs to perfection and grace). But the psalmist saw through the Spirit   24
what would be, and in the ardor of divine justice he desired and revealed what he foresaw so many centuries beforehand, although part of the second versicle could be explained quite appropriately, with no harm done to the law of charity, as the prayer of a peti-tioner. For although David, foreseeing the sin of the Jews, said "Add iniquity upon their iniquity," he did not understand by it that God would be the author of iniquity. Far be it from us to   25
believe that the highest and infinite Good might sometime be a cause of sin. For although God may concur in executing an act whereby sin is committed by us in our deficiency, our will evil and corrupt, nevertheless there is no question of God working any-thing through sinning. Yet while God is not the effector of evils,   26
he is their most just arranger. Hence the prophet says "Add iniq-uity upon their iniquity": this is the task of one arranging, not of

enim peccato peccatum apponitur cum alterum ad aggravationem alterius per iusticiam ordinatur.

27   Nam cum Iudei occidissent prophetas, nuntios regis ad nuptias invitantes, demum occiderunt et sponsum, qui et, in quantum homo, nuntius regni celorum erat, in quantum vero dei eterni fi-

28   lius, rex erat et sponsus. Que simul sunt a dei iusticia taliter ordinata quod, sublato filii nomine quo fuerant in Abraham et Ysaac adoptati, tanta dignitas transferretur ad gentes ut daret eis filios dei fieri, his qui credunt in nomine eius qui verbum caro factum

29   est et habitavit in nobis, ut sublimis evangelista testatur. Que cuncta cum videret in mentis excessu, propheta, quasi cum Christo suspirans, ait, 'Deleantur de libro viventium,' non quod videret propheta Iudeos de vite libro delendos, cum in illo dispositionis eterne volumine ubi cuncta sunt fixa nichil penitus deleatur, sed 'deleantur de libro viventium,' inquit, hoc est mundo moriantur, et peccatorum persona deposita, qui soli mundo dediti mundo vivunt, in rectos et iustos, qui se mundo occidunt, per dei misericor-

30   diam convertantur. Nam si rogavit Christus dum peccarent et dixit, 'Pater, dimitte illis quia nesciunt quid faciant,' nonne pie ex tunc potuit orare David quod delerentur de libro viventium mundo ut penitus non peccarent? Quantum autem carnaliter et mundo Iudei viverent consilium ipsorum declarat. Dicebant enim: 'Quid facimus quia hic homo multa signa facit? Si dimittemus eum sic, omnes credent in eum et venient Romani et tollent nostrum lo-

31   cum et gentem.' Optabat ergo propheta ne sic mundo viverent sed

one effecting. Then is sin added to sin, when one sin is arranged for the aggravation of the other through justice.

The Jews killed the prophets, who were messengers inviting 27 them to the king's wedding feast. In the end they also killed the Bridegroom, who too, insofar as he was a man, was a messenger of the King of Heaven; insofar as he was the Son of the eternal God, he was King and Bridegroom. These things were simultaneously 28 arranged by God's justice in such a way that the name of *son* (which they had gained through adoption in Abraham and Isaac) was withdrawn, and such a great honor was transferred to the gentiles, in order that he might give to those who believe in the name of him, who, as the Word, was made flesh and dwelt among us (as the sublime evangelist attests),[108] to become sons of God. When he saw all of this in his inspired mind, as if sighing with 29 Christ, the prophet said, "May they be erased from the book of the living." This was not because the prophet saw that the Jews were to be erased from the book of life, since in that volume of the eternal order where all things are fixed, nothing at all is erased. Rather, he said, "May they be erased from the book of the living," that is, may they die to the world, and, their mask of sins laid aside, may those who live dedicated to the world alone be converted through God's mercy into righteous and just people who kill themselves to the world. For if Christ prayed when they were 30 sinning and said, "Father, forgive them for they know not what they do,"[109] could not David piously pray that they be erased from the book of those living for the world, in order that they not sin at all? The extent to which the Jews were living carnally and for the world is made clear by their council. For they were saying, "How do we proceed, since this man performs many signs? If we release him, everyone will believe in him, and the Romans will come and destroy our land and our people."[110] Therefore, the prophet was 31

de libro viventium delerentur et cum iustis non scribantur, scilicet in mundo isto. Iusti enim in eternitatis libro non scribuntur sed scripti sunt. Hic autem inter iustos scribimus quos postea inter iniquissimos reputamus. Hoc igitur et quicquid simile in divinarum scripturarum pelago reperitur ad sane intelligentie regulam exponatur.

32   Sed unde paulisper evagati sumus sermonis institutio revertatur. Non solum igitur caritatem habere debet orator sed etiam oportet ipsum fidei lumine refulgere. Quis enim deum oraret quem esse non crederet? Quis orationibus insisteret si deum exau-
33 dire non posse desideria nostra putaret? Credere itaque debemus deum sed, quoniam hoc parum est (credit enim diabolus et contremiscit), credere debemus et in deum, credere quidem fide viva et assertione certissima. Sicut enim fides in specie sua certitudinem intuitivam non recepit, ita et opinionis ambiguum non admittit.
34 Nichil equidem dubitat vera fides, nichil videt; non tamen minus assentit quam si manibus tangeret oculisque videret. Et quia, licet bonum sit deum credere, non tamen satis est nisi credamus et in deum (est autem in deum credere que sunt dei fideliter operari), credamus in deum nosque credere bonis operibus confirmemus, ut per adoptionis beneficium pater noster qui in celis est in filios re-
35 cipere nos dignetur nosque nostris in orationibus exaudire. Non sufficit enim nobis habere deum in creatorem nisi et habeamus in patrem. Creationis quidem donum tanquam pluvia super iustos et iniustos est. Paternitatis autem beneficium solum illis convenit
36 quos fide renatos in filios adoptavit. In hac igitur fide orandum est ut audiamus vocem illam suavissimam, 'Fides tua salvum te fecit.'

wishing that they not live for the world in this way, but that they might be erased from the book of the living and that they might not be inscribed with the just, namely in this world. For the just are not being inscribed, but have been inscribed, in the book of eternity. Here, however, we inscribe among the just those whom we consider later to be among the most unjust. This, then, and whatever similar thing is found in the sea of divine scripture, should be explained according to the rule of sound understanding.

But let the plan of our discussion return to the point from 32 which we briefly strayed. The person who prays, then, ought not only to have charity; he should also shine with the light of faith. For who prays to a God that he doesn't believe exists? Who persists in prayers if he thinks that God is unable to hear and answer our desires? And so we should believe that God exists. But since 33 this is too little (for even the devil believes and trembles), we should also believe *in* God, indeed, believe with a living faith and unshakable affirmation. Just as faith does not accept intuitive certitude in its own outer appearance, so it does not admit the wavering of opinion. Indeed true faith doubts nothing, sees nothing; yet 34 it assents no less than if it were touching with hands and seeing with eyes. Granted, it is good to believe that God exists; but it is not enough unless we also believe in God (and believing in God is to faithfully do the things that are of God). Let us believe in God, then, and by good works let us prove that we believe, so that through the favor of adoption our Father who is in heaven may deign to receive us as children and to hear us in our prayers. It is 35 not enough to have God as our Creator unless we also have him as our Father. The gift of creation is like the rain falling on just and unjust alike.[111] But the favor of paternity only comes to those whom, born again in faith, God has adopted as children. In this 36 faith, therefore, we must pray so that we hear that sweetest of utterances, "Your faith has made you well."[112] For the Truth says,

313

'Quicquid enim,' inquit veritas, 'petieritis a patre meo in nomine meo dabit vobis,' ut ex hoc moneamur quod postulare debeamus in fide, nedum nichil hesitantes sed etiam fidelissimam spem ha-

37 bentes. Scio enim quod, nisi speraveris, non orabis. Quod si desiderium tuum ostendendo forsan oraveris sicut ille dives in inferno positus qui petebat ut Lazarus unam aque guttam digito suis faucibus instillaret, audies verbum illud, 'Inter vos et nos est magnum chaos.' Nam nisi pennis spei sublevetur oratio, nunquam immensum illud chaos quod inter creatorem et creaturam situm est oratio transire poterit et ad exauditionis auditorium pervenire.

38 Nec minus quam tres istas et illas alias quatuor debemus habere. Prudenter enim orandum est, ut mereamur, imo ut digni efficiamur, benignitate illius summi principis exaudiri; temperate vero, ne modum qui cunctarum virtutum mensura est in aliquo transeamus; fortiter autem, ne subito forsan oratio nostra deficiat; et demum iuste, ne contra formam dispositionis illius eterni numinis committamus.

39 Ut autem prudenter oremus, quod in eloquentie preceptis fere primum est, benivolum deum ad quem oratio nostra dirigitur habeamus. Hoc autem, ut plurima transeam que circa materiam eiusmodi tradi solent, quivis orans tripliciter assequetur si se primo componat taliter ad preterita quod deo non solum ore sed corde gratias referat et innumerabilia sue benignitatis dona suppli-

40 citer recognoscat. Nam, ut inquit divus Aurelius Augustinus, 'Quid melius et animo geramus et ore promamus et calamo exprimamus quam deo gratias?' et subdit, 'Hoc nec dici brevius nec intelligi grandius nec agi fructuosius potest.' Hec ille. Indignus est

"Whatever you ask my Father for in my name, he will give you."[113] By this we are advised that we ought to ask for things in faith; not only shouldn't we doubt, but we should even faithfully hope. I know that if you do not hope, you will not pray. But if in revealing   37 your request you should pray like that rich man who was sent to hell and begged Lazarus to let drip into his throat a single drop of water from his finger, you will hear these words: "Between you and us is a great chasm."[114] For unless prayer is raised on wings of hope, it will never be able to cross that immense chasm that lies between Creator and creature and arrive in the hall of reception.

We should have no fewer than these three things[115] and the   38 other four virtues as well. We must pray prudently, in order to deserve being heard (rather, to be made worthy of being heard) by the generosity of that supreme Ruler; temperately, lest we in some way overstep the limit that is the measure of all virtues; bravely, lest our prayer suddenly fall short; and finally, justly, lest we commit any offense against the form of the eternal Deity's disposition.

In order to pray prudently, we should have a benevolent God to   39 whom our prayer is directed. (This is more or less the first among the precepts of eloquence;[116] I will pass over this as well as a great many other things that are usually handed down regarding this kind of material.) Anyone who prays will attain this in three ways. First, he should set himself in relation to past events in such a way that he gives thanks to God not only with his lips but also with his heart, and in suppliant fashion acknowledges the innumerable gifts of his generosity. For, as the divine Aurelius Augustine says,   40 "What better thing do we render with our spirit, announce with our lips, and express with the pen than thanks to God?" And he adds, "Than this nothing briefer can be said, nothing grander can be understood, and nothing more fruitful can be done."[117] A person does not deserve to receive what he prays for if he neglects to

enim impetrare quod petit qui negligit debita gratitudine re-
41 cognoscere quod accepit. Ab ipso vero benigno patre de nichilo
secundum animam facti et ad sue maiestatis imaginem ordinati
non solum habemus hoc quod sumus sed etiam quicquid sumus.
Ipse enim fecit nos et non ipsi nos. Quicquid desumus culpa nostra desumus. Ipse nobiscum construit, nos soli destruimus. Ipse
42 plantat, nos vellimus. Ipse nos salvat dummodo recte velimus. Ut
non solum de beneficiis referende sint gratie sed etiam cuilibet
meditatione sit assidua recensendum quicquid errando commise-
rit, ut laborans in gemitu suo et lavando per singulas noctes lec-
tum suum et stratum suum lacrimis irrigando coram eo dicere
valeat: 'Discedite a me omnes qui operamini iniquitatem, quoniam
exaudivit dominus vocem fletus mei, exaudivit dominus depreca-
tionem meam, dominus orationem meam suscepit.'

43   Secundum est quod orans taliter se comparet elevatione mentis
quod ascendens in deum supra se positus obsecret, petat, supplicet, narret, et demum orationis gratiam consecutus (ipsum enim
orare nobis non nisi per gratiam datur) orando mereatur accipere
44 quod antequam oraret recte licuit exoptare. Caveatque ne de merito suo presumat, sed cum Daniele suppliciter dicat: 'Obsecro,
domine deus, magne et terribilis, custodiens pactum et misericordiam diligentibus te et custodientibus mandata tua, peccavimus,
iniquitatem fecimus, impie egimus et recessimus et declinavimus a
mandatis tuis ac iudiciis, non obedivimus servis tuis, prophetis,
qui locuti sunt nobis in nomine tuo. Nunc ergo exaudi, deus, orationem servi tui propter temet ipsum. Inclina, deus meus, aurem
tuam et audi. Non enim in iustificationibus nostris prosternimus
preces ante faciem tuam, sed in miserationibus tuis multis. Exaudi,

acknowledge with due gratitude what he has received. Made in the   41
soul out of nothing by that kind Father himself and ordered to the
image of his majesty, we have not only the fact that we are, but
whatever we are. For he himself made us and not we ourselves.[118]
In whatsoever we fail, we fail through our own fault. He builds
with us; we destroy alone. He propagates from cuttings; we up-
root. He saves us, as long as our will is correct. So not only must   42
we render thanks for favors, but every one of us must evaluate
with assiduous reflection what sin he has committed in straying
from the path. Toiling in his groaning as he washes his bed night
after night, watering his couch with his tears, he should be able to
say before God "Depart from me all you who do evil, since the
Lord has heard the voice of my lament, the Lord has heard my
entreaty, the Lord has taken up my prayer."[119]

The second instruction is that the person praying should so   43
prepare himself by lifting up his mind that, ascending to God and
placed above himself, he beseeches, petitions, supplicates, tells,
and finally, having attained the grace of prayer (for praying itself is
not given to us except through grace), by praying merits to receive
what he was permitted to desire correctly before he prayed. Let   44
him be watchful that he does not make presumptions about his
merit, but rather let him say in suppliant fashion with Daniel: "I
beg, Lord God, great and terrible, you who carefully guard your
covenant and your mercy for those who love you and keep your
commandments, we have sinned, we have committed iniquity, we
have acted impiously, and withdrawn and turned from your commandments and judgments, we have not obeyed your servants, the
prophets, who have spoken to us in your name. Now therefore,
hear, God, your servant's prayer, for your own sake. My God, incline your ear and listen. For we have not strewn prayers before
your face for our own justification, but for your many acts of

domine, placare, domine. Attende et fac, ne moreris propter temet ipsum, deus meus.'

45   Tertium erit ut id postulet orator quod non debeat denegari. Quid autem illud sit superius attigi, vite scilicet eterne immarcescibilis beatitudo, ut elevati per gratiam in lumine suo videamus inextinguibile lumen ipsius. Dicas igitur cum propheta, 'Unam petii a deo, hanc requiram, ut inhabitem in domo domini omnibus 46 diebus vite mee.' Hoc igitur petat, hoc supplicet, hoc exoret. Hoc unum, cum ab aliis plurima alia consequamur, nobis a solo domino dari potest. Hoc unum summum humani generis bonum est. Victus autem, potus, et vestitus ad illud ordinari debent, non precipue queri, non orationibus principaliter postulari, sed ad hoc petenda et optanda sunt, ut vivere possimus et viventes regni dei iusticiam facere, facientes autem ad divini regni gloriam pervenire. 'Querite enim,' dixit veritas, 'primum regnum dei et iusticiam eius, et hec omnia adicientur vobis.'

47   Et quoniam in maxima cecitate versatur nostra condicio, si forte quid petere debeas dubitaveris, habes salvatoris nostri documentum, qui discipulos non solum monuit quod orarent sed dedit etiam quam formam tenere conveniat cum orarent. Hec est enim oratio dominica, a perfectissimo magistro taliter edita quod, si recte et congruenter orare voluerimus, nichil aliud quam in ipsa sit 48 positum dicere debeamus. Que quoniam a multis diffusissime sunt tractata, cum presentis operis intentio non sit disputare de singulis, cumque festinem ad exitum, nedum consulte sed etiam quadam quodam modo necessitate dimittam. Hoc tamen dixisse suffecerit, quod, cum hec oratio brevissima sit, nichil queas tamen animo cogitare ad gloriam pertinens obtinendam quod non sit hoc 49 breviloquio comprehensum. Cum enim oratio nichil aliud sit quam elevatio nostri intellectus in deum ut, quo pervenire non

mercy. Hear, Lord; be placated, Lord. Give ear and act, don't delay, for your own sake, my God."[120]

The third instruction will be that the person praying should ask 45 for what ought not to be denied. Earlier I touched on what that is, namely unfading blessedness of eternal life, so that lifted through grace we see in his light his own inextinguishable light.[121] Therefore, say with the prophet "One thing have I asked of the Lord, for this I long, to live in the house of the Lord all the days of my life."[122] Let him ask for this, let him beg for it, let him win it by 46 entreaty. This one thing, although we obtain many other things from other people, can be given to us by the Lord alone. This is the one supreme good of the human race. Food, drink, and clothing must be ordered to that one thing, not sought especially, not asked for first and foremost in our prayers. Rather, we must seek and long for them for this reason, that we may live, and in living, do the justice of the kingdom of God, and in doing it, reach the glory of the divine kingdom. "Seek," says the Truth, "first the kingdom of God and its righteousness, and all these things will be added unto you."[123]

And since our condition is marked by extreme blindness, if you 47 are in doubt about what you should ask for, you have the example of our Savior, who not only warned his disciples to pray, but also gave them an appropriate form to use when they prayed. This is the Lord's Prayer, uttered by the perfect teacher in such a way that, if we want to pray correctly and appropriately, we should say nothing other than what is found in it. Many have treated these 48 things extensively; since the intention of the present work is not to debate about details, and since I am hastening to the end, I will leave them aside — deliberately, but even more by a kind of necessity. It will suffice to have said this, that although this prayer is extremely brief, in your mind you can think of nothing relevant to obtaining glory that is not included in this short utterance. Prayer 49 is nothing other than the raising of our understanding to God, so

possumus corpore, spiritu saltem ascendamus et mente, nonne prima orationis istius verba nos excitant ad dei contemplationem, quem bonitatis magnitudine confitemur in patrem et celum tes-
50 tamur incolere per excellentie maiestatem? Et quoniam oratio desiderii nostri mediatrix et interpres est coram deo, ut solum id recte possimus petere quod recte licet optare, et postquam appellando deum patrem exultavit spiritus noster in deo salutari nostro, nichil primum potest occurrere nisi ut cum apostolis dicamus, 'Domine, bonum est hic esse. Faciamus tria tabernacula,' deo videlicet unum tabernaculum, scilicet caritatis, ut in deo maneamus et deus in nobis; unum Moysi, hoc est legi iusticie, que ultimo dei iudicio eternaliter puniet malos, remunerabit et bonos; Helye
51 unum, id est veritati. Videbimus enim tunc sicuti est. Nec immerito Christus figuram caritatis, cum deus caritas sit, et Moyses legis, qui legem a deo acceptam populo dei dedit, et Helyas, prophetes eximius, typum obtinet veritatis, qui veritati testimonium ferens rapi promeruit ubi diutius vivens demum in fine temporum pro veritate pugnans ab Antichristo creditur occidendus.
52 Et quoniam illa stature caritatis extensio et ipsa veritatis revelatio non nisi per dei misericordiam fiet, ipsa vero iusticia sine misericordia non erit, non immerito propheta per spiritum tempus illud aspiciens inquit: 'Misericordia et veritas obviaverunt sibi. Iusticia et pax osculate sunt.' Hec enim sunt regnum dei. Nam, ut inquit apostolus, 'Regnum dei non est esca et potus, sed iusticia et pax et gaudium in spiritu sancto.'

53 Quod quidem advenire nobis tanquam ultimum nostrum finem secunde petitionis oraculo petimus prout dei gloria frui et illam participare beatitudinem exoptamus. Nam prime petitionis intentio, qua sanctificationem divini nominis poscimus, ad solam dei

that we may at least rise in spirit and in mind to a place where we are unable to go in body. Shouldn't the first words of that prayer stir us to the contemplation of God, whom we acknowledge as a Father for the magnitude of his goodness and testify that he dwells in heaven through the majesty of his excellence? Prayer is the me- 50 diator and interpreter of our desire before God, so that we can only rightly ask for what it is permitted to desire rightly; in calling God *Father* our spirit exults in God our Savior.[124] Therefore, the first thing that can occur to us is to say with the apostles "Lord, it is good to be here. Let us make three tents":[125] one for God, the tent of charity, so that we remain in God and he in us; one for Moses, that is for the law of justice, which in the Last Judgment of God will punish the wicked eternally and reward the good; one for Elijah, that is, for truth. For then we will see God as he is.[126] It is 51 right and proper that Christ has the figure of love, since God is love; and Moses has the figure of law, since he gave to the people of God the law he had received from God; and Elijah, outstanding prophet, has the type of truth, since bearing witness to the truth, he merited to be snatched away to a place where he is believed to live for a long time, destined at the end of time to fight for the truth and finally be killed by the Antichrist. And since that exten- 52 sion of the stature of charity and the very revelation of truth will not happen except through God's mercy, and without mercy, jus- tice itself will not exist, the prophet, beholding that time through the Spirit, rightly said, "Mercy and truth have met. Justice and peace have kissed."[127] For these things are the kingdom of God. As the apostle says, "The kingdom of God is not food and drink, but righteousness and peace and joy in the Holy Spirit."[128]

In the second petition of the Lord's Prayer, we ask that the 53 kingdom come to us as our final end, as we desire to enjoy the glory of God and have a share in that beatitude. The purpose of the first petition, by which we pray for sanctification of the divine

pertinet caritatem prout ipsum in se diligimus, et ob id ante omnia
54 confirmationem sui nominis flagitamus. Post finem vero nostrum,
per dilectionem et frui, sicut convenit peroratum, eiusdem sancte
orationis eulogio, ad reliqua que nos in finem dirigunt pervenimus,
quorum principaliter effectivum est obedientie meritum, qua voluntati dei, que sola, sicut supra memini, nostrorum esse debet
actuum regulatrix, conformes effecti in omni virtute divine iussionis imperium adimplemus, et ius ad eterne vite beatitudinem viventes acquirimus secundum legis ordinate gratiam, quam tandem
55 gratuito dei munere possidemus. Unde voluntatem eius impleri
tam in celo quam in terra rogamus ut sic in mundo possimus deo
obedientes vivere quod in celo valeamus gratie sue divitias ob-
56 tinere. Verum, quia non nisi in presenti vita bonum meritorie
possumus operari, consequens est ut vite necessaria deposcamus.
Quotidianum igitur panem petimus, sine quo quidem vivere non
possemus. Et, quoniam Christus etiam panis est, debemus et panem spiritualem petere, sine cuius participatione certum est nos ad
illam non posse gloriam pervenire.

57 Nam tria ultima que sequuntur ad id solum pertinent, ut viatores sic expediti reddamur ad viam quod venire non prohibeamur
in patriam. Dimitti quidem nobis peccata nostra volumus, que
non solum nos prohiberent celo sed cruciari facerent in inferno.
Nolumus etiam in temptationem trahi, qua possimus facile sine
suffragio divine gratie superari, sed ab omni malo liberari petimus,
58 quo nichil orandum sequentes Christi monita relinquamus. Illud
in tota oratione precipue considerandum est, quod nichil pro orantibus singulariter petitur sed totum sicuti peteretur a pluribus explicatur, quo facile possumus admoneri non solum orandum esse

name, relates only to God's charity, as we love God in himself, and for that reason we call for the confirmation of his name above all things. After our final end, involving love and enjoyment, has been 54 mentioned, as is fitting, with the blessing of the same holy prayer, we come to the remainder, which directs us to the end.[129] The most practically operative of these things is the merit of obedience. By obedience, we are conformed to the divine will, which alone (as I have mentioned above)[130] ought to be the regulator of our actions; thus we fulfill the power of the divine command in every virtue. Living for the beatitude of eternal life, we also acquire righteousness, according to the grace of the ordained law, which we finally possess by God's free gift. For this reason, we ask that his 55 will be done both in heaven and on earth, so that, obeying God, we can live in the world in such a way that in heaven we can obtain the riches of his grace. Yet, since we cannot do good meritoriously 56 except in this present life, it follows that we pray for the necessities of life. Therefore, we ask for our daily bread, without which we could not live. And since Christ is also bread, we ought to ask for our spiritual bread, too, since without sharing in it, we certainly cannot come to glory.

For the three final petitions that follow pertain to only one 57 thing, that as travelers we be returned to the path so unencumbered that we cannot be prevented from coming into our homeland. We want our sins to be forgiven: they not only keep us out of heaven but cause us to be tortured in hell. We don't want to be drawn into temptation, which can easily overcome us without the help of divine grace; but we ask to be freed from every evil, so that, following the teachings of Christ, we leave nothing to be prayed for. In the entire prayer, we should especially consider that 58 we are seeking nothing for ourselves individually. The whole discourse is unfolded as if it were being prayed by many people; hence we can easily be reminded that we must not only pray for

59 pro nobis sed etiam pro cunctis universaliter supplicandum. Orare
quidem debemus pro peccatoribus ut a malo resiliant, pro bonis
autem ut ab incepte bonitatis officio non desistant. Debemus
etiam omnes orare pro iustis, quia, cum a multis gratia deo refer-
tur, salus ipsorum facilius impetratur, et illi discunt se per insolentiam minus efferre cum viderint etiam minorum suffragia se iu-

60 vare. Nec debemus ab orationibus nostris inimicos excludere, quos
divine monitionis oraculo nobis non est licitum non amare.

Ceterum, ne virtutes reliquas excludamus, curemus moderati-
onem nostris orationibus adhibere ut, sicut mediator dei et hominum, Iesus Christus, admonuit, in orando multiloquium fugiamus.
Nam vix, ut inquit sapiens, in multiloquio potest evitari peccatum,
quo putant insipientes se forsitan per importunitatis tedium a deo

61 recipere quod brevisermo poterat longe placidius obtinere. Nam
cum iubeat nobis Christus orando verborum multitudinem fugere,
qui tantus et talis orandi nobis doctor extitit, cur inanem laborem
assumimus et quasi carnalis hominis voluntatem flectere deum in

62 nostra beneplacita importunis orationibus cogitamus? Immobilis
est enim dei voluntas, nec ideo nobis est orationibus insistendum
ut illam ad nostra desideria deflectamus sed, sicut veritas docuit et
sicut ipse idem salvator noster oravit, debemus orando petere pe-
tendoque desiderare, non quod nostra voluntas fiat, sed ut summi
creatoris placitum impleatur.

63 Nec, quamvis quod ab eterno deus voluit et previdit omnino sit
futurum, quoniam illius voluntas rerum est necessitas, debemus
propterea supervacuum orationis officium reputare. Nam, sicut
futuros effectus immutabili rerum serie et successione decrevit, sic

ourselves but also make supplication for all alike. We should indeed pray for sinners, that they may recoil from evil; but for the good, that they not cease from the service of goodness they have embarked upon. And all of us ought to pray for righteous people also: when thanks are given to God by many people, their salvation is more easily obtained; they learn to exalt themselves less through insolence when they see that even the petitions of lesser people help them. Nor should we exclude our enemies from our prayers, since according to the divine admonition, we not allowed not to love them.

But, so as not to leave out other virtues, let us take care to apply moderation to our prayers, so that (just as the mediator of God and men, Jesus Christ, warned) we flee garrulousness in praying.[131] For, as the wise man says, in garrulousness sin is scarcely to be avoided.[132] Foolish people think that they may receive from God through the tedium of importunity what succinct speech could far more peacefully obtain. For when Christ commands us to shun a multitude of words when we pray — he who is such a great and excellent teacher of prayer for us — why do we take on vain labor and think that we can by importunate prayers bend God to do what is pleasing to us, as if we were bending the will of a carnal human being? God's will is immovable. We must not focus with our prayers on turning his will to our desires, but (as the Truth has taught and as our Savior himself prayed) in praying we ought to seek, and in seeking, to desire, not that our will be done, but that the good pleasure of the Creator on high be fulfilled.

Moreover, we should not think that the duty of prayer is superfluous because what God wanted and foresaw from eternity will come about in every respect, since his will constitutes the necessity of events. Just as he has decreed future effects in an immutable series and succession of events, so also he has ordained their

59

60

61

62

63

et illorum certas et effectivas causas ordinavit, inter quas oratio non est inferior. Nam quid in eius affectu exauditurus esset in

64 tempore, dignatus est ante tempora providere. Et ideo ferventer orandum est ut, quod instituit deus nobis in oratione concedere, mereamur per sue benignitatis gratiam obtinere. Quod eo propensius faciendum est, quia, cum relique inferiores cause nedum plerumque non prosint sed quandoque manifestum etiam afferant nocumentum, sola tamen oratio semper prodest, nunquam nocet, sola nunquam frustra porrigitur sed semper aliquid promeretur.

65 Nam licet plerumque deus in eo quod petimus pro nobis aut aliis nos non audiat, oratio tamen nostra in sinu nostro convertitur, nobisque aliud ex ipsa premium reservatur. Deus enim quedam nobis denegat quandoque propitius que, si concederet, videretur iratus, ut exauditi gaudere debeamus recta vota nostra cum dei providentia concurrisse, non exauditi vero moneamur non omnia, licet nobis iustissima videantur, ab illa ineffabili bonitate et innarrabili iusticia concedenda, ut quotiens rogantibus optatum non conceditur nobiscum equanimiter consolemur.

66 Iusta sit etiam oratio nostra si volumus exaudiri. Inefficax est enim oratio qua petitur quod non licet. Nam, quamvis hec sit fiducia quam habemus ad deum, quia quodcunque petierimus secundum voluntatem eius audiat nos, quoniam, ut et ipsa testatur veritas, 'Quecunque orantes petitis, credite quia accipietis et venient vobis,' nichilominus tamen, ut inquit apostolus, 'Petimus et

67 non accipimus eo quod male petamus.' Tunc autem male petimus cum non secundum dei iusticiam sed secundum concupiscentias que militant in membris nostris petimus. Ut autem iuste possimus orare, iusti et innocentes simus aut cum vera cordis penitentia nostras iniusticias fateamur. Quis enim magis exaudiri meretur

certain and effective causes, among which prayer is not the least. What was in his heart to hear and fulfill in time he also deigned to foresee in advance. We must pray fervently so that, through the grace of his generosity, we deserve to obtain what God has decided to grant to us in prayer. This we must do all the more keenly, since, while the other, inferior causes are generally not advantageous, but sometimes even bring about manifest harm, prayer alone is always of benefit and never harms; prayer alone is never offered in vain but always earns some merit. Even though God often may not grant our prayers for something that we are seeking for ourselves or for others, our prayer nevertheless is transformed in our breast, and some other reward is reserved for us as a result of it. For God graciously denies us certain things sometimes; and if he were to grant these things, he would in fact seem to be angry. So when our prayers are answered, we should rejoice that our correct petitions coincided with God's providence. When our prayers are not answered, we are warned that not everything—even if it seems utterly just to us—must be granted by that ineffable goodness and justice beyond words; we should console ourselves with equanimity that our wish was not granted to us, despite our asking so many times.

If we want to be heard, let our prayer be just. Prayer is ineffectual when we ask for what is not allowed. We have this trust in God, that he will hear us when we ask for something according to his will; as the Truth itself attests, "Whatever you ask for in prayer, believe that you will receive it and it will come to you."[133] Nevertheless, as the apostle says, "We ask and we do not receive, because we ask badly."[134] We ask badly when we ask not according to God's justice but according to the desires that struggle in our bodies. In order to be able to pray justly, let us be just and innocent, or let us confess our acts of injustice with true repentance of heart. For who deserves to have his prayers answered more

64

65

66

67

quam qui potest cum psalmista dicere, 'Iudica me, domine, secundum iusticiam meam, et secundum innocentiam meam super
68 me'? Declinantes enim a malo et facientes bonitatem precipueque in optimis operibus misericordie, de quibus reddituri sumus in extremo iudicio rationem, totis affectibus occupati iustos nos coram deo exhibebimus oratores deique benignitate continget nos supra meritorum habitum exaudiri.

69 Memento quidem Tobie senioris, cui dixit angelus, 'Quando orabas cum lacrimis et sepeliebas mortuos et derelinquebas prandium et mortuos abscondebas in domo tua et nocte sepeliebas, ego obtuli orationem tuam domino,' ut manifestum sit orando devote cum bonorum operum suffragio nostras orationes ad dominum
70 sursum ferri. Nec putes Tobiam illum, singulare pietatis exemplum, licet ipsum angelus solum de sepultura commendet, non etiam aliis misericordie cultibus claruisse. Plane quidem per sepulture memoriam reliqua dedit intelligi; nam quem in mortuos tante misericordie fuisse proposuit in vivos etiam effusissimum intel-
71 lexit. Nudus enim vestiri, famelicus pasci, sitibundus potari, visitari infirmus, redimi carceratus, et hospitari peregrinus dum clamat, dum petit, dum rogat, dum gemitus emittit, dum lacrimis effluit vel humiliter deprecatur, tum aspicientium misericordia consequitur, tum importunitate rogaminum promeretur. Et hec illum sepius contingit accipere quem vicissim speramus aliquando
72 posse nobis in maioribus subvenire. Mortui vero iacent exanimes nec a tacentibus eis quicquam accipitur nisi quod in solius miserationis affectibus exhibetur, ut tanto magis putandum sit Tobiam

than the person who can say with the psalmist, "Judge me, Lord, according to my justice, and according to my innocence"?[135] If we turn away from evil and do good[136] (especially if we are wholeheartedly occupied with the most excellent works of mercy, of which we will render an account at the Last Judgment), we will show ourselves before God to be just in our prayers, and through God's generosity it will befall us to be heard over and above what we deserve.   68

Remember the elder Tobias, to whom an angel said, "When you were praying with tears and were burying the dead and were leaving your dinner behind and were hiding the dead in your house and burying them by night, I offered your prayer to the Lord."[137] Clearly, if we pray with devotion and have the support of good works, our prayers are borne on high to the Lord. And do not think that Tobias, a singular example of piety, did not shine also in other works of mercy, even though the angel commends him only for the burial. With the mention of the burial, the angel clearly gave us to understand the rest of his works; for the man whom he declared had been so merciful to the dead, he understood to have been most generous to the living also. As long as a naked person cries to be clothed; as long as a famished person begs to be fed; as long as a parched person asks to be given a drink; as long as a sick person groans for a visit; as long as the prisoner overflows with tears for his release; as long as the wayfarer humbly beseeches to be given accommodation: then the mercy of those who behold these people ensues, then merit is earned by importunity of prayers. And it happens quite often that the person who receives these things is one whom we hope will one day be able to help us in turn in greater things. But the dead lie inanimate, and we can receive nothing from those silent ones except what is granted in the merciful impulse alone. All the more, then, must we consider Tobias to have had a propensity toward   69   70   71   72

ad alia fuisse propensum quanto liberius legimus eum ad sepelien-
73 dos mortuos inclinatum. Sed, o te iustissimum oratorem, si circumventus ab inimicis dicere poteris, 'Eripe me de inimicis meis,
deus meus, et ab insurgentibus in me libera me,' et in veritate
subicere quod paulo post sequitur, 'neque iniquitas mea neque
peccatum meum, domine. Sine iniquitate cucurri et direxi.'

74   Nec nos ab orando deterreat, quamvis iustam esse debere dixerim orationem, quod per ipsam oporteat eterne vite premium
postulare, quam ex nostra iusticia non possumus promereri. Nam
deposcendo premium et illa omnia petimus sine quibus illud asse-
75 qui non possemus. Non est igitur iniusta petitio si desideria nostra
dirigamus in finem in quo perficimur et ad quem obtinendum ab
illo rerum omnium principe procreamur. Orantes enim vitam eternam actus nostros informari necessaria sancti spiritus gratia postu-
76 lamus. Nam licet per se ipsos exclusa dei gratia considerati, ad altitudinem illius glorie, que tantum supra nos est quod illam nec
oculus vidit et in cor etiam hominis non ascendit, nos non possimus extollere, si tamen illius ineffabilis trinitatis gratia sociemur,
divini numinis sublimitate levati digni efficimur nos supra nos ex-
77 tollere et in illam altitudinem glorie per iusticiam collocare. Ius-
tum est igitur orare pro gloria quam deus ab eterno rationali creature sue perfectionis terminum ordinavit; iustius autem orantes id
petere sine quo non possumus illud bonum ultimum obtinere;
iustissimum vero nedum bonis operibus sed etiam oratione conari
quod infinita dei bonitate ad suscipiendam illam iustificationis
nostre gratiam preparemur, sperareque in multitudine miseratio-
num suarum, in quibus solis nos salvandos fore cognoscere debeamus.

other good works, the more generously he was inclined (as we read) to bury the dead. But you will pray most righteously if you are able to say, surrounded by your enemies, "Snatch me away from my enemies, my God, and free me from those rising up against me," and to truthfully add what follows shortly thereafter, "neither my iniquity and nor my sin, Lord. Without iniquity I have run and directed my course."[138] 73

This shouldn't deter us from praying, even though I said that our prayer ought to be righteous, because through our prayer we ought to ask for the reward of eternal life — which we cannot earn by our own righteousness. For by asking for the reward, we are also seeking all those things without which we would be unable to attain it. Therefore, a petition is not unjust if we direct our desires to the end in which we are perfected and for the obtaining of which we have been created by the Ruler of all. Praying for eternal life, we are asking that our actions may be informed by the necessary grace of the Holy Spirit. We alone, without God's grace, cannot raise ourselves to the heights of his glory that is so much above us that eye has not seen it, and it has not even entered into the heart of man.[139] However, if we are accompanied by the grace of the ineffable Trinity, raised by the sublimity of divine power we are made worthy to raise ourselves above ourselves, and through righteousness to reach that height of glory. It is righteous, therefore, to pray for the glory that God has ordained from eternity for the rational creature as the end of his perfection. It is more righteous, however, to seek in prayer that without which we cannot obtain that ultimate good. But it is most righteous to try not only with good works but also with prayer to be prepared for receiving the grace of our justification by God's infinite goodness, and to hope in the multitude of his mercies, by which alone we should know we shall be saved. 74 75 76 77

78   Nec solum orator caritatem habeat ut mereatur, fidem ut exau-
diatur, spem ut ad orandum confidentius excitetur aut prudentiam
ut petenda discernat, temperantiam ut modum in aliquo non exce-
dat, iusticiam ut institutis divine maiestatis adhereat, sed etiam
fortitudinem ut ab orationis sancte proposito non discedat.

79   Non igitur quodam impetu levitatis aut subiti timoris instantia
vel repentine cuiuspiam voluntatis motu nos debemus orationibus
implicare, ut mox, impetu refrigescente vel postquam evanuerit timor aut illa fuerit immutata voluntas, incipiamus ab orando deficere, vel non, sicut precipimur, orationi totis affectibus intendatur.

80   Illam enim orationem deus non audit cui per mentis evagationem
orantis animus non intendit. Nam, cum per orationem animus
feratur in deum, damnande levitatis est ab illo mente discedere

81   quem ex tota nostra fortitudine debemus amare. Si autem propter
humane condicionis fragilitatem non possumus elevatam in deum
mentem quantum decet quantumque volumus sustinere, cum corpus quod corrumpitur aggravet animam et deprimat terrena inha-
bitatio sensum multa cogitantem, conemur tamen pro viribus ut
ab illius altitudinis culmine non cadamus, videatque deus in hoc
nos non voluntate deficere sed solum fragilitate nature non posse
durare, sicque nos benignus exaudiat et illius evagationis necessita-

82   tem nobis ad culpe demeritum non ascribat. Omnino tamen orationem intentissimis affectibus inchoemus, ne loquentes ad quod
non attendimus deum, quasi ludentes cum homine, rideamus.
Nunquam autem orantes mereri possumus vel id quod petimus
impetrare nisi in vi maxime ferventisque attentionis nos contigerit

83   deprecari. Scriptum est enim: 'Scitote quoniam exaudiet deus
preces vestras si manentes permanseritis in ieiuniis et orationibus
in conspectu domini.' Unde et apostolus inquit: 'Semper gaudete,
sine intermissione orate.' Nam, ut veritas suadet, 'Oportet semper

The person who prays should have charity, in order to earn   78
merit; faith, in order to be heard; hope, in order to be more confi-
dently motivated to pray; discretion, in order to discern what to
pray for; temperance, in order not to exceed good measure in anything; justice, in order to adhere to the ordinances of the divine
majesty; fortitude, in order not to abandon his plan of holy prayer.

Our prayers, therefore, should not be bound up with a fickle   79
impulse, an onset of sudden fear, or a sudden act of will: soon,
when the impulse has cooled, or the fear has vanished, or the will
has changed, we begin to fall away from prayer, or we do not exert
ourselves in prayer with all our heart as we are instructed to do.
God does not hear the prayer to which the spirit of the person   80
praying, through a wandering of mind, does not attend. For, when
the spirit is carried through prayer to God, it is damnable fickleness to mentally depart from him, whom we should love with all
our strength. But if on account of the fragility of the human con-   81
dition, we cannot sustain a mind raised to God as much as is fitting and as much as we want, since the corruptible body weighs
down the soul and our dwelling on earth presses down our sense
so that it thinks of many things, let us strive nevertheless, according to our strength, not to fall from the summit of that great
height, so that God sees in this that we are not deficient in will,
but only unable to endure because of the fragility of our nature
and thus may hear us with benevolence and not ascribe the necessity of that mental wandering of ours to the fault of guilt. Let us   82
begin our prayer with the most focused feelings, lest in speaking
words we are not attending to, we mock God as if we were playing
with a human being. When we pray, we can never earn merit or
obtain what we are seeking unless we beseech with the force of
utmost and fervent attention. For it is written, "Know that God   83
will hear your prayers if you consistently persevere in fasting and
prayers in the Lord's sight."[140] Hence the apostle says, "Rejoice always, pray without ceasing."[141] For, as the Truth persuades us,

84 orare et non deficere.' Non quod nichil aliud omnino faciendum
sit (impossibile quidem est), sed donec compleveris quod orare
proposuisti, penitus non desistas, et si forsitan id facere prohibebe-
ris, quantum tamen potes perseveres affectu. 'Semper enim,' ut dicit glosa super antedictis apostoli verbis, 'orat qui semper bene fa-

85 cit.' Ipsum enim desiderium bonum oratio est, et si continuum est
desiderium, continua est oratio, ut manifestum sit nec Christum
nec apostolum impossibile persuasisse. Nam licet semper actuali-
ter nequeamus orare, caritatis tamen iusticiam, que orationis est
seminarium, debemus habere servareque nobiscum in habitu quod
omnino tenere non valemus in actu.

86 Nec solum attente et continue putemus orandum sed etiam
orationem sciamus totis viribus intendendam, ut orantes effunda-
mus animam nostram in conspectu domini. Manasses enim coan-
gustatus oravit dominum et demum obsecravit intente, et exaudi-

87 vit deus orationes eius. Verum quia oramus spiritu, oramus et
mente, oramus etiam et lingua, simus attenti ad verba ne erremus.
Attendamus et spiritu taliter quod significata verborum quasi rerum imagines capiamus. Sed sublimis attentio mentis est qua in
deum ferimur et ab eo quod orantes intendimus non movemur.

88 Nam si lingua solum oremus, spiritus noster orat, spiritus scilicet
oris nostri, mens autem nostra sine fructu est; vel spiritus noster
orat, hoc est pars mentis inferior que sensibus proxima simulacra

89 rerum accipiens superiori parti mentis exhibet speculanda. Nec,
quamvis vera oratio sit cordis et non oris, negligenda est et vocalis
oratio. Moveat tamen devotio voces ut simul deo tam corpore
quam animo serviamus, excitemusque vocibus torpentem spiritum

"One must always pray and not grow weak."[142] Not that nothing   84
else at all should be done (that is impossible), but until you have
fulfilled what you proposed to pray for, do not cease, and if you
should be prevented from doing that, at least persevere in your effort as much as you can. As the gloss on the words of the apostle
(quoted above) says, "The person who always does good always
prays."[143] A good desire is itself prayer, and if the desire is continu-   85
ous, prayer is continuous. So it is clear that neither Christ nor the
apostle argued for something impossible. Although we are unable
in actuality to pray always, we ought nevertheless to have the righteousness of charity, which is the seedbed of prayer; we ought to
have and keep with us in disposition what we cannot completely
maintain in action.

Let us not only consider that we must pray attentively and con-   86
tinuously: we should also know that we must apply ourselves to
prayer with all our strength, so that when we pray, we pour out
our spirit in the Lord's sight. When in dire straits, Manasseh
prayed to the Lord and finally begged urgently; and the Lord answered his prayers. Since we pray with our spirit, with our mind,   87
and also with our tongue, let us be attentive to the words, lest we
make a mistake. Let us attend also with our spirit in such a way
that we grasp the significances of the words, like the images of
things. But the attention of the mind is elevated by which we are
carried to God and are not moved from the intention of our
prayer. If we pray only with the tongue, our spirit prays (that is,   88
the breath of our mouth), but our mind is without fruit; or our
spirit prays, that is, the inferior part of the mind which, nearest to
the senses and receiving the images of things, presents these images to the superior part of the mind for examination. Although   89
true prayer is of the heart and not the mouth, vocal prayer must
not be neglected. Let devotion move our voices so that we serve
God both in body and spirit; let us rouse our numb spirit with

ut mens nostra levetur in deum, et circumstantium animos ad orandum, sicut in ecclesia fieri cernimus, quasi quibusdam stimulis incitemus, ut simul intense caritatis fervore intus et extra coram

90 domino redundemus. Comprimamus tamen vocem si mentis illam elevationem clamore senserimus impediri. Cum vero ceperit mens hebescere, bonum erit vocibus adiuvare ut sic vicissitudine quadam interior homo exteriorem non deserat et exterior illum torpescere

91 non permittat. Taliter enim affecti, si in ipsa societate virtutum et per omnes ipsarum nervos effusi mentes nostras ante dominum prosternamus, quicquid iuste petierimus in dei benignitate dabitur nos per gratiam obtinere.

92 Nec nos ab orando deterreant nostrorum macule peccatorum. Licet enim peccatores extra gratiam positi pie et meritorie non possint orare cum careant illa virtute pietatis, caritate videlicet, sine qua vacua sunt opera nostra coram domino (scimus enim quod peccatores deus non exaudit), pia tamen esse potest ipsorum

93 oratio. Cumque pro salute orabit sua perseveranter atque devote, licet exaudiri non mereatur per iusticiam, in infinita tamen dei clementia poterit per gratiam impetrare. Publicanus enim ille, cum ascendisset in templum et oraret ac stans a longe nollet oculos ad celum levare sed percutiens pectus suum diceret, 'Deus, propitius esto michi peccatori,' teste veritate, descendit iustificatus in domum suam.

94 Unde, mi Ieronime, te moneo teque exhortor ut continuus in oratione sis, teque et totam mentem tuam in deum munus orationis implendo convertas. Nam cum oratio sit actus rationis que ad assecutionem nostri desiderii et finis ultimi qui prepositus est

our voice so that our mind is raised to God; let us, as if with a sort of goad, inspire the spirits of those around us to pray (just as we observe occurring in church), so that together we overflow in the Lord's presence with the fervor of intense love within and without. Let us, however, check our voice if we sense that our mind's eleva- 90 tion is being impeded by the clamor. But when the mind begins to grow dull, it will be good to assist with vocalization so that in this way, with a kind of reciprocity, the inner man does not desert the outer, and the outer does not allow the inner to grow numb. If, 91 so disposed in that union of virtues, we pour our minds through all of the sinews of the virtues and prostrate our minds before the Lord, whatever we justly ask for in God's generosity will be granted us to obtain through grace.

Nor should the blemishes of our sins deter us from praying. 92 Placed outside of grace, sinners cannot pray piously and meritori- ously since they lack the virtue of piety — that is, charity — without which our works are empty before the Lord (for we know that God does not hear the prayers of sinners). Nevertheless, the prayer of sinners can be pious. When a person prays for his own 93 salvation with perseverance and devotion, he may not merit a hearing on grounds of justice, but in God's infinite clemency he will, through grace, be able to obtain what he asks for. The publi- can went up to the temple and prayed; standing far off, he couldn't raise his eyes to heaven, but striking his chest, he said, "God, be merciful to me, a sinner." As the Truth attests, he went down to his home justified.[144]

For this reason, dear Girolamo, I advise and urge you to be 94 unceasing in prayer, and to turn yourself and all your mind to God in fulfilling the duty of prayer. Prayer is an act of the reason that is oriented toward the attainment of our desire and of the final goal

mortalibus ordinatur, sitque ascensus intellectus in deum, a quo per hanc nostre affectionis interpretem decentia postulamus, nichil magis rationali creature conveniet quam orare. Quod facientes deo deferimus nosque sue benignitatis indigere gratia confitemur. Oratio quidem deum placat, benignum facit, iratum mitigat, dura iudicia frangit, sententias revocat, irrevocabiles differt, ne labamur adiuvat, erigit lapsos, confirmat erectos, consolatur in adversis, monet in prosperis, virtutes edificat, dissipat vitia, reprimit temptatorem, superat hostem, mentem erigit, nos supra nos ponit, deo coniungit, fugat nocua, impetrat exoptanda. Hec superbos humiliat, conciliat invidos, frangit iratos, excitat desides, confirmat molles, illuminat cecos, resolvit avaros, et denique pulsantibus aperit, querentibus offert, petentibus donat, et sue fortitudinis vehementia violentis celestia regna concedit. Quid enim violentius oratione, que divine iusticie rigorem emollit dumque celo manum inicit et deum inflectit, polorum ianuam reserat, et tutum ab inferni penis mira defensione conservat? Quod quidem securius atque certius nos assecuturos esse credamus si orationem habitus devotionis associat nec ipsam actus adorationis et humilitatis cum reverentia derelinquat. De quibus, quoniam specialiter nichil dictum est, paucissima sub suis titulis videamus.

95

96

97

that has been set for mortals; it is the ascent of the understanding to God, from whom, through this interpreter of our feeling, we ask for things that are fitting. Nothing is more appropriate for a rational creature than to pray. When we do, we defer to God and acknowledge that we need the grace of his kindness. Indeed, 95 prayer appeases God, it makes him well disposed, softens him when he is angry, breaks his hard judgments, revokes his sentences, postpones those that are irrevocable; prayer supports us lest we fall, raises up the fallen, strengthens the upright, consoles us in adversity, warns us in prosperity, builds up virtues, dissipates vices, suppresses the tempter, overcomes the Enemy, lifts the mind, places us above ourselves, joins us to God, puts to flight what is harmful, obtains for us what we must long for. Prayer 96 humbles the proud, reconciles the envious, crushes the wrathful, rouses the idle, hardens the soft, gives sight to the blind, relaxes the misers, and finally opens to those who knock, offers to those who seek, gives to those who ask,[145] and yields the kingdom of heaven to the violent in the vehemence of their fortitude.[146] For 97 what is more violent than prayer, which softens the rigor of divine justice? When prayer takes possession of heaven and moves God, it unbolts the door of the poles and by a miraculous defense keeps one safe from the punishments of hell. We should safely and certainly believe that we will attain this if a disposition of devotion is linked to our prayer and the act of adoration and humility with reverence does not leave it. Since nothing has been specifically said about these things, let us look at a very few things under these headings.

: XII :

De devotione.

1 Religiosus enim animus, mi Ieronime, cum elevato mentis intuitu infinitam dei bonitatem et eius beneficia contemplatur, qui nos ad imaginem et similitudinem suam creavit, pro nobis mundum fecit, nos in filii sui morte preciosissimoque cruore redemit, nobisque beatitudinis sue gloriam preparavit quique solus in nobis virtutes et actus quos remuneret operatur, deum diligat necesse est, dumque plenitudinem illius et sue mortalitatis indigentiam intuetur, oritur ex dilectione devotio, per quam sopita voluntas accenditur

2 ut in dei servitio mancipetur. Hec autem in habitus recepta vigorem promptitudine mira quasi centrum ad omnem nostrorum operum ambitum coexistit, ut tanto sit acceptius deo quicquid

3 agimus quanto pleniore consecrate mentis spiritu faciamus. Devoverunt se nonnulli Romani principes, sicut bello Latino de duobus Deciis legitur, fallentibus diis quos illi maxima cecitate colebant, et pro salute suorum exercituum in hostes confertissimos procedentes mortem voluntariam acceperunt. Devovit et se regius iuvenis, Meneceus, pro salute Thebarum ex profano responso Tyresie suoque sanguine ruitura menia manu propria mortem accipiens

4 perlustravit. Nos ergo vero et immortali deo mentes nostras pro salutis eterne premio tanto lumine veritatis per revelationem sancti spiritus tantaque claritate perfusi non curabimus devovere? Ordinemus itaque mentes nostras in deum et non solum eas in

: XII :

Devotion.

A religious spirit, dear Girolamo, must love God, when with ele-   1
vated mental gaze it contemplates God's infinite goodness and his
gifts to us. For God created us in his own image and likeness; he
made the world for us; he redeemed us by the death and most precious blood of his own Son; he has prepared for us the glory of his
beatitude; he alone works in us the virtues and actions that he rewards. When the spirit beholds God's plenitude and the indigence
of its own mortality, devotion arises out of love, and through devotion the somnolent will is kindled with desire to be sold into the
service of God. Once welcomed into our character, devotion coex-   2
ists with vigor in a wonderful readiness as the center to the entire
circumference of our works, so to speak. So whatever we do is the
more acceptable to God the more the spirit with which we do it is
filled with consecrated intent. Several Roman leaders (as we read   3
of the two Decii in the Latin War) devoted themselves to the
fraudulent gods they worshipped with extreme blindness; for the
safety of their own armies they marched against an enemy that
was arrayed in close order and accepted death willingly.[147] The
royal youth Menoeceus also devoted himself for the safety of
Thebes: after hearing the unholy response of Tiresias, he received
death by his own hand, thus hallowing by his own blood the walls
that were on the verge of falling.[148] Therefore, shall we not make   4
an effort to devote our minds to the true and immortal God for
the reward of eternal salvation, flooded as we are by such a great
light of truth through the revelation of the Holy Spirit, and by
such a great brightness? And so let us orient our minds toward
God; let us not only hold them fixed and dedicated in a habit of

devotionis habitu fixas et deditas teneamus sed redundet noster
affectus exterius, et quantum deum revereamur quantumque sibi
simus uniti per actus forinsecos ostendamus.

: XIII :

De adoratione.

1 Uniamur itaque deo non presumentes ut socii sed humiliter tanquam servi et illam eius immensam maiestatem supra nos nulla
proportione manentem nostre mentis oculis intuentes procidamus
2 in terram et altitudinis sue gloriam adoremus. Adoremus equidem
non solum in corpore sed in spiritu et veritate, non solummodo
cor nostrum tradidisse contenti sed corpus ipsum exhibere parati,
exhibere quidem non solum in inclinatione capitis, poplitis flexu,
vel telluris osculatu, quo noster incitetur affectus ad nos humiliter
domino submittendos, sed etiam ad corpus ipsum pro Christo in
3 cruce et in omni supplicio protendendum. Adoramus in hac conversatione mortalium quoscunque videmus dignitatibus eminere,
capita detegimus, cervicem inflectimus, latus incurvamus, nec solum genibus terram attingimus sed provolvimur ante pedes dominantium humoque pretacta labiis tremebunda pedibus oscula
4 replicamus. Cum igitur tantum creature prebeamus, quantum debemus concedere creatori? Hominibus siquidem in hac humi-
liationis cumulatione deferimus vel dum pudet inurbanos haberi
vel dum nichil solite reverentie detrahere volumus dignitati; in
conspectu vero domini, qui verus rex est et dominus, rex quidem

devotion, but let our feelings overflow outwardly. Let us show through our public acts how much we revere God, and how much we are united to him.

: XIII :

Adoration.

Let us, then, be united to God not presumptuously, as if we 1 were his associates, but humbly, like servants. Beholding with our mind's eye his immense majesty abiding above us so disproportionately, let us fall to the ground and adore the glory of his sublimity. Indeed, let us adore him not only in body, but in spirit and 2 in truth,[149] not only content to have handed over our hearts, but prepared to offer our very bodies — to offer them not only in the bowing of the head, the bending of the knee, the kissing of the earth (by which our feeling is stirred for submitting ourselves humbly to the Lord), but also to stretch out our body itself for Christ on the cross and in all punishment. In this life of interac- 3 tion with mortals, we adore anyone we see who is prominent in marks of distinction: we uncover our heads, bend our necks, curve our body; not only do we touch the ground with our knees, but grovel before the feet of the powerful, touching the earth beforehand with our lips, and plant a series of tremulous kisses upon their feet. When we offer so much to a creature, how much ought 4 we to give to our Creator? We defer to human beings with this heap of humiliation because we are ashamed to be held uncouth, or because we don't want to detract from the honor of the reverence they are used to receiving. Yet in the sight of the Lord, who is

regum et dominus dominantium, debite reverentie sibi nullum of-
5 ficium exhibemus. Hei michi, pudet dicere! Quid est videre Christianos in templis ubi propter consecrationis misterium debemus
propensius sublimitatis divine glorie reminisci, quid est, inquam,
videre Christianos in templis cervicibus erectos, oculis vagos, col-
locutionibus impudicos, pene dum celebratur supersubstantialis
panis misterium conficiturque dominici corporis sacramentum
dumque verus Christi sanguis et caro sub accidentibus alienis
6 ostenditur, adorare? Qui cum adeo sint insolentes in deum, cui
pro eterne glorie munere supplicamus, terrenis principibus, a quibus sint aliquid transitorium petituri, se humiliant et cunctis ado-
7 rationum actibus adulantur. Quid dicam cum fuerint apud potestates istas mundanas ob aliquid commissum vel delatum de vita
solliciti? Nonne pallent, ingemunt, lacrimas effundunt adorantque
terre prostrati, adiurant et per omnia ferventis humilitatis officia
8 penam quam metuunt deprecantur? Pro eterna vero salute, cum
etiam iustissime viventes de ipsa non possint esse securi, imo penitus illam nequeant humanis viribus promereri, illi divine maiestati,
coram qua teste conscientia propria rei sunt, nec prebent adorationis officium nec humilitatis exhibent famulatum. Qui si exaltatio-
nem desiderant, ut opinor, deberent illam solum per humilitatis
officia procurare.

the true King and Lord—indeed, King of Kings and Lord of Lords—we show no service of due reverence. Alas, how shameful 5 it is to say it! What is it to see Christians in churches, where on account of the mystery of the consecration we ought to be the more ready to remember the sublimity of divine glory—what is it, I say, to see Christians in churches, worshipping with necks craning, wandering eyes, and immodest conversations, right when the mystery of transubstantiation is being celebrated, the sacrament of the Lord's body is being enacted, and the true flesh and blood of Christ is being revealed under accidents that are foreign to it? Al- 6 though these people are so insolent toward God, to whom we pray for the gift of eternal glory, they humble themselves before earthly rulers, from whom they intend to beg some transitory thing, and fawn on them with every possible act of adoration. What shall I 7 say when they are worried for their life before those potentates of the world on account of something they have done or been accused of? Do they not grow pale, moan, pour forth tears, and worship prostrate upon the earth? Do they not beg earnestly and by all the duties of fervent humility try to beg off the punishment they fear? Even those living most righteously cannot be secure 8 about eternal salvation; rather, they cannot in any way earn it by human strength. Yet for eternal salvation, people neither perform their duty of adoration nor display the service of humility to the divine majesty, before which they are accused, with their own conscience as a witness. If these people desire exaltation, they ought, in my opinion, to procure it only through the offices of humility.

: XIV :

De humilitate.

1 Quid enim magis necessarium excelsa petenti quam humilitas, que moderatio spiritus est, animo frenum iniciens ne plus quam conveniat elevetur, que superbiam pedibus calcans hominem ordinat re-

2 verenter in deum et cunctarum ponit fundamenta virtutum? Humilitas enim subit cum miseriam nostram agnoscimus nosque peccati deformitate corruptos contemptibiles iudicamus. Veraque gressibus suis incedit humilitas si incipimus de miseria nostra dolere, si non solum illam mente tacita confitemur sed in detestationem peccati taliter aliis persuademus quod id ipsos etiam credere cupiamus, et non solum patienter sustineamus hoc proferri sed

3 etiam amemus contemptibiliter nos tractari. His enim gradibus completa in suam perfectionem humilitas in dei timore totis innixa radicibus divina precepta memorie suggerit taliterque per reverentiam dei voluntatem amplectitur quod voluntate propria

4 nullatenus delectetur. Humilitas facit ut in observatione regule religionisque Christiane subditi simus obediendo maioribus nichilque recusemus durum vel asperum dum paremus. Hec multiloquium prohibet, taciturnitatem iubet, clamorem reprimit, non nisi iussa loquitur, rationabilia narrat, verecundos reddit, risum

5 frenat, oculos ad terram flectit sed mentem elevat in excelsis. Hec, ut perfecta sit, hominem maioribus subicit nec tamen equalibus anteponit. Hec in sua perfectione redundans paribus subditur et minoribus non prefertur. Sed illa demum humilitas in summam consumationem evadit que propter deum didicit etiam minoribus subiacere.

: XIV :

Humility.

What is more necessary to one seeking the heights than humility,   1
which is moderation of spirit, putting a bridle on the soul so that
it is not raised up higher than is appropriate, and which, trampling
arrogance under foot, orients man toward God in reverence, and
lays the foundation of all virtues? Humility comes into play when   2
we acknowledge our wretchedness and judge ourselves contempt-
ible, corrupted by the deformity of sin. And true humility ad-
vances by its own steps if we begin to feel pain on account of our
wretchedness; if we not only confess our wretchedness silently in
our mind, but also persuade others to detest sin in such a way that
we desire that they too believe in our sin; if we not only patiently
tolerate our sin to be broadcast, but even love to be treated with
contempt. Humility that has been made complete in its perfection   3
by these grades calls to mind divine precepts that are rooted in the
fear of God. This humility embraces God's will with such reverence that it in no wise takes pleasure in its own will. Humility   4
brings it about that in our observation of the rule and of the
Christian religion we are subject by obedience to our superiors,
and we refuse nothing hard or harsh when we obey. Humility pro-
hibits garrulity, commands quiet, suppresses shouting, does not
speak unless bidden to do so, gives a reasonable account, makes
people modest, bridles laughter, bends eyes to the ground but ele-
vates the mind to the heights. Humility, to be perfect, subjects a   5
person to his betters and does not place him above his equals.
Overflowing in its perfection, humility is subject to equals and is
not given preference above lesser. But humility finally reaches its
highest consummation when it has learned to be subject even to
lesser people for God's sake.

6 His igitur habitibus in humilitatis spiritu mens affecta mortalium de consideratione sue fragilitatis elevatur ad deum fideique
illuminata splendoribus deum credit esse per fidem, deo credit per
7 spem, in deum vero credit per plenissimam caritatem. Hinc est
principium quo nos cognoscimus et supra nos posita vestigamus.
Hinc nostros continemus affectus nec plus quam deceat de imper-
fectione nostra presumimus, qui nos inutiles et indignos ad omnia
8 iudicamus. Hec facit ut mensura debita convertamur ad alios, in
deum vero relaxatis habenis totis affectibus effundamur. Hec in
erratorum nostrorum memoria in adversis tolerantiam suggerit et
in prosperis effluere non permittit, ut quodam modo possimus
veraciter affirmare humilitatem esse virtutum omnium genitricem
et omnium actuum quibus aliquid per gratiam divini numinis or-
9 dinatione meremur verum et stabile fundamentum. Ut conari
debeamus, karissime mi Ieronime, taliter in hac humilitate profi-
cere quod deo in cunctis nostris actibus placeamus, quod inter ea
que recte facimus nullus assurgat obducturus lumen mentis superbie fumus, imo illa non nobis sed autori deo, qui solus ea in nobis
10 et per nos operatur ac perficit, imputemus. Cetera quidem vitia
singula singulis virtutibus opponuntur. Sola vero superbia cunctis
virtutibus insidiatur, ut, nisi nobis continue presto sit humilitatis
vere perfectio, facillime, dum bonis actionibus delectamur dumque
bene fecisse nobis reputamus ad gloriam, totum quod bene facimus corrumpatur.
11 Hec habui, conversus ad ea que sequeris, vir religiosissime, pro
secunda nostre promissionis parte que dicerem, que, si pauca sunt

By these habits in the spirit of humility, the mind of mortals is 6
affected by the consideration of its own fragility and is raised to
God; illuminated by the splendors of faith, it believes through
faith that God exists, through hope trusts in God, and believes in
God through superabundant charity. From humility comes the 7
principle by which we know ourselves and discover those things
that have been placed above us. Out of humility we contain our
emotions and do not presume more than is fitting concerning our
imperfection, since we judge ourselves to be useless and not worthy of anything. Humility brings it about that we turn to others in 8
due measure, but pour ourselves out unreservedly with our whole
heart to God. Humility in the recollection of our errors supplies
endurance in adversity; in prosperity, it does not permit us to let
ourselves go. Consequently, we can truly assert that humility is, so
to speak, the mother of all virtues and the true and stable foundation of all actions by which we earn any merit through grace according to the divine ordinance. We should try, then, dearest Gi- 9
rolamo, to make such progress in humility that we please God in
all our actions. Among the things that we do correctly, no smoke
of vanity must rise to obscure the light of the mind: rather, let us
ascribe those things not to ourselves, but to God as the author,
who alone works and perfects those things in us and through us.
Other vices are individually opposed to individual virtues, but only 10
pride plots against all virtues. So unless we have the perfection of
humility continually available, all the good we do is very easily corrupted, as we take delight in our good actions and reckon that we
have done well, to our own glory.

This is what I had to say with reference to the life you are pur- 11
suing, my most religious man, as the second part of my promise.
If these matters are scanty for those who desire much, may such

multa desiderantibus, patienter ferant ignorantiam meam; si vero sint nimia multa brevitate gaudentibus, dignentur meas ineptias tolerare; illique benigne hec pauciora suscipiant, isti vero mente pacata que longiuscula viderint pretermittant. Nunc autem his exactis tertium id quod restat, ut te videlicet ad inceptum exhortemur, totum opusculum concludentes unico capitulo, quanta brevitate poterimus, absolvemus.

12

: XV :

Brevissima exhortatio ad religionem.

1 In hac ultima voluminis nostri parte, qua te debemus ad religionem iuxta promissionis debitum exhortari, licet hoc sparsim hinc inde confecerim, sicut inter ea que diximus occurrebat, pauca tamen simul conabor que michi munus istud efficiant congregare.

2 Quod ut facillime faciam, libet paulisper supra sensus mentem attollere, rogoque te, dulcissime mi Ieronime, rogo et omnes qui forsan ista perlegerint, ut vos ad eandem mentis altitudinem sublevetis et mecum placeat ex illa sublimitatis specula primum infra

3 vos aliquantulum intueri. Hinc, si placet, a dextris religionem ponite, religionem, inquam, mundam et immaculatam apud deum, et tria religionis eiusdem vota, castitatem, obedientiam, paupertatem. Inde vero mundum a sinistris et eius plenitudinem collocate, concupiscentiam videlicet carnis, concupiscentiam oculorum, et super-

4 biam vite. Considerate parumper inter hec diabolum undique conversari et omnibus istis uti quo decipiat; inter illa vero tanquam

people patiently endure my ignorance; on the other hand, if they are excessive for those who rejoice in brevity, may such people deign to tolerate my ineptitude. May the former receive these few things kindly; may the latter pass over with equanimity what they perceive as rather lengthy. Now that this has been accomplished, I 12 will discharge the third duty, which remains — namely, to encourage you in your undertaking. I will now conclude the entire work with a single chapter, with as much brevity as I am capable of.

: XV :

Very brief exhortation to the religious life.

In this last part of our volume, I am to exhort you, in accordance 1 with my promise, to the religious life. I have done this here and there throughout the work, as the topic came up among the matters under discussion; yet I will try to gather a few things together to complete that service. In order that I may do that easily, I 2 would like to raise my mind above the senses for a little while. So I ask you, dearest Girolamo, and I also ask all who may perhaps read this work, to lift yourselves to the same heights of the mind and from that tower of sublimity first look with me a little while, please, at what lies below you. On the one side — on the right — if 3 you please, put the religious life, religious life, I repeat, pure and immaculate before God — and the three vows of religious life, chastity, obedience, and poverty. On the other side — on the left — place the world and its fullness, namely, concupiscence of the flesh, concupiscence of the eyes, and arrogance of life. Consider for a 4 little while that the devil stalks everywhere in the midst of the latter and uses all three of them to deceive; but among the former it

hostem quasi in inimicis finibus insidiari, cunctisque religionis ar-
5 ceri muneribus ut nocere non queat. Respicite denique quomodo
mundus deprimat et nos quasi miseranda diaboli mancipia ad impia Tartara mittat. Videte quo religio nos extollat et qualiter nos in
finem ultimum dirigat in eternam beatitudinem locatura.

6   Erigite nunc etiam mentis oculos supra vos et deum super hec
omnia cogitate religioni coniunctum, mundo adversum, hinc iu-
vantem ut proficias, inde retrahentem ut fugias, hinc premia polli-
centem, inde vero nobis eterna supplicia comminantem. In mundo
cogitetis omnium vitiorum exercitum, in religione vero letam
7 aciem militare virtutum. Non incongrue potestis etiam, nisi fallor,
que de mundo disserui vobis ante mentem proponere queve de
religione scribendo retuli cogitare, quod cum feceritis tu et alii religionem professi non solum eritis ad prosequendum militie vestre
munera promptiores, sed vobiscum gaudebitis decipientis mundi
fallacias cognovisse et de tam procelloso naufragio gratia superni
numinis liberati sola securitatis delectatione vos in robur super-
8 andi duriciam et asperitatem itineris componetis. Et quoniam in
hac carne fragillima et ipso mundo, licet mente fugerimus, tamen
corporaliter habitamus, exurget in nos de mundo tumor inflate
superbie, nec solum infestis signis contra nos veniet sed impercep-
tibili quadam insidiatione subrepet, que, nisi vere humilitatis habitu contundatur, quasi fecundissima mater cetera vitia generabit.
9 A mundo livor exibit invidie, ab hac vero caritas orietur; ille gignet
avariciam, ista voluntariam preferet paupertatem; iste movebit

is as if the Enemy waits in ambush in enemy territory and is fended off by all religious duties so that he cannot do any harm. Reflect, finally, on how the world presses us down and sends us to 5 impious Tartarus like piteous slaves of the devil. See the heights to which religion raises us, and how, directing us to our final goal, it will set us in eternal blessedness.

Now lift the eyes of the mind above you and think about God 6 above all these things, God who is joined to religious life and set against the world. On the one side he helps you to progress, on the other he draws you back so that you may flee; now on the one side he promises rewards, on the other he threatens us with eternal punishments. In the world, you may think you are serving in an army of all the vices, while in religious life you may think you are serving in a happy band of virtues. You can, I believe, appro- 7 priately place before your mind's eye what I have discussed regarding the world and think about what I have written concerning religious life. When you and other professed religious have done this, not only will you be more ready to discharge the duties of your military service, but you will inwardly rejoice that you have recognized the tricks of the deceiving world, and, liberated by the grace of the supernal Deity from such a storm-beaten shipwreck, you will, for the pleasure of security alone, prepare yourselves in strength for conquering the hardness and asperity of the journey. Physically we dwell in this most fragile flesh and in the world it- 8 self, though we may flee it mentally; consequently, the swelling of inflated pride will rise up against us from the world. Pride will not only attack us, but it will also creep in with an imperceptible insinuation, which, unless it is beaten down by the habit of humility, will, like a very fecund mother, generate other vices. From the 9 world the bruise of envy will emerge, but from religious life, charity will arise; the world will bring forth avarice, but religious life will produce voluntary poverty; the world will stir up wrath,

10   iram, illa mansuetudinem excitabit. Et denique quicquid contra legis eterne iusticiam mundus corruptibilis et corrumpens oculis nostre mentis obiecerit religio sancta atque sanctificans cunctis

11   armata virtutibus propulsabit. Surgamus igitur miseri mortales nec mundi decipientis illecebris retardemur. Surgamus, inquam, qui manducamus panem doloris, et corporis nostri sarcinam abhorrentes mente, quantum possumus, elevemur, nichilque in hac vita mortali salubrius reputemus, postquam hic corruptibili corpore cives sumus, quam spiritu peregrinari et deo per quanto maiorem perfectionis habitum possumus adherere.

12   Quando nascimur successione primi parentis, cuius omnes heredes sumus et filii, nascimur ire vasa moxque institutione sancte

13   matris, ecclesie, per baptismi lavacrum renovamur in gratia. Prima quidem et vera religio, in qua diabolo suisque pompis caratherem Christianitatis accipiens abrenuntiat, fides est nostra, plene quidem, si rite servetur, via perfectionis ad deum, adeo tamen perversa consuetudine temporalibus permixta negociis quod, nisi dei benignitas superet iniusticiam nostram, licet multi vocentur, pauci tamen sunt ad electionis beneficium perventuri. Plenior autem est quando quotidianis divine maiestatis servitiis, in copia tamen rerum nos extra seculum per clericatus ordinem obligamus. Plenis-

14   sima vero perfectio est in via cum non solum deum sequimur diabolum fugientes, non solum in dei servitio famulamur relinquentes mundum (non enim debet clericus secularibus se negociis permiscere), sed etiam nos ipsos per castitatis, obedientie, et paupertatis votum deo offerimus et verum holocaustum in religionis altario consecramus, ut non incongrue dici possit, quod et superius attigi, omnibus Christianis tanquam in terram bonam seminantibus

religious life will incite gentleness. Finally, sacred and sanctifying 10
religious life, armed with all the virtues, will drive away whatever
the corruptible and corrupting world puts before our mind's eye
that is against the justice of the eternal law. Let us rise, then, 11
wretched mortals, let us not be delayed by the snares of the deceiving world. Let us rise, I say, we who eat the bread of sorrow:
mentally abhorring our body's burden, as far as we are able, let us
be lifted up, and let us think that nothing in this mortal life is
more wholesome, when we are citizens here in a corruptible body,
than to be pilgrims in the spirit and adhere to God through a
greater habit of perfection than we are capable of.

Since we are born in the line of our first parent, whose heirs 12
and children all of us are, we are born as vessels of wrath; soon, by
the instruction of our holy mother, the church, we are renewed in
grace by the bath of baptism. The first and true religious bond, by 13
which a person renounces the devil and his works and receives the
mark of Christianity, is our faith; indeed, if it is preserved properly, it is a way of full perfection leading to God. Yet by perverse
custom it is so adulterated by temporal affairs that unless God's
generosity overcomes our injustice, few will attain the favor of
election, although many are called. The perfection is fuller, however, when by daily acts of service to the divine majesty, yet in an
abundance of material goods, we bind ourselves outside of the
secular world through clerical orders. But the fullest perfection lies 14
in this path: when we not only flee the devil and follow God, not
only abandon the world and serve among God's attendants (for a
cleric ought not to involve himself in secular business), but also
offer our very selves to God through a vow of chastity, obedience,
and poverty, consecrating ourselves as a true sacrificial offering on
religion's altar. Therefore, as I mentioned above, it can be aptly
said that thirtyfold fruit is reserved for all Christians sowing in

trigesimum fructum, clericis sexagesimum, religiosis vero centesimum reservari.

15 Iosep enim, qui 'filius auctus' vel 'appositus filius' interpretatur, secundum hunc sensum Christianos non incongrue poterit figurare, quoniam, cum omnes homines filii dei sint, soli Christiani
16 aucti per gratiam, appositi vero per adoptionem esse dicuntur. Hic itaque, ut primi fructus similitudinem aliquam assumamus, treginta annorum erat quando stetit in conspectu regis Pharaonis carcereque solutus circuivit omnes regiones Egipti. Et qui iam usque in diem illam a fratribus treginta argenteis invidia venditus et domine sue malicia coniectus in carcerem multis fuerat infelicitatibus circumventus, demum trigesimum fructum illo anno sue etatis accepit et, donec postea mansit apud mortales, felicissime dies
17 transegit. Ysaac vero, qui 'risus' interpretatur et 'gaudium,' quod quidem maxime conveniet Christianis (scriptum est enim, 'Beati eritis cum vos oderint homines et cum separaverint vos et exprobraverint et eiecerint nomen vestrum tanquam malum propter filium hominis,' et subditur, 'Gaudete in illa die et exultate; ecce enim merces vestra multa est in celo'); iste igitur Ysaac sexagenarius erat quando nati sunt ei parvuli Esau et Iacob, qui testamentum fuerunt benedictionis sue et fructus orationis eius. Deprecatus est enim Ysaac dominum pro uxore sua eo quod esset
18 sterilis; qui exaudivit eum. Et quoniam habitabat iuxta puteum nomine Viventis et Videntis, quis non fateatur ipsum habere similitudinem ordinis clericalis? Nam etsi cunctorum sit orare deum et apud illum puteum habitare, hoc tamen munus est precipue clericorum, qui apud puteum Viventis et Videntis, hoc est iuxta deum, vere puteum profundissimum sapientia, viventem eterne, viventem immense, videlicet in dei templis assidue commorantur. Quorum
19 primum, illud Salomonis, habebat sexaginta cubitos in longitudine, ut sic per huius mensure numerum et illius patriarche sexagesimum annum fructus sexagesimus designetur.

good soil, so to speak; sixtyfold is for clerics; and a hundredfold is reserved for religious.[150]

Joseph (which means "son increased" or "added son")[151] could in 15 this sense be a fitting figure for Christians, since, while all human beings are children of God, only Christians are said to be increased through grace and "added" through adoption.[152] And so 16 this Joseph (to take up the parable of the first fruit) was thirty years old when he stood in the sight of Pharaoh; once released from prison, he went around all the regions of Egypt. And he who up until that day had been surrounded by many misfortunes — having been sold by his brothers for thirty pieces of silver out of envy and cast into prison by the malice of his mistress — at last received thirtyfold fruit in that year of his age, and, as long as he remained among mortals thereafter, he passed his days most happily. To move on to Isaac: his name signifies "laughter" and 17 "joy"[153] — which will be especially appropriate for Christians, for it is written, "You will be blessed when people hate and shun and curse you and cast out your name as evil on account of the Son of Man," and then, "Rejoice and exult on that day; for see, your reward is great in heaven."[154] This Isaac, then, was sixty years old when little Esau and Jacob were born to him, who were a testament to his blessing and the fruit of his prayer. For Isaac prayed to the Lord for his wife because she was sterile; and the Lord answered his prayer. And since he lived next to a well called *Of the* 18 *Living and Seeing*, who wouldn't attest that Isaac bears a likeness to the clerical order? For even though anyone might pray to God and live near that well, nevertheless this is the particular duty of clerics, who linger constantly by the well *Of the Living and Seeing* — that is, by God, truly a well very deep in wisdom, living eternally, living unfathomably — that is, in the temples of God. The first of these 19 temples, that of Solomon, was sixty cubits in length, so that through the number of this measure and the sixtieth year of the patriarch the sixtyfold fruit is signified.

Verum quia et in hoc statu fames oritur super terram, perfectissimi scilicet status desiderium, abit Ysaac ad Abimalech, regem

20 Palestinorum in Geraris. Videamus, si placet, et horum nominum rationem. Abimalech 'pater rex' vel 'regnum patris,' Palestini 'sanguinem bibentes,' Gerara vero 'incolatus' vel 'maceria,' sicut ad in-

21 terpretationes recurrens videre poteris, exponuntur. Quid igitur est ad Abimalech, hoc est patrem regem, qui Palestinis, id est sanguinem bibentibus, dominatur, Ysaac famescentem ire, nisi deo, qui verus est pater et rex bibentium sanguinem, Christianorum videlicet, quibus datum est in corpore et sanguine domini nostri

22 Iesu Christi spiritualiter refici, quantum possumus adherere? Quid est manere in Geraris, hoc est in maceria, nisi in monasterio degere, ubi religiose deo in omnibus nostris actibus serviamus? Sed fructum queris. Ecce inquit scriptura: 'Seminavit autem Ysaac in terra illa et invenit in ipso anno centuplum.' Quod quidem sicut pleraque sub figura in Veteri Testamento positum veritas evangelica declaravit. Inquit enim salvator noster: 'Omnis qui reliquerit domum vel fratres aut sorores aut patrem aut matrem aut uxorem aut filios aut agros propter nomen meum centuplum accipiet et

23 vitam eternam possidebit.' Ut, cum non unum aliquod sed omnia predicta tu et alii religiosi Christum crucifixum sequendo reliqueritis, veritate promittente, que nec fallitur nec fallit, vobis cum eterne vite possessione fructus centesimus reservetur.

24 Nec putet aliquis centuplicatum premium illi qui solum unum ex enumeratis fecerit preparari. Non enim potest unum perfecte fieri quin reliqua comprendantur. Ad perfectionem quidem unius

25 cetera requiruntur. Quis enim perfecte relinquit agros nisi carnales dimiserit necessitudines quarum gratia divitie comparantur? Quis perfecte propter deum relinquit cognationem suam quin relinquat

But since even in this state famine arises over the land (that is, the desire for the most perfect state), Isaac goes to Abimelech, king of the Philistines, in Gerara. Let us, if you please, also look at 20 the sense of these names. As you will be able to see if you have recourse to interpretations, Abimelech is explained as "father king" or "father's kingdom"; the Philistines as "drinking blood"; and Gerara as "habitation" or "wall."[155] What is it, then, for the famished 21 Isaac to go to Abimelech — that is, the father king who rules over the Philistines, i.e., those who drink blood — but to adhere as much as we can to God, who is the true Father and King of those who drink blood, namely Christians, to whom it has been given to be spiritually refreshed by the body and blood of our Lord Jesus Christ? What is it to stay in Gerara — that is, in the wall — but to 22 spend one's life in the monastery, where we religiously serve God in all our actions? But you ask about the fruit. See, scripture says, "Isaac sowed in that land and found in that very year a hundredfold."[156] This the gospel truth has brought to light, though it is placed (like many things), under the guise of an Old Testament figure. For our Savior says, "Everyone who leaves his home, or his brothers, or sisters, or father, or mother, or wife, or children, or fields on account of my name will receive a hundredfold and possess eternal life."[157] Since you and other religious have left not 23 some one thing, but all of the aforesaid, by following Christ crucified, a hundredfold fruit is reserved for you with the possession of eternal life. The Truth, which neither is deceived nor deceives, promises this.

But no one should think that a hundredfold reward is prepared 24 for the one who has done only one of the things listed. For it is not possible for one thing to be done perfectly without the rest being included. Indeed, for the perfection of one, the others are required. Who perfectly leaves his fields if he has not rid himself 25 of the carnal relationships for the sake of which wealth is acquired? Who perfectly leaves his relations for God's sake without

et divitias que suis congregantur, cognatorum favoribus parantur,
26 defenduntur, augentur? Voluit igitur perfectionis magister sub illarum disiunctivarum serie non illud innuere quod unicum alternativorum ad fructum quem pollicetur sufficiat, sed quod unum sine reliquis fieri non valeat demonstrare. Qui alibi quidem dixit: 'Qui amat patrem aut matrem plus quam me non est me dignus, et qui amat filium aut filiam super me non est me dignus, et qui non ac-
27 cipit crucem suam et sequitur me non est me dignus.' Videsne qualiter hic cuncta pene coniunxit que sub disiunctione dissimulanter alibi numeravit, et taliter illa duo paria, patrem et matrem, filium et filiam, enuntiando disiunxit quod ea virtute subiecte negationis intelligi conveniat coniunctive? Centuplum itaque religiosorum premium est et eterne glorie certissimum additamentum.

28 Quid igitur propositis cum tanto fenore religionis premiis facere debemus, nisi quod ego et alii Christiani qui seculi sumus negociis implicati nos in multo lacrimarum profluvio coram domino prosternamus conemurque taliter vivere quod fructum saltem il-
29 lum trigesimum non perdamus? Quid clerici, quorum est occupationes mundi relinquere quique deo per sacrorum castissimas cerimonias deservire pro utilitate omnium elegerunt, si recte vixerint, agent nisi sic fructum custodire sexagesimum quod etiam, si fieri
30 possit, centesimum assequantur? Tibi vero et reliquis qui religionem arctissimam estis laudabiliter auspicati, quid restat agendum nisi quod in fervore caritatis quilibet inceptum taliter urgeat quod in fine dierum qui vobis constituti sunt et in illo migrationis articulo qui vere in solius divine et ineffabilis dispositionis et necessitatis ordine continetur, citra quem nunquam aut frustra temptamus deficere et ultra quem stulte querimus penetrare, ad illam gloriam atque pacem que superat omnem sensum ab hac terrestri

also leaving the wealth that has been accumulated for his family—
wealth acquired, defended, and increased by the favors of his relations? Therefore, with that series of disjunctives the Teacher of   26
perfection did not to wish imply that only one of the options suf-
fices to attain the fruit he promises, but he wanted to demonstrate
that one thing cannot occur without the rest. Elsewhere he said,
"He who loves father or mother more than me is not worthy of
me, and he who loves son or daughter above me is not worthy of
me, and he who does not take up his cross and follow me is not
worthy of me."[158] Do you see that just as here he has connected   27
almost everything that he elsewhere listed dissemblingly as separate, so in his discourse he separated those two pairs (father and
mother, son and daughter) in such a way that it is appropriate to
understand them conjunctively, by virtue of the underlying nega-
tion? And so the hundredfold reward of the religious is also the
most certain addition of eternal glory.

Since, therefore, the rewards of religious life have been set be-   28
fore us at such a high rate of interest, what should we do except
for me and other Christians who are entangled in secular business
to prostrate ourselves before the Lord in a great flood of tears and
try to live in such a way that at least we do not lose that thirtyfold
fruit? What will clerics do (whose characteristic it is to leave be-   29
hind worldly occupations and who have chosen to serve God
through the pure celebration of holy rites for the good of all), if
they have lived properly, but guard their sixtyfold fruit in such a
way that they may also attain, if possible, the hundredfold? But   30
for you and the rest, who have most laudably embarked upon the
narrowest path, religious life, what remains to be done but that in
charity's fervor someone or other encourage your undertaking in
such a way that at the end of the days allotted to you, in that junc-
ture of migration that is truly contained in the order of the divine
and ineffable disposition and necessity alone—short of this order
we never (or in vain attempt to) fall, and beyond it we foolishly

militia per infinite bonitatis dei gratiam ascendatis, ad cuius perpetue glorie statum illa celestis numinis insuperanda benignitas cunctos qui confessi sunt nomen eius et me, miserum peccatorem, disponere quamvis devios et perducere dispositos non recuset. Que cum infinita illa bonitate vere et ineffabilis trinitatis in sue eternitatis indivisibili unitate perseverat. Amen.

Explicit feliciter liber secundus et ultimus De seculo et religione *compositus a Colucio Pyeri de Stignano cancellario Florentino ad fratrem Ieronimum de Uzano, ordinis Camaldulensis in monasterio Sancte Marie de Angelis de Florentia.*

seek to penetrate — you ascend, through the grace of God's infinite goodness, from this earthly military service to that glory and peace that surpasses all understanding.[159] To the state of this perpetual glory the unconquerable generosity of the celestial Divinity does not refuse to dispose and lead all who have confessed his name (even me, a wretched sinner), errant though they be. May that generosity persist, with the infinite goodness of the true and ineffable Trinity in the indivisible unity of its eternity. Amen.

Here ends the second and final book On the World and Religious Life, *composed by Coluccio di Piero of Stignano, chancellor of Florence, for Brother Girolamo of Uzzano of the Camaldolese Order, of the Monastery of Santa Maria degli Angeli, Florence.*

Note on the Text

❧❧❧

The Latin text in this volume is based, with very few changes, on the edition of B. L. Ullman, *Coluccii Salutati De seculo et religione* (Florence: L. S. Olschki, 1957). Paragraph divisions have been introduced for ease of reading. Apart from slight adjustments to the punctuation, all changes to Ullman's edition are listed below. References are to the book, chapter, and paragraph numbers of this edition, followed by the page and line number of the Ullman edition in parentheses.

1.3.3 (p. 6, 24)	⟨spretis⟩ *added after* iudicio
1.6.4 (p. 15, 17)	⟨quaecumque⟩ *added after* corrumpit
1.8.9 (p. 18, 28)	faustu *emended to* fastu
1.13.5 (p. 30, 4)	rerum opulentia *corrected to* rerum opulentie; *cf.* rerum opulentia *at 1.14.3 (p. 31, 4)*
1.19.4 (p. 41, 13)	excitavit *emended to* excitaverit
1.22.3 (p. 47, 22)	contagio *emended to* contagione
1.26.4 (p. 58, 11)	usque *changed to* usque ad (*the reading of C; cf. p. 61, 8*)
1.29.16 (p. 68, 27–28)	pro genitoribus *corrected to* progenitoribus
2.prohemium.10 (p. 91, 5)	⟨habuisti⟩ *added after* doctorem
2.10.16 (p. 134, 11)	⟨et⟩ *added before* precipientis
2.11.25 (p. 142, 16)	efficiendo *emended to* efficiendum
2.11.70 (p. 151, 21)	Plene *emended to* Plane
2.15.16 (p. 164, 2)	religiones *emended to* regiones

The bulk of these changes were suggested by Andrew R. Dyke, who kindly read the volume for the series. Readers interested in an account of the manuscript evidence for the text and a full critical apparatus are advised to consult Ullman's excellent edition.

Notes to the Translation

࿓࿓࿓

The Psalms and Ecclesiastes are cited by their numbering in the Vulgate, with the alternate numeration indicated in parentheses. The following abbreviation has been used:

Migne   Jacques-Paul Migne, ed., *Patrologiae cursus completus, Series Latina*, 221 vols. (Paris: Migne, 1844–1891).

BOOK I

1. Luke 10:27.

2. 1 Peter 5:8.

3. Isidore of Seville, *Etymologies* 18.24.

4. Ibid. 11.2.1–7.

5. I.e., *Doli capax*, having knowledge of right and wrong; a legal phrase from the *Digest* of Justinian 43.4.1.6.

6. Cf. Galatians 6:3.

7. Ibid. 6:4.

8. Matthew 6:16.

9. Ibid. 25:9.

10. Ibid. 25:12.

11. Justinian, *Institutes* 2.17.8.

12. Jeremiah 6:13.

13. Cf. 2.9.47, with note.

14. Propertius 1.1.5–6.

15. Ovid, *Metamorphoses* 7.20–21 (Medea is the speaker).

16. Vergil, *Aeneid* 6.625–27.

17. By "bodies" (*corpora*) in the following, Salutati means the four elements: earth, water, air, and fire.

18. Cf. Matthew 26:24.

19. Cicero, *Tusculan Disputations* 4.13.

20. I.e., the Adriatic, separating Italy ("us") from Greece.

21. Response of Manius Curius Dentatus to a Samnite offer of god, reported by Cicero, *On Old Age* 56.

22. Matthew 22:13.

23. Wisdom of Solomon 3:7.

24. Matthew 22:12.

25. Valerius Maximus 1.8ex.16 (perhaps from Cicero, *On Fate* 5, where the text is damaged); Pliny, *Natural History* 7.172.

26. A variation on the more familiar saying, *homo homini lupus est*, found in Plautus' *Asinaria* 495 and many later sources. Salutati repeats his version of the saying at 1.16.4.

27. Proverbs 24:16.

28. Job 14:2.

29. Psalms 13(14):1.

30. I.e., baptism. Salutati goes on to paraphrase part of the liturgy of baptism. He then alludes to the sacraments of confirmation, communion, confession, i.e., the universal sacraments of the *viator*, as they will be transcended when the Christian enters the future state of immortality.

31. Cf. Matthew 22:15–22; Mark 12:13–17; Luke 20:20–26.

32. Luke 11:23.

33. I.e., the highest good, or *summum bonum*; see Aristotle, *Nicomachean Ethics*, 1.2 (1094a).

34. Ullman (p. 28n) cites Aristotle, *Eudemian Ethics* 3.2.12 (1231a15), concluding from the anecdote that Salutati must somehow have known this text of Aristotle in 1381, a complete version of which is usually believed to have been first brought to the West from Byzantium by Giovanni Aurispa in 1423. However, the same anecdote is preserved in the *recensio pura* (26.2.1) of Robert Grosseteste's Latin version of Aristotle's *Nicomachean Ethics* 3.13 (1118b), which contains also excerpts from the Greek commen-

tary tradition. In Grosseteste's notes to this passage, the glutton is also referred to as Philoxenus Erixius. See *Aristoteles Latinus* 26.1–3, fasc. tertius, ed. R. A. Gautier (1972), 198. This version of the medieval *Liber Ethicorum* enjoyed very wide circulation and is likely to be Salutati's source.

35. Genesis 1:31.

36. Matthew 26:41; Mark 14:38.

37. Matthew 19:24; Mark 10:25; Luke 18:25.

38. See n. 26, above.

39. For the lower and higher powers of reason, see Aristotle, *Nicomachean Ethics* 6.1–2 (1139a), though the distinction was widely diffused in scholastic literature.

40. Romans 7:15ff.

41. See 1.13.2 note.

42. Salutati refers respectively to the Arab astronomer Atimad ibn al-Farghani, active in Baghdad circa 800, and Campanus of Novara (ca. 1220–96), a mathematician and astronomer best known for a Latin edition of Euclid.

43. The following catalogue of personified virtues and vices doing battle is inspired, perhaps indirectly, by Prudentius' *Psychomachia*, in which the conceit is greatly elaborated.

44. Cicero, *Catilinarians* 1.1.

45. *Satires* 2.2.92–93.

46. 1 Corinthians 15:33.

47. Genesis 3:19.

48. Namely, 1.18.5–10.

49. Cf. Cicero, *On Duties* 1.65.

50. Matthew 6:1–2, also alluded to in the following lines.

51. 1 John 2:16.

52. Sallust, *Catiline* 52.22.

53. Psalms 8:7–8(6–7).

54. John 18:36.

55. Psalms 48:13, 21(49:12, 20).

56. Luke 15:16–18.

57. Acts 2:28.

58. Cicero, *Tusculan Disputations* 4.14.

59. Juvenal 10.243–45.

60. Salutati's elaboration of this story is based on Cicero, *Tusculan Disputations* 5.21.61–62.

61. Psalms 103(104):25.

62. Genesis 1:10.

63. Isidore, *Etymologies* 13.14.1.

64. Isaiah 17:12.

65. Ibid. 57:20.

66. Cf., for example, the *Glossa ordinaria*, in Migne 113:72–74.

67. Matthew 14:23–33.

68. Cf. John 14:30.

69. Ibid. 8:23.

70. 1 John 2:15.

71. John Balbus, *Catholicon*, and Papias s.v.

72. Possibly referring to the *Corpus iuris civilis, Codex* 3.33.17.2, or *Digest* 11.7.36, or a commentary on the same.

73. See above, 1.3.9, with note.

74. *Tusculan Disputations* 4.18.

75. Balbus, *Catholicon* s.v. *erumna*.

76. Cf. Luke 8:21, 11:27–28.

77. Psalms 101:26–28(102:25–27).

78. Exodus 3:14.

79. Psalms 101:27(102:26).

80. 1 Corinthians 13:12.

81. Vergil, *Eclogue* 1.24–25.

82. Justinus 10.1.

83. Ibid. 39.5.

84. Livy 2.50.11.

85. Servius, *Commentary on the Aeneid* 10.497.

86. Ovid, *Heroides* 6; Statius, *Thebiad* 5.28–721; possibly Hyginus, *Fabulae* 15.

87. Florus, *Epitome* 1.34.

88. Exodus 14:21–29 and 15:4.

89. See 2.8.16, with note.

90. For this expression, see, e.g., 1 Samuel 25:22.

91. Justinus, Book 1.

92. Vergil, *Aeneid* 6.540–43.

93. Ibid. 6.744.

94. Cf. Psalms 88:16–18.

95. Cf. ibid. 139:6.

96. Matthew 5:3.

97. Juvenal 6.268–69. Modern texts of Juvenal have *iurgia* (quarrels) rather than *prelia*.

98. Job 2:9.

99. Tobit 2:22; the Vulgate (Stuttgart, 1994) has *modo paruerunt* (have just now appeared), not *perierunt* (have disappeared).

100. Persius 1:1.

101. See 1.21.2, with n. 51.

102. Genesis 3:1–3.

103. Ibid. 2:17.

104. Ibid. 3:4–6.

105. 1 Timothy 2:14.

106. Genesis 3:22.

107. Cf. Matthew 7:2.

108. Matthew 22:39; Mark 12:31.

109. Juvenal 13.1–2.

110. Psalms 129(130):3.

111. Numbers 16:31–33.

112. Vergil, *Aeneid* 6.743.

113. Luke 9:60; cf. Matthew 8:22.

114. Aristotle, *Meteorology* 2.8 (368b28).

115. Cf., e.g., Augustine, *City of God* 20.16.

116. Based on Plato, *Timaeus* 38b–c, according to Ullman (p. 75), but probably mediated by Aristotle, *On the Heavens* 1.10 (280a19); see Hankins, "Salutati, Plato and Socrates," 288. Nevertheless, the doctrine elaborated below, of the radical dependence of the being of created things on God, is Neoplatonic in origin, probably mediated by Aquinas or another scholastic source.

117. Aristotle, *On the Heavens* 1.10 (280a19).

118. Varro, *On Agriculture* 1.2.14.

119. Augustine, *City of God passim*, especially 6.2–9.

120. Proverbs 4:25.

121. Job 8:9.

122. Balbus, *Catholicon* s.v. *diversorium*.

123. Cf. Cicero, *On Old Age* 5.

124. E.g., Vergil, *Eclogues* 4, 6, 9; Ovid, *Metamorphoses* 1.89–112, etc.

125. Boethius, *On the Consolation of Philosophy* 2.5, vv. 23–24.

126. Ibid. 25–26.

127. Daniel 1:12–16.

128. Cf. John 3:8.

129. Augustine, *Enarratio in Psalmos* 52.1 (Migne 36:613).

BOOK II

1. I.e., by taking holy orders, Girolamo has left behind the secular world, the topic of Book 1.

2. Papias, *Vocabularium* s.v. Nicholaus.

3. Luke 5:12–16; cf. 1.22.6, above.

4. 1 Corinthians 1:20.

5. Hieronymus, *On Hebrew Names* (Migne 23:829–30 s.v. Jerusalem ["vision of peace"]; 821 s.v. Jeroboam ["dividing the people"]; 833–34 s.v. Jeraia ["fearing the Lord"]).

6. Cf. Acts 8:26–39.

7. Cf. Jerome, *Against Jovinianum* 1.3, *Letter XXII, ad Eustochium* 15, 19.

8. "With fat Minerva" is proverbial for "with a dull intellect": Cicero, *On Friendship* 19. Like Cicero, Salutati seeks to disarm criticism by specialists — here probably scholastic theologians.

9. Actually, at *On the Nature of the Gods* 1.60, the skeptic Cotta says that in physics (which for the ancients included theology) he could more readily (*citius*) say what is not than what is. It is interesting, though, that Salutati thought Cicero worth citing on theology at all (cf. also 2.1.10).

10. Numbers 22:28.

11. An allusion to the so-called "ontological argument" invented by Saint Anselm, whose point of departure is David's utterance from Psalms (as below), "The fool has said in his heart there is no God." In general, Salutati's account of the attributes of God reflects the older, traditional synthesis of Christian Neoplatonism with Dionysian, Avicennian, and Aristotelian elements associated with the *via antiqua* of scholastic theologians like Aquinas.

12. Anselm's understanding of God in the ontological argument.

13. Psalms 13(14):1.

14. Salutati's arguments for the existence of God in this paragraph, though not formally worked out, to some extent track those of Aquinas

in the *Summa Theologiae* I q.2 a.3, the so-called Five Ways, including the argument from motion, the argument from necessary being, the argument from grades of being, and the argument from the governance of the world. The final argument, from Providence or the need for a standard of justice in the world, is not one of the Five Ways.

15. *On the Commonwealth* 6.13, known to Salutati via Macrobius' *Commentary on the Dream of Scipio* 5.

16. Ecclesiastes 11:10.

17. *Stoic Paradoxes* 14.

18. I.e., past, present, and future.

19. James 4:4.

20. Cf. 1.13.2 note.

21. James 1:13, 14.

22. Following the dubious etymology *Anthropos* ⟨ *ano kato dendros*.

23. *Iliad* 8.19, known to Salutati via Macrobius' *Commentary on the Dream of Scipio* 1.14.15.

24. See 1.21.2, with note.

25. Genesis 4:7.

26. Psalms 50:18–19(51:16–17).

27. The story was best known in Salutati's time via Ovid's *Metamorphoses*, Books 10 and 11.1–66.

28. Ecclesiastes 5:3(4).

29. Psalms 75:12(76:11).

30. 2 Corinthians 9:7.

31. See Book 2, n. 7, above.

32. Psalms 75:12(76:11).

33. Luke 17:10.

34. 1 Corinthians 15:10.

35. Ovid, *Amores* 3.4.7–8.

36. Matthew 5:28.

37. Cf. Cicero, *On Friendship* 19.

38. 1 Corinthians 6:18.

39. Wisdom 10:6. The Pentapolis refers to five cities of the Philistines.

40. Judges 20:15, 17, 35, 46.

41. Terence, *Eunuch* 732.

42. Vergil, *Georgics* 3.215–16.

43. Vergil, *Eclogues* 8.41.

44. Cf. Genesis 2:23–24.

45. Juvenal 14.139. Modern texts read *crescit amor nummi quantum ipsa pecunia creuit.*

46. Genesis 17:1. *Dimisit* here means "to leave as an inheritance"; see Genesis 24:36.

47. Ecclesiasticus 31:8–9.

48. Matthew 19:24–25.

49. Psalms 123(124):7.

50. Cicero, *Stoic Paradoxes* 8; Salutati's memory deceives him: it is Cicero who calls this sage Bias.

51. Mark 10:17, 21–23.

52. 1 Timothy 6:17.

53. Ecclesiasticus 10:9–10.

54. An allusion to the Holy Roman Empire.

55. Florus, *Epitome* 1.7.18.

56. Pliny the Elder, *Natural History* 35.158–59.

57. Livy 1.53.1–3, 1.57.1.

58. Publicola's triumph was over the Etruscans and Arruns Tarquinius, not Tarquinius Superbus, as Salutati might seem to imply.

59. Livy 2.16.7.

60. *Sic* for Quinctius.

61. I.e., the dictatorship.

62. Livy 3.26–29.

63. A mistake for Luscinus.

64. Salutati confuses Fabricius with Manius Curius Dentatus.

65. A mistake; see previous note.

66. Curius' second triumph in his consulship of 275 BCE was over King Pyrrhus of Epirus. Salutati may be following (ps. Aurelius Victor), *De viris illustribus* 33.3, which mentions a triumph over the Sabines and Samnites and suppresses that over Pyrrhus.

67. Cf. 1.8.8, with note.

68. Livy 2.33.10–11; Valerius Maximus 4.4.2.

69. Q. Aemilius Papus, mentioned as an even more frugal contemporary of Fabricius by Valerius Maximus 4.4.3.

70. Valerius Maximus 4.4.10.

71. Ibid.

72. Actually 40,000 *asses* = 4,000 *denarii*.

73. Sallust, *Catiline* 12.1.

74. Ibid. 10.1.

75. Ibid. 10.3.

76. Vergil, *Aeneid* 1.287.

77. Sallust, *Catiline* 12.2.

78. Matthew 8:20.

79. Acts 3:6.

80. 1 Thessalonians 2:9.

81. Acts 5:1–10.

82. Psalms 18:5(19:4).

83. The untranslatable pun (*non dotavit sed ditavit*) may imply that Salutati suspected the "Donation of Constantine," endowing the Church with extensive lands in Italy, was a forgery; rumors to that effect were rife even before Lorenzo Valla published his decisive proof in 1440 (*On the Dona-*

tion of Constantine, ed. G. W. Bowersock, ITRL 24 [Cambridge, MA, 2007]).

84. A reference to the Avignonese papacy (1305–67) and the Great Schism (1378–1417).

85. Tiberianus (poet, late 3rd/early 4th century CE), quoted by Servius on *Aeneid* 6.136.

86. 1 Timothy 6:9.

87. Genesis 12:1.

88. Ibid. 12:2.

89. Ibid. 22:2. In modern translations from the Hebrew, the "land of Vision" is the land of Moriah.

90. Ibid. 22:16–18.

91. Gregory, *Moralia in Iob* 35.28 (Migne 76:765).

92. *City of God* 14.12.

93. The distinction between use and enjoyment (*uti/frui*) of the virtues is Augustinian.

94. 1 Corinthians 13:3.

95. Ecclesiasticus 3:2.

96. Hebrews 13:17.

97. Cf. 1.13.2 note.

98. For a discussion of this important passage, see Trinkaus, *Image and Likeness*, 2:669–73.

99. Matthew 26:41.

100. Ibid. 17:21.

101. The phrase "queen of the virtues" derives from Cicero, *On Duties* 3.28 (there applied to justice).

102. Psalms 7:10(9); Jeremiah 11:20.

103. Isaiah 29:13.

104. Psalms 17:2–4(18:1–3).

105. Matthew 6:12.

106. Psalms 68:28–29(69:27–28).

107. Acts 13:22.

108. John 1:14.

109. Luke 23:34.

110. John 11:47–48.

111. Cf. Matthew 5:45.

112. Mark 10:52.

113. John 16:23.

114. Luke 16:26.

115. Namely, faith, hope, and charity.

116. Rhetoric taught that one of the functions of the exordium, the first part of a speech, was to render the hearer well-disposed (*benevolus*); hence its early position in handbooks; cf., e.g., Cicero, *On Invention* 1.20.

117. *Epistle* 41 (Migne 33:158).

118. Psalms 99(100):3.

119. Ibid. 6:9–10(8–9).

120. Daniel 9:4–6, 17–19.

121. Cf. Psalms 35:10(36:9).

122. Ibid. 26(27):4.

123. Matthew 6:33.

124. Cf. Luke 1:47.

125. Matthew 17:4.

126. 1 John 3:2.

127. Psalms 84:11(85:10).

128. Romans 14:17.

129. I.e., the following points in the prayer are steps leading toward participation in divine blessedness.

130. Namely, 2.10, especially 22–23.

131. Matthew 6:7.

132. Proverbs 10:19.

133. Mark 11:24.

134. James 4:3.

135. Psalms 7:9(8).

136. Psalms 33:15(34.14); 1 Peter 3:11.

137. Tobit 12:12.

138. Psalms 58:2, 5 (59:1, 3–4).

139. Cf. 1 Cor. 2:9.

140. Judith 4:12.

141. 1 Thessalonians 5:16–17.

142. Luke 18:1.

143. (Pseudo) Walafrid Strabo, *Glossa Ordinaria* (Migne 114:620).

144. Luke 18:13–14.

145. Matthew 7:7.

146. Cf. Matthew 11:12.

147. Florus 1.9.3, 1.12.7.

148. From the saga of the "seven against Thebes": Tiresias prophesied that Thebes must fall unless the walls were hallowed by the blood of a member of the family of one of the founders (the *Spartoi* "sown men"); hence the suicide of Menoeceus, son of Creon. Salutati could not have known the main ancient source for the legend (Euripides, *Phoenician Women* 834–1017), but he was familiar with Roman sources such as Statius, *Thebaid* 10.610–826, and possibly also Hyginus' *Fabulae* 67 (which referred the suicide to the homonymous grandfather).

149. Cf. John 4:23–24.

150. See Book 2, n. 7, above.

151. Alcuin, *Interpretations of Hebrew Names* (Migne 100:725).

152. Cf. Romans 8:15 and 23; Ephesians 1:5.

153. Hieronymus, *On Hebrew Names* (Migne 23:824).

154. Matthew 5:11–12.

155. Hieronymus, *On Hebrew Names* (Migne 23:780).

156. Genesis 26:12.

157. Matthew 19:29.

158. Ibid. 10:37–38.

159. Cf. Philippians 4:7.

Bibliography

EDITION

Colucii Salutati De seculo et religione ex codicibus manuscriptis primum edidit B. L. Ullman. (Nuova Collezione di testi umanistici inediti o rari 12). Florence: Leo S. Olschki, 1957.

STUDIES

Caby, Cécile. "À propos du *De seculo et religione*. Coluccio Salutati et Santa Maria degli Angeli." In *Vie active et vie contemplative au Moyen Âge et au seuil de la Renaissance*, edited by Christian Trottman, 483–529. Rome: École française de Rome, 2009.

——. "Coluccio Salutati e Santa Maria degli Angeli: nuovi documenti, nuovi approcci." In *Novità su Coluccio Salutati. Seminario a 600 anni dalla morte. Firenze, 4 dicembre 2006* = *Medioevo e Rinascimento: Annuario del Dipartimento di Studi sul Medioevo e il Rinascimento dell'Università di Firenze* XXII, n.s. XIX (2008): 87–103.

——. "Coluccio Salutati, Santa Maria degli Angeli e il *De seculo et religione*." In *Coluccio Salutati e l'invenzione dell'umanesimo. Atti*, 341–68.

Coluccio Salutati e l'invenzione dell'umanesimo. Atti del convegno internazionale di studi, Firenze, 29–31 ottobre 2008. Edited by Concetta Bianca. Rome: Edizioni di Storia e letteratura, 2010.

Coluccio Salutati e l'invenzione dell'Umanesimo. Catalogo della mostra (Firenze, Biblioteca Medicea Laurenziana, 2 novembre 2008 — 30 gennaio 2009). Edited by Teresa De Robertis, Giuliano Tanturli, and Stefano Zamponi. Florence: Mandragora, 2008.

Hankins, James. "Salutati, Plato and Socrates." In *Coluccio Salutati e l'invenzione dell'umanesimo. Atti*, 283–93.

Kahn, Victoria Ann. "Coluccio Salutati on the Active and Contemplative Lives." In *Arbeit, Musse, Meditation: Betrachtungen zur vita activa und vita contemplativa*, edited by Brian Vickers, 153–79. Zurich: Verlag der Fachvereine, 1985.

Lombardo, Paul A. "*Vita activa* versus *vita contemplativa* in Petrarch and Salutati." *Italica* 59 (1982): 83–92.

Petrucci, Armando. *Coluccio Salutati*. Rome: Istituto della Enciclopedia italiana, 1972.

Trinkaus, Charles. *In Our Image and Likeness: Humanity and Divinity in Italian Humanist Thought*. 2 vols. Chicago: University of Chicago Press, 1970. Reprint, Notre Dame, IN: University of Notre Dame Press, 1995.

Ullman, Berthold Louis. *The Humanism of Coluccio Salutati*. Padua: Antenore, 1963.

——. *Studies in the Renaissance*. 2nd ed. Rome: Edizioni di Storia e letteratura, 1973.

Witt, Ronald G. *Hercules at the Crossroads: The Life, Works, and Thought of Coluccio Salutati*. Duke Monographs in Medieval and Renaissance Studies, no. 8. Durham, NC: Duke University Press, 1983.

Index

❧❧❧

· INDEX ·

Publication of this volume has been made possible by

The Myron and Sheila Gilmore Publication Fund at I Tatti
The Robert Lehman Endowment Fund
The Jean-François Malle Scholarly Programs and Publications Fund
The Andrew W. Mellon Scholarly Publications Fund
The Craig and Barbara Smyth Fund
for Scholarly Programs and Publications
The Lila Wallace–Reader's Digest Endowment Fund
The Malcolm Wiener Fund for Scholarly Programs and Publications